T0320681

COORDINATION OF DISTRIBUTED
PROBLEM SOLVERS

**THE KLUWER INTERNATIONAL SERIES
IN ENGINEERING AND COMPUTER SCIENCE**

ARTIFICIAL INTELLIGENCE

Consulting Editor

Tom M. Mitchell
Carnegie Mellon University

Other books in the series:

AN ARTIFICIAL INTELLIGENCE APPROACH TO VLSI DESIGN
T. Kowalski ISBN 0-89838-169-X

AN ARTIFICIAL INTELLIGENCE APPROACH TO VLSI ROUTING
R. Joobbani ISBN 0-89838-205-X

AN ARTIFICIAL INTELLIGENCE APPROACH TO
TEST GENERATION
N. Singh ISBN 0-89838-185-1

LISP LORE: A GUIDE TO PROGRAMMING THE LISP
MACHINE, 2/E
H. Bromley, R. Lamson ISBN 0-89838-228-9

UNIVERSAL SUBGOALING AND CHUNKING OF GOAL
HIERARCHIES
J. Laird, P. Rosenbloom, A. Newell ISBN 0-89838-213-0

MACHINE LEARNING—A GUIDE TO CURRENT RESEARCH
T. Mitchell, J. Carbonell, R. Michalski ISBN 0-89838-214-9

MACHINE LEARNING OF INDUCTIVE BIAS
P. Utgoff ISBN 0-89838-223-8

A CONNECTIONIST MACHINE FOR GENETIC HILLCLIMBING
D.H. Ackley ISBN 0-89838-236-X

LEARNING FROM GOOD AND BAD DATA
P.D. Laird ISBN 0-89838-263-7

MACHINE LEARNING OF ROBOT ASSEMBLY PLANS
A.M. Segre ISBN 0-89838-269-6

COORDINATION OF DISTRIBUTED PROBLEM SOLVERS

by

Edmund H. Durfee
University of Massachusetts at Amherst

KLUWER ACADEMIC PUBLISHERS
Boston/Dordrecht/London

Distributors for North America:
Kluwer Academic Publishers
101 Philip Drive
Assinippi Park
Norwell, Massachusetts 02061 USA

Distributors for the UK and Ireland:
Kluwer Academic Publishers
Falcon House, Queen Square
Lancaster LA1 1RN, UNITED KINGDOM

Distributors for all other countries:
Kluwer Academic Publishers Group
Distribution Centre
Post Office Box 322
3300 AH Dordrecht, THE NETHERLANDS

Library of Congress Cataloging-in-Publication Data

Durfee, Edmund H., 1959—
    Coordination of distributed problem solvers.

    (Kluwer international series in engineering and
computer science ; 55)
    Bibliography: p.
    Includes index.
    1. Electronic data processing—Distributed pro-
cessing.   2. Problem solving—Data processing.
3. Artificial intelligence.   I. Title.   II. Series.
QA76.9.D5D87   1988   004'.36   88-13055
ISBN 0-89838-284-X

Contents

Foreword   vii

1 Overview   1
  1.1 Partial Global Planning: A Unified Approach to Dynamic
      Coordination 3
  1.2 Research Issues 11
  1.3 Relationship to Previous Research 15
  1.4 Guides for the Reader 26

2 Distributed Problem Solving and the DVMT   27
  2.1 The Experimental Domain 28
  2.2 The Problem-Solving Knowledge 29
  2.3 Control of Problem Solving 32
  2.4 Coordination and Organization of Nodes 35
  2.5 Specifying Problem-Solving Environments 37
  2.6 Network Simulation 38
  2.7 Problem-Solving Examples 38
  2.8 Limitations of the DVMT 42
  2.9 How This Work Builds on the DVMT 43

3 Identifying Local Goals Through Clustering   45
  3.1 Background 46
  3.2 Overview 48
  3.3 Details 51
  3.4 Generalizing 63

4 Planning Local Problem Solving   67
  4.1 Background 68
  4.2 Overview 71
  4.3 Details 74
  4.4 Generalizing 104

5 Local Planning: Experiments and Evaluation 111
  5.1 Local Planning Experiments 112
  5.2 Local Planning Evaluation 130

6 Recognizing Partial Global Goals 131
  6.1 Background 131
  6.2 Overview 133
  6.3 Details 137
  6.4 Generalizing 156

7 Coordination Through Partial Global Planning 159
  7.1 Background 159
  7.2 Overview 160
  7.3 Details 167
  7.4 Generalizing 202

8 Partial Global Planning: Experiments and Evaluation 209
  8.1 Partial Global Planning Experiments 209
  8.2 Evaluation 237

9 Conclusions 239
  9.1 Summary 239
  9.2 Research Issues Revisited 240
  9.3 Future Research Directions 244
  9.4 Contributions 248

Acknowledgments 251

Glossary 253

Bibliography 257

Index 265

vi

Foreword

As artificial intelligence (AI) is applied to more complex problems and a wider set of applications, the ability to take advantage of the computational power of distributed and parallel hardware architectures and to match these architectures with the inherent distributed aspects of applications (spatial, functional, or temporal) has become an important research issue. Out of these research concerns, an AI subdiscipline called distributed problem solving has emerged.

Distributed problem-solving systems are broadly defined as loosely-coupled, distributed networks of semi-autonomous problem-solving agents that perform sophisticated problem solving and cooperatively interact to solve problems. Nodes operate asynchronously and in parallel with limited internode communication. Limited internode communication stems from either inherent bandwidth limitations of the communication medium or from the high computational cost of packaging and assimilating information to be sent and received among agents. Structuring network problem solving to deal with consequences of limited communication—the lack of a global view and the possibility that the individual agents may not have all the information necessary to accurately and completely solve their subproblems—is one of the major focuses of distributed problem-solving research. It is this focus that also is one of the important distinguishing characteristics of distributed problem-solving research that sets it apart from previous research in AI. For example, early work in distributed problem solving was motivated by the desire to reproduce the type of cooperating expert problem solving that occurred in the Hearsay-II blackboard architecture without resorting to a globally-accessible blackboard for sharing information and a centralized scheduler (focus-of-attention mechanism) for coordinating the experts. This latter issue of achieving effective network coordination and global coherence is the major focus of this book.

The research presented in this book is an important milestone in developing an understanding of how to build effective distributed coordination mechanisms. This research not only has conceptual clarity and elegance in providing a unifying framework for previous work, but is also empirically grounded. In a research area such as distributed problem solving which is still in its initial stages of development, few systems exist in which ideas and intuitions can be verified, so it is essential that empirical feedback be a part of the research methodology. Durfee clearly shows, through experimental results, the benefits and limitations (directions for future research) of his framework for network coordination.

This new framework, which he calls partial global planning, represents an important step in our evolutionary understanding of coordinating a complex distributed problem-solving network. Durfee shows that a single coordination framework can handle the network control problems arising out of both a task-sharing (goal-directed) perspective for network problem solving exemplified by the contract-net protocol and also a result-sharing (data-directed) perspective exemplified by the functionally-accurate/cooperative paradigm. He suggests that the distinctions arising from these different approaches are artificial because both approaches may need to be employed concurrently to effectively control a complex situation, and in fact the different approaches often involve reasoning about similar information.

Another important idea exemplified by Durfee's approach is the distinction between "satisficing" network control and optimal network control. In environments which are highly dynamic and uncertain, and where an updated and consistent global view of the state of the network problem solving is very difficult to obtain, attempting optimal control at every moment is infeasible from both a computational and communicative perspective. Rather, he shows that a network control algorithm can be designed that achieves a reasonable balance between the interdependent requirements of global coherency, limited use of computational resources in computing network control, and responsiveness to dynamically changing conditions.

Two other ideas are exemplified in the partial global planning framework that are major contributions to our understanding of network coordination. The first is that the interplay between network and local control is an important ingredient in designing effective coordination strategies. Durfee shows that providing a local agent with the ability to (1) develop high-level problem-solving goals and plans, (2) make reasonably accurate predictions of the time required to achieve its planned steps, and (3) make predictions about likely future goals, all lead to more sophisticated network coordination. The second is the concept of network coordination as a distributed problem-solving task in its own right, distinct from domain-level distributed problem solving going on among agents. Durfee introduces the concept of meta-level organization to describe the organizational relationship among agents required to solve the network coordination problem and permits the coordination tasks to go on asynchronously and in parallel with domain problem solving.

In summary, this book will be an invaluable aid to researchers in AI and distributed systems who want to understand from both a conceptual and practical perspective the issues and the state-of-the-art in network coordination for distributed problem solving systems.

Victor R. Lesser, University of Massachusetts at Amherst

COORDINATION OF DISTRIBUTED
PROBLEM SOLVERS

The controlling intelligence understands its own nature, and what it does, and whereon it works. –Marcus Aurelius

Chapter 1

Overview

Distributed computing systems have several advantages over centralized, monolithic computing systems. They are often more cost effective, because n simple processors might be considerably cheaper than a single processor that is n times as powerful. A group of processors might also be more reliable, because the failure of some only reduces computing power, while if the single powerful processor fails then all computing power is lost. In addition, many computing tasks are inherently distributed. They might be spatially distributed, such as tasks to monitor different spatial areas or to process transactions at different branches of a bank. Or they might be functionally distributed, such as tasks to perform low-level processing of visual and tactile data, where processors with different functional capabilities might be used to process different types of data. These advantages have led to distributed computing systems being applied in increasingly complex domains.

As distributed computing systems are used in more diverse applications, however, the difficulties in controlling these systems become more pronounced. Not only must an individual computing element make control decisions about how it should most effectively apply its local resources, but the computing elements as a group must also coordinate their control decisions to effectively use network resources. Computing elements are more capable of helping or hindering each other when the interdependencies between their tasks are more complex, so distributed computing applications involving highly interdependent tasks require sophisticated control mechanisms to promote effective cooperation. This research develops control mechanisms for distributed computing systems with the following characteristics:

- The tasks performed in the network are highly interdependent.

- The tasks performed in the network can be grouped together based on their relationships, where a group of tasks leads to a single larger result.

- The computing elements can *roughly* predict the time (and other resource) needs of tasks and groups of tasks.

- The network situation is sufficiently predictable for computing elements to *tentatively* plan sequences of related tasks.

- The communication delays are of the same order of magnitude as the task times, so that computing elements can communicate about planned actions ahead of time, but synchronizing decisions about current activities is not feasible.

Distributed problem-solving networks often display these characteristics. In a distributed problem-solving network, the computing elements are problem solving **nodes** that are cooperatively trying to solve problems by individually solving subproblems and integrating subproblem solutions into overall solutions. These networks are typically used in applications such as distributed sensor networks [Lesser and Erman, 1980; Smith, 1980], distributed air traffic control [Cammarata *et al.*, 1983], and distributed robot systems [Fehling and Erman, 1983], where there is a natural spatial distribution of information but where each node has insufficient local information to completely and accurately solve its subproblems. The performance of the distributed problem-solving network depends on the control decisions that nodes make about their local actions (to solve relevant subproblems in a timely manner) and about their interactions (to share useful information and converge on overall solutions). The nodes pool their resources and expertise, work in parallel on different parts of a problem to solve it faster, avoid harmful interactions such as resource conflicts or working at cross-purposes, and promote helpful interactions such as moving information to where it is most needed or tasks to where they can best be performed.

To make coordination decisions, the nodes need knowledge about the **goals of cooperation**: whether they should avoid redundant work (to save on computation) or promote this work (to verify each other's results); whether they should assign important tasks to multiple nodes (in case those nodes fail) or should avoid this (so that nodes do not unnecessarily duplicate each other's activities); whether they should exchange predictive partial results (to focus each other on forming compatible results) or not (to avoid overly influencing each other). In complex domains, the goals of cooperation may differ as circumstances change, so mechanisms for coordination must be flexible for nodes to achieve appropriate goals of cooperation in a given situation.

Similarly, the nodes' **style of cooperation** depends on the problem domain and on the environmental characteristics. Sometimes the nodes should channel information about their local activities to "controller" nodes that make coordination decisions for the network. At other times, the nodes might broadcast this information to each other and individually form more global views about how their local activities fit into network problem solving. When communication is very expensive or integrating information into more global views is costly, however, nodes should work relatively independently and selectively exchange their local solutions to converge on global solutions. Alternatively, they may negotiate in small groups to contract out tasks in the network. To work in a wide variety of situations, the coordination mechanisms must be flexible enough for the nodes to coordinate in different styles.

The focus of this research is on developing, implementing, and evaluating a new approach for coordinating cooperating problem solvers (and, more generally, computing elements with interdependent tasks). This approach, called partial global planning, is significant because it provides a unified framework where nodes can achieve various goals of cooperation using different styles of cooperation. The remainder of this chapter introduces our approach and related information, while the rest of this book concentrates on details of local planning, partial global planning, and experiments. More details can be found in the dissertation upon which this book is based [Durfee, 1987].

1.1   Partial Global Planning: A Unified Approach to Dynamic Coordination

Partial global planning is a new approach to coordination in which interacting nodes explicitly plan their actions and interactions in complex and dynamically changing situations. Through partial global planning, each node can represent and reason about the activities of groups of nodes and about how local activities fit into this more global view. These representations are called partial global plans (PGPs) because they specify how different *parts* of the network (subsets of nodes) *plan* to work together to achieve more *global* goals. A partial global plan thus indicates the concurrent actions of individual nodes (planned sequences of actions each node should pursue) and the important interactions between nodes (planned communication of partial solutions to help other nodes perform their tasks or build more complete solutions). Each node maintains a set of PGPs that represents its own local view of network activity, and the nodes can exchange information about their local plans and PGPs to improve each other's view.

Different problem situations may call for different styles of cooperation, and partial global planning allows versatility in how nodes coordinate because nodes may exchange and reason about plan information in a variety of ways. Because the network may be capable of achieving only some of its objectives, the approach also incorporates flexibility in how the network balances different goals of cooperation. Finally, coordination in dynamic, uncertain, distributed domains must be based on possibly inaccurate, incomplete, and out-of-date information. Partial global planning allows cooperating nodes to use whatever information they have and to spend whatever computing time they can afford in order to dynamically plan satisfactory (not necessarily optimal) actions and interactions to meet network goals.

1.1.1 Conceptual Contributions

Conceptually, partial global planning is at the same time both simple to understand and versatile. It is simple to understand because it is so familiar—it resembles coordination among humans: (1) each node determines its own goals and forms plans to achieve them; (2) nodes exchange information to identify cases where their goals and plans interact; and (3) nodes change their planned local actions and interactions to coordinate better based on their view of group activity. It is versatile because it has the flexibility to coordinate nodes in a variety of situations: individual nodes are free to form local goals and plans based on their local knowledge and priorities, and the nodes' coordination responsibilities and their criteria for choosing what plans to communicate can be changed to modify how (and whether) nodes decide to coordinate. Whereas previous approaches to coordination, such as contracting [Smith, 1980] and multi-agent planning [Cammarata *et al.*, 1983], are specialized for particular situations (discussed in Section 1.3), partial global planning consolidates these different approaches into a unified and versatile framework for dynamically coordinating independent nodes.

The flexibility of partial global planning means that nodes can coordinate in many different ways, but this flexibility can lead to incoherent network behavior when nodes have different views of how to develop and use PGPs. An important new concept introduced in this research is the use of an explicit **meta-level organization** to structure how nodes form, exchange, manipulate, and react to PGPs. Unlike a **domain-level organization** that nodes use to guide problem solving [Corkill and Lesser, 1983], the meta-level organization guides coordination. Partial global planning reduces the need for relatively static, domain-level organizations because information to coordinate problem solving is dynamically formed and represented in PGPs. Instead, the network needs a relatively static, meta-level organization to delimit coordination roles and responsibilities. By representing the meta-level organization explicitly and declaratively, the partial global planning mechanisms can be used appropriately for different situations to achieve effective coordination.

Partial global planning coordinates nodes working in dynamic situations, and this also leads to important conceptual contributions. Because nodes cannot fully predict their future situations, their local plans are tentative and uncertain. Individual nodes must: resolve uncertainty about long-term goals to pursue; monitor and repair plans; modify plans in response to changing circumstances; and possibly meet deadlines. Our local planning framework that underlies partial global planning is a conceptually new approach for controlling problem solving in dynamic and uncertain domains.

Because local plans are tentative, so are PGPs. The conceptual development and experimental evaluation of partial global planning provide initial answers to important questions about how nodes should coordinate in a tentative, uncertain domain. We explore conceptual issues such as how much detail about their plans nodes should exchange and when a change to a local plan is worth communicating about. In addition, we examine the ramifications of frequently modifying and communicating about plans in dynamic situations. We study issues in how and when nodes should build more resilient PGPs, and how they can build PGPs that assign tasks to better exploit network resources. Our work also explores the complexities involved in coordinating larger networks, and how the complexity can be reduced. Most importantly, we recognize that local and partial global planning are tools that are more or less cost effective depending on the situation: although useful in a wide range of situations, they do introduce overhead that makes them impractical in either very simple situations (where cheaper and less sophisticated control mechanisms would suffice) or in very ambiguous, complicated situations (where nodes either cannot distinguish promising plans or else the cost of forming useful plans is prohibitively large).

Partial global planning also makes reasoning about coordination an integral part of a node's activity. Unlike approaches where coordination mechanisms are added as an afterthought to stand-alone systems, partial global planning recognizes that, to cooperate effectively, nodes need to reason in depth about network activity when making local control decisions. Partial global planning thus represents an important conceptual contribution in that it integrates local and network control into a single control structure: nodes are essentially independent and determine their own tentative goals and plans, and yet they can exchange information about their plans to develop and use a more global view of the network. The result is a new understanding about how a node's local awareness can lead to better network awareness among nodes, how local and network awareness call for representing and reasoning about actions and interactions at multiple levels of detail, and how using this awareness can improve coordination.

More generally, partial global planning has implications for control in other types of distributed systems. Our research indicates that effective cooperation among computing nodes requires that each node be capable of representing and reasoning about network activity as an integral part of local decisionmaking. Even if the computing nodes are not knowledge-based systems, partial global planning techniques could still be incorporated into their control mechanisms to improve coordination when they work on highly interdependent tasks.

1.1.2   Technical Contributions

To evaluate partial global planning from a practical as well as a conceptual viewpoint, we have implemented the approach in a testbed that simulates a distributed problem-solving network working in the vehicle monitoring domain.[1] During implementation, we have encountered many technical issues and obstacles that could be overlooked in a more speculative, conceptual treatment. As a result, a large proportion of this book is devoted to technical aspects of how partial global planning can be implemented into specific control mechanisms. The technical details contribute to our understanding of partial global planning and provide a basis for implementation in other domains.

The technical development has two main thrusts. One thrust is developing local planning mechanisms, because before it can cooperate with others, a node must first identify its local goals and possible actions to achieve those goals. That is, to determine how it fits into more global activities, a node must have a certain amount of *self-awareness*. Subsequent chapters are devoted to describing how nodes recognize local goals (Chapter 3) and build plans for achieving them (Chapter 4). The other thrust is developing partial global planning mechanisms. Given self-awareness of its own plans and, through communication, network awareness about others' plans, a node must reason about the plans and the goals of cooperation to develop PGPs to coordinate group activity. Later chapters describe how nodes develop greater network awareness (Chapter 6) and use it to form PGPs (Chapter 7).

An important assumption behind our mechanisms is that nodes can plan future actions and interactions, and that dynamic changes to their situations are not so fast and unpredictable that planning is not worthwhile. In some domains, nodes cannot plan their activities, or plans are obsolete before significant progress is made, or the overhead for local and partial global planning is excessive. Partial global planning should not be applied when coordination using a relatively static, general, domain-level organization is more cost-effective than attempting to dynamically coordinate for specific situations. Our mechanisms allow nodes to resort to domain-level organizations in such situations.

The basic components of our new mechanisms are shown in Figure 1. Initially, we begin with a problem solver having a queue of possible pending actions (tasks), a dispatcher that chooses the next action to take, and an executor that takes that action. The action might change the problem state and trigger new actions to be placed on the queue. To the basic problem solver, we add a local planner that plans sequences of actions and associates pending actions with their corresponding plans. Plans are stored on a plan queue, and the plan dispatcher chooses the pending plan to follow. The plan executor pursues that

---

[1] The testbed and all of the new mechanisms for local and partial global planning, except where noted, have been implemented in a local dialect of Lisp, comprising roughly 20,000 lines of code. Experiments are run on a VAX 11/750. The mechanisms are currently being reimplemented in CommonLisp on TI Explorers.

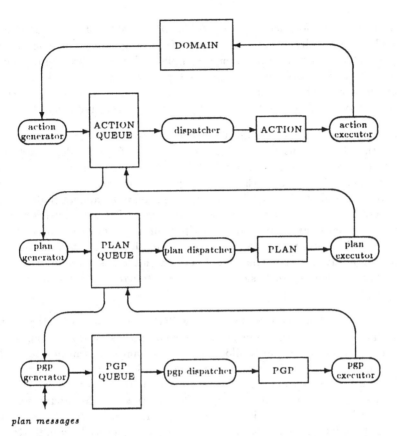

plan messages

The control components of the basic problem solver form and execute problem-solving actions. The local planner combines related pending actions into plans, and executes the best plan on the queue by inserting the appropriate action at the top of the action queue. The partial global planner builds PGPs from local plans and received plan information, and executes the best PGP by inserting the relevant local plan at the top of the plan queue. The different control activities can be pursued concurrently and asynchronously.

Figure 1: An Overview of the Levels of Control.

plan by rearranging the queue of pending actions so that the next action for the chosen plan is taken. Finally, to the problem solver and local planner we add a partial global planner that uses local plans and plan information received from other nodes to form PGPs. It maintains a queue of PGPs and has a dispatcher that chooses the PGP that the node should follow. The partial global planner modifies the local plan associated with the chosen PGP to improve coordination, and the local plan queue is reordered to ensure that the appropriate local plan is dispatched next.

The local planning mechanisms use the relationships between actions to form and incrementally update local plans. Even in domains where actions are interdependent, however, it is often a complicated process to identify larger groups of related actions, develop promising sequences of actions, and form predictions about when those actions will be done and what kind of results they will likely generate. Nodes therefore make only tentative local plans.

The partial global planner must adequately coordinate local plans despite the fact that these plans can change over time. To form PGPs, a node uses its current view of other nodes' plans, but because nodes may be in the process of changing their plans, this view may be incomplete or obsolete. As a result, partial global planning is a complex process, balancing nodes' needs for predictability with their needs for responsiveness. The mechanisms work by grouping together nodes' plans that participate in larger, more global long-term goals and finding ways that nodes could revise their local plans to improve coordination. In addition, the partial global planning mechanisms build predictions about when and where nodes should communicate partial results to construct more global results.

Because several nodes may be forming PGPs simultaneously, the partial global planning mechanisms must tolerate some inconsistency among nodes' views of coordination and must allow them to exchange information to resolve inconsistencies. How nodes do this depends on the meta-level organization, specifying what nodes a node should inform about its local plans and PGPs, what nodes are responsible for forming PGPs and for what other nodes, and how much credibility a node has in information it gets from another node. Although partial global planning lets nodes cooperate in whatever style is indicated by the meta-level organization, an important (and open) research issue is how the nodes can reorganize their coordination roles when circumstances change.

Problem solving, local planning, and partial global planning can be done asynchronously and in parallel: the local planner follows the top-ranked local plan whether or not the partial global planner has altered the queue, and similarly the problem solver executes the top-ranked action whether or not the local planner has influenced this choice. In the current implementation, however, problem solving, local planning, and partial global planning are done on a single processor, so a node's control activities step through these mechanisms (Figure 2). The dispatcher for choosing the next action is replaced with the local planner which finds the next action for the best local plan. In turn, the dispatcher for choosing the best local plan is replaced with the partial global planner which finds the local plan of the best PGP. The detailed description of the planning and coordination mechanisms in the next chapters use this view when describing the sequence of control activities performed by a node. However, in the final chapter, we briefly return to issues in performing problem solving, local planning, and partial global planning in parallel.

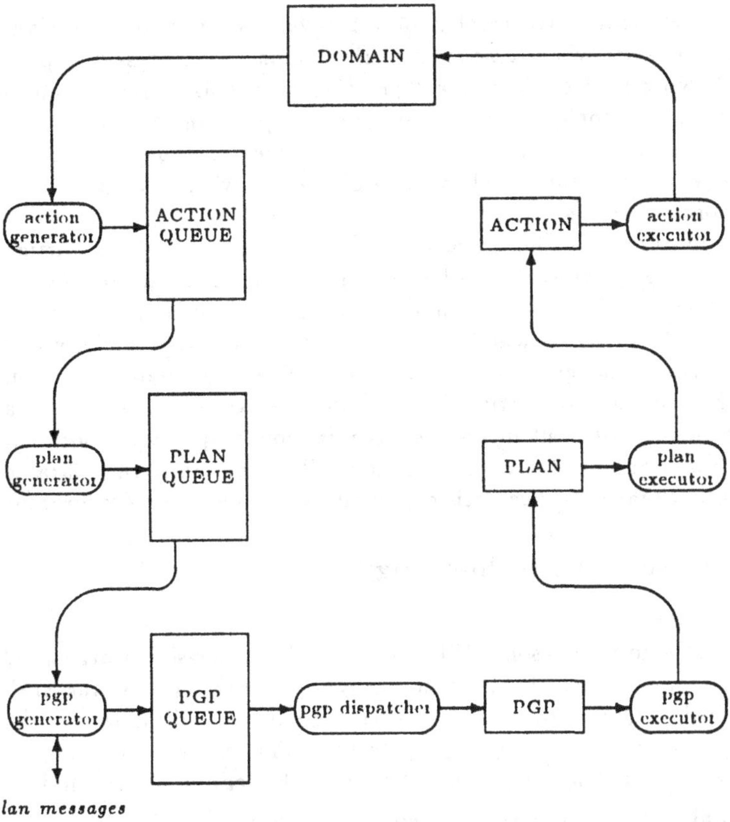

plan messages

In a serial view of control, the control components of the basic problem solver first form problem-solving actions. The local planner then combines related pending actions into plans, which the partial global planner uses, along with received plan information, to build PGPs. The partial global planner executes the best PGP by making the relevant local plan the current plan, and the local planner executes this local plan by making the appropriate action the current action. This action is taken, causing changes to the domain information that may trigger the generation of new potential actions, and the cycle repeats.

Figure 2: A Serial Overview of the Levels of Control.

1.1.3 Empirical Contributions

To more fully understand the benefits, costs, and limitations of partial global planning, it should be evaluated from both a conceptual and a practical perspective. Because we have implemented the approach in a complex domain, we can experimentally evaluate its performance in a variety of situations, measuring not only the improvements to control due to the new mechanisms, but also the overhead costs the mechanisms incur.

Our experiments with local planning (Chapter 5) show that planning is advantageous even when a node is working alone. We present experimental results showing how our new local planning mechanisms resolve uncertainty about goals, monitor and repair plans, modify plans in response to changing circumstances, and allow a node to meet deadlines. The overhead of planning is generally offset by the saved effort in problem solving, because a node takes fewer incorrect actions.

While local planning makes each node a better problem solver, partial global planning makes nodes work as a better team. In our experimental problem situations (Chapter 8), we show that partial global planning improves control decisions in the network, usually with acceptable overhead. Moreover, our experiments verify that nodes should coordinate differently in different situations, so that the versatility of partial global planning is extremely useful. For a given situation, we use different meta-level organizations to promote coordination in different ways, and use the experimental results to recognize the characteristics of a situation that influence decisions about how nodes should coordinate.

1.1.4   Research Methodology

A fable by Aesop:

> A crab said to her son, "Why do you walk so one-sided, my child? It is far more becoming to go straightforward." The young crab replied: "Quite true, dear mother; and if you will show me the straight way, I will promise to walk in it." The mother tried in vain, and submitted without remonstrance to the reproof of her child.
>
> Moral: *Example is more powerful than precept.*

Experimentation plays a major role in our research because an approach to coordination should be evaluated from a practical as well as a conceptual standpoint. In fact, experimentation and conceptualization are concurrent activities. Concepts guide the experiments, but experimental results (especially unexpected results) cause revision and extensions to concepts.

An advantage of coupling experimental and conceptual development is that it forces concepts to be well-defined, otherwise they cannot be implemented. Moreover, experimental verification can point out holes in a conceptual approach, and its costs and limitations. Working with concrete, experimental examples also allows us to anchor our concepts in reality, so that we can better characterize and understand phenomena. Developing a conceptual and experimental approach concurrently has disadvantages, however, and the most important of these is the danger of forming concepts that are only applicable in the experimental domain. To some extent, this is unavoidable: examples lead to seeing issues in certain ways, and the concurrent evolution of concepts and implementations make disassociating the two difficult.

The design, implementation, and evaluation of our approach has been (and still is) an iterative process. The high-level concepts behind partial global

planning—building plans for groups of nodes from plans of individual nodes—
are by themselves not particularly enlightening, but making these ideas actually
work in a non-trivial domain is an interesting and exciting problem. For this
reason, the bulk of this book is concerned with *how* things work. We mostly
transmit our ideas through implementation details and examples, although at
intervals we also highlight how our mechanisms are more generally applicable.
The result, hopefully, is a balance between details and generalizations, so that
the reader can develop an understanding of how we have made things work and
how we believe similar things could be done elsewhere.

1.2 Research Issues

1.2.1 Local Node Sophistication

When a computing node is working alone, it can afford to be less sophisticated
because it need not *explicitly* represent its current and expected future states
and actions. However, for nodes to recognize possible future interactions (desirable or undesirable), they must have explicit representations for themselves
and others. An interesting (but on reflection not surprising) common thread in
much distributed computing research is that, to use better coordination techniques, individual computing nodes need more self-awareness than when they
work alone.

Our research similarly needs local node sophistication, and an important
thrust of our work has been to improve control in individual nodes. When
working alone, a node can explore possible solution paths in an erratic manner, possibly switching frequently among a number of paths depending on the
promise of the next step of each. When coordinating with others, however, a
node should attempt to be more predictable so that others can anticipate its
actions and can coordinate interactions. A node should consider the long-term
promise of the various paths and should plan purposeful sequences of actions.
We give a node the ability to inexpensively form the view it needs to recognize
promising long-term goals, and then to plan actions to achieve them. Because it
works in a dynamic domain, a node's long-term goals are uncertain and changing, so a node cannot simply plan sequences of actions based on the initial
situation. Instead, it should interleave building, modifying, monitoring, and
repairing plans with executing them. A node should plan *incrementally* by
sketching out a general sequence of activities but adding detailed actions over
time since the results of earlier actions affect how (and whether) later actions
should be taken.

Local node sophistication is thus crucial to coordination because without
the ability to plan local actions the nodes cannot predict and plan coordinated
interactions. The increased self-awareness achieved through local planning also
helps a node behave more purposefully, and can improve local problem solving.
Because it is important and difficult to achieve, much of the research described

in later chapters (especially Chapters 3–5) is concerned with increasing local node sophistication.

1.2.2 Goals of Cooperation

The form that cooperation takes depends on the situation, and cooperative actions in one situation may be undesirable in other situations. For example, students may cooperate to improve each other's exam grades by discussing the material *before* an exam, but discussion *during* the exam is likely to achieve the opposite effect. Before the exam, the students cooperate by sharing resources (ideas and information), while during the exam they should cooperate by avoiding harmful interactions (that might lead to accusations of cheating).

Choosing appropriate actions therefore requires an understanding of the goals of cooperation. The generic goals of cooperation include:

1. To increase task completion rate through parallelism.

2. To increase the set or scope of achievable tasks by sharing resources (physical devices, information, expertise, etc.).

3. To increase the likelihood of completing tasks (reliability) by undertaking duplicate tasks, possibly using different methods to perform those tasks.

4. To decrease interference between tasks by avoiding harmful interactions.

In particular applications, specific variations and combinations of these generic goals of cooperation determine how nodes interact. In a distributed problem-solving application, for example, these generic goals are refined into a set of more specific goals. Associated with their related generic goals of cooperation (numbers in parentheses refer to generic goals above), these goals include:

- To increase solution creation rate by forming subsolutions in parallel (1).

- To minimize time nodes must wait for results from each other by coordinating activity (1,4).

- To improve overall problem solving by permitting nodes to exchange predictive information (2).

- To increase the probability that a solution will be found despite node failures by assigning important tasks to multiple nodes (3).

- To improve computing resource use by allowing task exchanges (2).

- To improve use of individual node expertise by allowing nodes to exchange tasks (2).

- To reduce the amount of unnecessary duplication of effort by letting nodes recognize and avoid useless redundant activities (4).

- To increase confidence of a (sub)solution by having nodes verify each other's results through rederivation using their potentially different expertise and information (2,3).

- To increase the variety of solutions by allowing nodes to form local solutions without being overly influenced by other nodes (1,4).

- To reduce communication resource use by being more selective about what messages are exchanged (4).

Because all of these goals cannot be achieved simultaneously, nodes must cooperate differently depending on the particular situation. For example, if a solution must be found quickly, the nodes should not spend time verifying each other's results or developing a wide variety of solutions. Because of the diversity in the forms that cooperation can take in a distributed problem-solving system, distributed problem solving is an appropriate context in which to study how different goals of cooperation can be met.

1.2.3   Styles of Cooperation

The purpose of the coordination mechanisms is to control problem solving so that cooperating nodes work together as a coherent team. However, the question arises about how to control coordination activity: before they can coordinate their problem-solving, nodes must first decide how they will coordinate their activities to form this coordinated view. There are several different ways of controlling how nodes coordinate [Cammarata *et al.*, 1983; Corkill, 1983; Davis and Smith, 1983; Steeb *et al.*, 1986].   For example, the nodes could send coordination information to a single coordinator node. Or the nodes could broadcast their information and individually develop views about how they should all cooperate. Or pairs of nodes could exchange information to decide on task reassignments, forming shared plans (contracts) with each other. Or the nodes could avoid exchanging any coordination information and instead fall back on any domain-level organizational knowledge.

Each style of cooperation has advantages and disadvantages. Having a single coordinator node has advantages such as having only one node spend its resources on reasoning about coordination and having that node enforce consistent views, but has disadvantages such as this node being a potential bottleneck and the entire network being prone to collapse if it fails. On the other hand, having each node coordinate itself, though more reliable, may incur large amounts of overhead because more information must be exchanged and because nodes may duplicate each other's reasoning about coordination.   Forming contracts between pairs of nodes can be very cost effective when some nodes must pass tasks to others, but when larger groups of nodes already have tasks distributed among them they may not gain a suitably global view of how to interact if they only consider how pairs can coordinate. The advantage of not exchanging any information at all is that the coordination overhead (computation and communication) is eliminated, but at the potential cost of a lack of network coherence (duplication of effort, working at cross-purposes, poorly timed interactions) leading to poor network performance. Therefore, no single style of cooperation is appropriate for all distributed problem-solving situations [Smith and Davis, 1981].

In fact, some distributed problem-solving situations may call for several styles of cooperation simultaneously. As nodes are identifying possible overall solutions to work toward and deciding which local subproblems to individually pursue and which partial results to share, they might also coordinate the transfer of subproblems from overburdened nodes to nodes with available resources or expertise. The nodes should coordinate to avoid duplication of effort on common subproblems, but should also solve closely related subproblems to share relevant partial results in a timely manner. In short, because subproblems, expertise, and other resources may be inherently but possibly unevenly distributed, nodes need to coordinate in several styles to share results *and* tasks.

1.2.4   Predictability and Responsiveness

The conflict between predictability and responsiveness is a recurring problem in coordination. Before it coordinates with others, a node can respond to dynamic changes in its situation in any way that its local control component considers best. So long as it need not coordinate with others, in fact, a node can and should be responsive. However, to cooperatively solve problems, nodes should exchange information about their plans and goals, and what they send determines how other nodes will perceive them. When a node changes its local plans and goals, it deviates from the view that other nodes have, which is the view that they use when making coordination decisions. Delays in communication mean that other nodes will continue to use obsolete views of the node for some interval of time until they receive an update, and the coordination decisions are thus not as effective as they might be over this interval. Ineffective coordination can cause nodes to work at cross-purposes or on unimportant tasks, and the best overall solutions may be found later than if the node had not changed its local plans. On the other hand, when the changes to its plans can substantially impact network behavior (trigger working in completely different areas or in different ways), then the node should change its plans. The network can tolerate an interval of uncoordinated activity if the network performs significantly better after the changes have been made known to others.

Deciding when a change to local plans is substantial enough to warrant a response is a difficult problem, but one which our approach takes initial steps toward solving. Our approach to coordination has nodes plan their interactions—not only *how* they will interact but also approximately *when* they will interact. When a node changes its local plans, therefore, it can compare how these changes will affect planned interactions: can the node still interact in the expected way at about the same time? When nodes can no longer interact in the expected way, then it is important to respond to the situation. However, if the change indicates that they will interact at about the same time (where the tolerance to time deviations can be adjusted), then the node need not change its plans. Tolerance for minor variations in interactions increases predictability at the cost of possibly degrading performance (since nodes might have cooperated more effectively had they responded to these variations). However, being responsive can itself degrade performance, not only because of intervals where nodes have inconsistent views of each other but also because reformulating how they should coordinate incurs overhead and the costs of this overhead might outweigh its benefits. Our approach allows us to adjust the tolerance and observe the effects to better understand how predictability and responsiveness should be balanced.

1.2.5 Negotiation

To coordinate effectively, nodes must *negotiate* over their use of local resources, information, and expertise. Sometimes they negotiate to decide which *local* problem-solving tasks to pursue, while at other times they negotiate over the exchange of tasks. Nodes negotiate to solve the **connection problem**: they match problems to solve with nodes having the resources (expertise, data, computing power) to solve them. To solve the **decomposition problem**, nodes should negotiate over decomposing their problems in the first place. Or when subproblems are inherently distributed, nodes must solve the **association problem** by communicating to discover which nodes are working on associated subproblems, and negotiating over how, when, and where to form complete solutions by sharing results. Any framework for coordination, including partial global planning, must provide a protocol (means of communication) and reasoning mechanisms that use this protocol in order to allow nodes to negotiate in an appropriate manner given their situation. Our research uses PGPs as the protocol, and we develop mechanisms that use PGPs for negotiation to address the problems of connection, decomposition, and association.

1.3 Relationship to Previous Research

The relevant previous research in cooperation and coordination among independent nodes can be divided into three basic categories. The first of these is distributed artificial intelligence. Because we are interested in cooperation between artificially-intelligent problem solvers, and because we view coordination decisions as knowledge-based (knowledge about local plans, plans of other nodes, and goals of cooperation), previous research in distributed artificial intelligence is very relevant. The second category of related research is in distributed operating systems and distributed control in general. Although principally interested in domains with much less interdependence between tasks (where avoiding resource conflicts is the primary objective), distributed operating systems research is evolving toward distributed artificial intelligence research as it faces similar issues in coordinating nodes with tasks that are related in more complicated ways. Finally, the third category of related research is studies of cooperation in natural systems. This includes social, biological, game theoretic, and economic views of cooperation, each of which can enrich our understanding of cooperation among complex agents.

1.3.1   Distributed Artificial Intelligence

Distributed Artificial Intelligence (DAI) research, in our view, studies how intelligent agents can combine their resources so that the intelligence of the group is more than the sum of the individual agents' intelligence. This view assumes that the individuals do have some intelligence (as opposed to connectionist views where simple, unintelligent computing elements combine to form an intelligent whole [Feldman and Ballard, 1982]). For our purposes, we define intelligence as the ability to flexibly respond to situations: an intelligent agent (or network) does not simply react to its environment but instead uses knowledge (possibly heuristic) to make informed decisions about how to act. When they cooperate with others, the combined abilities of the agents transcend their individual capabilities so that the size and scope of the problems they can solve as a group increases dramatically.

Many crucial issues in DAI revolve around providing agents with the ability to control how they cooperate:

- Agents need to decompose high-level tasks, assign subtasks among themselves, and combine the results of these subtasks.

- Agents need to represent and reason about their own actions, the actions of other agents, and the interactions between agents.

- Agents need to recognize when they have conflicting or inconsistent goals and respond appropriately by, for example, negotiating, competing, or appealing to a higher authority.

- Agents need to coordinate their interactions so that they work as a coherent team when cooperating to achieve shared goals.

The emphasis of this section is to review past approaches to control in DAI systems so that we can contrast our approach with these. For more complete information about DAI in general, the reader is referred to the surveys by Rosenschein [Rosenschein, 1985] and Corkill and Lesser [Corkill and Lesser, 1987], and the DAI annotated bibliography by Jagannathan and Dodhiawala [Jagannathan and Dodhiawala, 1986].

Control of Closely Cooperating Experts

Early DAI research dealt with closely cooperating agents. Because these agents cannot be considered intelligent in themselves, these systems do not fit in the definition of DAI given above. Nevertheless, they do represent some initial explorations into issues of cooperation between independent computing agents.

In Hearsay-II, the computing elements are knowledge sources (KSs) that interact through a blackboard data structure [Erman *et al.*, 1980; Fennell and Lesser, 1977]. A KS monitors a portion of the blackboard, waiting for particular patterns of data. When such a pattern occurs, the KS takes the data and manipulates it, typically forming new combinations of data which it places on other portions of the blackboard. A KS cannot be construed as an intelligent agent by itself because it responds in a set way to expected patterns of data. However, by acting asynchronously and by communicating through the blackboard, a group of cooperating KSs can respond flexibly to data so that their overall behavior can be viewed as being intelligent. Control of cooperation is effected in several ways: the specificity of KSs (in terms of the data they respond to and produce) limit how they interact; the structure of the blackboard allows KSs to work concurrently in different areas of the blackboard; and a blackboard monitor resolves contentions between KSs attempting to modify the same part of the blackboard.

In the ACTOR system, simple, unintelligent computing agents very similar to KSs (but often of much smaller granularity) cooperate through a communication channel [Hewitt, 1977]. An ACTOR monitors the communication channel, waiting for messages fitting its desired pattern. The ACTOR responds to such a message by performing some computation on that message and possibly generating new messages during and after this computation. These new messages in turn trigger other ACTORs to act, and so the network of communicating ACTORs, which are individually simple, can flexibly interact to different situations (patterns of messages) to form complex, intelligent computations. Control of cooperation in this system is based on: ACTORs responding to highly specialized patterns and generating specialized results; patterns of messages triggering concurrent activities; and a communication channel that has the speed and capacity for ACTORs to freely broadcast messages in a timely manner.

The two systems are extremely similar. Both work toward deriving intelligent overall behavior from groups of unintelligent agents, and depend on concurrency and close coupling to achieve this. Concurrent activity of a number of agents allows these systems to perform adequately despite a lack of explicit coordination. The incoherent behavior of many of the agents can be tolerated because the odds are that some of the agents are doing useful work at any given time. The close-coupling allows large amounts of relatively simple information to be exchanged, and this means that agents communicate often to maintain a more global view of their activity. In blackboard-based cooperation, this view is maintained on the blackboard, while in the ACTOR system, this view is maintained by the constant flow of messages in the system. In both systems, an important source of contention is for the information passing mechanisms, whether a shared blackboard or a shared communication channel.

The view of cooperation afforded by these mechanisms is based on agents simply responding to information and publicizing their results. These mechanisms have limited application in loosely-coupled systems, because the costs and delays of communication make the broadcasting of all results impractical. If the loosely-coupled agents are as simple as KSs or ACTORs and need to frequently exchange simple information, then they would spend most of their time waiting for messages from each other. The agents should therefore have more local intelligence so that they perform more local computation and interact less frequently. The less frequent interactions should also be more directed: to make effective use of their communication channels, the agents should make better decisions about what information to communicate and where to communicate it. Research in closely-coupled systems therefore developed an initial view of control that, through its failure in loosely-coupled systems, helped direct later development of control mechanisms.

Control Through Contracts

Consider a network of loosely-coupled agents with various resources. If one of these agents receives a large problem to solve, then either it can apply its own resources and solve the problem as best it can by itself, or it can decompose the large problem into smaller subproblems and convince other agents to pursue these subproblems. The latter approach makes better use of network resources. The contract-net protocol developed by Smith develops a framework for this form of cooperation [Smith, 1980]. Given a task to perform, a node first breaks the task into subtasks if possible. If it forms such subtasks, or it is locally unable to perform the initial task, then the node must coordinate with others to decide where to transfer tasks. It employs the contract-net protocol to announce the tasks that could be transferred and request that nodes that could perform any of those tasks submit bids. A node that receives a task announcement message can reply with a bid for that task, indicating how well it believes it can perform the task. The node that announced the task collects these bids and awards the task to the "best" bidder. The contract-net protocol allows nodes to broadcast bid-requests to all others or to focus bid-requests to a likely subset of nodes. Nodes can also communicate about their availability, so that focusing information (and decisions about whether it is worth advertising a task in the first place) can be based on dynamic views of the network.

The contract-net protocol promotes control based on negotiating over task assignments to form manager-contractor relationships [Davis and Smith, 1983] that determine how nodes will work together. Because nodes exchange information about tasks and availability, they make dynamic control decisions about how they will cooperatively pursue tasks. Thus, in applications where the principal mode of interactions between nodes fits into the contracting model, the contract-net protocol is an effective approach for coordination. Unfortunately, some applications do not fit cleanly into this model: tasks may be inherently distributed among nodes, and coordination is not a matter of decomposing and assigning tasks but instead is a matter of recognizing when distributed tasks (or partial results) are part of some larger overall task (or result) and, if so, how to interact to achieve the larger task (or result).

Control Through Organization

The organizational approach to coordination developed by Corkill and Lesser stems from a different view of cooperative problem solving [Corkill, 1983; Corkill and Lesser, 1983; Lesser and Corkill, 1983]. In domains where related subproblems are inherently distributed, the nodes do not need to coordinate subproblem assignments, but they do need to coordinate how they combine subproblem solutions. When the nodes decompose problems and assign subproblems themselves, they know how the subproblem solutions should be integrated, but when subproblems are inherently distributed, nodes do not know what subproblems other nodes are working on and how those subproblems are related. To cooperate, these nodes exchange partial solutions in a functionally-accurate, cooperative manner [Lesser and Corkill, 1981] so that despite some incorrect control decisions they eventually converge on overall problem solutions. Without any knowledge about the possible activities of other nodes, nodes can do no better than to broadcast partial solutions in the hope that they will eventually converge on overall solutions. In loosely-coupled networks, however, such a communication-intensive approach would be infeasible, and so the organizational approach to coordination was devised.

An organization indicates the general interests, responsibilities, and capabilities of the nodes. Each node has a copy of this organization, and uses it to guide local decisions. For example, given local tasks (to process local data), a node gives preference to tasks that coincide with its organizational roles. Once it has formed some partial solution, it can also use the organization to identify nodes that could possibly use (extend, improve) this partial solution. An organization therefore promotes cooperation by guiding nodes into working on complementary tasks and selectively exchanging partial results. However, because an organization represents common knowledge shared by the nodes, forming an organization can be costly and time-consuming. Organizations are thus relatively static, and must be general enough to allow acceptable coordination in a range of situations that could be encountered. This generality has drawbacks, because nodes are unable to coordinate in the best way for a given situation. Later extensions to the organizational approach (and preliminary steps in this research [Durfee et al., 1985a]) allowed nodes to exchange information to refine the organization based on current circumstances, but even so the nodes could not cooperate with complete flexibility, such as transferring tasks among themselves.

Control Through Multi-Agent Planning

In a multi-agent planning approach to cooperation, nodes together form a multi-agent plan that specifies the future actions and interactions for each of them.

Typically, one of the nodes acts as the group planner, and each of the other nodes sends this node all pertinent information. The planning node forms and distributes a multi-agent plan. Because this plan is based on a global view of the problem, all important interactions between nodes can be predicted. Such prediction can be crucial in domains such as air-traffic control where it is imperative that detrimental node interactions (vehicle collisions) are predicted and avoided [Cammarata *et al.*, 1983]. Unfortunately, achieving a global view of the problem might be extremely costly both in communication resources and in time, and the performance of the entire network depends on the planning node and would be compromised if that node fails. Multi-agent planning by a single node may thus be infeasible in many realistic situations.

When multi-agent planning is done in a distributed manner, there may be no single node with a global view of network activities, so detecting and dealing with interactions among agents is much more difficult. The general approach is to provide each agent with a model of other agent's plans (for example, Corkill's MODEL nodes [Corkill, 1979], Georgeff's process models [Georgeff, 1984], Konolige's belief subsystems [Konolige, 1984], and Rosenschein and Genesereth's exchange of tentative multi-agent plans [Rosenschein and Genesereth, 1987]). Interactions between plans are usually reconciled by synchronizing critical regions of the plans.

How nodes coordinate in multi-agent planning systems is explicitly specified in the multi-agent plan that identifies all actions and interactions of nodes. The strength of this approach is that the nodes form a plan for a given situation and can therefore cooperate effectively in that situation. However, in dynamic domains where situations change over time, the multi-agent planning approach would be less effective: whenever the situation changes, the nodes would have to stop their activities and recompute (in either a centralized or distributed fashion) a new multi-agent plan. Depending on globally-shared plans for coordination can thus have its drawbacks. To work in dynamic domains, nodes need the ability to cooperate despite having inconsistent views of planned actions and interactions, and should be able to form and communicate about plans asynchronously as problem solving proceeds.

Finally, the multi-agent planning approach to cooperation has been combined with other approaches in a two stage coordination process for controlling fleets of vehicles [Steeb *et al.*, 1986]. Each node (vehicle) has a copy of a pre-established type of organization, where the organization has a single coordinating node that plans for the entire group. However, the assignment of organizational roles is not static: although they know that they will have a leader, the nodes must communicate to determine which node will assume that role. Thus, in the first phase nodes exchange information to converge on a choice for leader, and then in the second phase they send information to the leader, which forms a multi-agent plan (possibly by assigning sub-planning tasks to other nodes). Therefore, although coordination is predominantly based on multi-agent planning, other techniques are fit in around this approach to increase its flexibility, resulting in a hybrid system.

Formalisms for Control of Cooperation

Several research efforts have been directed toward developing a more formal foundation for views of coordination. In general, these have been grounded in predicate logic, focusing on the beliefs, goals, intentions, and actions of nodes. For example, Georgeff has proposed formal representations for reasoning about interacting plans and for representing how agents view each other to develop multi-agent plans [Georgeff, 1983; Georgeff, 1984]. More recently, Georgeff and Lansky have extended these ideas [Lansky, 1985]. Another formal approach for agents to represent each other's beliefs has been developed by Konolige [Konolige, 1984]. Halpern and Moses have explored questions of common knowledge that are very relevant to DAI [Halpern and Moses, 1984]. For example, they have shown that agents may never converge on common views in certain distributed environments.

Rosenschein and Genesereth have similarly been developing formal models of cooperative (and not so cooperative) activity [Rosenschein and Genesereth, 1985; Rosenschein, 1985]. Much of their work is based on game theoretic views, where the payoff an agent receives for an action depends on the actions concurrently being taken by other agents. Assuming that each agent knows about how every possible combination of actions will affect the payoffs of each of the agents, Rosenschein and Genesereth study issues in what agents need to know about how other agents make their decisions (are they rational?) in order to coordinate their decisions. They have also examined issues in converging on common plans in distributed environments, concerned not so much with mechanisms for forming these plans as with identifying situations where convergence is possible [Rosenschein and Genesereth, 1987].

Formal models of cooperation allow researchers to mathematically prove theories about what cooperating agents can and cannot do, and about how assumptions about their domains and characteristics affect their capabilities. As a result, formal models are useful for delimiting problems and identifying research issues. However, bridging the gap between theories and implemented mechanisms is not a simple matter, and the formalisms currently provide little help for developing practical systems.

1.3.2 Distributed Operating Systems

Distributed control is also of crucial importance to distributed operating systems research. Among the issues of concern are control of resources to avoid contention and deadlock, control of scheduling decisions to maximize concurrency and meet performance needs, and control of memory to insure integrity of distributed data. These concerns overlap with many issues in DAI, but take a different perspective because tasks are typically considered to be independent.

Recently, research in domains where tasks are more interdependent (related by precedence) have emphasized the link between distributed operating systems and DAI [Zhao, 1986; Zhao *et al.*, 1987].

This section discusses important general issues and approaches to control in distributed operating systems without going into details about specific systems. For a more information see the survey by Stankovic [Stankovic, 1984].

Control of Network Resources

Tasks in a computer system require resources such as memory, files, devices, and CPU time. The operating system must manage and allocate resources so that tasks have access to resources they need. Tasks that contend for resources might prevent each other from proceeding and lead to deadlock. Detecting contention and avoiding deadlock becomes particularly difficult in distributed computing systems since information about tasks and resource needs is itself distributed.

In centralized resource management approaches, a single manager coordinates all accesses to a network resource. Unfortunately, this manager can be a bottleneck (since all accesses must pass through it) and dependence on a single manager makes the system unreliable. This second drawback can be reduced by having backup managers for the resource—but this adds the overhead of having the manager update the backup managers. More decentralized approaches allow access to resources to be granted based on local views. This reduces the time costs and bottleneck problems, but might not prevent contention for a resource (because local views may be inconsistent). In this case, the mechanisms must also be able to detect and recover from contentions that may lead to deadlock, usually by aborting and restarting some of the tasks. Coordinating access to network resources based on local views, therefore, is useful in domains where recovery is relatively inexpensive and infrequent compared to the cost of maintaining global views of resource access.

Control Through Distributed Scheduling

A related area of research is distributed scheduling. Tasks arrive at nodes over time, and associated with these tasks may be their resource needs, expected computation times, priorities, and deadlines. A node schedules its tasks to maximize some performance criteria, such as completing as many high-priority tasks to meet deadlines as possible. In the network of nodes, however, some nodes might have more high-priority tasks to complete over a given interval of time than others, and transferring tasks might improve overall network performance. For reasons of reliability and to avoid bottlenecks, a centralized network task scheduler is impractical. Instead, schedulers at each node should control both local activity and possible task transfers. The distributed schedulers contract out tasks: a local scheduler that cannot adequately schedule a task might contract that task out to another, less overburdened node. Distributed scheduling systems have borrowed and extended DAI techniques to do this contracting [Ramamritham and Stankovic, 1984; Stankovic *et al.*, 1985].

Control of Data Consistency

Controlling data consistency is much like controlling access to resources. A piece of data could reside at only a single node which controls how it is manipulated, but then this node could become a bottleneck (if that data is particularly popular) and reliability would be reduced (if that node fails, the data is lost). However, if the data is replicated at several nodes, then they must coordinate changes to that data, otherwise the data at the nodes might be manipulated differently leading to inconsistencies. To control data consistency, nodes either should coordinate changes so they all commit to certain changes and modify their copies simultaneously, or they could make local changes and then detect whether inconsistencies have arisen. In the latter case, nodes must negotiate about which of the different views to adopt, and then activities based on inconsistent views must be retracted. Coordination thus must either incur the overhead for continually insuring against inconsistencies, or incur the less frequent (but possibly more substantial) overhead of correcting the effects of any inconsistencies that may occur.

1.3.3   Natural Metaphors for Cooperation

Social Metaphors for Cooperation

Cooperation is an integral part of social interaction [Chandrasekaran, 1981]. A group of agents (people, companies) often achieve more by working together than by working alone. In an economy, for example, agents interact by exchanging goods and services: by finding a suitable exchange, they each benefit because the utility each assigns to what it trades away is less than the utility it assigns to what it gets in return. A market represents a forum for making coordination decisions, a place where agents can communicate to make deals. Decisions about cooperation are (usually) made locally, not imposed from some other authority. Control in an economy thus emerges from local decisionmaking and is usually communication intensive. Only after a series of messages and input from the more global market database do the agents arrive at a decision. Nonetheless, economic models provide one view of how independent agents can choose to cooperate, and these models have been applied to computer systems [Kurose *et al.*, 1985].

Another important model for social interaction is game theory [Axelrod, 1984; Shubik, 1982]. Given information about possible actions and payoffs for those actions, agents reason about how their local choices can affect and can be affected by the choices of others. They recognize situations where cooperation (or competition) will give them the highest payoffs. Game theory uses formal representations, and various properties of interactions can be developed based on certain assumptions. In fact, these game theoretic approaches have been used in DAI formalisms to understand various types of cooperation [Rosenschein and Genesereth, 1985]. However, game theory generally provides descriptive information (why some control decisions are better than others) rather than prescriptive information (how to make good control decisions) except in very trivial domains.

Organizational theory [Fox, 1983; Malone and Smith, 1984; March and Simon, 1958] assumes that participants are part of some overall team, and the purpose of an organization is to define the types of actions each should take and the patterns of interactions between them. An organization is thus established to serve a particular purpose—to coordinate agents working together in some basic way—and gives structure to the decisions that agents make that leads them to work together more effectively. Control is imposed on the agents through knowledge of their roles and the roles of others that constrain how they act and interact. The work of Malone addresses issues common to human and computer organizations and helps bridge the gap between these types of organizations [Malone and Smith, 1984].

Biological Metaphors for Cooperation

While social metaphors are concerned with cooperation between intelligent agents, biological metaphors address cooperation between much simpler agents. Therefore, it differs from the thrust of this research and we only briefly address it here by mentioning some representative work. First, the work by Dawkins views genes as self-interested agents that, through mutation and combination, can form cooperative groups [Dawkins, 1976]. Cooperation in this domain is accidental, not intentional, and control is not an issue. As a second example, neurons and neuron-like elements interact through their connections, and they can change their interactions by modifying these connections [Barto, 1985]. Rewards are propagated among the agents to reinforce patterns of activity that led to favorable responses (based on environmental feedback). Thus, cooperation is controlled by having agents make local adjustments to their connections which, over many iterations, eventually generates a connection structure (an organization) that leads to good performance by the overall network. Again, cooperation is not intentional (the agents are too simple to recognize how their decisions affect other agents).

Natural Language and Cooperation

Research in natural language processing, and particularly in dialogues, addresses many issues concerning cooperation and building common views. To communicate effectively, agents must use models of each other to plan their speech acts [Cohen, 1978; Cohen and Levesque, 1986]. The work by Grosz, for example, is concerned with discourse between potentially cooperating agents, and considers how a dialogue between agents exchanges sufficient information for them to develop a shared plan of action [Grosz and Sidner, 1985]. Coordination is achieved through discourse (to share information) and by assumptions that agents share about each other's goals and planning abilities that allow them to infer each other's (and hence their shared) plans. The common (or assumed common) knowledge gives structure to their interactions so that they can coordinate without exchanging extensive amounts of information.

Stories also deal with how characters' interactions are colored by a desire to cooperate, compete, conflict, etc. Understanding a story requires the ability to infer and represent the beliefs and goals of the characters. The approach by Bruce and Newman, for example, uses models of characters when attempting to interpret their actions [Bruce and Newman, 1978]. Although the focus is more on how to recognize relationships (including cooperative relationships) than on how to develop them, many of the issues in representing and reasoning about goals and beliefs are shared by other areas of research in cooperation.

1.3.4 Where Partial Global Planning Fits In

Our approach synthesizes and extends many of the previous approaches to DAI by building a unified framework for dynamically coordinating nodes. Rather than using contracting mechanisms for some situations and multi-agent planning mechanisms for others, our approach uses PGPs as a versatile coordination mechanism that permits dynamic control of coordination in each of these various styles. This dynamic control is coupled with the more static organizational techniques so that nodes have a basic structure for interactions which they can modify and refine dynamically.[2]

This approach emphasizes sophisticated local control that leads to making intelligent coordination decisions. An important aspect of coordination in social systems is the ability of the agents to make assumptions about each other—they have so much in common that they can infer most of each other's goals and beliefs without exchanging any information at all (often simply by hypothesizing what their goals and beliefs would be if they were in another's situation). Providing artificial agents with better local control mechanisms and thereby increasing their self-awareness can lead to better cooperative reasoning.

---

[2] Each technique for coordination must have some underlying organization to provide a framework for the more dynamic mechanisms. In contracting, for example, the underlying organization is the preferences that each node has for bidding on tasks. If nodes have incompatible preferences, so that nodes capable of performing some tasks do not bid on those tasks, then some tasks may remain uncompleted and the network cannot converge on overall solutions. The network should reorganize, causing nodes to change how they bid on tasks so that network performance improves. Similarly, the multi-agent planning approach assumes an underlying organization about the planning roles of nodes (or of how they will decide on the planning roles).

Once a node has intelligent local control, it can intelligently reason about coordination with others. In particular, it can *plan* how to coordinate with others. Although it has ramifications to distributed computing systems research in general and might even shed light on aspects of natural forms of cooperation, our research is predominantly interested in extending DAI research by integrating and improving upon several DAI approaches. We need to address issues in contracting out tasks, in multi-agent planning, and in organizing agents to guide decisions about problem solving and about how they should coordinate their problem solving. Many of these ideas are not new, and in particular Davis outlined many of the same issues [Davis, 1981]. Our research differs, however, in that it goes beyond speculation about how agents might coordinate their plans—we implement an approach that lays out exactly how coordination occurs, and we experimentally evaluate whether, in fact, the approach is practical.

1.4   Guides for the Reader

This book can be divided into four major parts. The first part is comprised of Chapter 1, providing an introduction to the research, and Chapter 2, introducing the experimental domain and testbed. The second part covers local planning: Chapter 3 describes how local goals are recognized, Chapter 4 discusses how local plans are constructed and executed, and Chapter 5 summarizes experimental results and evaluation. The third part is concerned with partial global planning: Chapter 6 discusses how more global goals are identified, Chapter 7 describes how partial global plans are formed and pursued, and Chapter 8 presents experimental results and evaluates the mechanisms. Finally, the fourth part, Chapter 9, contains concluding remarks and outlines avenues for future research.

The chapters about the mechanisms, Chapters 3, 4, 6, and 7, are all structured to first provide background information, then give an overview of the mechanisms developed in the chapter, then present those mechanisms in detail along with detailed examples, and then finally generalize the mechanisms to point out how they could be used in other domains. These chapters thus cycle through overview to detail to generalizations and back again. The purpose of these cycles is to put details and generalizations for important subgroups of mechanisms together to give the reader a more complete view.

This is as strange a maze as e'er men trod,
And there is in this business more than nature
Was ever conduct of. Some oracle
Must rectify our knowledge.
          –Shakespeare *(The Tempest)*

Chapter 2

Distributed Problem Solving and the DVMT

A distributed problem solving network is composed of semi-autonomous problem-solving nodes that can communicate with each other. Nodes work together to solve a single problem by individually solving interacting subproblems and integrating their subproblem solutions into an overall solution. Because each node may have a limited local view of the overall problem, nodes must share subproblem solutions; cooperation thus requires intelligent local control decisions so that each node performs tasks which generate useful subproblem solutions. The use of a global "controller" to make these decisions for the nodes is not an option because it would be a severe communication and computational bottleneck and would make the network susceptible to complete collapse if it fails. Because nodes must make these decisions based only on their local information, well-coordinated or *coherent* cooperation is difficult to achieve [Davis and Smith, 1983; Lesser and Corkill, 1981].

The **distributed vehicle monitoring testbed** (DVMT) simulates a distributed problem-solving network so that approaches for distributed problem solving can be developed and evaluated. In this chapter, we introduce the DVMT: the problem domain, the problem-solving knowledge and architecture

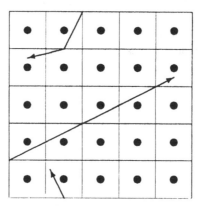

A simple view of a vehicle monitoring task. Each dot represents an acoustic sensor and the small square surrounding each is its range. Together, the sensors cover the overall area and vehicles moving through the area (indicated by arrows) pass within the ranges of different sensors at different times.

Figure 3: A Vehicle Monitoring Task.

of a node, the local problem-solving actions, the network interactions, and some examples of distributed vehicle monitoring problems. In the final section, we motivate the need for local and partial global planning in the DVMT.

2.1   The Experimental Domain

The experimental domain is vehicle monitoring. Acoustic sensors are dispersed in a two-dimensional area, where each sensor has a limited range. By distributing the sensors throughout the area, each part of the area is sensed by at least one sensor (Figure 3) As vehicles pass through the overall area, they move through the subregions of various sensors, so each sensor only detects part of the overall vehicle path. By combining the data from each sensor, the vehicle can be tracked through the entire region.

Two basic approaches can be taken to correlating the sensor data. In a centralized approach, all of the sensors are connected to a single processor that interprets all of the data. In a distributed approach, several processors are distributed among the sensors and subsets of sensors are connected to each processor. The distributed approach: exploits parallelism since the processors can work on different data concurrently; reduces communication since the large amounts of raw data are sent a shorter distance (to a nearby processor) and only abstract views are passed longer distances; and increases reliability since much of the overall area can be monitored despite the loss of a processor. The major disadvantage of the distributed approach is the difficulty in coordinating problem solving: since the processor's have limited views of the overall problem, they lack the context for deciding how and where their individual pieces of a solution should be combined. Because of the difficulties in coordination, distributed vehicle monitoring is a fertile domain for studying control of cooperation.

2.2 The Problem-Solving Knowledge

In the DVMT, a vehicle monitoring node applies simplified signal processing knowledge to the acoustically sensed data in an attempt to identify, locate, and track patterns of vehicles moving through the two-dimensional space [Lesser and Corkill, 1983]. The vehicles' characteristic acoustic signals are detected at discrete time intervals, and these signals indicate the types of vehicles passing through the area and their approximate locations at each sensed time. An acoustic sensor's range and accuracy are limited, and the raw data it generates can be errorful, causing non-existent (ghost) vehicles to be "identified" and causing actual vehicles to be located incorrectly, misidentified, or missed completely. A node applies signal processing knowledge to correlate the data, attempting to recognize and eliminate incorrect noisy sensor data as it integrates the correct data into solution tracks.

Each node has a blackboard-based architecture, with knowledge sources and levels of abstraction appropriate for vehicle monitoring. A **knowledge source** (KS) performs the basic tasks of extending and refining **hypotheses**, where a hypothesis represents a partial interpretation of some signal data. A hypothesis is characterized by one or more **time-locations** (where the vehicle was at discrete sensed times), by an **event-class** (classifying the frequency or vehicle type), by a **belief** (the confidence in the accuracy of the hypothesis), and by a **blackboard-level** (corresponding to the amount of processing performed on the data).

The blackboard has four principal blackboard-levels: **signal** (for low-level analyses of the sensory data), **group** (for collections of harmonically-related signals), **vehicle** (for collections of groups that correspond to given vehicle types), and **pattern** (for collections of spatially-related vehicle types such as vehicles moving in a formation). Each of these blackboard-levels is split into a blackboard-level for location hypotheses (which have one time-location) and a blackboard-level for track hypotheses (which have a sequence of time-locations). In total, nodes have eight blackboard-levels with appropriate KSs for combining hypotheses on one level to generate more encompassing hypotheses on the same or on a higher level (Figure 4).

The KSs can be divided into three basic types: synthesis, integration (or extension), and communication. A synthesis KS uses knowledge about how different distributions of frequencies are indicative of certain types of vehicles. It finds combinations of compatible data and filters out noisy data to identify likely vehicles based on a signal grammar. An example grammar is shown in

solution

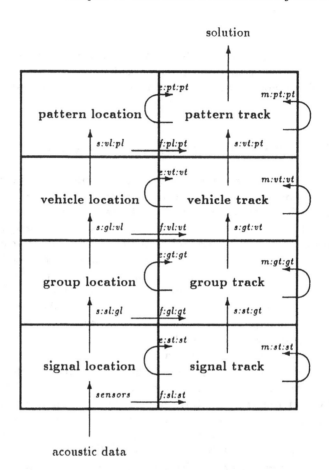

acoustic data

KSs combine hypotheses to form more encompassing hypotheses on the same or higher levels. KS names have the form $k{:}ib{:}ob$, where k is the type of KS, ib is the (highest) blackboard-level of the input hypotheses, and ob is the blackboard-level of the output hypotheses. Synthesis ($s{:}$) KSs generate higher level hypotheses out of compatible lower level hypotheses. Formation ($f{:}$) KSs form a track hypothesis from two combinable location hypotheses. Extension ($e{:}$) KSs combine a track hypothesis with a compatible location hypothesis to extend the track. Merge ($m{:}$) KSs combine two shorter track hypotheses that are compatible into a single longer track. The sensors KS creates signal location hypotheses out of sensed data. Communication KSs are not shown.

Figure 4: Blackboard-levels and Knowledge Sources.

Figure 5. To form a hypothesis at the vehicle blackboard-level with event-class 1, the node should first form hypotheses at the group blackboard-level with event-classes 2 and 6. In turn, to form these hypotheses it must use hypotheses with relevant event-classes at the signal blackboard-level (signal event-classes 2 and 6 lead to group event-class 2, for example). By looking for suitable combinations of hypotheses based on event-classes, the synthesis KSs can filter

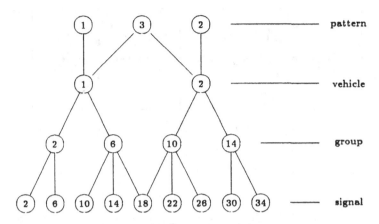

The signal grammar is represented graphically. For example, event-class 1 at
the vehicle blackboard-level is composed of event-classes 2 and 6 at the group
blackboard-level.

Figure 5: An Example Signal Grammar

out data at spurious frequencies and can increase the confidence in hypotheses
with a large degree of support (a large proportion of the supporting hypotheses
at corroborating event-classes are present).

An integration KS (formation, extension, or merge) takes several hypotheses
that each indicate where a particular type of vehicle may have been at some
sequence of sensed times, and uses vehicle movement (velocity and acceleration)
constraints to combine the hypotheses into a single hypothesis with a longer
track. For example, after applying synthesis KSs to data at sensed times 1–5
(Figure 6a), the node then uses integration KSs to join points together into
longer tracks. After it has formed some of the partial tracks, the node might
have the situation shown in Figure 6b. It attempts to combine the track d_1–
d_3 with the possible tracks for sensed times 4–5. It cannot join d_1–d_3 with
d_4''–d_5'' because of velocity constraints: according to knowledge about how fast
vehicles can move, a vehicle could not move from d_3 to d_4'' in a single time unit.
Similarly, it cannot join d_1–d_3 with d_4'–d_5' because of acceleration constraints:
although a vehicle could get from d_3 to d_4' in one time unit, it could not then
turn fast enough to get to d_5'. Thus, the only extension to d_1–d_3 possible is to
d_4–d_5 (Figure 6c).

Communication KSs (which are not shown in Figure 4) exist for each
blackboard-level and allow nodes to exchange information from their black-
boards. Transmission KSs access a hypothesis on the blackboard and build a
message out of its attributes. This message is then sent to some other node. Reception KSs construct new hypotheses from received messages and insert these
hypotheses on the blackboard. How the communication KSs decide what infor-

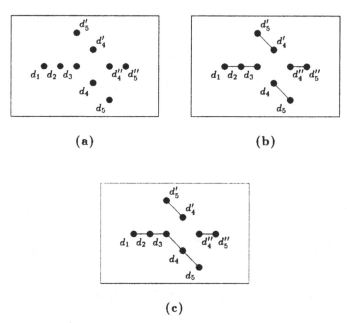

(a)   (b)

(c)

In (a), the individual data locations are shown (where d_i is data for sensed time
i). In (b), some locations at adjacent sensed times have been combined into
tracks, and the node then attempts to combine d_1-d_3 with each of the other
tracks. Because of velocity and acceleration constraints, only one combination
is possible, shown in (c).

Figure 6: An Example of Integrating Partial Tracks.

mation to exchange with other nodes depends on the organizational structure,
which we describe later in this chapter.

2.3   Control of Problem Solving

At any given time, a node must make control decisions about what KS to apply
to which hypotheses. Since the node's objective is to form credible hypotheses
at the top (pattern) blackboard-level, the control mechanisms should invoke
KSs that extend and refine the best (highest belief) hypotheses.

A **knowledge source instantiation** (KSI) represents the potential application of a particular KS to specific hypotheses. Each node maintains a queue
of pending KSIs and, at any given time, must rank the KSIs to decide which one
to invoke next. When the next action must be taken, the dispatcher retrieves
the most highly-rated KSI and invokes it. We use an extended Hearsay-II architecture (Figure 7) that lets nodes reason more fully about the intentions
or **goals** of the KSIs [Corkill *et al.*, 1982]. When a hypothesis is formed, the

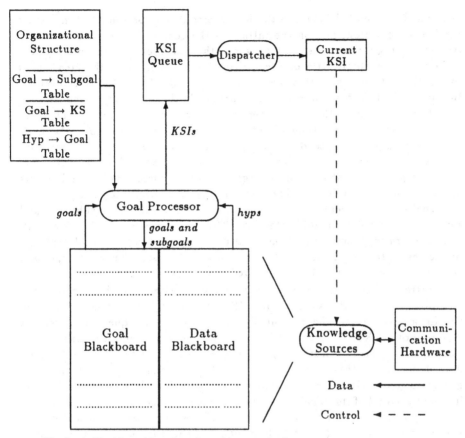

The basic blackboard-based node architecture is shown.

Figure 7: The Problem-Solving Architecture of a Node.

node builds goals to explicitly represent how the hypothesis can be extended and abstracted. The goals are stored on a separate goal blackboard and are given importance ratings. Goal ratings, KSI ratings, and hypothesis beliefs have values in the range of 0 to 10000 (the DVMT belief/rating range), where 0 represents no confidence and 10000 represents complete confidence.[1]

The **goal processor** performs the bulk of the control reasoning. Given new goals to satisfy, the goal processor steps through possible KSs and applies their preconditions to find any that could potentially achieve those goals. If a KS precondition indicates that it might generate the desired hypotheses to satisfy goals, the goal processor forms a KSI. A KSI is rated, where this rating is based

---

[1] This is for efficiency reasons, so numerical calculations are done on integers rather than real numbers between 0 and 1.

both on the estimated beliefs of the hypotheses it may produce (estimated by the KS precondition) and on the ratings of the goals it is expected to satisfy. By recognizing interactions between goals, the goal processor can modify KSI ratings. For example, two different hypotheses might cause the creation of two goals that are trying to achieve the same thing—their objectives overlap. Because a KSI that satisfies one may satisfy both goals, the rating of such a KSI is increased so that it is given precedence over other KSIs. The goal processor can also form subgoals of some goals. As an example, the node might form a goal to extend a track at a high blackboard-level, but the data that would extend the track only exists at low blackboard-levels. The goal processor generates subgoals of the high-level goal, where a subgoal represents an intention to develop data that might lead to achieving the high-level goal. The goal processor identifies other goals that overlap with these subgoals, and since the subgoals are highly rated, the KSIs to satisfy the overlapping goals have their ratings increased. Thus, goal processing improves control decisions by increasing the ratings of KSIs that may lead to the achievement of important goals such as extending a highly-believed hypothesis.

Control and problem solving are interleaved. After a KS is executed, the goal processor generates subgoals and KSIs. When goal processing is complete, the dispatcher extracts the most highly-rated KSI from the queue and executes the appropriate KS. Thus, the DVMT simulates the nodes' activities as follows.[2] Each node begins by transforming any sensed data into a set of signal location hypotheses (using the sensors KS). For each new signal hypothesis, the node generates goals to improve upon it and forms KSIs to achieve these goals. After it has created all of its signal hypotheses, a node then chooses a KSI to invoke. The KSI invocation may cause the creation of new hypotheses, which stimulate the generation of more goals, which in turn may cause more KSIs to be formed. The node then chooses another KSI and the cycle repeats until the node generates acceptable solutions. The criteria for deciding whether a hypothesis at the pattern blackboard-level represents an acceptable solution is statically defined before problem solving begins: the user specifies some minimum belief, expected spatial and temporal characteristics, etc.[3]

A snapshot of the contents of the signal, group, and vehicle blackboard-levels while solving a sample problem is shown in Figure 8, where each blackboard-level is represented as a surface with spatial dimensions x and y. At the signal blackboard-level s, there are 10 hypotheses, each for a single time-location (the time is indicated for each). Two of these hypotheses have been synthesized to the group blackboard-level g. In turn, these hypotheses have been synthesized to the vehicle blackboard-level v, where they have been connected into a single

---

[2] More details can be found elsewhere [Corkill, 1983; Lesser and Corkill, 1983].

[3] In many cases, the user specifies exactly the solution that the node should find, but this information is treated as an "oracle" that only tells the node when a solution has been found—the information cannot be used to guide a node's decisions.

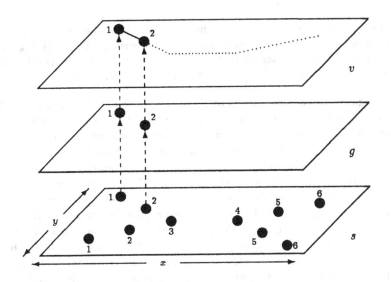

Blackboard-levels are represented as surfaces containing hypotheses (with associated sensed times). Hypotheses at higher blackboard-levels are synthesized from lower level data, and a potential solution is illustrated with a dotted track at blackboard-level v.

Figure 8: An Example Problem-Solving State.

track hypothesis (graphically, the two locations are linked). Problem solving proceeds from this point by having the goal processing component form goals (and subgoals) to extend this track to time 3 and instantiating KSIs to achieve these goals. The most highly-rated pending KSI is then invoked and triggers the appropriate KS to execute. New hypotheses are posted on the blackboard, causing further goal processing and the cycle repeats until an acceptable track incorporating data at each time is created. One of the potential solutions is indicated at blackboard-level v in Figure 8.

2.4 Coordination and Organization of Nodes

Each node is an independent problem solver and makes its own control decisions. When different nodes have data for tracking the same vehicle, however, they must cooperate to share information so that they form an overall solution. To coordinate, the nodes must have knowledge about each other so that they know how to interact. In the DVMT, the nodes share common knowledge in the form of an organizational structure.

An **organizational structure** specifies a set of long-term responsibilities and interaction patterns for the nodes. This information guides local control decisions of each node and increases the likelihood that the nodes will behave coherently by providing a global strategy for network problem solving. Currently in the DVMT, we assume that the organizational structure is established at network creation and is never altered [Pattison *et al.*, 1985].

The organizational structure is implemented in the DVMT as a set of data structures called **interest areas**. As implied by its name, an interest area specifies the node's interest (represented as a set of parameters) in a particular area of the partial solution space (characterized by blackboard-levels, times, locations, and event-classes). A node's interest areas specify its general roles and responsibilities in network problem solving. The goal processor uses the interest areas to modify the ratings of goals, so that goals to generate hypotheses in desirable areas of the blackboard have their ratings increased. Since the goal rating is a factor in rating KSIs, the interest areas can influence node activity, but because there are other factors in rating KSIs (such as the expected beliefs of the output hypotheses), a node still preserves a certain level of flexibility in its local control decisions. The organizational structure thus provides guidance without dictating local decisions, and can be used to control the amount of overlap and problem-solving redundancy among nodes, the problem-solving roles of the nodes (such as "integrator", "specialist", and "middle manager"), the authority relations between nodes, and the potential problem-solving paths in the network [Corkill and Lesser, 1983].

Because nodes know of each other's interest areas, the communication KSIs can decide which hypotheses (and goals) could be of interest to other nodes. The organization indicates communication blackboard-levels (to enforce communication of only more fully processed information). When it forms a new hypothesis on a communication blackboard-level, the node checks this hypothesis against the other nodes' interest areas, and if another node may be able to use (extend or refine) the hypothesis, a KSI to send it is formed. When this KSI becomes the most highly-rated KSI on the queue (a separate queue is maintained for communication KSIs [Durfee *et al.*, 1984]), the hypothesis is sent.

Because it affects both the local control decisions of nodes and decisions about how they interact through communication, an organizational structure can guide nodes into coordinating effectively. When it assigns appropriate responsibilities (interest areas) to nodes, the organization can lead to acceptable network behavior over the long term. However, an organization that is specialized for one short-term situation may be inappropriate for another. Because we assume that network reorganization is costly and time consuming, and since specific problem characteristics cannot be predicted beforehand, an organizational structure should thus be chosen which can achieve acceptable and consistent performance in the long-term rather than being very good in a limited range of situations and very bad in others [Durfee *et al.*, 1985a].

2.5   Specifying Problem-Solving Environments

Information about a particular network configuration and about the problem characteristics are contained in an **environment file**. The contents of an environment file (which are detailed elsewhere [Corkill, 1983]) are:

global tuning parameters: control parameters indicating such things as the relative weight of goal and data ratings in KSI ratings and whether subgoaling should be performed;

signal grammar: how hypotheses with different event-classes are related at the various blackboard-levels;

movement constraints: the maximum velocity and acceleration of vehicles;

node specifications: the nodes that comprise the network;

interest areas specifications: the problem-solving roles of the nodes;

knowledge source assignments: the KSs assigned to each node;

subgoaling specifications: how hypotheses at higher blackboard-levels should be subgoaled to lower blackboard-levels;

sensor assignments: which sensors send data to which nodes;

communication information: the communication delays and error rates between nodes;

solution specifications: the characteristics of desired solutions;

signal data: the simulated sensor data received by each sensor and when it is simulated to arrive.

To experiment with a particular distributed problem-solving situation, the user can build an environment file with the suitable characteristics. Because different aspects of the environment can be changed independently, the user can flexibly experiment with many aspects of the distributed vehicle monitoring domain, including the size of the network, the sensor configurations, the control strategies, the signal data to be interpreted, the rate at which that data arrives, and the communication topology. It is this flexibility that makes the DVMT such a valuable research tool: by modifying aspects of the environment, we can simulate an extremely wide range of distributed problem-solving scenarios, including situations that would not likely occur in the vehicle monitoring domain but which may be of interest in other domains. The DVMT is thus more general than a testbed for studying distributed vehicle monitoring. In fact, because the goal of our research is to study more general issues in distributed problem solving, the emphasis in the DVMT has been on providing opportunities for experimenting with distributed problem-solving situations, and has not been on accurately simulating the vehicle monitoring task itself.

2.6　　Network Simulation

The DVMT runs on a serial machine, and must interleave node activities to simulate the concurrent actions of the nodes [Durfee *et al.*, 1984]. The DVMT does this by cycling through the nodes and performing a **node execution** for each. A node execution corresponds to a node invoking a single local KS, and includes the activities that go into choosing that KS and that are triggered as a result of that KS. In the DVMT, the execution of a KS takes a certain amount of simulated time. Each time it executes a KS, therefore, a node updates its simulated clock to reflect this time need. At any given time, the DVMT performs a node execution for the node that is furthest behind.

In a simplified view sufficient for understanding the later chapters, a node execution has four basic phases:

1. The sensor information is checked and any KSIs corresponding to the simulated arrival of new sensor data are formed and placed on the queue;

2. Reception KSIs are invoked until all of the data that should arrive before the next local KS is invoked has been incorporated and processed (it might trigger new KSIs);

3. The most highly-rated local KSI is invoked, causing new hypotheses to be placed on the blackboard and triggering goal processing to form new goals and KSIs;

4. Transmission KSIs are invoked to send out any relevant hypotheses formed by the local KSI.

A node execution has a duration corresponding to the amount of simulated time that the node takes to execute. Because this duration depends on the KSI invoked and is unaffected by the control activities (how many goals and subgoals were formed, how many KSI preconditions were run), the simulated time needs of nodes in the DVMT do not completely reflect the node's activities during the node execution. Instead, the duration of the KSI is simply calculated as $ax + b$ where a and b are constants associated with KSs (defined in the environment file) and x is the number of hypotheses produced by the KSI. The DVMT's current inability to simulate the time needs for control limit our ability to measure control overhead in the experiments in Chapters 5 and 8.

2.7　　Problem-Solving Examples

To more completely understand problem solving in the DVMT, we now go through two examples in some detail. In the first example, we consider how a single node processes the data shown in Figure 9a. Data is received for 5 sensed times, and data for two locations exists for sensed time 4. Although not represented in the figure, we assume that each of the data points actually has 5 hypotheses in the same location, where these hypotheses have different

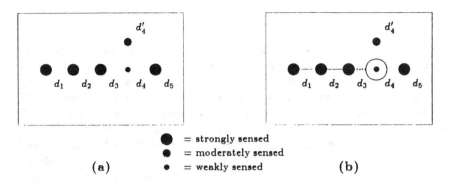

Figure 9: Single Node DVMT Problem-Solving Example.

event-classes. The event-classes are 2, 6, 10, 14, and 18, corresponding to the signals caused by a vehicle of type 1 (Figure 5). Furthermore, note that the data at times 1, 2, 3, and 5 are strongly sensed, while d_4 is weakly sensed and d'_4 is moderately sensed. We assume that all KSs take 1 time unit to execute, and that the interval between discrete sensed times equals one time unit (although in Chapters 5 and 8, we experiment with larger intervals so that nodes can run several KSs before they receive data for the next sensed time).

The sensor KSs run over the first 5 time intervals, from simulated time 1 to simulated time 6. For each of these KSs, the goal processing generates goals based on the new hypotheses and instantiates KSIs to achieve these goals. Because we only allow the node to form tracks at the vehicle and pattern blackboard-levels (by not giving it certain KSs), the node forms KSIs to generate group-level hypotheses from the signal-level hypotheses rather than to generate tracks from these hypotheses. At time 6, the node invokes the most highly-rated of these KSIs, and forms a group-level hypothesis with group event-class 2 out of data in d_1. At time 7, it does the same for data in d_2, at time 8 it does the same for data in d_3, and at time 9 it does the same for data in d_5. It skips over the data for sensed time 4 because it is less strongly sensed (and so less highly-believed). The node then invokes KSIs to form the group-level hypothesis with group event-class 6: at time 10 it works in d_1, at time 11 in d_2, at time 12 in d_3, and at time 13 in d_5. Using the group-level hypotheses, it forms vehicle-level hypotheses with vehicle event-class 1: at time 14 in d_1, at time 15 in d_2, at time 16 in d_3, and at time 17 in d_5.

The node then begins to combine the data into tracks. When it had formed the vehicle-level hypothesis at d_2 (time 15), the goal processor built a goal to combine it with data at d_1 (formed at time 14). Since the KS precondition for forming the track out of separate locations found a vehicle-level hypothesis at d_1 that could be used, the goal processor instantiated a KSI to form d_1–d_2. Similarly, at time 16 a KSI is formed to combine d_3 with d_2. At time 18, the node invokes the first KSI and forms d_1–d_2. The goal processor instantiates a KSI to combine this result with d_3, but because the KSI to form d_2–d_3 was on the queue first, it is invoked at time 19. With this result, the goal processor forms a goal to extend it to d_1, and and forms a KSI to merge these two short tracks. At time 20, the node invokes the KSI to extend d_1-d_2 into d_3 and forms d_1-d_3, and forming this track causes the goal processor to delete the KSI to merge the two short tracks since it would generate redundant results. The node also has d_5 at the vehicle-level, but cannot combine it with anything yet because the data at adjacent sensed times is not at a suitable blackboard-level.

When the node forms d_1-d_3, it generates a goal to extend this track into sensed time 4. Using the vehicle movement constraints, the goal processor is able to identify an area of allowable extensions to this track, shown in Figure 9b. When the goal processor forms subgoals of this goal, these subgoals overlap with goals to process d_4 but not with goals to process d_4'. Before subgoaling, the KSIs to process d_4' were more highly rated than those to process d_4, but because the subgoals increase KSI ratings the opposite is true after subgoaling. Thus, at time 21 the node invokes the KSI to form the group-level hypothesis for group event-class 2 in d_4, and at time 22 it forms the hypothesis for group event-class 6. The node forms the vehicle-level hypothesis for vehicle event-class 1 in d_4 at time 23, and when it does it forms goals to combine this hypothesis with data at both earlier and later sensed times. At time 24, the node forms d_1-d_4. At time 25, it forms d_4-d_5. The node builds a goal to combine these and at time 26 invokes a KSI to generate d_1-d_5. This hypothesis is at the vehicle blackboard-level, while solution specifications indicate that overall problem solutions must be pattern-level hypotheses. The node invokes a KSI to synthesize the track to the pattern-level at time 27. This KSI is completed at time 28, so the simulated solution time is 28.

This one-node example shows the basic activities of a node. It also illustrates how subgoaling can improve performance: without subgoaling, the node would have worked on d_4' before d_4. Because of vehicle movement constraints, it would have failed when trying to combine d_4' with the other tracks, and would eventually have pursued d_4. Subgoaling allows it to base expectations on highly-believed hypotheses and to use these expectations to focus low-level activity. However, the experiment did not reflect the costs of performing subgoaling, since this extra processing does introduce overhead.

We next turn to a simple two-node environment, shown in Figure 10. Each node receives data for 2 sensed times, and we assume again that each data point represents 5 hypotheses. KSs again take 1 time unit to execute. We assume that nodes can exchange track hypotheses at the vehicle-track blackboard-level (exchanging only high level tracks can reduce communication).

Both nodes invoke sensor KSs over the first 4 time intervals, even though each node does not necessarily get data for all 4 times. Until it runs the sensor KS for a particular sensed time, a node does not know what if any data has been sensed at that time, so it must run sensor KSs for every sensed time. The problem solving thus begins at time 5. At time 5, node 1 forms the group-level hypothesis at group event-class 2 in d_1 while node 2 forms a similar hypothesis

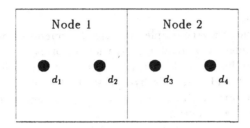

Figure 10: Multi-Node DVMT Problem-Solving Example.

for d_3. Similarly, at time 6 node 1 forms the hypothesis for group event-class 2 in d_2 while node 2 does the same in d_4. At time 7, node 1 forms the hypothesis at group event-class 6 in d_1 while node 2 makes the corresponding hypothesis in d_3, and at time 8 the nodes work in d_2 and d_4 concurrently. The nodes then develop vehicle-level hypotheses for vehicle event-class 1: at time 9, node 1 works in d_1 while node 2 works in d_3, and at time 10 nodes 1 and 2 work in d_2 and d_4 respectively.

At time 11, the nodes form tracks from their vehicle-location hypotheses. Node 1 builds d_1–d_2 while node 2 builds d_3–d_4. They complete these hypotheses at time 12. Each then checks the goal for extending its local hypothesis against the organizational structure, and determines that the other node is responsible for the area in which the track should be extended. Each node thus sends its hypothesis to the other. Because of communication delays, they will not receive results from each other until time 14. When they invoke local KSIs at time 12, therefore, the nodes cannot continue on their highly-rated data. Because they received data for signal-level hypotheses at signal event-class 18, and because this event-class supports vehicles of type 2 as well (see Figure 5), the nodes begin invoking KSIs to build a vehicle track of event-class 2. When they had formed group-level hypotheses with event-class 6, they also formed hypotheses with event-class 10 (the synthesis KS formed all possible hypotheses from the signal-level hypotheses with event-classes 10, 14, and 18). Because there were no signal-level hypotheses with event-class 22 or 26, these group-level hypotheses have low belief (they lack full support). Moreover, the nodes cannot build any group-level hypotheses with event-class 14 since they have no suitable signal data. At time 12, therefore, node 1 builds the vehicle-level hypothesis with vehicle event-class 2 in d_1, and this has very low belief because it lacks support. Node 2 builds a similar hypothesis for d_3. At time 13, they do the same for d_2 and d_4 respectively.

At time 14, the nodes receive the hypotheses they sent to each other. Each forms goals from its received hypothesis, and forms a KSI to combine them. At time 14, the nodes concurrently form the vehicle-track hypothesis d_1–d_4. Once again, they then invoke synthesis KSs at time 15 to form pattern track hypotheses. Since these KSs end at time 16, both nodes have formed the solution at time 16.

This example shows a very simple example of cooperation among the nodes. Each works independently on its data, but when it forms a transmittable result (at the vehicle-track blackboard-level) it checks the organizational structure to decide whether it should send this hypothesis to the other. An appropriate organizational structure can thus lead nodes to exchange sufficient results so that they can converge on overall solutions.

2.8   Limitations of the DVMT

As mentioned, the DVMT is a flexible research tool for simulating and experimenting with a wide range of distributed problem-solving situations. However, the DVMT does have limitations. Some limitations stem from its relatively static view of coordination (through organization) and from the way that nodes make control decisions. As we describe more fully in the next section, the principal focus of this research is on improving control and coordination in the DVMT. However, other limitations that are beyond the scope of this research nonetheless influence how we evaluate our new mechanisms.

One limitation mentioned before is the inability to simulate the costs of control. Potentially very costly control activities such as subgoaling and invoking KS preconditions are not adequately represented within the simulated runtime calculations for KSs. We are therefore unable to simulate different relative costs of problem solving and control to determine when control is and is not worthwhile. Because the costs of control are important to its practicality, the empirical evaluation in this research compares the *actual* computation costs of experiments with and without various control mechanisms. The overall computational runtime (CPU time) represents the total time spent on problem solving and control. Thus, although we cannot simulate situations where control is more or less costly, we can use the the computation time to recognize, with the mechanisms as implemented, whether the overhead added by the additional control mechanisms is offset by the savings in time spent on problem solving and goal processing because of better control decisions.

Another limitation is in the representation and calculation of confidence values (beliefs) for hypotheses. The calculations of belief are relatively simple, and a hypothesis's belief is often computed as a weighted average of its supporting hypotheses's beliefs. In particular, the belief computations lack the ability to factor in "independent verification" when computing beliefs. For example, say two nodes form identical hypotheses in an area where their independent sensors overlap. If they exchange these hypotheses, each will set the belief of this hypothesis as the maximum of the beliefs of the two versions. The belief calculations thus do not allow nodes to increase their confidence in results because of corroboration, or for that matter to decrease the beliefs of results because of "negative" evidence. The DVMT does not reflect the advantages of working together to independently verify results, so we cannot experimentally test coordination mechanisms in such scenarios.

Therefore, the DVMT does have some limitations that affect its use as a tool for experimentation and evaluation in the context of this research. However, these limitations are fairly minor compared to the flexibility that the DVMT does provide: despite its limitations, the DVMT provides a rich framework for experimenting with a wide range of issues in distributed problem solving, and this research makes use of much, but certainly not all, of this versatility.

2.9 How This Work Builds on the DVMT

Local control in the DVMT is based on a combination of data-driven and goal-directed forces. Because nodes typically process their best data in a data-driven manner, they are likely to eventually form highly-believed results. Because they also can subgoal important goals to trigger short sequences of actions (KSIs) to achieve those goals, they are somewhat goal-directed as well. However, the goal-directed component basically works toward relatively short-term goals (single extensions to a hypothesis). As a consequence, a node is never working toward any particular long-term goals: it takes actions that show promise in the near-term under the assumption that near-term promise leads to long-term gains. Because nodes make control decisions with such a short-sighted view, it is common for a node to jump among different partial solutions, doing a little work on one and then moving on to another when the first looks less promising.

Coordination through a static organization can also lead to erratic behavior. Because they only know of each other's general roles and responsibilities, nodes might not coordinate effectively: they can work at cross-purposes (on different overall solutions); they can unnecessarily duplicate each other's work (where their responsibilities overlap); they can distract each other into doing less important activities (by transmitting partial results of lowly-rated overall results, causing other nodes to work on extending those results); and they can fail to adapt to inefficient situations (where some nodes sit idle while others are overburdened). Although the network will coordinate better with a static organization than with no organization at all, the organization might not accommodate the needs of a particular situation, and the short-term network behavior may be ineffective.

These methods of local control and coordination depend on eventual convergence: although local problem solving might jump among solution paths, the drive toward forming highly-believed results will eventually lead a node into generating useful results; and although network activity might be erratic and poorly coordinated, the organizational structure slowly pushes nodes into converging on acceptable solutions. With short-sighted views of control and with general organizations, one cannot expect any more than such functionally-accurate behavior.

When experimenting with the DVMT, however, it became obvious that we need not settle for control and coordination at this level. Nodes could cooperate more effectively if they could communicate about their local activities and *plan* how they should work together. But before they can plan as a group, they need to be able to plan their local activities so that they can exchange plans to converge on more global plans. And before they can plan their local activities, nodes need to develop more long-term views of what solutions they should work toward forming. Because nodes in the DVMT initially could not do any of these things, we have developed mechanisms for identifying local long-term goals though clustering data, then for forming local plans, then for recognizing more global goals, and then for building more global plans—each set of mechanisms building upon the previous ones. These mechanisms are covered in turn in the next chapters.

The first step is to identify possible solutions to work toward. In a blackboard-based problem solver such as a node in the DVMT, this first step is difficult. Because the problem solver explicitly represents complete solutions only *after* it has solved the problem, any planning mechanisms must generate a new representation that allow them to recognize potential solutions in advance. This representation should be formed quickly and inexpensively to minimize the overhead for developing this view, but it still should be adequate for identifying important solutions to work toward. The first phase of this research thus concentrates on using approximate knowledge to cheaply form a representation that allows a node to recognize its long-term goals, and this is addressed next.

"Cheshire Puss," she began ... "would you tell me, please, which way I ought to go from here?"

"That depends a good deal on where you want to get to," said the Cat.

"I don't much care where—" said Alice.

"Then it doesn't much matter which way you go," said the Cat.

"—so long as I get somewhere," Alice added as an explanation.

"Oh, you're sure to do that," said the Cat, "if you only walk long enough."

–Lewis Carrol *(Alice in Wonderland)*

Chapter 3

Identifying Local Goals Through Clustering

A problem solver that more clearly defines its goals can make better decisions about the activities it should pursue. The problem solver can use the specific attributes of a more well-defined goal to constrain the possible steps leading up to that goal: it can back-propagate the desired characteristics of the goal to formulate a specific sequence of subgoals leading to the solution, and in turn can use these well-defined subgoals as context for determining what actions to take. In short, a *goal-directed* problem solver can identify and perform actions that lead toward its well-defined long-term goals, whereas a *data-driven* problem solver takes actions that seem promising based on its current state without any view of the long-term significance of those actions.

In this chapter, we describe mechanisms that allow a blackboard-based problem solver, which typically performs data-driven problem solving, to identify its long-term goals. By building a suitable representation of its problem situation—a representation specifically intended to improve its control decisions—the problem solver can recognize the areas where it should expend effort and how working in those areas can affect its future activities as it pursues its long-term goals. However, it must balance the benefits of having this view against the costs of forming it, and we focus on how a node can build an adequate view by applying approximate knowledge.

3.1   Background

Although goal-directed and data-driven problem solvers both begin with goals to achieve, the specificity of their goals is what sets them apart. A data-driven problem solver begins with the vague and often implicit goal of developing "good" solutions, where goodness is often measured as some rating (belief, confidence) of how well the data associated with the initial problem situation combines to lead to the solution. Because the problem solver essentially begins with no prior knowledge about which possible solutions are more or less likely, it takes any actions that might form promising combinations of data, possibly generating a very large number of such combinations as it explores a variety of solution paths. A goal-directed problem solver has more specific, explicit goals that let it prefer some solution paths to others, so it works more purposefully toward desirable solutions.

Goal-directed problem solving is more purposeful and usually less costly than data-driven problem solving, but it assumes that more specific goals are in fact available to the problem solver. These goals might be provided by the user (usually human) desiring a problem solution, but of course this would defeat the whole purpose of having an autonomous problem solver. Alternatively, the problem solver might enumerate each of the possible goals and attempt to achieve each in turn. This approach is used in MYCIN, for example, where to diagnose a patient's diseases the problem solver sequentially attempts to confirm whether the patient has each of the diseases known to it [Shortliffe, 1976]. Exhaustively considering each possible goal in this way can be costly, and alternative approaches have combined aspects of goal-directed and data-driven reasoning, attempting to use the data in the problem situation to prune the set of goals considered. For example, Aikins used "prototypical" rules that could hypothesize whether each goal (disease) was feasible based on a rough view of the situation (patient symptoms) [Aikins, 1980]. The NEOMYCIN system extended this idea by using prototypical rules to trigger possible diagnoses, and then reasoning about the relationships between diagnoses when trying to differentiate between them as it worked toward solutions [Clancey and Letsinger, 1981]. As another example, in Hayes-Roth's blackboard architecture for control, the gross characteristics of the problem situation trigger one out of a small number of problem solving strategies to be adopted [Hayes-Roth, 1985].

These methods for combining goal-directed and data-driven reasoning are useful in domains where the set of possible goals can be enumerated (so criteria for when to consider each can be specified) and where this set is relatively small (since each must have its criteria checked in the course of problem solving). Unfortunately, there are many types of problems where the set of possible goals is very large, and possibly not enumerable. For these problems, specifying goals demands more sophisticated and flexible techniques that can exploit current information to generate a set of possible, situation-specific goals rather than choosing from a previously established set.

After initially developing partial solutions, a problem solver can form specific goals from expectations about how these partial solutions could be enlarged. Through goal processing (forming subgoals), the problem solver can trigger sequences of actions that achieve the goals (enlarge the partial solutions), thereby coupling data-driven and goal-directed processing [Corkill *et al.*, 1982]. Unfortunately, the subgoal sequences represent relatively short-term intentions—single extensions to partial solutions—rather than long-term views of potential overall solutions. Moreover, before subgoals can be formed, a certain amount of purely data-driven processing must generate the initial high-level partial solutions to be extended. To develop long-term goals about potential overall solutions more quickly requires different mechanisms.

To generate a set of possible goals in a complex situation, a problem solver must transform its problem situation (data) into a form that is specifically intended to let it see these goals. For example, a problem solver attempting to interpret an image (perhaps represented as an array of pixel data) usually cannot simply match the data against predefined templates because the set of possible objects and combinations of objects seen in a non-trivial environment can be enormous. The problem solver may be expected to eventually identify each object in the image, but if it can start with a more specific goal such as "determine if the image is a house in a forest" then it has context that lets it focus more quickly on looking for features that fit into this goal. To find this goal in the first place, the problem solver could simplify the data, averaging the attributes of spatially adjacent pixels into a smaller, less exact representation of the same information. By successively doing this, a "visions cone" is created where the most abstracted image data (at the top of the cone) can be matched against simple knowledge of images [Hanson and Riseman, 1978]. For example, if the most abstracted image has a band of blue pixels above a band of green pixels, the problem solver might develop a goal to prove whether the image is in fact of an outdoor scene with blue sky above green forest. By abstracting the data using knowledge about images (that nearby pixels are more likely to correspond to the same object), the problem solver builds a representation that helps it identify possible goals to work toward—a representation that improves its control decisions.

A vehicle monitoring problem solver must use similar techniques to recognize its local goals. The set of possible goals (to form solutions for each of the different ways that vehicles could move through its sensed area) is extremely large, so rather than explore each possible goal in turn, the problem solver should abstract the data for its current situation to identify potential goals that it might work toward. Conceptually, therefore, the vehicle monitoring problem solver's techniques for identifying its goals are very similar to those of an image interpretation problem solver. However, abstraction in image interpretation can be based on the spatial relationships between pixel data, while the data used in vehicle monitoring has a richer set of relationships, such as temporal, spatial, harmonic (event-class), and signal strength (belief).

By building a suitable abstraction hierarchy, a problem solver can not only identify possible long-term goals, but also can find relationships among these goals. For example, if two goals call for different interpretations of the same data, the goals represent competing solutions since both cannot simultaneously be true. By reasoning about such relationships, the problem solver can approach solving the problem in a more informed way.

3.2   Overview

Transforming the node's problem situation into a suitable representation for control requires domain knowledge to recognize relationships—in particular, long-term relationships—in the data. This transformation is accomplished by incrementally clustering data into increasingly abstract groups based on the attributes of the data: the hypotheses can be clustered based on one attribute, the resulting clusters can be further clustered based on another attribute, and so on. The transformed representation is thus a hierarchy of clusters where higher-level clusters abstract the information of lower-level clusters. More or less detailed views of the problem situation are found by accessing the appropriate level of this abstraction hierarchy, and clusters at the same level are linked by their relationships (such as having adjacent time frames or blackboard-levels, or corresponding to nearby spatial regions).

A set of knowledge-based clustering mechanisms for vehicle monitoring has been implemented, each of which takes clusters at one level as input and forms output clusters at a new level. Each mechanism uses different domain-dependent relationships, including:

- **temporal relationships:** the output cluster combines any input clusters that represent data in adjacent time frames and that are spatially near enough to satisfy simple constraints about how far a vehicle can travel in one time unit.

- **spatial relationships:** the output cluster combines any input clusters that represent data for the same time frames and that are spatially near enough to represent sensor noise around a single vehicle.

- **blackboard-level relationships:** the output cluster combines any input clusters that represent the same data at different blackboard-levels.

- **event-class relationships:** the output cluster combines any input clusters that represent data corresponding to the same event-class at a higher blackboard-level.

- **belief relationships:** the output cluster combines any input clusters that represent data with similar beliefs.

The abstraction hierarchy is formed by sequentially applying the clustering mechanisms. The order of application depends on the *bias* of the problem solver: since the order of clustering affects which relationships are most emphasized at the highest levels of the abstraction hierarchy, the problem solver should cluster to emphasize the relationships it expects to most significantly influence its control decisions. This emphasis helps it make control decisions that lead it to efficiently form good solutions.

To illustrate clustering, consider the clustering sequence in Figure 11, which has been simplified by ignoring many cluster attributes such as event-classes, beliefs, volume of data, and amount of pending work; only a cluster's blackboard-levels (a cluster can incorporate more than one) and its time-regions (indicating a region rather than a specific location for a certain time) are discussed. Initially, the situation is nearly identical to that in Figure 8, except that for each hypothesis in Figure 8 there are now two hypotheses at the same sensed time and slightly different locations. In Figure 11a, each cluster c_n^l (where l is the level in the abstraction hierarchy) corresponds to a single hypothesis, and the graphical representation of the clusters mirrors a representation of the hypotheses. By clustering based on blackboard-level, a second level of the abstraction hierarchy is formed with 19 clusters (Figure 11b). As is shown graphically, this clustering "collapses" the blackboard by combining clusters at the previous abstraction level that correspond to the same data at different blackboard-levels. In Figure 11c, clustering by spatial relationships forms 9 clusters. Clusters at the second abstraction level whose regions were close spatially for a given sensed time are combined. Finally, clustering by temporal relationships in Figure 11d combines any clusters at the third abstraction level that correspond to adjacent sensed times and whose regions satisfy weak vehicle velocity constraints.

The highest level clusters, as illustrated in Figure 11d, indicate four rough estimates about potential solutions: a vehicle moving through regions $R_1 R_2 R_3 R_4 R_5 R_6$, through $R_1 R_2 R_3 R_4 R_5' R_6'$, through $R_1' R_2' R_3 R_4 R_5 R_6$, or through $R_1' R_2' R_3 R_4 R_5' R_6'$. The problem solver could use this view to improve its control decisions about what short-term actions to pursue. For example, this view allows the problem solver to recognize that all potential solutions pass through R_3 at sensed time 3 and R_4 at sensed time 4. By boosting the ratings of KSIs in these regions, the problem solver can focus on building high-level results that are most likely to be part of any eventual solution.

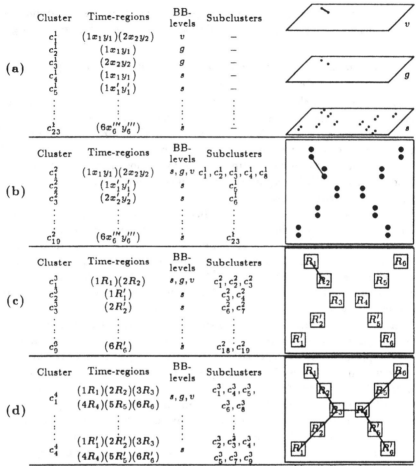

A sequence of clustering steps is illustrated both with tables (left) and graphically (right). c_i^l represents cluster i at level l of the abstraction hierarchy. In (a), each cluster is a hypothesis. These are clustered by blackboard-level to get (b); note that graphically the levels have been collapsed into one. These clusters are then grouped by spatial relationships to form (c), which in turn is clustered by temporal relationships to form (d).

Figure 11: An Example of Incremental Clustering.

In some respects, the formation of the abstraction hierarchy is akin to a rough pass at solving the problem, as indeed it must be if it is to indicate where the possible solutions may lie. However, abstraction differs from problem solving because it ignores many important constraints needed to solve the problem. Forming the abstraction hierarchy is thus much less computationally expensive than problem solving, and results in a representation that is too inexact as a solution but is suitable for control. For example, although the high-level clusters in Figure 11d indicate that there are four potential solutions, three of these are actually impossible based on the more stringent constraints applied by the KSs. The high-level view afforded by the abstraction hierarchy therefore does not provide answers but only rough indications about the long-term promise of various areas of the solution space, and this additional knowledge can be employed by the problem solver to make better control decisions as it chooses its next task.

3.3 Details

The mechanisms for developing an abstract view of the problem situation evolved considerably over the course of this research. Initially, the abstraction hierarchy was intended to emphasize "problem solving situations" that could be planned for. Thus, the hierarchy was constructed until such a situation was recognized, at which point a planning mechanism developed for that situation was employed to find actions (KSIs) suitable for the situation. The mechanisms were therefore extensions to earlier research that abstracted the problem state and made plans in response to particular situations [Durfee *et al.*, 1985a], where the extensions added flexibility in how abstractions and plans were formed.

As the more sophisticated planning techniques that are outlined in later chapters were introduced, many of the mechanisms initially employed in forming the abstraction hierarchy became unnecessary, either because other planning mechanisms took on tasks initially performed during abstraction or because the planning mechanisms, in their current state of development, assumed that the abstraction hierarchy had a certain form, so that the flexibility for abstracting in different ways became unused. This section describes the abstraction data structures and the mechanisms for forming the clustering hierarchy as currently implemented in the DVMT's planner, and does not address how the mechanisms evolved or how their capabilities could be extended.

3.3.1 The Clustering Data Structures

The clustering hierarchy is composed of individual clusters (Figure 12), where each cluster summarizes the characteristics of some set of hypotheses and indicates how this set of hypotheses is related to other sets (clusters). The clusters are grouped together into levels of abstraction, depending on how much abstraction has been applied. The clustering hierarchy is a list $(clusters_n \; clusters_{n-1} \; ... \; clusters_i \; ... \; clusters_1)$ where $clusters_i$ is a set of clusters at level i of the clustering hierarchy.

The structure of an individual cluster is based on how it can be related to other clusters. In the previous section that gave an overview of clustering are listed a set of relationships: temporal, spatial, blackboard-level, event-class, and

data-list	A list of the hypotheses summarized in the cluster.
blackboard-levels	A list of the blackboard-levels covered by the data.
time-regions	The combined time-locations of the data.
event-classes	A list of the event-classes of the data.
belief-range	A range (lowest-highest) of beliefs covered by the data.
past-work	A list of previously invoked KSIs that were stimulated by the hypotheses in the data-list.
pending-work	A list of not yet invoked KSIs that were stimulated by the hypotheses in the data-list.
vehicle-event-classes	A list of event-classes at a high blackboard-level (the vehicle level) that could potentially be derived from the event-classes of the data.
forward-cluster-list	A list of clusters where each contains data that could extend the cluster's data forward in time.
backward-cluster-list	A list of clusters where each contains data that could extend the cluster's data backward in time.
near-to-cluster-list	A list of clusters where each contains data that is for the same sensed time and for nearby locations as some of the cluster's data.
greater-cluster-list	A list of clusters where each has similar blackboard-level and time-region characteristics to the cluster and where the belief-range of each is greater than the cluster's belief-range.
lesser-cluster-list	A list of clusters where each has similar blackboard-level and time-region characteristics to the cluster and where the belief-range of each is less than the cluster's belief-range.
above-cluster-list	A list of clusters where each summarizes some hypotheses that may be derived from (are on the adjacent blackboard-level above) some hypotheses in the cluster's data-list.
below-cluster-list	A list of clusters where each summarizes some hypotheses that may have been used to derive (are on the adjacent blackboard-level below) some hypotheses in the cluster's data-list.
super-cluster-list	A list of clusters at the next higher level of the clustering hierarchy where each subsumes this cluster.
sub-cluster-list	A list of clusters at the next lower level of the clustering hierarchy where each is subsumed by this cluster.

Figure 12: The Contents of a Cluster.

belief. For some of these relationships, either two clusters are related or they are not—two clusters either represent the same data at different blackboard-levels or they do not. Other relationships depend on additional knowledge, and often knowledge used by the KSs as well. An example relationship of this type is how close the locations of hypotheses at adjacent sensed times must be for them to be temporally related (that is, how close they must be to conceivably be the same vehicle moving over time).

The parameters controlling such relationships are contained in the cluster-data structure. These parameters represent approximate knowledge about the domain, and for vehicle monitoring they are:

forward-backward-distance Maximum distance between regions covered by

clusters at adjacent sensed times for those clusters to be related temporally (the clusters could represent the same vehicle moving over time).

near-to-distance Maximum distance between regions covered by clusters at
the same sensed times for those clusters to be related spatially (the clusters
could represent spatially displaced data about the same vehicle at a given
sensed time).

belief-range For hypotheses whose time-locations and blackboard-levels
match, specifies how close their beliefs must be for them to be grouped
together in the same cluster.

A cluster then has two principal types of information: information about
the data that it summarizes and information about its relationships with other
clusters (Figure 12). The information about the data includes the time-regions
covered by the hypotheses (their combined time-locations), their blackboard-
levels, their event-classes, and the range of beliefs they cover. The information about relationships includes clusters related by time (both forward (later)
and backward (earlier)), by space (near-to clusters), by blackboard-level (levels above and below), and by belief (greater and lesser belief). Also, a cluster
is related to clusters at adjacent levels of the clustering hierarchy, pointing to
its sub-clusters (clusters at the level below that this cluster subsumes) and its
super-clusters (clusters at the level above that subsume this cluster).

3.3.2 Forming the Initial Clusters

The base-clusters (clusters at the bottom of the clustering hierarchy) are constructed directly from the hypotheses on the blackboard. The initial set of
these clusters is formed when the node has some hypotheses on its blackboard
and must make control decisions about which KSs to invoke in order to process
those hypotheses.

The base-clusters group hypotheses together to a very small extent. To be
clustered together at this level, hypotheses must have identical time-locations,
be at exactly the same blackboard-level, have beliefs within the range specified
in the cluster-data, and have a common vehicle-event-class. This last require-
ment means that the clustered hypotheses indicate that the same type of vehicle
may have been detected. To determine vehicle-event-classes for a given hypothesis, a simplified version of the signal grammar that maps each event-class at
an arbitrary blackboard-level to a set of possible event-classes at the vehicle
blackboard-level is employed. This simplified version of the grammar ignores
aspects such as how different event-classes collaborate and how much support
they give each other, but is sufficient for grouping hypotheses that could potentially support each other.

The node maps through all of the hypotheses on its data blackboard, and
for each first determines the vehicle-event-classes of that hypothesis. For each
vehicle-event-class, the node determines whether the hypothesis fits into an

already existing cluster (with matching vehicle-event-classes, time-locations, levels, and a belief-range that could be extended to fit the hypothesis's belief without exceeding the limits expressed in the cluster-data). If so, the cluster is updated accordingly (its data-list includes the hypothesis, its event-classes include the hypothesis's event-class, its belief-range is extended suitably). Otherwise, a new cluster is formed for the hypothesis and vehicle-event-class combination, the values for its characteristics are taken straight from the hypothesis, and it is inserted in the list of clusters at this clustering level.

After all of the clusters have been formed, the next step is to determine their relationships to each other. For each pair of clusters, their attributes are compared to determine whether any of the relationships hold. Figure 13 gives examples of how relationships between clusters are found. Cluster-1 and cluster-2 share some time-regions, have vehicle-event-classes in common, but have different blackboard-levels, so they are linked by blackboard-level relationships indicating that cluster-1 is *above* cluster-2 and cluster-2 is *below* cluster-1. (Figure 13, relationship a). Similarly, cluster-4 is above cluster-3 and cluster-3 is below cluster-4 (Figure 13, relationship b). One cluster can extend another forward in time if the time-regions of the clusters overlap (have one or more time-regions in common) or abut (the time of one cluster's last time-region is adjacent to the time of the other cluster's first time-region and their regions fall within the forward-backward-distance specified in the cluster-data structure). In Figure 13, relationship c, the time-regions of cluster-2 abut with those of cluster-3, and since the regions of their adjacent time-regions are within the forward-backward-distance and their vehicle-event-classes intersect, cluster-3 points to cluster-2 as a forward cluster and cluster-2 points to cluster-3 as a backward cluster. In the same way, cluster-4 points to cluster-2 as a forward cluster and cluster-2 points to cluster-4 as a backward cluster. Relationships need not be symmetric, however. For example, in Figure 13, relationship c, cluster-1 and cluster-2 have overlapping time-regions. Cluster-2 points at cluster-1 as a forward cluster (since cluster-1 shares time-region $(2\ R_2)$ and also has time-region $(3\ R_3)$), but cluster-1 does not point to cluster-2 as a backward cluster since cluster-2 cannot extend cluster-1's time-regions backward in time. Similarly, cluster-2 points to cluster-1 as a backward cluster but the reciprocal relationship does not hold. Finally, note that cluster-1 is not related temporally with either cluster-3 or cluster-4 because of its different region at time 1.

Because there are on the order of n^2 pairs of clusters given n clusters, and because the relationships between clusters may be asymmetric, the determination of relationships can be a costly procedure as the number of clusters increases. Even by implementing the procedures to check less costly requirements for a relationship first (so that failure to relate clusters will be found as cheaply as possible), the volume of comparisons between clusters can be quite large. Fortunately, only the relationships between the base-clusters need to be found in this way—clusters at higher levels of the clustering hierarchy can inherit relationships from the lower levels as will be described shortly.

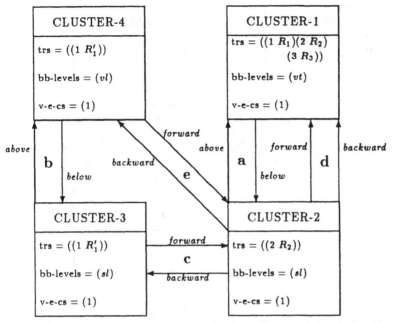

Four clusters are shown, indicating some of their attributes and the relationships
between them (marked with letters).

Figure 13: Sample Relationships Between Clusters.

3.3.3   Forming the Clustering Hierarchy

The clustering hierarchy is generated by successively grouping together clusters
at one level to form new clusters at the next higher level.[1] A set of functions for
merging clusters based on various relationships has been implemented, where
each function takes as input the cluster-set for one level and returns a cluster-set
for the next level. In essence, each function concentrates on one relationship
that differentiates clusters from each other in the input cluster-set and "ignores" that relationship in the output cluster-set, merging clusters together
which are no longer different when the particular relationship is ignored. Each
function concentrates on different relationships, and the current set of functions
are merge-by-level, merge-by-time, merge-by-time-split, merge-by-near-to, and
merge-by-event-class.

---

[1] Even when the attributes of a cluster are unchanged from one level of the clustering
hierarchy to the next, we still form a new cluster because the new cluster will have different
relationships to other clusters.

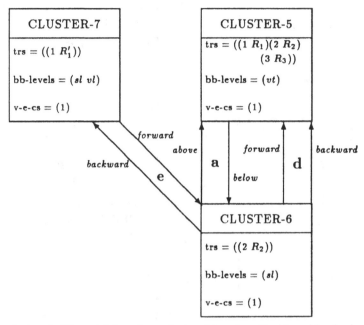

The clusters in Figure 13 have been clustered based on blackboard-level relationships. The resulting clusters at the new level of the clustering hierarchy and their relationships are shown.

Figure 14: Clusters Merged by Level.

Merge-by-level. This merges clusters that correspond to the same information at different blackboard-levels, where these clusters point at each other in their above-cluster and below-cluster relationships. The purpose of merging by level is to no longer differentiate between clusters based on the blackboard-level of their data. Clusters linked by the above-below relationship may only be clustered together if their other relationships are consistent. For example, in Figure 13, cluster-3 and cluster-4 can be merged by blackboard-level relationships since their other pointers are consistent (they both point to cluster-2 as a forward cluster), but cluster-2 and cluster-1 cannot be merged by blackboard-level since their forward-backward pointers are inconsistent. More specifically, if cluster-1 and cluster-2 were merged, their merged time-regions $((1\ R_1)\ (2\ R_2)$ $(3\ R_3))$ could not be related to the time-regions of cluster-3 or cluster-4 since they have different regions for sensed time 1. Merging them would thus lose the possible combination of cluster-3 and cluster-2 to form time-regions $((1\ R_1')$ $(2\ R_2))$. The result of applying merge-by-level to the clusters in Figure 13 is shown in Figure 14.

Merge-by-time. This merges clusters that are linked *unambiguously* by forward-backward relationships. If cluster-a can only be extended forward (backward) by cluster-b, and cluster-b either can be extended backward (forward) by cluster-a or cannot be extended backward (forward) by any clusters, then the clusters can be combined unambiguously into a single cluster with a possibly longer set of time-regions. The purpose of merging by time is to recognize sequences of time-regions (tracks) that could not be part of alternative sequences. For example, if in Figure 14 there were no cluster-7, then cluster-5 and cluster-6 could be merged by time. Similarly, if there were no cluster-5, cluster-6 and cluster-7 could be merged by time. However, because cluster-6 is temporally related to both cluster-5 and cluster-7, and because cluster-5 and cluster-7 have incompatible time-regions, merge-by-time will not change the situation shown in Figure 14: the cluster-set returned by this function in this case mirrors the cluster-set it received as input.

Merge-by-time-split. This merges clusters that are linked by forward-backward relationships and finds all possible sequences of time-regions—all possible tracks—by splitting up ambiguous sequences into a set of specific, unambiguous sequences.[2] In the situation of Figure 14, for example, the function takes the three clusters as input and returns two clusters as output: one cluster that combines cluster-7 and cluster-6 and another cluster that combines cluster-5 and cluster-6. The result is shown in Figure 15. Note that the two resulting clusters, cluster-8 and cluster-9, are unrelated, representing alternative tracks. Furthermore, the function to merge-by-time-split can in the worst case (a highly ambiguous situation) create a very large number of output clusters because the same input cluster could map to a number of output clusters depending on how many possible sequences of time-regions it can participate in.

Merge-by-near-to. This merges clusters which point at each other by the near-to (spatial) relationship—a symmetric relationship—and which have consistent other relationships such as forward-backward relationships (as were considered in the merge-by-level function). The purpose of merging by near-to is to ignore minor spatial offsets in the data (possibly caused by inexact detection by the sensor). Note that this function only considers the "nearness" of pairs: if cluster-a is near cluster-b which is near cluster-c, then the three are clustered together even if cluster-a is not near cluster-c. The assumption underlying this simple (and inexpensive) clustering criterion is that noisy data will center around actual signals rather than being distributed randomly in space.

---

[2] This description accounts for the name of this clustering mechanism in the DVMT. More generally, the mechanism represents the need to generate alternative clusters when a single cluster can be part of multiple, incompatible combinations.

CLUSTER-9
trs $= ((1\ R_1')(2\ R_2))$
bb-levels $= (sl\ vl)$
v-e-cs $= (1)$

CLUSTER-8
trs $= ((1\ R_1)(2\ R_2)$ $(3\ R_3))$
bb-levels $= (sl\ vt)$
v-e-cs $= (1)$

The clusters in Figure 14 have been clustered based on temporal relationships. The resulting clusters at the new level of the clustering hierarchy and their relationships are shown.

Figure 15: Clusters Merged by Time-split.

Merge-by-event-class. This merges clusters that have consistent time-regions and overlapping blackboard-levels but that have different vehicle-event-classes (recall that hypotheses with event-classes that could potentially contribute to the same vehicle-event-class are clustered in the base-clusters). The purpose of merging by event-class is to ignore the particular type of the vehicle being tracked.

The clusters returned by one of these functions represent the next level of the clustering hierarchy. Before they can be passed to the next function to be merged by another relationship, they must be related to each other. Recall that the base-clusters are related to each other by considering how each pair is related. Above the bottom level of the clustering hierarchy, however, such a costly set of comparisons need not be performed. Instead, the relationships between the new clusters are inherited from their sub-clusters. For example, to find the forward-clusters of a new cluster, the new cluster's sub-clusters are found, the forward-clusters of the sub-clusters are retrieved, and the super-clusters of these clusters are found. If there are any super-clusters, then the new cluster will point at each as a forward-cluster (except if one of the super-clusters is the same as the new-cluster, which can occur when clusters are merged by time or time-split).

The clustering hierarchy is thus formed by applying the functions in some order, and the form that the hierarchy takes depends on that order. At higher levels of the clustering hierarchy, more relationships in the data are ignored so that those relationships that have yet to be merged are emphasized. That is, the mechanisms that use the clustering hierarchy typically start at the highest, most abstract level and work their way down to lower levels until the desired relationship in the data is recognized. Therefore, relationships clustered later are more prominent (seen at higher levels) in the clustering hierarchy. It is thus important to generate the clustering hierarchy with a view to the relationships that are most important to planning. If the planner were rewritten to focus on other relationships, however, the clustering mechanisms would simply have to be applied in a different order to form a suitable clustering hierarchy.

The planner, whose implementation is described in the next chapter, emphasizes building solution tracks by processing data in an area (time-region) and then using the results to extend any solution track currently being developed. The most important relationships therefore are temporal and spatial, with blackboard-level and event-classes taking a back seat. The clustering functions are applied in the order: merge-by-event-class, merge-by-blackboard-level, merge-by-near-to, merge-by-time, and merge-by-time-split. By eliminating event-class, then blackboard-level, and then near-to relationships, the number of clusters that have to be considered during the more costly temporal merging steps can be significantly reduced. Merging by time then groups together clusters that form unambiguous partial tracks, and finally merging by time-split generates clusters representing potential complete tracks. These clusters correspond to *potential* solutions that the problem solver can work toward, but because clusters are developed using only approximate domain knowledge, they may not represent viable solutions. Clustering thus allows nodes to cheaply develop rough views of the data that they use to improve control decisions, but they must use their KSs to generate actual solutions from the data. As will be seen in the next chapter, having information about unambiguous partial tracks can be useful for finding areas where potential solution tracks share information, and so, places to initially investigate that avoid commitment to a single potential solution.

3.3.4   Updating the Clustering Hierarchy

In any dynamic environment, problem information will change over time. A vehicle monitoring problem solver, for example, might get new data from its sensors or might receive data from other problem solvers. To adequately represent the problem situation, therefore, the clustering hierarchy must be updated when relevant new information arrives at the node.

In the preliminary research, every new hypothesis was incorporated into the abstraction, whether the hypothesis was formed from local activity or from received information from sensors or other problem solvers [Durfee *et al.*, 1985a]. In the current implementation, the mechanisms do not need to incorporate hypotheses formed from local activity into the clustering hierarchy, because these hypotheses do not alter the scope of potential solutions to be pursued. That is, the locally generated hypotheses all fall within the scope of clusters already in the clustering hierarchy. Hence, the clustering hierarchy is only updated when new information is received from the sensors or from another problem solver.

The initial approach to updating the clustering hierarchy was simply to discard the existing hierarchy and to build a new one. This simple strategy proved very expensive: although the new information might alter certain clusters and relationships between clusters, most of the clustering hierarchy was often unaffected by the new information. Discarding all of this still valid information and deriving it all over again was very inefficient, so new mechanisms were added for appropriately modifying the base-clusters and then propagating any changes to higher levels of the abstraction hierarchy.

The first step is to map through the new hypotheses and either incorporate each into existing clusters or form new clusters. The functions used are the same as those described in Section 3.3.2 above. The next step is to take any new or modified clusters and determine how they relate to each of the other clusters. Thus, once again a pairwise comparison is made between base-clusters but this time only pairs involving new or modified clusters need be considered (since relationships between pairs of unaltered clusters will not change). When the set of base-clusters has been fully updated, there will be some set of new-or-modified-clusters, including clusters whose data-lists have not changed but whose relationships with other clusters have.

The clustering functions for merging based on various relationships are then once again employed, but this time they are given a list of the new-or-modified-clusters of the input cluster-set. When merging clusters to build the updated output cluster-set, only the new-or-modified-clusters are considered. These clusters might in turn cause new-or-modified-clusters to be formed in the output cluster-set, and this new list of new-or-modified-clusters is passed on to the next clustering function.

3.3.5   Identifying Local Goals

The clusters at the highest level of the clustering hierarchy—clusters that correspond to potential solution tracks—represent the long-term goals of the problem solver. An **alternative-goal** is developed for each of these clusters, and the alternative-goal points to the cluster upon which it is based and points to any *competing* alternative-goals. Two alternative-goals are competing if they specify alternative solutions which cannot both be true at the same time. For example, if two tracks have some common time-regions, then both cannot be simultaneously valid solutions because that would imply two vehicles being in the same place at the same time. To recognize competing alternative-goals, the mechanisms simply compare the sub-clusters of the alternative-goals' clusters, and if they have common sub-clusters then the alternative-goals are competing.

An alternative-goal is a goal for local problem solving. The clustering mechanisms allow the problem solver to identify the alternative-goals. The planning mechanisms outlined in the next chapter determine what sequence of actions should be taken to recognize which alternative-goals are most important to achieve and to achieve them.

3.3.6   A Clustering Example

Some simple examples of clusters and clustering were presented in Section 3.3.3. We now present a slightly more elaborate example showing how a clustering hierarchy changes when new data arrives, extending potential solutions and joining previously unrelated clusters.

A problem solver receives sensory information and creates hypotheses at the signal blackboard-level (sl) based on this information. A vehicle passing through the sensed area typically generates a set of signals—frequency event-classes—and a separate hypothesis is generated for each. For example, if a vehicle of type 1 passes through the area, it generates several frequencies corresponding to signal blackboard-level event-classes 2, 6, 10, 14, and 18 (see Figure 5), usually all detected at the same location. Each of these different signals is represented as a separate hypothesis at the signal blackboard-level.

The base-clusters group together hypotheses with the same time and location attributes and that could contribute to a compatible vehicle type. Therefore, the base-clusters in Figure 16 that have vehicle-event-class 1 each have five hypotheses in their data-list. However, because a hypothesis at signal event-class 18 is also a characteristic of vehicles of type 2, a separate cluster is made for this possibility at each time-location. Therefore, two base clusters are formed for each of the four distinct time-regions in Figure 16.

The first step in clustering, merge-by-event-class, brings together the pairs of clusters for separate vehicle-event-classes, and the vehicle-event-classes attribute of these clusters reflects both possibilities. The next step, merge-by-level generates copies of the clusters at the next level since all of the clusters contained data at the same blackboard-level (sl). Merge-by-near-to is applied next, and again generates copies of the clusters at the next clustering hierarchy level, this time because there is no spatial ambiguity. Merge-by-time combines the clusters for sensed times 3 and 4 since their temporal combination is unambiguous. Merge-by-time-split cannot merge clusters any further, and the result is three unrelated top-level clusters, each corresponding to a different potential solution that could be developed.

After some time has elapsed, the node receives new information (possibly from another node): a hypothesis at the vehicle blackboard-level, where the hypothesis indicates a short track for sensed times 2 and 3. This track fills the gap between the local data for sensed time 1 and the data for sensed time 3, as is shown in Figure 17. The base-clusters are updated by generating a new cluster (since the received hypothesis does not fit any existing base-clusters), which is related to the clusters for sensed times 1, 3, and 4. Merge-by-event-class has no effect on the new cluster, but merge-by-level combines the new cluster with the existing cluster at sensed time 3—they have common time-regions and their relationships to other clusters are consistent. The modified existing cluster is then used by merge-by-near-to which cannot combine it with any clusters. Merge-by-time combines the modified cluster with the existing cluster

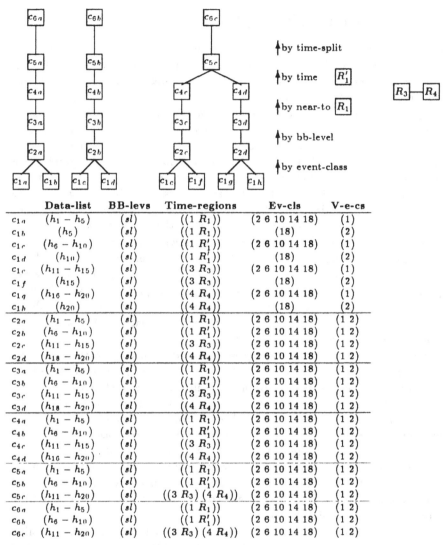

	Data-list	BB-levs	Time-regions	Ev-cls	V-e-cs
c_{1a}	$(h_1 - h_5)$	(sl)	$((1\ R_1))$	$(2\ 6\ 10\ 14\ 18)$	(1)
c_{1b}	(h_5)	(sl)	$((1\ R_1))$	(18)	(2)
c_{1c}	$(h_6 - h_{10})$	(sl)	$((1\ R_1'))$	$(2\ 6\ 10\ 14\ 18)$	(1)
c_{1d}	(h_{10})	(sl)	$((1\ R_1'))$	(18)	(2)
c_{1e}	$(h_{11} - h_{15})$	(sl)	$((3\ R_3))$	$(2\ 6\ 10\ 14\ 18)$	(1)
c_{1f}	(h_{15})	(sl)	$((3\ R_3))$	(18)	(2)
c_{1g}	$(h_{16} - h_{20})$	(sl)	$((4\ R_4))$	$(2\ 6\ 10\ 14\ 18)$	(1)
c_{1h}	(h_{20})	(sl)	$((4\ R_4))$	(18)	(2)
c_{2a}	$(h_1 - h_5)$	(sl)	$((1\ R_1))$	$(2\ 6\ 10\ 14\ 18)$	$(1\ 2)$
c_{2b}	$(h_6 - h_{10})$	(sl)	$((1\ R_1'))$	$(2\ 6\ 10\ 14\ 18)$	$(1\ 2)$
c_{2c}	$(h_{11} - h_{15})$	(sl)	$((3\ R_3))$	$(2\ 6\ 10\ 14\ 18)$	$(1\ 2)$
c_{2d}	$(h_{18} - h_{20})$	(sl)	$((4\ R_4))$	$(2\ 6\ 10\ 14\ 18)$	$(1\ 2)$
c_{3a}	$(h_1 - h_5)$	(sl)	$((1\ R_1))$	$(2\ 6\ 10\ 14\ 18)$	$(1\ 2)$
c_{3b}	$(h_6 - h_{10})$	(sl)	$((1\ R_1'))$	$(2\ 6\ 10\ 14\ 18)$	$(1\ 2)$
c_{3c}	$(h_{11} - h_{15})$	(sl)	$((3\ R_3))$	$(2\ 6\ 10\ 14\ 18)$	$(1\ 2)$
c_{3d}	$(h_{18} - h_{20})$	(sl)	$((4\ R_4))$	$(2\ 6\ 10\ 14\ 18)$	$(1\ 2)$
c_{4a}	$(h_1 - h_5)$	(sl)	$((1\ R_1))$	$(2\ 6\ 10\ 14\ 18)$	$(1\ 2)$
c_{4b}	$(h_6 - h_{10})$	(sl)	$((1\ R_1'))$	$(2\ 6\ 10\ 14\ 18)$	$(1\ 2)$
c_{4c}	$(h_{11} - h_{15})$	(sl)	$((3\ R_3))$	$(2\ 6\ 10\ 14\ 18)$	$(1\ 2)$
c_{4d}	$(h_{16} - h_{20})$	(sl)	$((4\ R_4))$	$(2\ 6\ 10\ 14\ 18)$	$(1\ 2)$
c_{5a}	$(h_1 - h_5)$	(sl)	$((1\ R_1))$	$(2\ 6\ 10\ 14\ 18)$	$(1\ 2)$
c_{5b}	$(h_6 - h_{10})$	(sl)	$((1\ R_1'))$	$(2\ 6\ 10\ 14\ 18)$	$(1\ 2)$
c_{5c}	$(h_{11} - h_{20})$	(sl)	$((3\ R_3)\ (4\ R_4))$	$(2\ 6\ 10\ 14\ 18)$	$(1\ 2)$
c_{6a}	$(h_1 - h_5)$	(sl)	$((1\ R_1))$	$(2\ 6\ 10\ 14\ 18)$	$(1\ 2)$
c_{6b}	$(h_6 - h_{10})$	(sl)	$((1\ R_1'))$	$(2\ 6\ 10\ 14\ 18)$	$(1\ 2)$
c_{6c}	$(h_{11} - h_{20})$	(sl)	$((3\ R_3)\ (4\ R_4))$	$(2\ 6\ 10\ 14\ 18)$	$(1\ 2)$

Clustering hierarchy is shown graphically above left, and the relationships between regions is shown above right. For each cluster is given the hypotheses it summarizes, their blackboard-levels, time-regions, and event-classes, and the vehicle-event-classes that the clustered data supports.

Figure 16: Clustering Example Hierarchy.

for sensed time 4, and generates a modified cluster indicating the unambiguous track for sensed times 2 through 4. Finally, merge-by-time-split can combine this modified cluster with the (previously unrelated) clusters at sensed time 1, forming two top-level clusters representing potential solution tracks.

The addition of new information therefore may both extend potential solutions and collapse the clustering hierarchy. By providing information that relates previously unrelated clusters—by filling in gaps between clusters—the new information can reduce the number of top-level clusters. The clustering mechanisms at times need to increase the scope of existing clusters, eliminate other clusters that are obsolete, and propagate the changes to affect relationships between the clusters that remain. In turn, as top-level clusters are created, modified, and deleted, the set of alternative-goals must be updated in the same way: by creating new, modifying existing, and deleting obsolete alternative goals when the top-level clusters change.

3.4 Generalizing

The clustering hierarchy serves two major purposes. First, it groups together related data to indicate where potential solutions may lie. In a problem solver that begins with only vague goals, identifying potential solutions can help resolve uncertainty about what hypotheses to develop and how to develop them. The second (and related) purpose of the clustering hierarchy is to identify important subgoals (sub-solutions) that provide the problem solver with even more information about how to develop the complete potential solutions. When forming the overall potential solutions, the clustering mechanisms automatically generate likely sub-solutions (smaller groupings of related data) at lower levels of the clustering hierarchy. Identifying potential solutions and their important subgoals is the first step toward planning effective sequences of actions.

These mechanisms are necessary in the vehicle monitoring domain because a vehicle monitoring problem solver begins with a quantity of data to be processed and little direction other than to develop a "good" interpretation of that data. Not all domains are like this, however. The attributes of the domain that make clustering appropriate are:

- The problem solver begins with a vague goal (such as to develop a "good" interpretation of some data).

- The set of specific goals is so large that enumerating them and trying each in turn is infeasible.

- The set of specific goals is so large that enumerating them and applying some predefined criteria for each to decide whether to pursue it is infeasible.

- The set possible subgoals of each goal is so large that, even if it were given specific goals, the problem solver lacks the information it needs to determine how to satisfy those goals (what subgoals to pursue).

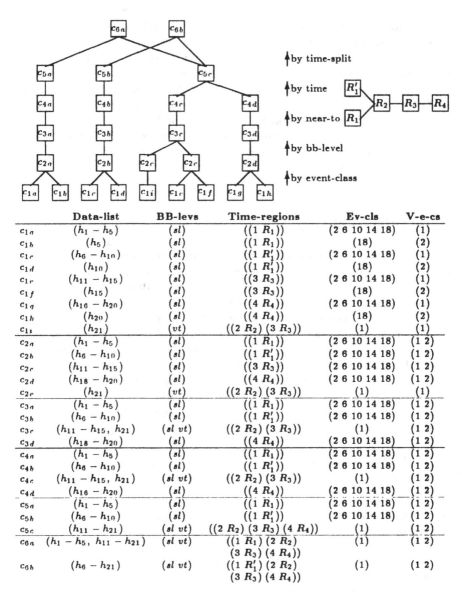

	Data-list	BB-levs	Time-regions	Ev-cls	V-e-cs
c_{1a}	$(h_1 - h_5)$	(sl)	$((1\ R_1))$	(2 6 10 14 18)	(1)
c_{1b}	(h_5)	(sl)	$((1\ R_1))$	(18)	(2)
c_{1c}	$(h_6 - h_{10})$	(sl)	$((1\ R_1'))$	(2 6 10 14 18)	(1)
c_{1d}	(h_{10})	(sl)	$((1\ R_1'))$	(18)	(2)
c_{1e}	$(h_{11} - h_{15})$	(sl)	$((3\ R_3))$	(2 6 10 14 18)	(1)
c_{1f}	(h_{15})	(sl)	$((3\ R_3))$	(18)	(2)
c_{1g}	$(h_{16} - h_{20})$	(sl)	$((4\ R_4))$	(2 6 10 14 18)	(1)
c_{1h}	(h_{20})	(sl)	$((4\ R_4))$	(18)	(2)
c_{1i}	(h_{21})	(vt)	$((2\ R_2)\ (3\ R_3))$	(1)	(1)
c_{2a}	$(h_1 - h_5)$	(sl)	$((1\ R_1))$	(2 6 10 14 18)	(1 2)
c_{2b}	$(h_6 - h_{10})$	(sl)	$((1\ R_1'))$	(2 6 10 14 18)	(1 2)
c_{2c}	$(h_{11} - h_{15})$	(sl)	$((3\ R_3))$	(2 6 10 14 18)	(1 2)
c_{2d}	$(h_{18} - h_{20})$	(sl)	$((4\ R_4))$	(2 6 10 14 18)	(1 2)
c_{2e}	(h_{21})	(vt)	$((2\ R_2)\ (3\ R_3))$	(1)	(1)
c_{3a}	$(h_1 - h_5)$	(sl)	$((1\ R_1))$	(2 6 10 14 18)	(1 2)
c_{3b}	$(h_6 - h_{10})$	(sl)	$((1\ R_1'))$	(2 6 10 14 18)	(1 2)
c_{3c}	$(h_{11} - h_{15},\ h_{21})$	$(sl\ vt)$	$((2\ R_2)\ (3\ R_3))$	(1)	(1 2)
c_{3d}	$(h_{18} - h_{20})$	(sl)	$((4\ R_4))$	(2 6 10 14 18)	(1 2)
c_{4a}	$(h_1 - h_5)$	(sl)	$((1\ R_1))$	(2 6 10 14 18)	(1 2)
c_{4b}	$(h_6 - h_{10})$	(sl)	$((1\ R_1'))$	(2 6 10 14 18)	(1 2)
c_{4c}	$(h_{11} - h_{15},\ h_{21})$	$(sl\ vt)$	$((2\ R_2)\ (3\ R_3))$	(1)	(1 2)
c_{4d}	$(h_{16} - h_{20})$	(sl)	$((4\ R_4))$	(2 6 10 14 18)	(1 2)
c_{5a}	$(h_1 - h_5)$	(sl)	$((1\ R_1))$	(2 6 10 14 18)	(1 2)
c_{5b}	$(h_6 - h_{10})$	(sl)	$((1\ R_1'))$	(2 6 10 14 18)	(1 2)
c_{5c}	$(h_{11} - h_{21})$	$(sl\ vt)$	$((2\ R_2)\ (3\ R_3)\ (4\ R_4))$	(1)	(1 2)
c_{6a}	$(h_1 - h_5,\ h_{11} - h_{21})$	$(sl\ vt)$	$((1\ R_1)\ (2\ R_2)$ $(3\ R_3)\ (4\ R_4))$	(1)	(1 2)
c_{6b}	$(h_6 - h_{21})$	$(sl\ vt)$	$((1\ R_1')\ (2\ R_2)$ $(3\ R_3)\ (4\ R_4))$	(1)	(1 2)

Clustering hierarchy is shown graphically above left, and the relationships between regions is shown above right. For each cluster is given the hypotheses it summarizes, their blackboard-levels, time-regions, and event-classes, and the vehicle-event-classes that the clustered data supports.

Figure 17: Clustering Example Hierarchy Incorporating New Data

- The problem situation provides sufficient information for the problem solver to identify a small set of likely goals and subgoals by applying approximate domain knowledge.

Domains that do not have these attributes probably will not need the clustering mechanisms described in this chapter. Given specified goals and the ability to break them down into subgoals, a problem solver could bypass these mechanisms and go straight to the planning mechanisms covered in the next chapter. However, in many real-world domains the problem solver cannot start with a complete list of possible specific goals: in an unpredictable world, the set of situations the problem solver may encounter cannot be predicted, and hence the set of possible specific goals it will need to achieve cannot be enumerated. In these circumstances, the problem solver must have the ability to develop specific goals "on the fly" based on the situation it faces. If the problem solver develops solutions by investigating how different pieces of problem information are related, it can use clustering mechanisms like those described in this chapter.

The most important prerequisite for building similar mechanisms in another domain is identifying the relationships in the problem information to exploit in clustering. In a blackboard-based problem solver, the inherent organization of the blackboard provides many useful relationships: certain attributes of the units placed on the blackboard are used as indices that facilitate storing and retrieving the units. In a well-designed blackboard architecture, these attributes correspond to the important relationships between units.[3] In the DVMT, for example, the hypothesis blackboard has blackboard-level, time, and location indices: these same relationships (blackboard-level, temporal, and spatial) are exactly those emphasized in the clustering hierarchy.

Problem solvers that do not employ a blackboard architecture can also have important relationships between pieces of problem information. For example, a problem solver to schedule tasks (perhaps in a job-shop) can use relationships between tasks: temporal relationships (some tasks may need to be performed before others, some tasks may have to execute simultaneously); spatial relationships (tasks may be spatially distributed); and resource relationships (tasks may compete for processing resources)—just to name a few. To build a high-level view of such a situation, the problem solver can exploit these relationships to cluster information (tasks) into related groups to recognize the important long-term goals of problem solving (such as how a group of tasks all contribute to a final product).

Once the relationships have been identified, functions to generate the set of base-clusters and functions to merge clusters based on certain relationships can

---

[3] The principal function of a KS in an interpretation task is to combine related hypotheses into larger, more encompassing hypotheses. A well-designed blackboard architecture will store hypotheses so that a KS can efficiently retrieve related hypotheses, so the hypotheses are stored based on their attributes that determine their relationships.

be implemented very much like those described above. Although the concepts involved in developing these mechanisms is straightforward, the implementation is not always simple. For example, the merge-by-time-split function described above is complicated by the bookkeeping involved in keeping track of what combinations of time-regions have been developed and the desire to avoid developing redundant combinations (by combining the same clusters in a different order) while not missing any new combinations. Similarly, the functions to update the clustering hierarchy are conceptually straightforward, but keeping track of new and modified clusters and propagating changes to relationships as clusters are formed, modified, and deleted complicate the functions. The description of the functions implemented as part of the DVMT provide the conceptual framework; the rest is a matter of software engineering, understanding the complexity of algorithms, and good programming practice.

Forming a clustering hierarchy requires the clustering functions to be applied in some order. The order used in the DVMT, as described in this chapter, was chosen based on knowledge about how problem solving is done by the system and how the planning mechanisms described in the next chapter are expected to behave. In fact, there may be no order that consistently generates the most useful clustering hierarchy for every problem situation, and our clustering mechanisms were developed to be applicable in any order. In a given application domain, therefore, the decisions about what relationships to emphasize in the clustering hierarchy must be made by the implementer of the problem solver using an understanding of what aspects of a problem situation are most important for making intelligent local decisions. Fortunately, by implementing clustering mechanisms that can be applied in any order (like those described in this chapter), different clustering hierarchies can be easily developed to gain experience and insight into which is the most effective.

The planning mechanisms described in subsequent chapters can use local goals independently of how they are generated by a node or supplied to the node from an outside source. However, forming a clustering hierarchy is an appropriate technique for recognizing goals in domains such as data interpretation, where identifying specific goals and their subgoals cannot otherwise be accomplished. The mechanisms and data structures described in this chapter provide an example of how clustering hierarchies can be formed in a particular domain, and this example helps suggest a framework for implementing clustering hierarchies in other domains. Finally, by identifying more specific local goals and their subgoals, the problem solver can then proceed to develop plans for determining which of the goals are worth pursuing and how to go about pursuing them.

It is a bad plan that admits of no modification. –Publius

Chapter 4

Planning Local Problem Solving

Once the problem solver has identified a set of *possible* specific local goals, it should plan activities that not only achieve goals, but also resolve uncertainty about which goals to pursue. Some of these goals might represent alternative and conflicting solutions, and others, on further investigation, might prove to be incompatible with the problem information. By taking actions in pursuit of the goals, the problem solver can work toward acceptable solutions, and by ordering its actions appropriately, the problem solver may be able to more quickly recognize which goals are worthwhile.

An intelligent planner should not simply pursue goals one at a time, but should reason about goal interactions in order to develop a problem solving strategy that effectively resolves uncertainty about which goals to pursue at the same time that it pursues them. By working on subgoals shared by several goals, the planner can use subgoal solutions to better identify which of the larger goals are more important. The planner can also expend the minimum effort on the initial exploration of a plan by performing less costly actions first and then using the results of these actions to decide whether continued work on the plan is warranted. When it cannot decide between goals that have no common subgoals, the planner should work on subgoals that are most likely to help distinguish between the overall goals.

4.1   Background

If a planner has a complete and certain model of its environment and actions, then a plan should achieve its predicted results. The simplest type of planner assumes that only it changes the environment and that its actions have completely predictable effects. In essence, such a planner assumes that the actual environment always behaves exactly as its internal model of the environment does. Many early planners such as STRIPS were based on this assumption [Fikes and Nilsson, 1971]. Even with this assumption, planning can be a complex problem because of the potential interactions between goals (or subgoals) to be achieved: one action might undo the effects of an earlier action, causing previously achieved subgoals to be no longer satisfied. Later planning systems, such as INTERPLAN [Tate, 1975] and Waldinger's system [Waldinger, 1977], reordered goals to avoid harmful plan interactions; other planners, like NOAH [Sacerdoti, 1977] and NONLIN [Tate, 1977], only imposed an order on goals when interactions between plans to achieve the goals independently indicated that a particular ordering was necessary. In all of these systems, plans were formed assuming that the environment and actions could be modeled with complete certainty, so that choosing a plan step requires the planner only to explore the ramifications of its possible actions.

When the effects of an action cannot be predicted with certainty, or when events beyond the planner's control can change the environment, then the planner cannot assume that its plan will necessarily be successful. A planner like those discussed above develops a plan based on its internal models, and can monitor the actual execution of the plan to detect deviations between what was expected and what actually occurred. When the plan deviates, the planner creates a new plan or alters the remainder of the old plan to account for the unanticipated environment. As examples, NOAH [Sacerdoti, 1977] and SIPE [Wilkins, 1984] develop plan representations that facilitate execution monitoring and replanning, and Wesson describes a system that monitors and revises plans [Wesson, 1977]. When possible deviations are predictable, the planner can even plan in advance for different contingencies [Drummond *et al.*, 1987].

Sacerdoti has recognized that more advanced planners should integrate plan generation, execution, and repair [Sacerdoti, 1979]. In unpredictable and uncertain environments, it may be pointless to plan actions for the distant future [Chien and Weissman, 1975; Davis, 1981; Feldman and Sproull, 1977; McCalla *et al.*, 1982]. The planner should adopt a "wait and see" approach in these situations by only planning as far in the future as it can reasonably predict. After executing its partial plan (alternatively, its plan to achieve some set of subgoals), the planner can reconnoiter before developing its next partial plan. By interleaving planning and execution, the planner wastes less time forming plans that are unlikely to come to fruition; by maintaining a view of its overall goals, the planner can choose an effective sequence of partial plans to achieve these goals. Monitoring and repair are still needed since the partial plans may themselves deviate from expectations.

A planner that works in a dynamically changing world must therefore plan both reactively and strategically. *Reactive* planning means that the planner monitors the situation and takes appropriate actions in reaction to it, taking into account both expected and unexpected features of the situation. Reactive planning is thus data-driven. *Strategic* planning means that the planner maps out, at some level, an entire sequence of actions that will take it from its initial situation to some goal situation, and is thus goal-directed. To work effectively, a planner must balance reactive with strategic planning: if overly reactive, it will make short-sighted decisions in response to its current situation and may fail to work purposefully toward its long-term goals; but if overly strategic, it will lean toward following a planned sequence of actions that may no longer be suitable in its current situation.

The planners developed by AI researchers have fallen somewhere in the range between being purely reactive and purely strategic. At the purely reactive end are planners that simply map situations to actions, where planning is reduced to "if the situation is a and the goal is b , then take actions x, y, and z." These planners are arguably not planning at all since they simply follow such rules without the long-term view of how actions will lead to achieving goals that is usually associated with planning. At the purely strategic end are planners that assume that only they can affect their environment and that effects of their actions are completely predictable. Such planners map out detailed actions to achieve all their goals, recognizing before they begin any interactions between goals that force actions to be taken in a particular order. When planning complex sequences of actions, such as molecular genetics experiments for example, a planner may only be capable of developing plans that cannot tolerate any unexpected situations, due to the strong interactions between planned actions. The planner therefore must plan strategically [Stefik, 1981], and need not be reactive (since any need to react means that the only acceptable plan has failed).

The planner described in this chapter falls between the two extremes. The domain is predictable to the extent that the planner can formulate strategic plans at a high level, but unpredictable enough that it should not expend effort planning detailed actions too far in the future.[1] Because it generally has several ways to achieving each goal, the planner has the flexibility to react to unexpected situations by modifying its plans to achieve goals in a different way. With this flexibility, the planner can find plans that may pursue several of its goals simultaneously, thereby helping it resolve its uncertainty about which

---

[1] This can be compared with Wesson's approach of forming detailed plans up to some cut-off time in the future, but then pursuing only some of the planned actions before it replans [Wesson, 1977]. By planning far enough into the future, his system tries to recognize future situations that should be resolved by near-term actions. To keep this view of the more long-term future, his system occasionally looks ahead farther into the future. In contrast to this approach, our mechanisms generate a less detailed view of the entire plan, and use this view to plan short-term actions that lead to worthwhile results.

goals are in fact important. In short, planning involves not so much finding the only sequence of actions as finding the most appropriate sequence, where the appropriateness of a plan can change as the situation changes in unexpected ways.

Because the planner must control a problem solver that interacts with some "outside" world (other problem solvers—possibly human—that need solutions within some time), the planner must also have rudimentary capabilities for reasoning about time. In planners that do not associate actions with their durations, it is the order of plan steps that defines the temporal relationships between actions, and predictions about "when" an action will occur can only be expressed in terms of the actions that must precede it. To better interact with other problem solvers (consumers of a solution), the problem solver needs not only to plan its actions but to predict when those actions will take place so that it can meet deadlines or synchronize in some way with the outside world. Cheeseman, for example, describes a multi-agent planner that uses temporal reasoning to avoid resource conflicts and deadlocks [Cheeseman, 1984]. Other research in planning has incorporated temporal reasoning into planners [Allen, 1984; Lowrance and Friedman, 1977; McDermott, 1982; Vere, 1983]. For example, these planners can develop plans that allow agents to prevent the predicted actions of other agents from occurring [Allen, 1984], or to base planning steps around expected events [Vere, 1983]. The planner described in this chapter uses predictions about the time-costs for achieving different subgoals as a factor in ordering how it will attempt to achieve them. It also uses these predictions to estimate when actions will take place and results will be formed, so that it can respond to externally imposed deadlines by recognizing when its plans may exceed deadlines and altering those plans appropriately.

Our planner is useful in domains where:

- Unpredictable changes to the problem situation can occur at any time.

- There are several ways to achieve goals (different orderings of subgoals or different sets of subgoals), although some ways may be better (faster, cheaper) than others, so that when plans fail it is possible to form new plans to achieve desired goals.

- The node is initially uncertain about which goals to pursue and how to pursue them, but taking appropriate actions can reduce this uncertainty.

- The possible goals may have related subgoals so the planner could reason about how subgoals should be pursued to further several goals.

- A node could interact with other nodes, and so must reason about the time needs of actions to meet deadlines and to coordinate with others.

4.2   Overview

Even with the high-level view provided by the clustering mechanisms, the planner has uncertainty about whether each long-term goal can actually be achieved, whether an action that might contribute to achieving a long-term goal will actually do so (since long-term goals are inexact), and how to most economically form a desired result (since the same result can often be derived in different ways). The planner reduces control uncertainty in two ways. First, it orders the intermediate goals for achieving long-term goals so that the results of earlier intermediate goals can diminish the uncertainty about how (and whether) to work on later intermediate goals. Second, the planner details the least costly sequence of steps to achieve the next intermediate goal. The planner thus both sketches out long-term intentions and details short-term actions.

A long-term vehicle monitoring goal to generate a track consisting of several time-locations can be reduced to a series of **intermediate-goals** (i-goals) where each i-goal represents a desire to extend the track satisfying the previous i-goal into a new time-location.[2] To determine an order for pursuing the possible i-goals, the planner currently uses three domain-independent heuristics:

Heuristic-1: *Prefer common intermediate-goals.* Some intermediate-goals may be common to several long-term goals. If uncertain about which of these long-term goals to pursue, the planner can postpone its decision by working on common intermediate-goals and then can use these results to better distinguish between the long-term goals. This heuristic is a variation of least-commitment [Stefik, 1981].

Heuristic-2: *Prefer less costly intermediate-goals.* Some intermediate-goals may be more costly to achieve than others. The planner can quickly estimate the relative costs of developing results in different areas by comparing their corresponding clusters at a high level of the abstraction hierarchy: the number of event-classes and the spatial range of the data in a cluster roughly indicates how many potentially competing hypotheses might be produced. This heuristic causes the planner to develop results more quickly. If these results are creditable they provide predictive information, otherwise the planner can abandon the plan after minimal effort.

Heuristic-3: *Prefer discriminative intermediate-goals.* When the planner must discriminate between possible long-term goals, it should prefer to work on intermediate-goals that most effectively indicate the relative promise of each long-term goal. When no common intermediate-goals remain, therefore, this heuristic triggers work in the areas where the long-term goals differ most.

These heuristics are interdependent. For example, common i-goals may also be

---

[2]In general terms, an i-goal in any interpretation task is to process a new piece of information and to integrate it into the current partial interpretation.

more costly, as in one of the experiments described in the next chapter. The relative influence of each heuristic can be modified parametrically.

Having identified a sequence of i-goals to achieve one or more long-term goals, the planner can reduce its uncertainty about how to satisfy these i-goals by planning in more detail. If the planner possesses models of the KSs that roughly indicate both the costs of a particular action and the general characteristics of the output of that action (based on the characteristics of the input), then the planner can search for the best of the alternative ways to satisfy an i-goal. We have provided our planner with coarse KS models that allow it to make reasonable predictions about short sequences of actions to find the sequences that best achieve i-goals.[3] To reduce the effort spent on planning for an uncertain future, the planner only forms detailed plans for the next i-goal: since the results of earlier i-goals influence decisions about how and whether to pursue subsequent i-goals, the planner avoids expending effort forming detailed plans that may never be used.

Given the abstraction hierarchy in Figure 11, the planner recognizes that achieving each of the four long-term goals (Figure 11d) entails i-goals of tracking the vehicle through these regions. Influenced predominantly by Heuristic-1, the planner decides to initially work toward all four long-term goals at the same time by achieving their common i-goals. A detailed sequence of actions to drive the data in R_3 at the signal blackboard-level to the vehicle blackboard-level is then formulated. The planner creates a plan whose attributes (and their values in this example) are:

- the long-term goals of the plan (in the example, there are four);

- the predicted, underspecified time-regions of the eventual solution (in the example, the time regions are $(1 \quad R_1 or R_1')(2 \quad R_2 or R_2')(3 \quad R_3) \dots)$;

- the predicted vehicle type(s) of the eventual solution (in the example, there is only one type of vehicle considered);

- the order of i-goals (in the example, begin with sensed time 3, then time 4, then work backward to earlier and forward to later times);

- the blackboard-level for tracking, depending on the available knowledge sources (in the example, this is the vehicle blackboard-level);

- a record of past actions, updated as actions are taken (initially empty);

- a sequence of the specific actions to take in the short-term (in the example, the detailed plan is to process data in region R_3);

- a rating based on the number of long-term goals being worked on, the effort already invested in the plan, the ratings of pending short-term actions, and the predicted belief of the eventual result.

---

[3] If the predicted cost of satisfying an i-goal deviates substantially from the crude estimate based on the abstract view, the ordering of the i-goals may need to be revised.

As each predicted action is consecutively pursued, the record of past actions is updated and the actual results of the action are compared with the general characteristics predicted by the planner. When these agree, the next action in the detailed short-term sequence is performed if there is one; otherwise the planner develops another detailed sequence for the next i-goal. In our example, after forming results in R_3 at a high blackboard-level, the planner forms a sequence of actions to do the same in R_4. When the actual and predicted results disagree (since the planner's models of the KSs may be inaccurate), the planner must modify the plan by introducing additional actions that can get the plan back on track. If no such actions exist, the plan is aborted and the next most highly-rated plan is pursued. If the planner exhausts its plans before forming a complete solution, the node discontinues planning and pursues any pending highly-rated KSIs in an effort to eventually generate these results using its simpler control mechanisms.

The planner thus generates, monitors, and revises plans, and interleaves these activities with plan execution. In our example, the common i-goals are eventually satisfied and a separate plan must be formed for each of the alternative ways to proceed. After finding a partial track combining data from sensed times 3 and 4, the planner decides to extend this track backward to sensed time 2. The long-term goals indicate that work should be done in either R_2 or R'_2. A plan is generated for each of the two possibilities, and the more highly-rated of these plans is followed. Note, however, that the partial track already developed can provide predictive information that, through goal processing, can increase the rating of work in one of these regions and not the other. In this case, constraints that limit a vehicle's turning rate are used when goal processing (subgoaling) to increase the ratings of KSI's in R'_2, thus making the plan to work there next more highly rated.[4]

The planner and goal processing thus work in tandem to improve performance. The goal processing uses a detailed view of local interactions between hypotheses, goals, and KSIs to differentiate between alternative actions. Goal processing can be computationally wasteful, however, when it is invoked based on strictly local criteria. Without the knowledge of long-term reasons for building a hypothesis, the problem solver simply forms goals to extend and refine the hypothesis in all possible ways. These goals are further processed (subgoaled) if they are at certain blackboard-levels, again regardless of any long-term justification for doing so. With its long-term view, the planner can drastically reduce the amount of goal processing. As it pursues, monitors, and repairs plans, the planner identifies areas where goals and subgoals could improve its decisions and selectively invokes goal processing to form only those goals that it needs.

---

[4] In fact the turn to R_2 exceeds these constraints, as does the turn to R'_5, so that the only track that satisfies the constraints is $R'_1 R'_2 R_3 R_4 R_5 R_6$.

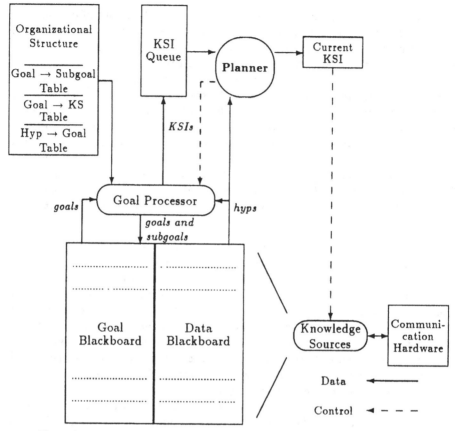

The node architecture incorporating the planner is shown. Note that the planner uses hypotheses, KSIs, and goals (through the goal processor) to generate plans and find the current KSI.

Figure 18: The Modified Problem-Solving Architecture of a Node.

4.3 Details

The planner is responsible for controlling problem solving, and so must decide what KSI should be invoked at any given time. Without the planner, a node has a KSI dispatcher that simply invokes the most highly-rated KSI at any time (Figure 7). The planner replaces this dispatcher so that a more intelligent choice of KSIs can be made (Figure 18). Moreover, because the planner controls the goal processing, it can trigger the creation of goals (and in turn KSIs) that it believes would be useful. The planner thus uses hypotheses, goals, and KSIs to plan sequences of actions to achieve goals and to invoke specific KSIs that correspond to the planned actions.

The architecture of the planner is sketched in Figure 19. The mechanisms that build a clustering hierarchy and recognize alternative-goals were described in the previous chapter. In this section, the other important components of the planner are detailed. First, the plan data structures are introduced in Section 4.3.1. The process of creating plans is described in Section 4.3.2 and Section 4.3.3, discusses the mechanisms for incrementally updating plans as they are being executed, for monitoring and repairing plans, and for determining what KSI should be invoked for a plan. Next, the other activity of the plan generator—to modify plans based on new problem situations—is discussed in Section 4.3.4, and mechanisms for updating plans so that they meet deadlines are described in Section 4.3.5. Section 4.3.6 puts all of these pieces together and Section 4.3.7 presents a detailed example of planning.

4.3.1 The Plan Data Structures

The attributes of a plan are summarized in Figure 20. The plan has a unique name, and the simulated node time when the plan is created (or later updated) is recorded. A single plan can pursue several alternative-goals if it works in their common areas, although once problem solving in common areas is complete the plan is divided into different plans for subsets of the original alternative-goals. The time-regions of the alternative-goals are combined into the plan's objective track. For example, the objective track might be $((1 \ (R_1))(2 \ (R_2 \ R'_2))(3 \ (R_3 \ R'_3)))$, where the track indicates that at time 1 the vehicle was in region R_1, at time 2 the vehicle was in region R_2 or R'_2, and so on. The plan also has an objective of tracking certain types of vehicles, indicated by a list of vehicle-event-classes. Finally, the plan maintains a list of competing-plans—plans working on competing alternative-goals.

For each plan, the planner forms strategic information about how the goals will be achieved: the order in which partial solutions will be formed and how they will be integrated into tracks. The *long-term* plan information sketches out a time-order (the order in which intermediate-goals will be pursued), determines the tracking-level (the level of the blackboard where hypotheses for individual locations or for partial tracks will be integrated into larger partial tracks), records time-predictions (about how long each i-goal is expected to take and how long the plan is expected to take as a whole), and summarizes the general activities performed for each i-goal.

A plan has *short-term* information, containing details about how i-goals have been or will be achieved. The short-term information indicates the base-clusters "used" for each i-goal so the planner keeps track of what clusters' data it has used to attempt to satisfy an i-goal so that if it fails with some data it knows what data it has not tried yet. The short-term:actions[5] is a list of

---

[5]The data structures often are themselves composed of substructures. We specify a particular field in a substructure by indicating the larger structure(s) as well, using the form

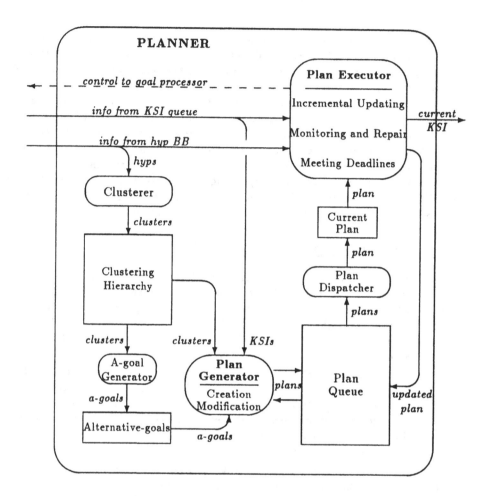

Figure 19: The Architecture of the Planner.

pending detailed actions that will be taken to satisfy the next i-goal, and the
short-term:record stores the actions that were taken in the past to achieve i-
goals so that the planner can refer to past actions and their results. When
executing a plan, the node pops the first action off the pending actions list,
takes that action, and then pushes the action onto the record list.

An action is a list containing: a KS-type which is a list of possible KSs

---

larger-structure:smaller-structure. For example, plans have short-term information, and this
information is itself a structure containing fields for actions, record, and used-clusters. The
short-term:actions are thus the actions field in the plan's short-term information.

name	A unique name (symbol) pointing at the plan structure	
creation-time	When the plan was created or last updated	
objective	alternative-goals	A list of the alternative-goals to achieve
	track	The expected track for the plan, formed by combining alternative-goals' time-regions
	v-event-classes	The vehicle-event-classes (types of vehicles) being tracked
	competing-plans	A list of plans that have competing alternative-goals as objectives
long-term	time-order	The order for pursuing i-goals, where each i-goal is identified by its data's sensed time
	tracking-levels	The blackboard-level(s) where hypotheses will be integrated into tracks
	time-predictions	The predicted or actual time needs of each i-goal and for the entire plan
	activity-per-time	The basic activities (KSs) executed to achieve an i-goal
short-term	actions	The detailed actions remaining to be done to achieve the current i-goal
	record	The detailed actions already taken for the current i-goal and any past i-goals
	used-clusters	The base-clusters used to achieve each past i-goal and the current i-goal
prediction	result-belief	The predicted belief of the eventual result
	runtimes	The predicted or actual time costs for each i-goal
	prediction-time	When the prediction was formed
rating	rating	The overall rating for the plan
rating-factors	prediction	The predicted belief of the eventual result
	fraction-completed	The fraction of the overall result that has been completed
	alternatives	The number of alternative-goals the plan is concurrently pursuing
	next-result	The predicted belief of the next i-goal's result
	max-ksi	The maximum rating of the KSIs in the short-term actions

Figure 20: The Attributes of a Plan.

that could be invoked; a KSI which is the specific KSI to be invoked (if it has been instantiated); a duration which is the expected duration of the action; and a result which indicates the expected attributes of a hypothesis generated by the action. These attributes include time-regions, an expected *belief-range*, a blackboard-level, a list of event-classes, a *volume* (how many hypotheses are expected to be generated by the action), and a list of *sat-hyps*. When the action is taken, a list of hypotheses that satisfy the expectations is inserted into the sat-hyps slot, so that past actions (in the short-term:record) will point to the hypotheses that they generated.

A plan has prediction information. It maintains a list of hypotheses at the tracking-level that have some time-locations matching the plan's objective track. The planner uses this list when predicting the belief of the plan's eventual result and the time needed to form it. The prediction information contains the simulated time that the prediction was made, the predicted belief of the plan's eventual result, and the predicted time needs for each of the plan's i-goals.

A plan has a rating, which is computed as a combination of several rating-factors. These factors include: a prediction about the belief of the plan's eventual result (which comes from the prediction information); the fraction of the plan already completed (indicating both the effort invested in the plan and the distance to completing the plan); the number of alternative-goals that the plan is concurrently working toward (the length of the objective:alternative-goals list); and information about the more near-term qualities of the plan—how highly believed it expects the result satisfying the next i-goal to be and how highly-rated the KSIs it has to work with in the near future are.

4.3.2   Creating Plans

Given a set of alternative-goals to achieve, the planner extracts the most highly-rated alternative-goals (those with the most highly-believed data) in order to generate only the most promising plans. A parameter specifies the allowable range of ratings for the most highly-rated alternative-goals. Next, the planner forms groups of competing alternative-goals. Since competing alternative-goals by definition share common sub-clusters—which means that they share i-goals—they are initially grouped together so that the combination can be concurrently pursued by working first on their common i-goals. A plan name and structure are then generated for each group, and the attributes of the plan are computed.

Computing Plan Objectives

The objective:alternative-goals are simply the group of competing alternative-goals that the plan has been generated to achieve. The objective:vehicle-event-classes are initially the union of the vehicle-event-classes lists of the clusters associated with the alternative-goals.

The objective:track is a combination of the alternative-goals' time-regions. For example, if the time-regions of alternative-goal-1 are $((1\ R_1)(2\ R_2)(3\ R_3))$ and the time-regions for alternative-goal-2 are $((1\ R_1)(2\ R_2'))$, then their combined track is $((1\ (R_1))(2\ (R_2\ R_2'))(3\ (R_3)))$. This combined track indicates that for each time there are one or more regions that could be developed: at sensed time 1 the vehicle passes through region R_1, at sensed time 2 the vehicle passes through R_2 or R_2', and so on. If the planner decides to work on data for sensed time 1 first, then it need not decide yet which of the regions for the other times it will explore—the track indicates several possibilities so that the planner need not commit itself before it has to. When it needs to work at other sensed times, the planner will divide the plan into alternative plans to explore the different regions.

Initially, the plan will have no competing-plans because it is attempting to achieve an entire group of competing alternative-goals. However, as the plan is pursued (and modified when the alternative-goals change), the plan may be divided into different plans to achieve subsets of the original competing alternative-goals. The planner keeps track of what plans are working on competing alternative-goals in its objective:competing-plans.

Computing Plan Long-term Information

The most important long-term plan information is the order in which the plan will pursue the various i-goals. Since the node is attempting to process all of the appropriate data and integrate it all together into a solution, it can process and integrate the data in any order. However, by processing some data before other data, the node can substantially reduce the time it needs to form a solution: partial solutions provide predictive information that guides processing to extend those partial solutions. Therefore, although the node could pursue the i-goals of a plan in any order and eventually complete the plan (if it can be completed), finding a good ordering of the i-goals can reduce the time needed to achieve a plan or the time needed to recognize that the plan is not worth pursuing.

The order of i-goals is called the **time-order** because each i-goal is represented as a sensed time. By a time-order of $(i\ j\ k\ ...)$ is indicated that the node will form a partial track from data for sensed time i, then attempt to integrate data for sensed time j into that track, then try to integrate data for sensed time k into the track composed by i and j, and so on. To generate a time-order, the planner uses several heuristics about how it is best to go about pursuing a set of long-term goals in domains where the goals may interact and possibly be unachievable. These heuristics were briefly described in Section 4.2, and are incorporated into the i-goal ordering function as follows:

1. The top-level clusters that are associated with the alternative-goals may have some common sub-clusters, where the sub-clusters represent data that is unambiguously related by time. For example, the top three levels of a sample clustering hierarchy are shown in Figure 21a. By stepping through the alternative-goals' top-level clusters, the function counts the occurrences of each of their sub-clusters, building a list that associates sub-clusters and their occurrence-counts (Figure 21b).

2. For each sub-cluster, the function finds a cost-value to roughly estimate the effort needed to achieve the i-goal associated with the cluster. The cost-value is a function of event-class uncertainty (ambiguity), spatial uncertainty (ambiguity), the distance from the tracking-levels (remaining processing), and the occurrence-count. The cost-values for the example sub-clusters are shown in Figure 21c, where each cost-value is computed as the product of the three factors divided by the occurrence-count. Dividing by the occurrence-count distributes the cost among the relevant alternative-goals, so that more costly sub-clusters can still be preferred if they contribute toward achieving enough alternative-goals.

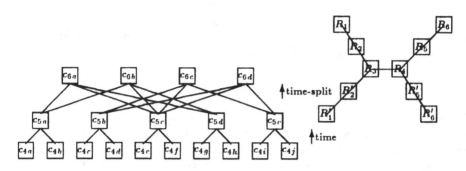

	Time-regions	BB-levs	V-e-cs	Sub-clusters	Super-clusters
c_{4a}	$((1\ R_1))$	(sl)	(1 2)	$(\cdots)$	(cl_{5a})
c_{4b}	$((2\ R_2))$	(sl)	(1 2)	$(\cdots)$	(cl_{5a})
c_{4c}	$((1\ R_1'))$	(sl)	(1 2)	$(\cdots)$	(cl_{5b})
c_{4d}	$((2\ R_2'))$	(sl)	(1 2)	$(\cdots)$	(cl_{5b})
c_{4e}	$((3\ R_3))$	(sl)	(1 2)	$(\cdots)$	(cl_{5c})
c_{4f}	$((4\ R_4))$	(sl)	(1 2)	$(\cdots)$	(cl_{5c})
c_{4g}	$((5\ R_5))$	(sl)	(1 2)	$(\cdots)$	(cl_{5d})
c_{4h}	$((6\ R_6))$	(sl)	(1 2)	$(\cdots)$	(cl_{5d})
c_{4i}	$((5\ R_5'))$	(sl)	(1 2)	$(\cdots)$	(cl_{5e})
c_{4j}	$((6\ R_6'))$	(sl)	(1 2)	$(\cdots)$	(cl_{5e})
c_{5a}	$((1\ R_1)(2\ R_2))$	(sl)	(1 2)	$(cl_{4a}\ cl_{4b})$	$(cl_{6a}\ cl_{6b})$
c_{5b}	$((1\ R_1')(2\ R_2'))$	(sl)	(1 2)	$(cl_{4c}\ cl_{4d})$	$(cl_{6c}\ cl_{6d})$
c_{5c}	$((3\ R_3)(4\ R_4))$	(sl)	(1 2)	$(cl_{4e}\ cl_{4f})$	$(cl_{6a}\ cl_{6b}\ cl_{6c}\ cl_{6d})$
c_{5d}	$((5\ R_5)(6\ R_6))$	(sl)	(1 2)	$(cl_{4g}\ cl_{4h})$	$(cl_{6a}\ cl_{6c})$
c_{5e}	$((5\ R_5')(6\ R_6'))$	(sl)	(1 2)	$(cl_{4i}\ cl_{4j})$	$(cl_{6b}\ cl_{6d})$
c_{6a}	$((1\ R_1)(2\ R_2)(3\ R_3)$ $(4\ R_4)(5\ R_5)(6\ R_6))$	(sl)	(1 2)	$(cl_{5a}\ cl_{5c}\ cl_{5d})$	$()$
c_{6b}	$((1\ R_1)(2\ R_2)(3\ R_3)$ $(4\ R_4)(5\ R_5')(6\ R_6'))$	(sl)	(1 2)	$(cl_{5a}\ cl_{5c}\ cl_{5e})$	$()$
c_{6c}	$((1\ R_1')(2\ R_2')(3\ R_3)$ $(4\ R_4)(5\ R_5)(6\ R_6))$	(sl)	(1 2)	$(cl_{5b}\ cl_{5c}\ cl_{5d})$	$()$
c_{6d}	$((1\ R_1')(2\ R_2')(3\ R_3)$ $(4\ R_4)(5\ R_5')(6\ R_6'))$	(sl)	(1 2)	$(cl_{5b}\ cl_{5c}\ cl_{5e})$	$()$

(a)

$$((cl_{5c}\ 4)(cl_{5a}\ 2)(cl_{5b}\ 2)(cl_{5d}\ 2)(cl_{5e}\ 2))$$
(b)

$$((cl_{5c}\ 4\ 1)(cl_{5a}\ 2\ 2)(cl_{5b}\ 2\ 2)(cl_{5d}\ 2\ 2)(cl_{5c}\ 2\ 2))$$
where each entry has (cluster occurrence-count cost-value)
and
Vehicle-event-class uncertainty (each cluster) = 2　　(v-ev-cls = (1 2))
Spatial uncertainty (each cluster) = 1　　(each region covers 1 location)
Distance to tracking-levels (each cluster) = 2　　(distance from *sl* to *vl*)
(c)

Figure 21: Ordering I-goals for Sample Situation.

3. The function orders the sub-clusters based on their occurrence-counts and cost-values. The relative importance of these two factors is controlled by a user-supplied parameter *cost-heuristic-weight* (*chw), which balances the heuristics to prefer common i-goals and to prefer less costly i-goals. The overall rating for each cluster is computed as:

overall-cost = (*chw × cost-value) − [(1 − *chw) × occurrence-count].

The sub-clusters are ordered from lowest to highest overall-cost. Since the cost-value is computed from both the cost factors and the occurrence-count, a *cost-heuristic-weight of 1 is typically used to balance the heuristics, but values of 0 are also studied in Chapter 5.

4. The function then steps through the sub-clusters and for each identifies its sub-clusters (which do *not* cluster hypotheses by time) and orders them by their cost-values. It forms the time-order beginning with the least costly i-goals, and then adding other i-goals, giving preference to those with times adjacent to those earliest in the time-order (if any). This promotes extending existing partial solutions rather than generating new partial solutions, and extending partial solutions outward in both directions. For example, given the information in Figure 21c and using a *cost-heuristic-weight of 1, the planner first adds times 3 and 4 to the time-order. Next, since the remaining clusters have equal cost-values, the planner takes the cluster-group times (1 2 5 6) and adds them to the time-order: first 2 is added (both it and 5 are adjacent to (3 4) but 2 is closer to 3), then 5 is added (both it and 1 are adjacent to (3 4 2) and equally close to 3 but 5 is closer to 4), then 1 is added (both it and 6 are adjacent to (3 4 2 5) but 1 is closer to 3), and finally 6 is added.

The function only considers cost and commonality when building the time-order. The third heuristic—to prefer i-goals that help discriminate between competing plans—is not needed yet since a single plan is created for the entire set of competing alternative-goals. If the plan is later divided into several plans for subsets of the alternative-goals, this heuristic is employed by having the different plans use a common time-order so that they work in competing areas for the same sensed times. For example, if $plan_1$ is pursuing an i-goal to determine whether a partial track passed through region R_i at sensed time i, then it makes sense to have $plan_2$, which wants to extend the same partial track, pursue its i-goal to extend the track into R'_i so that the planner can directly compare the results made by each plan to decide which plan shows more promise.

The long-term tracking-levels specify the blackboard-levels where tracks are constructed: where locations are combined into short tracks, where tracks and locations are extended to form longer tracks, and where tracks are merged to form longer tracks. The choice of appropriate tracking-levels depends on the available KSs (the node may only have KSs for forming, extending, and merging tracks at certain levels), the branching of the grammar (by constructing tracks at levels where the number of event-classes is least, the number of tracks can be minimized), and the communication blackboard-levels (integrating results from several nodes is most efficient if tracking is done at the same blackboard-level as communication). The planner as currently implemented does not make sophisticated decisions about the tracking-levels. Because the grammars used in the experiments to date have had the smallest number of event-classes at the vehicle blackboard-level, and because communication between nodes is at this blackboard-level as well, the planner computes the tracking-levels as the communication blackboard-levels (when the node is part of a network) or as the vt blackboard-level otherwise. In all of the experiments we discuss, the tracking-levels is the list (vt), although the mechanisms that use the tracking-levels can work with other blackboard-levels as well. Our future research directions include modifying the planner so that it determines what blackboard-level is best for tracking based on the node's capabilities and the type of information it can communicate.

The long-term:time-predictions and long-term:activity-per-time are computed after the short-term information and the predictions have been computed. In essence, the time-predictions indicate for each i-goal the expected time needed to achieve that i-goal (or if the i-goal has already been achieved, how long it took). These are taken directly from the plan's prediction:runtimes slot once the predictions about the plan have been made. The sum of these times is also computed as the expected overall time needs for the plan. The activity-per-time attempts to generalize the typical activities (KSs) that are needed to achieve an i-goal, and are extracted from the short-term actions: each action has a KS-type associated with it, and the mechanisms simply step through the plan's short-term:actions when they have been computed and lists together the sequence of KS-types to be pursued. Since both the long-term:time-predictions and the long-term:activity-per-time information are used primarily for communicating with other nodes about plans, they are not discussed any further in this chapter.

Computing Plan Short-term Information

The long-term information indicates the planner's long-term approach for achieving the plan's objectives. By achieving the i-goals in order, the node will hopefully arrive at an acceptable overall solution in an efficient manner. However, before problem solving can occur, the planner must translate the i-goals into specific actions.

The short-term information is computed whenever a plan needs details for achieving an i-goal, which includes when a plan is created and when it has successfully achieved an i-goal and needs to incrementally add details for the next. For its current i-goal, the planner computes detailed actions using a repetitive procedure: the node should process data to generate the most highly-believed hypotheses in the area, and then should integrate these hypotheses with any compatible hypotheses it made previously to generate larger, more encompassing hypotheses. By always following these basic steps for achieving an i-goal, the planner simplifies its task of finding an appropriate sequence of actions.

The planner therefore faces little uncertainty about which actions should be taken, but it faces considerable uncertainty about what data will be needed by the actions and what results those actions will generate. As it works through the basic sequence of phases for generating a detailed *action-list* for the current i-goal, the planner must use models of the KSs and knowledge about precedence relationships between actions (so that all of the actions to generate results needed by an action are completed before that action is attempted).

Models of the KSs. The planner uses models of the KSs to predict the results and durations of its actions.[6] There are two types of models: a model for synthesis KSs and a model for integration (extension) KSs. A synthesis KS finds a group of hypotheses at one blackboard-level and combines them to generate hypotheses at the next higher blackboard-level. To generate output hypotheses, the KS must not only determine what hypotheses should be combined, but also *how well* they combine—indicated by the output hypotheses' beliefs. Given a set of input results from preceding actions, the model for synthesis KSs predicts the output results': blackboard-level (the next higher blackboard-level above the input results); time-regions (the same as the input results); event-classes (computed from the grammar, mapping the event-classes of the input results to event-classes at the next higher blackboard-level); volume-of-data (the number of expected output hypotheses equals the number of output event-classes); and belief-range (approximated as described below).

Whereas a KS computes how highly believed the output hypotheses should be, based on more complex knowledge about how beliefs should be combined, the model for synthesis KSs uses a much simpler computation that only roughly approximates the KS calculations. The KS-model uses the grammar to determine how many possible event-classes at the input blackboard-level can lead to any of the output event-classes, and then examines the input results to find out how many actual event-classes it has at the input blackboard-level. It computes the likely output belief as a function of the maximum of the input result belief-ranges and the proportion of support (actual to possible input event-classes). The belief-range for the output result has a minimum and maximum both equal to the estimated output belief.

For integration KSs, the model must also determine both what results to combine and how highly to believe their combination. The integration KSs generate hypotheses at the same blackboard-level as the input hypotheses, but

---

[6]These are similar to Hearsay-II's precondition functions that compute a *response frame* (stylized description of the KS's results) based on a *stimulus frame* [Erman et al., 1980].

the scope (time-locations) of the output hypotheses is extended. The characteristics of the output results based on input results are estimated by the model of integration KSs: blackboard-level (same as the input results); time-regions (combination of the input results' time-regions); event-classes (same as the event-classes of the input results); volume of data (number of output event-classes); and belief-range (average of the beliefs of the input results).

The models of KSs estimate the volume of hypotheses that they expect to produce, and they compute their expected duration using the function $ax + b$, where x equals the volume of data and where a and b are retrieved from the node's data about its KSs.

The models of KSs are much less costly than the KSs themselves, and cheaply develop an expectation about the duration and results of a sequence of actions. However, since the models only crudely estimate the characteristics of the results, and since the results estimated for one action are used as input to estimate the results of the next action, the potential for generating poor estimates increases proportionally with the length of a sequence of actions. By only finding detailed sequences of actions to achieve the next i-goal, the planner avoids forming long sequences that could introduce such errors.

Finding Hypotheses to Develop. The planner must first locate the data that it should use to achieve an i-goal. It takes the plan's alternative-goals' clusters, the plan's objective:vehicle-event-classes (which can change as problem solving proceeds), and the current i-goal, and works its way down the clustering hierarchy following a path of clusters that are compatible with the i-goal and vehicle-event-classes. Having arrived at a set of base-clusters that satisfy the required characteristics, the planner removes from these any already used clusters (from the short-term:used-clusters information). The planner then chooses from the remaining base-clusters the cluster with the highest belief-range (the cluster with the most highly-believed hypotheses), and this cluster specifies the hypotheses to start with. Note, however, that this base-cluster might *not* be common to all of the alternative-goals: as the planner pursues successive i-goals in a plan to achieve multiple alternative-goals, it will eventually attempt an i-goal that is not shared by the alternative-goals. When working on a cluster that is not shared by all alternative-goals, the planner changes the plan's alternative-goals to the subset that do share the chosen cluster, and the remaining alternative-goals are saved for the last stage of short-term planning, where they trigger the creation of new plans.

Improving the Initial Hypotheses. Before it starts synthesizing the initial hypotheses to a tracking-level, the planner should first take any actions that will improve the initial hypotheses' beliefs, because the beliefs of later hypotheses depend on the beliefs of the initial hypotheses. To increase the belief in a hypothesis, the planner should find actions that increase the support for that hypothesis. Support comes from hypotheses at lower blackboard-levels whose attributes (time-regions and event-classes) corroborate the hypothesis, based on the KSs. The planner determines whether there are any pending KSIs that may synthesize hypotheses at lower blackboard-levels to increase the belief in any of the initial hypotheses. It does this by inspecting related clusters for data at lower blackboard-levels and examining their pending KSIs.

Given a KSI that should be invoked, the planner builds an action whose KS-type is the KS associated with the KSI, whose KSI is the KSI, and whose duration and result it predicts by using its models of synthesis KSs. The planner appends these actions to the action-list that it is building. Finally, because the subsequent planning phases work from the actions and results in the action-list, this phase must generate some action. If it found KSIs to improve the initial hypotheses, then these serve. However, if there were no such KSIs, the planner creates a "dummy" action directly from the initial cluster. This action specifies that an action of KS-type "dummy", with no KSI and a duration of 0, generates a result with exactly the characteristics of the initial cluster (belief-range, time-regions, event-classes, blackboard-levels, a volume equal to the length of the data-list, and sat-hyps is the data-list).

Generating the Hypotheses at a Tracking-level. The planner next finds actions to synthesize the (possibly improved) initial hypotheses up to a tracking-level specified in the plan's long-term:tracking-levels. It first checks the results of the last action taken (possibly a "dummy" action) and determines whether the results are already at a tracking-level. If so, this phase is completed, but otherwise the planner must form actions to synthesize previous results to higher blackboard-levels. These actions are formed using the KS models, and are appended onto the action-list. The planner then once again checks the blackboard-level of the last result and determines whether it now has a result at the tracking-level. If not, then the planner forms more actions. This cycle continues until the planner has generated all the actions needed to synthesize the data up to a tracking-level.

The planner uses models of the synthesis KSs to estimate, given some set of input results (the results of the relevant previous actions), the results of the action as well as its predicted duration. Also, if the relevant previous actions have already been taken (for example, "dummy" actions), then the planner examines their sat-hyps to find any KSIs that were formed to work on those hypotheses. If it finds a KSI that may achieve the action's result, then that KSI is used as the action's KSI, otherwise the action's KSI is initially nil. When forming the synthesis action, the planner also finds *all* of the relevant previous actions in the action-list. Because a KS can combine the results of several previous actions, the planner must find all of these actions. For example, the actions for generating hypotheses at the *vl* blackboard-level based on the grammar of Figure 5 are shown in Figure 22. When planning the action to synthesize a hypothesis with event-class 1 at *vl* ($action_3$), the planner should use the results not only of the last action ($action_2$) but also of the other action

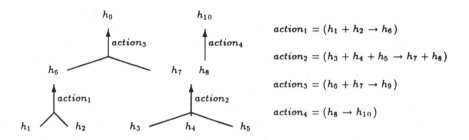

Hypothesis	BB-level	Event-class	Hypothesis	BB-level	Event-class
h_1	sl	2	h_6	gl	2
h_2	sl	6	h_7	gl	6
h_3	sl	10	h_8	gl	10
h_4	sl	14	h_9	vl	1
h_5	sl	18	h_{10}	vl	2

Figure 22: Actions for Synthesizing VL Hypotheses.

that formed hypotheses at gl ($action_1$).

As it develops synthesis actions, the planner also keeps track of the vehicle-event-classes being planned for. As described above, the models of the KSs can hypothesize that several actions may lead to the same result and that one action can lead to more than one result. For example, in Figure 22, $action_2$ generates two hypotheses: one with vehicle-event-class 1 and the other with vehicle-event-class 2. Instead of generating for this action a result with both event-classes, the planner uses models of the KSs to identify that, in fact, the result for vehicle-event-class 2 will be substantially inferior to that of vehicle-event-class 1. The planner can therefore decide to concentrate on the better choice rather than pursuing both simultaneously. Currently, the criterion is that the expected beliefs of better results must be more than twice that of others. The planner modifies the plan for the better subset of vehicle-event-classes (in this case, vehicle-event-class 1), and subsequently only develops actions that work toward it (only actions 1–3 are included in the detailed plan). The planner later creates a plan for the cast aside vehicle-event-classes, as described shortly.

Integrating the Hypotheses into Tracks. Having developed results at a tracking-level, the planner then forms actions to integrate these results with any of the results it has formed in the past. To plan these actions, the planner uses both the action-list that it is currently developing and the record of past actions (for previous i-goals) stored in short-term:record. It determines what adjacent i-goals (for adjacent sensed times) have been pursued in the past (if none, no tracking actions are planned). For the current i-goal and any adjacent i-goals, the planner finds actions in action-list that are to generate the most complete results (results with the most time-regions) at the tracking-level. The planner then applies its model of the integration KSs to these results, builds an action for each result returned by the model (since there may have been several different combinations of results), and adds these actions to the action-list.

Generating the Solution Hypotheses. This planning phase is performed when the planner has exhausted a plan's i-goals—when it has formed a complete track. A complete track at a tracking-level is *not* necessarily tantamount to being a solution. Solution hypotheses are hypotheses that represent complete interpretations *at the highest blackboard-level*. Therefore, the planner must synthesize its complete tracks up to the *pt* blackboard-level. It retrieves the past actions resulting in complete solutions and plans synthesis activities (as previously described) to form solution hypotheses.

Developing Alternative Plans. In the course of detailing the actions for the short-term, the planner may have constrained the plan. When choosing the initial cluster, the planner may have modified the plan so that it only works toward a subset of its original alternative-goals. When determining what results to generate when working toward a tracking-level, the planner may have decided that some vehicle-event-classes appear more promising (have substantially more support) than others, and thus may have changed the plan's objective:vehicle-event-classes to this promising subset.

After it has planned the detailed actions for the plan, therefore, the planner must check to see if there are now any alternative-goals or vehicle-event-classes or both that are no longer planned for. The alternative-goals that were dropped from the current plan are grouped together into competing subsets, and a new plan is created for each subset. These plans inherit some of the information from the original plan: the relevant actions in the short-term:record (that worked toward i-goals that these plans did have in common), the short-term:used-clusters for common i-goals pursued in the past, and, most importantly, aspects of the long-term:time-order. The new plans cannot always directly inherit the long-term:time-order since there is no guarantee that the alternative-goals have time-regions for all of each other's sensed times. However, when they have the same next sensed time, the plans both work on it. In the discussion about ordering i-goals, the third heuristic is to prefer working on discriminating i-goals. This heuristic is implemented not when choosing an initial ordering of i-goals but when dividing a plan into competing plans: the planner forces the competing plans to work on i-goals for their common sensed times in the same order. By extending shared tracks into different data for the same sensed times, the plans are most likely to generate results that can be compared to discriminate between them.

A new plan is also created for any unused vehicle-event-classes. In this case, the plan also inherits the same alternative-goals as the plan that it is being created from. As with dividing a plan for separate alternative-goals, when a plan is divided for different vehicle-event-classes, the planner forces the plans to develop partial solutions that can be better compared.

Computing Plan Predictions

The planner uses information about the costs and results of the plan's past and current activities, and extrapolates over the future activities to predict the overall costs and results of the plan. By assuming that i-goals that process similar data will be pursued in similar ways, the planner bases predictions for future activities on the most similar past activities. However, the costs of achieving a particular i-goal and the quality of the result depend on the attributes of the data that must be processed (such as how strongly it is sensed, its frequency distribution, and its spatial distribution), and these attributes can vary from one i-goal to another [Pavlin, 1983].

The method of forming predictions for a simple plan to process the data shown in Figure 23a is illustrated in Figure 23b. The plan will meet its long-term goal of forming a track covering sensed times 1–4 by consecutively achieving its i-goals (generating partial results for each time). The base-cluster for an i-goal summarizes the attributes of its data, so to predict the costs and results for a future i-goal, the planner matches its cluster against the clusters for the current i-goal and any past i-goals, and then extrapolates based on the closest match. Since a plan always has a current i-goal, the mechanisms always have some basis for prediction.

Figure 23 shows the plan in a partially completed state: the i-goal for time 1 was achieved in the past, the i-goal for time 2 is currently being worked on, and the other i-goals are still pending. For a past i-goal (time 1), the results and the cost of forming those results are known. The planner finds the relationship between the attributes of that i-goal's cluster and the results achieved, representing the result as some function of the cluster's attributes. For the current i-goal (time 2), the planner has used models of the KSs to estimate the attributes of the results of a KS action (based on the attributes of its input data) and the costs of the action. The overall costs of the i-goal is the sum of the estimated KS costs, and its result is simply the estimated result of the last KS action. Once again, the relationship between this result and the i-goal's cluster is found.

To predict the results and costs for a future i-goal, the planner first determines whether any competing plans have already achieved the i-goal. If so, the planner treats the i-goal as a past i-goal, using the results and costs found by the other plan. If not, then it makes predictions based on past i-goals and its current i-goal. The first step is to match its cluster against the past and current i-goals' clusters to find the closest match. To simplify Figure 23, we represent the attributes as letters, and the closest match is the past or current cluster with the most letters in common: cl_3 (with attributes bcgh) is closer to cl_1 (abcd) than cl_2 (aefg) while cl_4 (bfgh) is more like cl_2 (aefg). In our im-

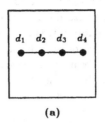

(a)

past	**current**	**future**	**future**
known:	**expected:**	**predicted:**	**predicted:**
$r_1 =$ actual results	$r_2 = r_e(KS_3)$	$r_3 = f_1(cl_3)$	$r_4 = f_2(cl_4)$
$= f_1(cl_1)$	$= f_2(cl_2)$	$c_3 = c_1$	$c_4 = c_2$
$c_1 =$ actual cost	$c_2 = \sum_{i=1}^{3} c_e(KS_i)$		

$$r_1 \quad\quad r_2 \quad\quad r_3 \quad\quad r_4$$

$$KS_3$$

$$KS_1 \quad\quad KS_2$$

cluster=cl_1	cluster=cl_2	cluster=cl_3	cluster=cl_4
$at(cl_1)=abcd$	$at(cl_2)=aefg$	$at(cl_3)=bcgh$	$at(cl_4)=bfgh$
		$match(cl_3)=cl_1$	$match(cl_4)=cl_2$

Overall predicted result (currently) $= average(r_1, r_2, r_3, r_4)$
Overall predicted cost (currently) $= c_1 + c_2 + c_3 + c_4 = 2c_1 + 2c_2$

(b)

Definitions:

r_i	result satisfying intermediate goal i
cl_i	initial clustered hypotheses for intermediate goal i
$at(cl_i)$	attributes of cl_i, here simply represented as letters
$match(cl_i)$	closest matching past or current i-goal cluster for cl_i
c_i	cost (in time) of forming r_i from cl_i
f_i	function relating cl_i with r_i for past and current i-goals
KS_j	KS activity j for achieving current i-goal
$r_e(KS_j)$	expected result generated by KS_j based on KS models
$c_e(KS_j)$	expected cost of performing KS_j based on KS models

The data (a) has a partially completed plan to form a track shown in (b). Results and costs for i-goal 1 are known, for i-goal 2 are estimated using models of KSs, and for i-goals 3 and 4 are predicted by matching their clusters against those of 1 and 2 and applying knowledge to the closest match. As more i-goals are achieved, knowledge about more closely matching clusters can improve predictions. To reduce cost by decreasing belief, either KS_1 or KS_2 might be ignored.

Figure 23: Simple Example of Making Predictions.

plementation, the algorithm scans the past and current clusters for those with the closest blackboard-levels (because data at close blackboard-levels undergo similar processing). If only one is found it is returned, but if several are equally close then of these, those with the closest volume of data are found (since more hypotheses may mean substantially more processing is needed). Again, if only one is found then it is returned, but if several are equally close then the one whose i-goal was most recently worked on is returned (because more recent activity probably reflects future activity better). When the closest match is found, the future i-goal's cost is predicted to be the same as the cost for the matching cluster's i-goal (Figure 23). To predict the result quality, the planner uses the relationship between the matching cluster and its result (relating the average belief of the cluster's hypotheses with the result's belief) and predicts that the same relationship will hold between the future i-goal's cluster and result (Figure 23). For example, if the matching i-goal's result has a belief twice that of the average of its cluster's hypotheses (because the distribution of clustered hypotheses fits the grammar well), then the belief of the future i-goal's result is predicted to be twice the average belief of its cluster's hypotheses.

The predicted overall cost of a plan is the sum of the i-goals' costs. The predicted belief of the plan's overall result is the average of the i-goals predicted beliefs. Because the actual KSs decrease belief based on unlikely vehicle movements, and because the plan's high-level view is to imprecise to recognize such movements, the prediction tends to overestimate rather than underestimate the actual result. However, as the plan is pursued, its predictions generally improve, both because actual costs and results replace those predicted so that overall predictions improve, and because more past experience increases the chances of finding more relevant past i-goals for making predictions about future i-goals. The plan in Figure 23, when it was just starting, could only base predictions on the expected result and cost of the i-goal for time 1 (which was its current i-goal at that time). Since it now can also base predictions on the i-goal for time 2, it can make better predictions about time 4's i-goal (which matches 2 more closely than 1), and when time 3 becomes the current i-goal, the predictions for 4 will be even better (since it most closely matches 3).

Computing Plan Ratings

A plan rating is based on several factors. One factor is the predicted belief of the plan's result (as determined by the prediction mechanisms). Because the node is attempting to generate acceptable results as quickly as possible, and because highly-believed results are more acceptable than lowly-believed results, the planner should rate plans to pursue highly-believed results sooner. Another rating factor is the fraction of the plan that has already been completed: the nearer a plan is to completion, the more emphasis there should be on completing it. By considering the fraction-completed, the planner not only makes problem solving more purposeful (by preferring to continue along a plan that it has been developing), but also can avoid being distracted by a plan that may generate a slightly better result but might require much more time. The number of alternative-goals a plan is pursuing should affect ratings: a plan that pursues several alternative-goals is attractive because by following that plan the node works concurrently on several potential solutions and can delay committing to a particular potential solution. Finally, the planner should consider the short-term advantages of a particular plan. The predicted results of the next i-goal and the ratings of the KSIs to pursue it give a short-term view of the plan's promise. This view can be very useful, for example, where choosing between plans that indicate alternative ways of extending the same track. Since goal processing uses knowledge about vehicle movements to form goals indicating where the track can most likely be extended, and since the subgoals of these goals may cause certain KSIs to have their ratings increased, it is useful for the modified ratings of these KSIs to influence the plan rating.

These separate factors are combined into a single plan rating using the formula:

$$rating = (w_{pr} \times pr) + (w_{fc} \times fc) + (w_{nr} \times (mk \times nr/mb)) + (w_{ag} \times ag).$$

The weights w_{pr}, w_{fc}, w_{nr}, and w_{ag} are normalized (they sum to 1). The predicted result belief, pr, has a value within the DVMT belief/rating range (0 to 10000). The fraction-completed, fc, is also expressed in terms of this range: if the plan is half done, its fraction-complete is 5000. The maximum-ksi rating, mk, falls within this range as does the next i-goal result's expected belief nr. When these are multiplied together, their product is divided by the maximum belief mb of any result (10000) so that their combination has a value within the DVMT belief/rating range. The last factor is the number of alternative-goals, ag, and has a value well under 10000 for the problem situations we examine. Since the weights are normalized, the weighted sum of these factors also falls within the DVMT belief/rating range: a plan can have a maximum rating of 10000. Typical ratings and beliefs in the system are between 1000 and 9000. A plan usually pursues less than a dozen alternative-goals, so if the factors are weighted equally (at .25) the plan rating is most influenced by the first three factors (predicted result belief, fraction-completed, and expected next result belief). In this case, the number of alternative-goals essentially acts only to break ties between otherwise equally-rated plans. In the next chapter (Section 5.1.2), several experiments are described where the relative weights are changed to examine how they affect problem solving.

4.3.3 Plan Execution, Monitoring, and Repair

Planning is interleaved with execution, occurring not only when i-goals are satisfied but also when each short-term action is performed. The planner monitors plans, repairs them when needed, and updates them as actions that are taken trigger KSIs for pending actions.

Monitoring Plans

Each time a short-term action is carried out by invoking its KSI, the planner monitors the action to determine whether the hypotheses generated by the KSI meet predictions for that action (which were computed using the KS-models). The monitor examines the KSI's created hypotheses and checks each against their expected attributes. The hypothesis's blackboard-level should match the expected result's blackboard-level, the hypothesis's event-class should be included in the expected result's event-classes, and the hypothesis's belief should fall within some user specified tolerance of the expected result's belief-range (currently that tolerance is at least half of the belief-range's minimum).

In addition, the hypothesis's track should have time-locations that at least cover the result's time-regions: for each of the time-regions, the track should have a time-location with the same time and whose location falls within the desired region. Cases of where the track matches or fails to match the expected result's time-regions are shown in Figure 24. If the track misses a time-region by having no time-location for the same time then the track does not match the time-regions (Figure 24a). Also, if the track misses a time-region by having a time-location whose location does not fall within the desired region, then the track does not satisfy the result (Figure 24b). If each of the tracks time-locations matches one of the expected result's time-regions, then the hypothesis's track satisfies the result's time-regions (Figure 24c). The final case is when the hypothesis's time-locations cover the result's time-regions, but also include time-locations for times not covered by the time-regions (Figure 24d). This can happen when the KSI finds on the blackboard a hypothesis with a longer track (formed by another plan or received from another node), and combines this hypothesis with the partial result generated by the plan's past actions. The overall track may or may not be acceptable: if the track's additional time-locations do *not* fall within the expected time-regions of *all* of the plan's alternative-goals, then the hypothesis is unacceptable because it does not represent a result that contributes to all of the plan's objectives. If the track's time-locations are consistent with the plan's objectives, however, then the planner adopts the more complete track as satisfying the action. The more complete track can make achieving some future i-goals (for extending the track into times already covered by the more complete track) trivial to achieve and therefore allows the plan to be finished sooner. The planner thus takes advantage of having more complete results being formed unexpectedly, so long as those results are consistent with all of the plan's objectives.

The planner compares all of the hypotheses created by the invoked KSI with the expected results, and builds a list of the hypotheses satisfying the expectations (the sat-hyps). This list replaces the previous value (an empty list) in the expected result's data structure, to record the actual results.

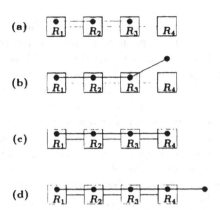

Four cases of attempting to match a hypothesis's time-locations (connected dots) with the expected result's time-regions $R_1 R_2 R_3 R_4$ (connected squares) are shown. In (a), the time-locations do not match because there is no time-location in R_4. In (b), the time-locations do not match because the location for time 4 does not fall within R_4. In (c), the time-locations match the time-regions. In (d), the time-locations extend beyond the time-regions, and whether they match or not depends on whether the additional time-location is consistent with the plan's objectives (its alternative-goals' tracks).

Figure 24: Matching Hypothesis Tracks to Expected Time-Regions.

Repairing Plans

As it monitors a plan's actions, the planner watches for actions that have no satisfying hypotheses. When such an action occurs, the plan has deviated from expectations. The planner attempts to repair the plan by inserting new short-term actions that it expects will generate the missed result. Because plan repair is a complex process that is not the focus of this research, the planner as currently implemented is equipped to only repair plans that fail in certain ways to illustrate how repair can be effected in this framework.

The planner is capable of repairing plans whose actions fail to generate hypotheses with the right time-location characteristics. For example, a KSI might find hypotheses on the blackboard that the plan did not anticipate (hypotheses formed by another plan or received from another node) and thus might generate hypotheses whose tracks are too long or too short or that deviate from the expected time-regions. When this happens, the planner is equipped to generate new actions that may lead to suitable hypotheses whenever possible. The planner begins by finding hypotheses that it may be able to combine into the desired results.[7] It examines the hypotheses produced by past actions, and

---

[7] Since the blackboard stores every hypothesis generated in the course of problem solving, the planner can retrieve any hypotheses that were formed at any time, even if these hypotheses have been used to generate other hypotheses. When trying to repair a plan, therefore, the planner can plan actions that use some or all of the hypotheses used by earlier plan steps. In

finds the hypothesis closest to the desired result: a hypothesis that correctly covers as many of the expected time-regions as possible. If the planner cannot find any such hypotheses, then it fails to repair the plan. Having found such a hypothesis, the planner triggers the goal processing to generate a goal to extend the hypothesis into the missing time-regions. In turn, this goal triggers the creation of KSIs to achieve it. If any KSIs are generated, then the planner takes the most highly-rated of these and creates a new detailed action based on the KSI. It inserts this action as the next short-term action, and the repair is completed. Of course, if this action also fails to produce the desired result, the planner once again attempts to repair the plan in the same way. Eventually, either the desired results will be formed or else the planner will run out of KSIs (ways of combining relevant hypotheses) to try, and no new actions are inserted. Whenever a plan's action fails to achieve its result and no new actions can be inserted to repair the plan, the plan is **aborted**.

Updating Plans

After the planner monitors the plan (and repairs it if necessary), it must find the next action and KSI. It starts by taking the first action from the list of pending short-term actions and checks whether the KSI for that action is already specified. If so, then that KSI is triggered as the next local activity and the action is pushed onto the short-term:record list. Otherwise, a KSI for the action was unavailable at the time the short-term:actions were detailed because the results of earlier short-term actions are expected to trigger the formation of this KSI. The planner therefore must cause the goal processing mechanisms to generate the appropriate KSI.

Given an action without an associated KSI, the planner first scans the short-term:record to find the actions that led up to this action: the results that this action is expected to use. The planner then compares the relevant past results to the current action to determine what type of activity is needed: synthesizing the past results, extending them forward, or extending them backward.[8] By passing the satisfying hypotheses (sat-hyps) of the relevant past results and the type of goals desired to the goal processor, the planner triggers new goals to combine the past results in the appropriate way. The new goals in turn trigger the instantiation of new KSIs to achieve the goals. The planner finds the most

---

other domains, such as assembly tasks, an action that combines two pieces into a subassembly causes those individual pieces to be no longer available: if a plan to form a subassembly fails, the planner cannot simply develop a new sequence of assembly steps but must also *disassemble* the faulty subassembly.

[8] In addition, if the planner is pursuing a plan to extend a track, and that plan is working toward competing alternative-goals that indicate different extensions, then the planner can invoke subgoaling on the extension goal so that it can better differentiate between KSI's that contribute to the different extensions. By being more selective about what goals are formed and when they are subgoaled, the planner reduces goal processing overhead.

promising KSI (the most highly-rated KSI whose goals are consistent with the expected result of the next action) and inserts that KSI into the action's KSI slot. Finally, the KSI is triggered as the next KSI and the action is pushed onto the short-term:record list.

When the planner invokes the goal processor to create goals that extend previous results, the goal processor might determine that such goals already exist—they were formed by another plan working on the same data. The planner then must check to see if these goals are already satisfied (hypotheses were formed that satisfy them) and, if so, whether the satisfying hypotheses already achieve the desired results of the next action. When this occurs, the action is trivially achieved and its attributes are updated (its result sat-hyps are set to the satisfying hypotheses, its KSI is set to the KSI that created those hypotheses). It is then pushed onto the short-term:record and the next action in the short-term:actions list is retrieved and pursued.

Finally, the goal processor may be unable to instantiate a suitable KSI. This typically occurs when the plan is attempting to generate a result that conflicts with the KSs' knowledge. For example, a plan may be attempting to extend a track into a new time-region (Figure 25a). Based on the clustering mechanisms' knowledge, this track should be possible because a vehicle in R_3 at time 3 could be in R_4 at time 4. The plan therefore details an action to join the track for times 1–3 with data at 4 into a track for times 1–4. The KSs, on the other hand, have more extensive knowledge about vehicle movements. In particular, given the track for times 1–3 and knowledge about a vehicles maximum turning rate (acceleration), the KSs identify that only data within a specific region can be combined with track 1–3 (Figure 25b). Because the data falls outside of this region, no KSI can be formed to generate the plan's desired result (Figure 25c). The plan is **suspended**; it is not aborted because new data may possibly arrive that can be used by the KSs to continue the plan. For example, new data that is located close enough to the old data to be clustered together might also overlap with the range of acceptable extensions and therefore allow the plan to continue (Figure 25d).

4.3.4 Modifying Plans

Not only do plans change as they are pursued, but they also change when relevant new information arrives at the node (from another node or from the sensors) that affects the plans' goals. In Section 3.3.4 the mechanisms for updating the clustering hierarchy based on new information were described.[9] When the clustering hierarchy changes, the top-level clusters may change: some

---

[9] The clustering mechanisms could also be triggered when a local KS generates completely unexpected hypotheses which would not fit into any existing plans. Extending the mechanisms to cluster such hypotheses would be straightforward, but is currently unnecessary since the KSs currently used in the DVMT cannot generate such hypotheses.

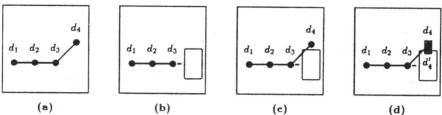

(a)   **(b)**   **(c)**   **(d)**

The plan data is shown in (a), and a partial track for $d_1 d_2 d_3$ is shown in (b) along with the acceptable range of extensions for that track. The possible range of extensions does not include the data for d_4, shown in (c), and no KSI can currently be formed to extend the partial track. If new data d_4' arrives, the planner clusters it with d_4 and modifies the plan's expected track. The new data does overlap with the range of extensions (d), so a KSI can be formed and the plan can be pursued.

Figure 25: Example of Suspended Plan and its Continuation.

existing clusters may be extended or joined together, and new top-level clusters may be added for new information. Because each top-level cluster corresponds to an alternative-goal, the planner must modify the set of alternative-goals as well, changing any existing alternative-goals whose clusters have changed and creating new alternative-goals for new clusters.

The planner then plans for any new or modified alternative-goals. It divides the new alternative-goals into groups of competing goals and creates a new plan for each group (see Section 4.3.2), recording the names of these new-plans. It then steps through the modified alternative-goals and, for each, determines what existing plans were pursuing that alternative-goal. The names of these modified plans are also recorded.

The planner then determines whether any of the new and modified plans should be merged: separate plans that were generated for previously non-competing alternative-goals may need to be merged if the new data has caused their alternative-goals to now become competing. For example, given the initial situation in Figure 26a, the planner identifies two alternative-goals: to form the track $d_1 d_2$ and the track $d_1' d_2'$. Because these alternative-goals have no common data, they are non-competing and a separate plan is made for each. Some time later, data arrives for sensed times 3 and 4—d_3 and d_4—that is compatible with both of the initial tracks (Figure 26b). The alternative-goals are modified to $d_1 d_2 d_3 d_4$ and $d_1' d_2' d_3 d_4$, and both of the initial plans therefore have modified alternative-goals. Whereas the plans were initially non-competing, now their alternative-goals overlap in $d_3 d_4$. The planner could pursue the now competing plans separately, but if it merges them into a single plan, it can reason about how both alternative-goals can be pursued by working on their common data.[10]

---

[10]Besides giving plans formed by dividing a single plan similar long-term:time-orders, the

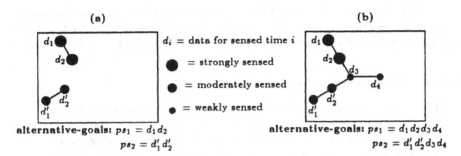

alternative-goals: $ps_1 = d_1 d_2$
$ps_2 = d'_1 d'_2$

alternative-goals: $ps_1 = d_1 d_2 d_3 d_4$
$ps_2 = d'_1 d'_2 d_3 d_4$

Initially, the planner has four data points: d_1, d'_1, d_2, and d'_2, shown in (a).
After some time, more data (d_3 and d_4) arrives and can be combined with the
previous data into modified alternative-goals, shown in (b). The separate plans
based on the initial (non-competing) alternative-goals in (a) should be merged
to pursue the competing alternative-goals in (b) by working on their common
data.

Figure 26: An Example of Modified Alternative-Goals.

When deciding whether to merge two plans, the planner considers their
objectives and past activities. They must have competing alternative-goals,
the same objective:vehicle-event-classes, and any past actions taken by either
plan should not interfere with their combined actions. For example, if the plan
to form track $d_1 d_2$ in Figure 26a has formed that track before the new data
arrives, then consider what would happen if the plans were merged because of
the common data in $d_3 d_4$. After the merged plan raises the data in d_3 to a
tracking-level, the planner recognizes that, in the past, a result was formed for
sensed time 2, so d_3 should be joined to that result, forming $d_1 d_2 d_3$. This result
is *not* appropriate because it is not shared by all of the objective alternative-
goals. As a result, only plans that have not yet formed results adjacent to shared
areas can be merged. When two plans are merged, their combined attributes
are assigned to one of them and the other is deleted from the set of plans. Their
alternative-goals are combined, and so are their short-term:records (their lists
of past actions are combined into a single list) and short-term:used-clusters.
When the merged plan is later divided up again for the different alternative-
goals, the planner extracts out and gives the divided plans only the short-term
information appropriate.

The final step in modifying the plans is to update the attributes of any
merged plans and modified plans, since their alternative-goals have changed.

planner does not reason about how pursuing one plan will affect other local plans. The
planner is implemented to pursue the most highly-rated plan without regard to other plans,
otherwise the complexity of the planning task (number of different combinations of plans
and ways of achieving them) would increase, along with the planning overhead. To have the
planner reason about achieving several alternative-goals simultaneously, the alternative-goals
must be part of the same plan, so related plans must be merged.

The objective:track is recomputed for the new combination of alternative-goals, as is the long-term:time-order. New short-term actions are found for the plan, and new predictions are made. The rating factors and rating are recalculated.

4.3.5   Deadlines and Termination

A problem solver is seldom given exactly as much time as it needs to solve a problem, especially when the costs of problem solving are initially uncertain. When given extra time, the problem solver should make intelligent decisions about when to terminate problem solving: it should sufficiently explore the possible solutions to be reasonably confident that it has found the best one, but should avoid wasting time generating solutions that could not possibly be of use [Hayes-Roth and Lesser, 1977; Woods, 1977]. When given less time than it needs, it should revise plans to generate inferior but acceptable solutions.

When a node has found a solution with time to spare and needs to decide whether to terminate problem solving, the planner compares the solution with the predicted results of competing plans. Since the node is attempting to form the best solution, any plans that predict better results should be pursued. Any plans that predict much worse results should not. Plans that predict somewhat worse results might still be worth pursuing, since the predictions may underestimate the actual results, especially when the plan's i-goals work with very dissimilar data. Our mechanisms allow the user to specify how close a competing plan's predicted results must be to the best solution already found for the plan to warrant further work. The planner can be conservative if the window of acceptable plans is so large that it is unlikely to miss any good solutions, or if the window is very small the node can more quickly propose a solution at the risk of missing a better solution had it kept looking. Unlike our earlier termination technique of using statically-defined criteria such as generating a hypothesis with certain predefined characteristics, the new mechanisms allow the node to dynamically compare the solutions it has developed with those it predicts it could develop and decide when it has found the best solutions.

Instead of having extra time and needing to decide whether it is worthwhile exploring alternative solutions, the node might have too little time to generate even a single solution. The node might face tight deadlines. Without the ability to predict how long a plan will take, the node would simply pursue a plan and hope to finish in time. Our new mechanisms, however, allow the node to roughly predict how long a plan will take. Before it gets far with a plan, the node can recognize that the predicted time needed by the plan will probably exceed the time available, and can do something about it. The planner can respond to this situation in any of a number of ways [Lesser *et al.*, 1988]: it can reduce the needs of the plan by making the plan's long-term goal less constrained (for example, instead of forming the entire track it may focus on only forming a shorter track for the most recently sensed data); it may replace costly activities with less costly activities which may produce inferior but acceptable results; or it may choose another, cheaper plan that can be finished.

Our current implementation has two simple mechanisms for revising a plan to meet deadlines. The first reduces the scope of the plan's long-term goals by ignoring data for some of the sensed times. Because a vehicle's more recent movements are usually most important (for recognizing pending collisions with other vehicles, for example), our mechanism drops i-goals for earlier sensed data until it predicts that the plan to process the remaining data will meet the deadlines. The other mechanism drops plan steps that corroborate hypotheses and increase the belief in the solution but do not affect the scope of the solution. For the current i-goal in Figure 23, for example, KS_1 and KS_2 both supply supporting hypotheses for KS_3. The results formed by KS_3 will be better (more highly believed) if both supporting KSs are executed, but an inferior result can still be made if one KS is dropped. When a plan will exceed deadlines, preferences about which of these mechanisms to try first depends on whether the agent needing the solution (currently the user) tells the node that belief is more important than scope or *vice versa*.[11]

4.3.6 Planning for Problem Solving

The planner is part of a node's control activities between KSI executions:

1. it forms or updates the clustering hierarchy with any new data, and creates and modifies plans given a new/updated clustering hierarchy;

2. it monitors the plan that was last pursued, determining whether the KSI invoked achieved the desired result, and if not, it repairs the plan;

3. it determines whether the plan last pursued has exhausted its set of detailed short-term:actions and needs detailed planning for its next i-goal;

4. it finds the best active plan to pursue next (ignoring aborted, suspended, or completed plans);

5. and it finds the appropriate KSI for the plan being pursued and puts that KSI at the top of the KSI-queue.

If for some reason the planner fails to find a KSI (there are no active plans), then the node reverts back to the simpler control scheme of executing the most highly-rated KSIs. Since the planner might have suppressed the goal processor from forming goals and subgoals that were not needed by the plans, and since some of these goals and subgoals might be needed by the simpler control scheme to form and rate useful KSIs, a node without active plans might retrigger goal processing on some of its hypotheses. Even when no plans are active, however,

---

[11]Since the KSs compute belief as essentially the average of the individual pieces of a track, belief does not necessarily increase with increasing scope—belief is more a function of the amount of processing done on each piece of a solution than of how many pieces have been processed. Thus, our two mechanisms can treat scope and belief as being relatively independent attributes of a solution.

the planner is still invoked between each KSI execution so that it can modify its plans based on any new sensor data or data received from another node. If it develops active plans, the planner once again controls node problem solving.

4.3.7   An Example of Local Planning

As an example of how the planning mechanisms work, we describe in more detail the example used in the overview (Section 4.2) and in the more complete description of the mechanisms above: the problem data is shown in Figure 27. Assume that the data for the six sensed times arrives over the first six simulated time intervals. Problem solving thus begins at time 7.

The planner begins by forming the clustering hierarchy. The top three levels of this particular clustering hierarchy were discussed in the previous chapter (Figure 21). When it has completed the clustering hierarchy, the planner then extracts the four top-level clusters and generates alternative-goals. All four alternative-goals are competing since they share common data in their clusters. The plan generator then groups the alternative-goals into groups of competing alternative-goals—in this case, into a single group.

The plan generator creates a plan for this group of alternative-goals. It computes the plan's objectives by combining the attributes of the alternative-goals. It then computes the long-term information for the plan. The long-term tracking-levels is set to (vt) because that is the lowest blackboard-level at which the node has KSs that can combine hypotheses into tracks. To order the plan's i-goals, the planner computes the overall-cost for the various sub-clusters (Figure 21) and identifies that the most cost effective area of the plan is the common area d_3d_4 (the *cost-heuristic-weight is 1 in these calculations). The planner starts the time-order with these i-goals: having no reason to prefer one to the other, it arbitrarily orders these i-goals as (3 4)—to work in d_3 and then d_4. By comparing the costs of the remaining clusters, it groups them together and orders the i-goals as (3 4 2 5 1 6).

Before it can determine the other long-term attributes of the plan, the planner must plan short-term activities and make predictions about the plan. The short-term actions are found for the first i-goal (to process data in d_3). Initially, the planner attempts to find actions that will develop hypotheses at the tracking-level at both vehicle-event-classes (1 and 2). It searches down the clustering hierarchy for appropriate base-clusters and forms actions to synthesize their data to the proper blackboard-level. Based on its models of KSs, however, the planner identifies that the hypotheses formed for vehicle-event-class 1 are likely to have a much higher belief. Therefore, it changes the plan's objectives to pursue only that type of vehicle, develops suitable short-term actions, updates the short-term used-clusters, and saves the ignored vehicle-event-class so that later it can produce a second plan for that vehicle-event-class.

The planner then forms predictions for the plan. Until it has pursued its plans further, it bases these predictions on the expected results of the short-

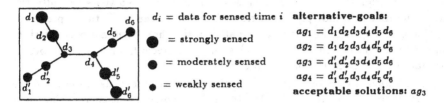

d_i = data for sensed time i

● = strongly sensed

● = moderately sensed

● = weakly sensed

alternative-goals:

$ag_1 = d_1 d_2 d_3 d_4 d_5 d_6$

$ag_2 = d_1 d_2 d_3 d_4 d'_5 d'_6$

$ag_3 = d'_1 d'_2 d_3 d_4 d_5 d_6$

$ag_4 = d'_1 d'_2 d_3 d_4 d'_5 d'_6$

acceptable solutions: ag_3

Time	Plan	Rating	A-goals	V-e-cs	Results	Pend I-gs
7	$plan_1$	2719	ag_1, ag_2, ag_3, ag_4	(1)	none	(3 4 2 5 1 6)
	$plan_2$	285	ag_1, ag_2, ag_3, ag_4	(2)	none	(3 4 2 5 1 6)
14	$plan_1$	4143	ag_1, ag_2	(1)	$d_3 d_4$	(2 5 1 6)
	$plan_2$	285	ag_1, ag_2, ag_3, ag_4	(2)	none	(3 4 2 5 1 6)
	$plan_3$	4213	ag_3, ag_4	(1)	$d_3 d_4$	(2 5 1 6)
18	$plan_1$	4143	ag_1, ag_2	(1)	$d_3 d_4$	(2 5 1 6)
	$plan_2$	285	ag_1, ag_2, ag_3, ag_4	(2)	none	(3 4 2 5 1 6)
	$plan_3$	4316	ag_4	(1)	$d'_2 d_3 d_4$	(5 1 6)
	$plan_4$	4344	ag_3	(1)	$d'_2 d_3 d_4$	(5 1 6)
22	$plan_1$	4143	ag_1, ag_2	(1)	$d_3 d_4$	(2 5 1 6)
	$plan_2$	285	ag_1, ag_2, ag_3, ag_4	(2)	none	(3 4 2 5 1 6)
	$plan_3$	4316	ag_4	(1)	$d'_2 d_3 d_4$	(5 1 6)
	$plan_4$	4240	ag_3	(1)	$d'_2 d_3 d_4 d_5$	(1 6)
26	$plan_1$	4143	ag_1, ag_2	(1)	$d_3 d_4$	(2 5 1 6)
	$plan_2$	285	ag_1, ag_2, ag_3, ag_4	(2)	none	(3 4 2 5 1 6)
	$plan_3$	0	ag_4	(1)	$d_4 d'_5$	(1 6)
	$plan_4$	4240	ag_3	(1)	$d'_2 d_3 d_4 d_5$	(1 6)
34	$plan_1$	4143	ag_1, ag_2	(1)	$d_3 d_4$	(2 5 1 6)
	$plan_2$	285	ag_1, ag_2, ag_3, ag_4	(2)	none	(3 4 2 5 1 6)
	$plan_3$	0	ag_4	(1)	$d_4 d'_5$	(1 6)
	$plan_4$	5906	ag_3	(1)	$d'_1 d'_2 d_3 d_4 d_5 d_6$	()

A problem environment is displayed, along with the possible solutions found by clustering the data and the acceptable solutions that can eventually be generated by the node. The plans at various times are shown to indicate the evolution of the plans as problem solving progresses. For each plan is given its rating (out of 10000), the alternative-goals that it is expected to work toward, the Vehicle-event-classes of the vehicles it is attempting to track, the result it has generated to this point, and the pending i-goals in the order that they will be attempted.

Figure 27: A Plan Summary for an Example Environment.

term actions (which were predicted by the models of KSs). It compares the expected results of i-goal 3 with that i-goal's base-clusters, and predicts the results of the future i-goals by identifying their base-clusters and expecting the same relationship to hold between their results and base-clusters as between i-goal 3's results and its base-clusters. The planner also predicts that the time costs for future i-goals will be comparable to the expected time needs (again predicted by the KS models) of i-goal 3.

The remaining long-term information is determined: the time-predictions are based on the predictions just found, and the activity-per-time is found by scanning through the short-term actions and listing their KS-types. Finally, the rating factors are found: predicted result belief from the predictions, predicted belief and KSI ratings for the next i-goal from the short-term actions, fraction-completed from the (initially empty) short-term record, and the number of alternative-goals from the plan's objectives.

The planner inserts this plan on the plan queue, where it also puts the more lowly-rated plan that it creates for the other vehicle-event-class. The plan dispatcher chooses the most highly-rated plan as the current plan, which gets passed to the plan executor. The plan executor first determines whether there are any short-term actions, and if not it sends the plan to the plan generator to form the detailed short-term actions for the next i-goal. If the next i-goal is not common to all of the plan's alternative-goals, then the plan generator will divide the plan: it generates actions that only pursue a subset of these goals, and builds new plans to achieve any remaining alternative-goals. These are placed in the plan queue and the plan dispatcher once again sends the most highly-rated plan to the plan executor.

If the plan has short-term actions, the plan executor then determines whether the predicted time needs of the plan exceed any deadlines, and if so it modifies the plan appropriately (reducing its goals, removing some of its short-term actions). If it changes the plan, the plan executor rerates the plan, reinserts it into the plan queue, and triggers the plan dispatcher to find the current plan once again. When it has a plan that needs no modification, the plan executor takes the next short-term action and determines whether it has a KSI associated with it. If not, the plan executor examines the plan's short-term actions to find relevant hypotheses formed in the past and triggers the goal processor to build appropriate goals from these hypotheses and KSIs to satisfy these goals. The plan executor selects the appropriate KSI for the action from the KSI queue. If no acceptable KSI is available, the plan executor gives the plan a rating of 0 and reinserts it into the plan queue: the plan is suspended and may be retriggered (rerated) if new data arrives at the node. When the plan executor can associate a KSI with the action, the planner then sets the node's top (current) KSI to this KSI, and the node invokes the KS.

When the KS has completed, the plan executor retrieves the new hypotheses from the blackboard and checks them against the predicted results of the action. It thus monitors the actions and detects when the actual hypotheses produced deviate from the expected results. When this occurs, it invokes the repairing functions, which in turn might trigger more goal processing to generate new KSIs. The plan repairing functions may be unable to generate alternative actions to achieve the desired result, and if that occurs then the plan is aborted: it is rated to 0 and reinserted on (the bottom of) the plan queue. If it can find a repairing action, the planner inserts this as the next short-term action and reinserts the plan into the plan queue.

After the initial plans are formed, therefore, the planning activity cycles through choosing a current plan, finding the appropriate KSI for that plan, invoking the KSI, monitoring (and repairing) the results, and then once again choosing a current plan. This cycle continues until the termination mechanisms end problem solving: either a hypothesis has been formed that meets the solution criteria, or there are no plans for which KSIs can be found, or none of the remaining plans are likely to generate better solutions than those already found. At any time, the plan generator can modify plans on the plan queue when new data arrives that changes the clustering hierarchy. When that happens, the plan generator modifies any existing plans on the plan queue and generates any needed new plans.

To illustrate how plans change over time, the plans on the plan queue at selected times are shown in Figure 27. The plans are created at time 7, and $plan_1$ is pursued until time 14, when the common i-goals have been achieved so the plan is divided into two plans: $plan_1$ now only extends d_3d_4 into d_2 and a new plan $plan_3$ is generated to extend d_3d_4 into d_2' (Figure 27, time 14). The track d_3d_4 is used by the goal processor to form a goal indicating where good data for sensed time 2 is most likely to lie, as is shown in Figure 28.

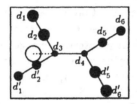

Figure 28: Expected Extension of Track d_3d_4.

This goal overlaps only with the data in d_2', so the KSIs to work on this data have their ratings increased while the ratings for KSIs in d_2 are unchanged. Although originally the KSIs for d_2 were more highly rated (since they work with more strongly sensed data), the KSIs to work in d_2' are now more highly rated. The plan to work on d_2' ($plan_3$) is therefore pursued because its more highly-rated KSIs cause its rating to be highest. Similarly, when this plan is divided into separate plans to extend either to d_5 or to d_5' (Figure 27, time 18), goal processing affects KSI ratings so that $plan_4$ (to work on d_5) is preferred. After generating the track $d_2'd_3d_4d_5$, however, the plan to continue developing this correct track is no longer the most highly-rated plan: because the track spanning times 2–5 has a lower belief than was predicted (the actual belief was reduced because of vehicle turns which the prediction mechanisms cannot take into account), $plan_3$ to extend the track $d_2'd_3d_4$ to d_5' becomes more highly rated (its predicted result's belief is higher and its fraction-complete is sufficiently high, so its overall rating is higher). This plan is pursued (Figure 27, time 22) until the node is unable to join d_5' to $d_2'd_3d_4$ because of vehicle turning constraints. This plan ($plan_3$) is aborted (its rating is set to 0), and $plan_4$ is resumed (Figure 27, time 26) and pursued until the solution is generated

(Figure 27, time 34).

4.4   Generalizing

The planner must concurrently reason at three different levels: it must reason about entire plans—rating alternative plans and following the best one at any time; it must reason about the intermediate goals for achieving plans—finding an ordering of these goals that allows it to efficiently form solutions or detect that solutions are not worth forming; and it must reason about detailed actions—identifying specific actions (KSIs) that may lead to desired results. Because plan ratings depend on the order of i-goals and the detailed actions, the i-goal ordering depends on the overall goals of the plan, and the detailed actions depend on previous i-goals, the planner must reason about all three levels interdependently.

The planner improves control decisions by reasoning in a top-down manner: it first chooses the most highly-rated plan, then the next i-goal of that plan, and then finally the next KSI for that i-goal. Top-down planning has been used in many other systems, but several aspects of our domain distinguish our planner. First, it must formulate its own goals, unlike typical planning systems where the planner begins with both a current "state" and a set of prioritized goal "states" to reach. Second, our planner faces uncertainty in its goals and must develop plans that efficiently resolve this uncertainty. Unlike differential diagnosis tasks [Clancey and Letsinger, 1981] where each solution has a well-defined set of "confirming" and "refuting" hypotheses, our planner must incrementally construct partial solutions in such a way that, over time, certain partial solutions make some overall solutions look more plausible than others.

Another important aspect of the task is that a problem solver can maintain a record of all partial solutions it has constructed, so that its reasoning is monotonic in the sense that any actions it could have taken in the past are still viable in the present. Unlike tasks where planned actions cause changes to the physical world, a problem solver's planner need not worry about "undoing" previous actions to recover an earlier state. The assumption that actions never have to be undone simplifies our planner, but if given information about actions to undo past actions, the planner could handle domains where an action not only generates an output result but also changes its inputs.

The task also allows flexibility in how results can be achieved, and the planner exploits this flexibility when planning incrementally. The drawback is that the planner might take actions that preclude important future actions because it did not look far enough ahead. The assumption behind the planner is that there is sufficient flexibility in how goals can be achieved, so that the planner can recover from unanticipated interactions between actions and from unexpected changes to the problem situation by pursuing an alternative set of actions that will achieve the desired result. The planner also assumes predictability in the task that lets it estimate future results and time needs based on past experience. In tasks where this assumption does not hold, the planner would need an alternative source of such information, such as a database that associates activities with predicted outcomes and costs.

Our planner is particularly suited to controlling the activities of a problem solver. Hence, besides its practical contributions to the DVMT, the planner more generally contributes to planning technology because it represents mechanisms that are useful in a new class of problems. The components of the planner can be generalized for use in problems sharing the characteristics outlined above.

4.4.1 Generalizing the Planner's Components

Generalizing the Plan Data Structures. The principal divisions of the plan data structure are intended to be domain-independent: plans have objectives (the purposes of the plans); long-term (strategic) activities and short-term (tactical or reactive) actions; predictions about what is expected to occur during the plan (action preconditions, postconditions, and expected durations); and rating information that helps prioritize them. Although in this domain only two levels of planning are needed, long-term and short-term, the plan structures could be extended to include more levels as well. Within these major divisions are the more domain-dependent plan attributes that allow plans for specific tasks to be represented.

The plan's objective attributes not only correspond to pointers to the plan's goals (which it either identifies for itself—as in this planner—or has provided to it by the user), but also give specifications for what the plan's intended solution will look like. The plan's long-term attributes provide an ordering of the major subgoals of the plan's overall goal, information about how the results of these subgoals should be combined, predictions about the costs of achieving each subgoal and the overall plan, and a summary of the activities that go into achieving the subgoals. The plan's short-term information links specific actions to the larger subgoals. The representation of these actions is the most domain specific aspect of the plans, which is not surprising since this is the level where the planner generates commands for the problem solver. The contents of these actions—KS-types, KSIs, specific expected result attributes (which correspond to attributes of the hypotheses generated by the actions)—are based on the actions and results in the task domain. The underlying structures for storing sequences of actions and records of past activities are domain-independent, however. The prediction information indicates the expected costs and results of the major subgoals of the plan, and in other domains, additional information might be useful as well, such as resource requirements other than computation time. Finally, the rating information outlines basic information that affects how important the planner should consider the plan, including the expected quality of the overall results, the amount of effort expended on the plan, how highly rated the next actions for the plan are, and the number of goals the plan concurrently pursues. These characteristics of plans are domain-independent, and other information might be useful in other domains, such as the resource costs for achieving the plan other than the computation time (which is considered in the plan's fraction-completed factor).

Generalizing Long-term Planning. The long-term planning functions order the major subgoals for achieving the plan's overall goals. The functions, as implemented, first identify the subgoals (i-goals) by scanning down the clustering hierarchy, and then use the relative cost and commonality of these subgoals to find an ordering. More generally, the planner need not have a clustering hierarchy, but could identify subgoals using other knowledge for decomposing goals into subgoals. Furthermore, the ordering decisions need not be based on cost and commonality. Unlike this domain where the subgoals can be pursued in any order (although the costs of pursuing them and their results can be affected by the order), in other domains there may be precedence constraints between the subgoals. The mechanisms detailed in this chapter could be extended to include such factors: by including the relevant factors in the computation of overall subgoal costs, an ordering that takes them all into account can be generated. Finally, the same knowledge the planner uses to decompose a goal into subgoals often indicates how the subgoals' results should be combined into an overall result. For example, if the planner knows how to decompose an assembly task into subassembly tasks (which in essence means that it disassembles the assembly into subtasks), then it knows how to reassemble the overall assembly.

Generalizing Short-term Planning. The purpose of short-term planning is to find domain-level actions that achieve the desired subgoals. From the perspective of the other planning components, how these actions are found is irrelevant. The mechanisms detailed in this chapter take one approach: they assume that basic sequence of activities will achieve the desired results, and expend most of their effort not on choosing a sequence of actions but on modeling those actions to predict what kind of results they will generate. In other domains, the detailed planning could be done quite differently. When a larger variety of actions is available and subgoals are more difficult to achieve, planning techniques involving propagating constraints about actions to find sequences that achieve the subgoals would be needed [Stefik, 1981].

Generalizing the Prediction Mechanisms. Our prediction mechanisms exploit the repetitive nature of constructing solutions, assuming that similar subgoals will be achieved in similar ways. In other domains, if subgoals with similar characteristics can be identified (subgoals with the same basic differences between the initial and goal states), then predictions for future activities can be based on past experience. However, achieving an overall goal might not always involve pursuing a sequence of similar subgoals. Or even if the subgoals are similar, the actions taken to achieve them may vary. In these cases, prediction information must come from somewhere else, if it can be derived at all. For example, other mechanisms and knowledge may be added to the system to generate predictions, or a database that matches situations and subgoals with costs and results may be provided to the system. Without the ability to predict costs and results for i-goals, the local planner can still function but its capabilities and sophistication are reduced. If it cannot predict result quality, it lacks an important factor in choosing among plans and in making termination decisions. If it cannot predict time needs for plans, the planner cannot anticipate difficulties in meeting deadlines. Prediction is especially important when the planner is attempting to coordinate with others, so that it can anticipate future interactions.

Generalizing Plan Ratings. The factors considered when rating plans (expected result quality, fraction-complete, rating of next actions, number of goals concurrently pursued) would generally be of interest when rating plans in any domain. The techniques for measuring these factors depend on information found by other mechanisms: the expected quality from the prediction mechanisms, the fraction-complete and rating of next actions from the short-term information, the number of goals from the plan's objectives. Assuming that this information was available (even if developed in different ways), the rating mechanisms could compute ratings in other domains as well. In addition, other factors might be important in other domains, such as information about needs for scarce resources. The choice of appropriate factors must be based on experience; and experience is also necessary when deciding how much each factor should contribute to the overall plan rating. To improve plan selection decisions, the decisionmaking might be based not simply on numeric factors but on more sophisticated methods for reasoning about the different influences that affect choice of plans. This remains an open research issue, but as long as the plans can be ranked in some way (prioritized on the plan queue), it is all the same to the rest of the planning mechanisms.

Generalizing Plan Monitoring and Repair. Since the short-term planning mechanisms generate expected results for each action, plan monitoring involves simply comparing actual results with those expected and recognizing when they do not agree. More generally, plan monitoring assumes that the planner has some model of expected behavior against which it can compare actual behavior to recognize anomalies. The mechanisms described in this chapter use the specifications of expected results from actions and determines whether the actual results meet these specifications, allowing some tolerance for error (particularly in the predicted belief) since the predictions are only estimates.

Our current repair mechanisms are rudimentary. In general terms, when the plan was expected to combine results from several subgoals into a single result and fails, the repairer finds the largest combined result made so far and develops actions that combine it with the results of the remaining subgoals. This approach to repair assumes that no actions need to be undone before the recovery actions can be attempted. In domains such as assembly tasks, before an alternative assembly action can be attempted, some disassembly might be needed to get back the subassemblies. More sophisticated reasoning is needed in the repairing mechanisms to handle such situations. Therefore, our current repair mechanisms represent a framework for repair in our type of domain, but much work needs to be done before the mechanisms more generally allow sophisticated recovery of failed plans.

Generalizing Plan Modification.   The plan modification mechanisms allow new problem data to affect plans. The clustering mechanisms that allow the clustering hierarchy to be updated enable the planner to identify when long-term goals have changed. Given new long-term goals, the planner modifies its set of plans to achieve those goals: it modifies existing plans whose goals have changed and adds new plans for new goals. It also recognizes when previously unrelated plans become related because their long-term goals now interact, and it may merge these plans. In more general terms, the modification mechanisms allow the planner to react to a changing environment by altering goals and plans when circumstances change. When a plan's goals change, the planner usually recomputes most of the plan's attributes, taking into consideration the actions already performed on the plan and the i-goals already achieved. Therefore, applying the modification mechanisms to other domains essentially reverts to applying the basic mechanisms for generating plans, with the added complication of merging plans when they now share subgoals and their completed subgoals do not conflict.

Generalizing Planning for Deadlines.   The mechanisms described above for meeting deadlines simply drop i-goals or actions from plans to generate less complete or less highly-believed solutions. Decisions about how to reduce the scope of goals—about what i-goals to drop—are domain dependent, as are decisions about what actions to drop. However, the basic reasoning behind them is more general. To meet deadlines, the planner must simplify the task by specifying a less difficult goal to achieve. This might entail reducing the size of the goal (dropping subgoals) or relaxing the constraints on an acceptable solution (allowing less highly-believed solutions to satisfy the overall goal). Our mechanisms represent a framework in which more complex reasoning about real-time constraints can be developed [Lesser *et al.*, 1988]. In particular, our termination mechanisms are very general. Given plans for tracking vehicles or for any other task, these mechanisms compare the predicted result quality—

the expected payoff of the plan—with the results formed by completed plans to determine whether a plan is worth pursuing.

4.4.2 Other Applications of the Planner

The planner described in this chapter has been implemented in the DVMT, and its success in improving performance in this domain (which is further discussed in the next chapter) indicates that it could be useful in other systems as well. In particular, the planner is well suited to blackboard-based interpretation systems, because these systems are usually data-driven and construct solutions through the repeated application of sequences of KSs. Many types of problems demand that solutions be *constructed*—problems ranging from design to diagnosis—and the planner is useful in such task domains. For example, a chemical-synthesis problem solver may be given a list of available chemicals (data), knowledge about possible synthetic reactions (KSs), and a rough goal of forming any compound so long as it has certain characteristics (insoluble in water, non-acidic, polar, and a melting point above 100°C, for example). Given the initial set of chemicals and rough knowledge about what types of chemicals can be combined, it can group these together to recognize more specific types of compounds that may fit the bill (for example, polystyrenes, polyesters, and polyphenylenes). Next, since some of these compounds may have common precursors, the planner can group them together so that it can be working on several at once by generating a stock of intermediate compounds. By considering both the expected cost of forming these intermediates and the likelihood that they will be of use in some eventual product, the planner can sketch out a high-level sequence of intermediate compounds that should be developed on the way to forming potentially desirable complete compounds. For the next intermediate compound, the planner could then detail the actions needed to synthesize that compound: what reagents to mix, how to mix and heat them, and so on. Because reactions all too often fail to produce the desired product, the planner should not plan subsequent steps in detail until the next intermediate compound is formed. By analyzing the products of a reaction, the planner can determine whether the desired intermediate compound has been made, and if not, can propose modifications to the reaction or an alternative reaction that might produce the desired product. Moreover, if new chemicals arrive at the laboratory, the planner should check to see whether different goal compounds can be proposed and whether these affect how the intermediate compounds currently under development should be synthesized. The chemical synthesis domain therefore needs a planner with essentially the same features as the planner developed for the DVMT, and many of the mechanisms developed for the DVMT could be reimplemented for the chemical domain. Our directions for future research (Chapter 9) include revising the planning mechanisms to better separate the domain-independent from the domain-dependent aspects to simplify implementing our mechanisms in other domains.

The planner could also be useful in a job-shop or other task scheduling system where the tasks are interdependent and where there is uncertainty about their time (resource) needs and about whether they will successfully generate useful results. For example, a task scheduler may be given a set of large tasks where each of these tasks can be broken down into subtasks. Associated with each of the large tasks is a deadline for completion. To decide what subtasks to execute and when is not simply a scheduling problem because of the uncertainty involved: the task scheduler cannot find an optimal (or even satisfactory) schedule of tasks at the outset because it is uncertain about how long they will take and whether they will succeed. The scheduler thus needs a planning component to roughly map out how each larger task should be pursued to best resolve uncertainty about whether it can be successfully completed in time to meet its deadline. The planner can also take advantage of cases where the large tasks share subtasks. For example, several of the larger tasks might need to access a database, and so they all include a *get-user-authorization* subtask. By first identifying that they share this subtask and then by planning to pursue it early on, the planner can more efficiently pursue several tasks (if the subtask succeeds) or identify tasks that it cannot complete (if the subtask fails). The more detailed actions for achieving this subtask may need to be planned as well, and these detailed actions should be monitored and repaired if they fail (trying alternative ways of getting authorization, for example). In addition, the task scheduler may work in a dynamic environment where the set of tasks may change, so the planner must be capable of modifying its plans for achieving tasks dynamically. A planner like the one outlined in this chapter could therefore be suitable for this domain.

Solutions did not appear so readily as before, and things were not so clear as they once seemed. Things were just not working out as planned. Nothing ran smoothly. Nothing was succeeding as planned. –Joseph Heller *(Good as Gold)*

Chapter 5

Local Planning: Experiments and Evaluation

Having described how the planner works in the previous chapter, we now examine how the planner affects problem solving. The first part of this chapter explores the activities of the planner and problem solver in a variety of experiments to better understand what the planner does. To fully understand the effects of the planner, these experiments not only examine how the planner improves control decisions, but also what the costs of those improvements are. It is important to remember that the planner's job is to reduce the time needed to solve problems by improving control decisions, but if the planner needs a lot of time to make these decisions, then the net result may be that the time needs increase—the time saved in problem solving is used up in planning! In many of these experiments, therefore, the discussion covers not only how the planner affects local decisions but also whether the costs of planning are acceptable.

The second part of this chapter presents an evaluation of the planner in terms of its costs, benefits, and limitations, drawing on the experimental results. The planner is summarized and open research issues are briefly discussed.

5.1   Local Planning Experiments

To simplify discussion, our different experimental situations emphasize certain aspects of the planning mechanisms. The first experiment set (Section 5.1.1) shows how the planner can rearrange activities to more quickly identify and generate promising solutions. In the second experiment set (Section 5.1.2), the emphasis is on how the various plan-rating factors influence the choice of plans to pursue, and how this in turn affects problem solving. The third experiment set (Section 5.1.3) illustrates how the planner monitors and repairs plans when planned actions fail to generate their expected results. To show how the planner modifies plans when new information arrives, the fourth experiment set (Section 5.1.4) examines how varying times that sensor data arrives at the node affects planning and problem solving. Finally, the fifth experiment set (Section 5.1.5) focuses on how the planner decides when to terminate problem solving and how it meets deadlines.

When evaluating the benefits and costs of the planner, the following factors are considered: how much does it improve control decisions (reduce the number of incorrect decisions), how much additional computation overhead does it require, and how much additional storage do the clustering-hierarchy and plans need. Since each control decision causes the invocation of a KSI, the first factor is measured using problem solving time: since each KSI is simulated to take 1 time unit, generating a solution at an earlier time means fewer KSIs were invoked so better control decisions were made. The second factor is measured as the actual computation time (runtime) needed to solve a problem, representing the combined costs of problem solving and control computation. The third factor is roughly measured as the number of problem solving and planning data structures formed in the course of an experiment. The planner generates clusters (to find long-term goals) and plans, but because it controls problem solving it might reduce the number of hypotheses, goals, and KSIs the node generates.

5.1.1   Experiment Set 5.1: Planning to Resolve Uncertainty

Several experiments to evaluate the benefits and costs of the planner in the environment studied in the previous chapters (see Figure 27) are summarized in Table 1. Experiments E5.1.1 and E5.1.2 illustrate how the planner can dramatically reduce the number of KSIs invoked during problem solving. Without the planner (E5.1.1), the node begins with the most highly sensed data (d_1, d_2, d_5', and d_6') that actually corresponds to *noise* and may have been formed due to sensor errors or echoes in the sensed area. The node attempts to combine this data through d_3 and d_4 but fails because of turning constraints, and then it uses the results from d_3 and d_4 to eventually work its way back out to the moderately sensed correct data. With the new mechanisms (E5.1.2), the planner begins in the area common to all four alternative-goals and then works outward (see Section 4.3.7). Through planning, the time needs to solve the problem are substantially reduced. The cost of planning is also acceptable in this case: the actual computation time required to solve the problem was reduced (E5.1.2 compared to E5.1.1); and the storage was also reduced because the planner forms fewer (only necessary) goals and KSIs, and the node builds fewer incorrect hypotheses.

The planner controls goal processing to generate and process only those goals that further the plan; if goal processing is done independently of the planner (E5.1.3), the overhead of the planner coupled with the only slightly diminished goal processing overhead (the number of goals is only modestly reduced, comparing E5.1.3 with E5.1.1) nullifies the computation time saved on actual problem solving. The amount of storage needed by the node is also increased (E5.1.3 compared with E5.1.1). In addition, without the planner to control it, the goal processing builds goals and subgoals based on less complete results, and these less precise subgoals do not selectively increase the ratings of appropriate KSIs. For example, with the planner controlling goal processing, a goal to find data for sensed time 2 is only generated when the track covering d_3d_4 is formed, and this goal selectively increases the KSI ratings for d_2' as described above. Without the planner controlling goal processing, a goal to find data for sensed time 2 is formed earlier, based only on the result from d_3. Because it has no information about later vehicle locations, the goal indicates that data in any direction around d_3 is equally likely to be useful, and so increases the ratings of KSIs in both d_2 and d_2': the KSIs in d_2 remain more highly rated and the planner then prefers the plan to work on d_2 over the correct plan, degrading performance.

The improvements in experiment E5.1.2 were due to the initial work done in the common areas d_3 and d_4. Because the expected cost of working in each area was expected to be the same, the preference for common i-goals dominated the ordering of the i-goals. In experiments E5.1.4–E5.1.6, areas d_3 and d_4 were flooded with numerous competing hypotheses at other event-classes. If the planner gives strong preference to working on common i-goals regardless of their cost (by setting the *cost-heuristic-weight to 0), then more KSIs are needed to develop all of these hypotheses (E5.1.5). In fact, the node would have solved the problem faster without the planner (E5.1.4). Since the planner developed an inefficient plan, the savings in computation and storage costs are very little. Estimating the relative costs of the alternative i-goals, the planner can determine that d_3 and d_4, although twice as common as the other areas, are likely to be more than twice as costly to work on. By considering both cost and commonality (*cost-heuristic-weight of 1), the planner develops the other areas first and then uses these results to more tightly control processing in d_3 and d_4. The simulated time needed to solve the problem is thus reduced (E5.1.6), along with the computation and storage overhead.

Table 1: Experiment Summary for Experiment Set 5.1.

Expt	Plan	STime	Rtime	Hyps	Goals	KSIs	Cls	Pls	Store	Other
E5.1.1	no	57	17.5	189	254	76	0	0	519	-
E5.1.2	yes	34	8.8	150	51	47	59	4	311	-
E5.1.3	yes	40	17.3	163	205	64	59	4	495	ind goal
E5.1.4	no	57	21.2	247	276	98	0	0	621	-
E5.1.5	yes	74	19.8	293	138	97	69	6	603	*chw=0
E5.1.6	yes	47	15.6	234	74	79	69	6	462	-

Abbreviations

Plan: Are the new planning mechanisms used?
Stime: The simulated time (number of KSIs invoked) to find solution.
Rtime: The total runtime (computation time) to find solution (in minutes).
Hyps: The number of hypotheses formed.
Goals: The number of goals formed and processed.
KSIs: The number of KSIs formed.
Cls: The number of clusters formed in the clustering-hierarchy.
Pls: The number of plans formed.
Store: The total number of structures stored (storage costs).
Other: Additional aspects of the experiment (whether goal processing is independent or the *cost-heuristic-weight is 0).

5.1.2 Experiment Set 5.2: Weighing Different Plan Rating Factors

This experiment set explores how weighing the rating factors differently helps us understand both the need for each factor and the choice of weights for the remaining experiments. In the earlier experiment E5.1.2 (Figure 27), the planner chose to pursue an alternative plan ($plan_3$) after it had already completed more of $plan_4$, when in fact it should have continued with $plan_4$. As a result, the solution was found at time 34. In Table 2, the experimental results for that environment without the planner (E5.2.1) and with the planner (E5.2.2) are summarized again. To elicit better behavior from the planner, the weight w_{fc}—the contribution of the fraction-complete rating factor—can be doubled: instead of each of the four normalized weights (see Section 4.3.2) being 0.25, w_{fc} is set to 0.4 and the other three are set to 0.2. In experiment E5.2.3 which is run with these weights (Figure 29), $plan_4$ is never interrupted—once the planner has proceeded down one plan, it is much less prone to change to another. As a result, the solution is generated at time 30, which is in fact the *optimal* time [Durfee *et al.*, 1985a].

In experiment E5.2.4, the weight for the predicted result belief (w_{pr}) is set to 0.4, twice what the other weights are (Figure 30). Performance degrades compared to both E5.2.2 and E5.2.3 because the planner rated plans to develop d_2 and d_5' highly: since strongly sensed data generally leads to more highly-believed results, and since the planner has insufficient information for predicting

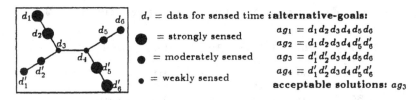

d_i = data for sensed time i **alternative-goals:**

● = strongly sensed

● = moderately sensed

● = weakly sensed

$$ag_1 = d_1 d_2 d_3 d_4 d_5 d_6$$
$$ag_2 = d_1 d_2 d_3 d_4 d_5' d_6'$$
$$ag_3 = d_1' d_2' d_3 d_4 d_5 d_6$$
$$ag_4 = d_1' d_2' d_3 d_4 d_5' d_6'$$

acceptable solutions: ag_3

Time	Plan	Rating	A-goals	V-e-cs	Results	Pend I-gs
7	$plan_1$	2176	ag_1, ag_2, ag_3, ag_4	(1)	none	(3 4 2 5 1 6)
	$plan_2$	229	ag_1, ag_2, ag_3, ag_4	(2)	none	(3 4 2 5 1 6)
14	$plan_1$	3966	ag_1, ag_2	(1)	$d_3 d_4$	(2 5 1 6)
	$plan_2$	229	ag_1, ag_2, ag_3, ag_4	(2)	none	(3 4 2 5 1 6)
	$plan_3$	4038	ag_3, ag_4	(1)	$d_3 d_4$	(2 5 1 6)
18	$plan_1$	3966	ag_1, ag_2	(1)	$d_3 d_4$	(2 5 1 6)
	$plan_2$	229	ag_1, ag_2, ag_3, ag_4	(2)	none	(3 4 2 5 1 6)
	$plan_3$	4434	ag_4	(1)	$d_2' d_3 d_4$	(5 1 6)
	$plan_4$	4476	ag_3	(1)	$d_2' d_3 d_4$	(5 1 6)
22	$plan_1$	3966	ag_1, ag_2	(1)	$d_3 d_4$	(2 5 1 6)
	$plan_2$	229	ag_1, ag_2, ag_3, ag_4	(2)	none	(3 4 2 5 1 6)
	$plan_3$	4434	ag_4	(1)	$d_2' d_3 d_4$	(5 1 6)
	$plan_4$	4726	ag_3	(1)	$d_2' d_3 d_4 d_5$	(1 6)
30	$plan_1$	3966	ag_1, ag_2	(1)	$d_3 d_4$	(2 5 1 6)
	$plan_2$	229	ag_1, ag_2, ag_3, ag_4	(2)	none	(3 4 2 5 1 6)
	$plan_3$	4434	ag_4	(1)	$d_2' d_3 d_4$	(5 1 6)
	$plan_4$	6588	ag_3	(1)	$d_1' d_2' d_3 d_4 d_5 d_6$	()

A problem environment is displayed, along with the possible solutions found by clustering the data and the acceptable solutions that can eventually be generated by the node. The plans at various node times are shown to indicate the evolution of the plans as problem solving progresses. For each plan is given its rating (out of 10000), the alternative-goals that it is expected to work toward, the Vehicle-event-classes of the vehicles it is attempting to track, the result it has generated to this point, and the pending i-goals in the order that they will be attempted.

Figure 29: Plan Summary for Experiment E5.2.3.

how beliefs will be affected by vehicle turns, the best predicted results are for tracks involving d_1, d_2, d_5', and d_6'. It is not until the plans involving this data fail that the correct plans are pursued.

Similarly, if the weight for the next result factor is twice the other weights, problem solving is also worse (E5.2.5). This time, the planner pursues plans that generate the correct partial track $d_2' d_3 d_4 d_5$ but then gets sidetracked because the KSIs to extend this track are less highly rated than the KSIs to extend $d_3 d_4$ into the strongly sensed data.[1] By giving the KSIs such a large influence on

---

[1] This is in part due to the planner's control of goal processing. The planner only triggers subgoaling when it faces uncertainty about how to extend a track—as is the case when it must decide whether to extend $d_3 d_4$ into d_2 or d_2'. Because subgoals alter KSI ratings, subgoaling in such situations can improve the planner's decisions. However, since the planner does not invoke subgoaling when there is no uncertainty—when it can only extend $d_2' d_3 d_4 d_5$ into d_1'

Table 2: Experiment Summary for Experiment Set 5.2.

Expt	Plan	STime	Rtime	Store	Comments
E5.2.1	no	57	17.5	519	-
E5.2.2	yes	34	8.8	311	-
E5.2.3	yes	30	8.0	293	$2 \times w_{fc}$
E5.2.4	yes	38	9.7	329	$2 \times w_{pr}$
E5.2.5	yes	38	9.9	329	$2 \times w_{nr}$
E5.2.6	yes	38	9.6	329	$0 \times w_{nr}$
E5.2.7	yes	45	11.3	361	$197 \times w_{ag}$
E5.2.8	no	68	20.3	578	-
E5.2.9	yes	38	10.2	346	-
E5.2.10	yes	48	19.9	411	$2 \times w_{fc}$
E5.2.11	yes	30	8.4	293	$2 \times 2_{pr}$

Abbreviations

Plan:	Are the new planning mechanisms used?
Stime:	The simulated time (number of KSIs invoked) to find solution.
Rtime:	The total runtime (computation time) to find solution (in minutes).
Store:	The total number of structures (hypotheses, goals, KSIs, clusters, plans) stored (storage costs).
Comments:	Additional aspects of the experiment.

plan ratings, the planner becomes much more likely to simply trigger the most highly-rated KSI to be pursued, which is exactly the decision that the node would have made without the planner. However, it is also wrong to completely ignore the KSIs. It is the influence of KSIs that causes the plan to extend d_3d_4 into the less strongly sensed but correct data at d'_2, for example. If the weight given to this rating factor is set to 0 ($w_{nr} = 0$), then performance also degrades (E5.2.6) relative to having the weights equal (E5.2.2).

Finally, the factor for the number of alternative-goals is generally a very minor factor: when it's weight is equal to the others, its influence is still very small (since it generally has values in the range of 1-10, compared with the other factors that often have values in the hundreds or thousands). The alternative-goals factor thus really acts as a tie-breaker between plans: if they are essentially identical in all other ways, the plan with the larger number of alternative-goals will be chosen. If the weight for this factor is set *very* high (.985) while the other weights are very low (.005), then alternative-goals do have a high influence. This experiment (E5.2.7) has very poor results: since the planner

---

and not d_1, for example—the KSIs for working in d'_1 may not be as highly rated as they might if subgoaling were performed. Therefore, when the KSI ratings have a disproportionately large influence on plan ratings, the lack of subgoaling can cause poor plan choices. This is not, however, an error in the planner's use of subgoaling: since the purpose of subgoaling is to resolve uncertainty about how to extend a partial solution, it should not be invoked when there is no uncertainty. Rather, the error is in giving KSI ratings such heavy influence on plan ratings when the other factors should be considered as well.

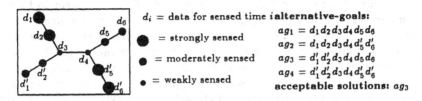

alternative-goals:

$$ag_1 = d_1 d_2 d_3 d_4 d_5 d_6$$
$$ag_2 = d_1 d_2 d_3 d_4 d_5' d_6'$$
$$ag_3 = d_1' d_2' d_3 d_4 d_5 d_6$$
$$ag_4 = d_1' d_2' d_3 d_4 d_5' d_6'$$

acceptable solutions: ag_3

Time	Plan	Rating	A-goals	V-e-cs	Results	Pend I-gs
7	$plan_1$	3980	ag_1, ag_2, ag_3, ag_4	(1)	none	(3 4 2 5 1 6)
	$plan_2$	429	ag_1, ag_2, ag_3, ag_4	(2)	none	(3 4 2 5 1 6)
14	$plan_1$	5045	ag_1, ag_2	(1)	$d_3 d_4$	(2 5 1 6)
	$plan_2$	429	ag_1, ag_2, ag_3, ag_4	(2)	none	(3 4 2 5 1 6)
	$plan_3$	5092	ag_3, ag_4	(1)	$d_3 d_4$	(2 5 1 6)
18	$plan_1$	5045	ag_1, ag_2	(1)	$d_3 d_4$	(2 5 1 6)
	$plan_2$	429	ag_1, ag_2, ag_3, ag_4	(2)	none	(3 4 2 5 1 6)
	$plan_3$	4981	ag_4	(1)	$d_2' d_3 d_4$	(5 1 6)
	$plan_4$	5002	ag_3	(1)	$d_2' d_3 d_4$	(5 1 6)
22	$plan_1$	0	ag_1, ag_2	(1)	$d_2 d_3$	(5 1 6)
	$plan_2$	429	ag_1, ag_2, ag_3, ag_4	(2)	none	(3 4 2 5 1 6)
	$plan_3$	4981	ag_4	(1)	$d_2' d_3 d_4$	(5 1 6)
	$plan_4$	5002	ag_3	(1)	$d_2' d_3 d_4$	(5 1 6)
26	$plan_1$	0	ag_1, ag_2	(1)	$d_2 d_3$	(5 1 6)
	$plan_2$	429	ag_1, ag_2, ag_3, ag_4	(2)	none	(3 4 2 5 1 6)
	$plan_3$	4981	ag_4	(1)	$d_2' d_3 d_4$	(5 1 6)
	$plan_4$	4763	ag_3	(1)	$d_2' d_3 d_4 d_5$	(1 6)
30	$plan_1$	0	ag_1, ag_2	(1)	$d_2 d_3$	(5 1 6)
	$plan_2$	429	ag_1, ag_2, ag_3, ag_4	(2)	none	(3 4 2 5 1 6)
	$plan_3$	0	ag_4	(1)	$d_4 d_5'$	(1 6)
	$plan_4$	4763	ag_3	(1)	$d_2' d_3 d_4 d_5$	(1 6)
38	$plan_1$	0	ag_1, ag_2	(1)	$d_2 d_3$	(5 1 6)
	$plan_2$	429	ag_1, ag_2, ag_3, ag_4	(2)	none	(3 4 2 5 1 6)
	$plan_3$	0	ag_4	(1)	$d_4 d_5'$	(1 6)
	$plan_4$	6069	ag_3	(1)	$d_1' d_2' d_3 d_4 d_5 d_6$	()

A problem environment is displayed, along with the possible solutions found by clustering the data and the acceptable solutions that can eventually be generated by the node. The plans at various node times are shown to indicate the evolution of the plans as problem solving progresses. For each plan is given its rating (out of 10000), the alternative-goals that it is expected to work toward, the Vehicle-event-classes of the vehicles it is attempting to track, the result it has generated to this point, and the pending i-goals in the order that they will be attempted.

Figure 30: Plan Summary for Experiment E5.2.4.

always pursues the plan with the largest number of alternative-goals, it begins by pursuing all of the plans until it has divided them all up so that each plan has one alternative-goal. Of the eight plans formed (one for each combination of the four alternative-goals and the two vehicle-event-classes), the planner then pursues the appropriate single plan, since once they have all been divided the other factors determine which will be pursued.

In this environment, the fraction-complete and KSI factors seem to be the most important for rating plans appropriately, but in other environments, other factors may be important. For example, in Figure 31 is an environment like the previous environment except that the tracks are symmetric (all turns are acceptable) and d_1 and d'_6 are *weakly* sensed. In this environment, the best solution is still $d'_1 d'_2 d_3 d_4 d_5 d_6$ because the overall belief of the moderately sensed data is higher than the combination of strongly and weakly sensed data. For comparison, the environment was run without the planner (E5.2.8) and with the planner weighing all factors equally (E5.2.9). The evolution of the plans for experiment E5.2.9 is shown in Figure 31, indicating that problem solving was not optimal: even though the predicted results for the correct track were higher, the influence of the more highly-rated KSIs in d_2 and d_5 caused plans to explore these areas to be more highly rated. However, these plans become less highly rated when data in d_1 and d'_6 must be developed because this data is so weakly sensed. If the weight for fraction-complete is set to twice the other weights—as it was when optimal performance was achieved in E5.2.3—then the performance is worse (E5.2.10). Because the turns to d_2 and d'_2 are equally sharp, the better KSIs belong to the plan to extend into the strongly-sensed data d_2. Similarly, the better KSIs belong to the plan to extend into d'_5 as well. As in Figure 31, the planner first forms $d_2 d_3 d_4 d'_5$. Because the fraction-complete weight is so high, instead of moving on to other plans (since the KSIs to extend $d_2 d_3 d_4 d'_5$ are so lowly rated), the planner continues working on the plans to extend into the weak data. The fraction-completed factor influences the planner to continue working on plans that it has already invested time into, but overly emphasizing this factor can cause the planner to continue pursuing bad plans. If instead the weight of the predicted result belief factor (w_{pr}) is twice the other weights, the planner pursues the correct plans from the start (since it predicts that the better result does not involve the most strongly sensed data) and the best solution is found in optimal time (E5.2.11).

One conclusion from these experiments is that no single set of weights will allow the planner to rate plans optimally in all situations. A static selection of weights for the rating factors may therefore provide good performance over a range of situations, but may be non-optimal for some of the situations. Because giving equal weights to the factors seems to generally result in good balance of the factors, the remaining experiments in this and later chapters have equal weights. Another conclusion is that giving plans numeric ratings may not be the best way of choosing between them. Different, more symbolic representations for reasoning about uncertainty may prove useful in our planner, but as a simple first approximation, rating plans using a combination of numeric factors appears to provide a good if non-optimal way of deciding between alternatives.

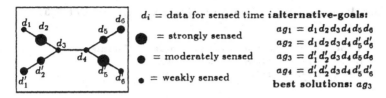

d_i = data for sensed time i

● = strongly sensed

● = moderately sensed

• = weakly sensed

alternative-goals:

$ag_1 = d_1 d_2 d_3 d_4 d_5 d_6$

$ag_2 = d_1 d_2 d_3 d_4 d_5' d_6'$

$ag_3 = d_1' d_2' d_3 d_4 d_5 d_6$

$ag_4 = d_1' d_2' d_3 d_4 d_5' d_6'$

best solutions: ag_3

Time	Plan	Rating	A-goals	V-e-cs	Results	Pend I-gs
7	$plan_1$	2647	ag_1, ag_2, ag_3, ag_4	(1)	none	(3 4 2 5 1 6)
	$plan_2$	306	ag_1, ag_2, ag_3, ag_4	(2)	none	(3 4 2 5 1 6)
14	$plan_1$	4398	ag_1, ag_2	(1)	$d_3 d_4$	(2 5 1 6)
	$plan_2$	306	ag_1, ag_2, ag_3, ag_4	(2)	none	(3 4 2 5 1 6)
	$plan_3$	4010	ag_3, ag_4	(1)	$d_3 d_4$	(2 5 1 6)
18	$plan_1$	4257	ag_2	(1)	$d_2 d_3 d_4$	(5 1 6)
	$plan_2$	306	ag_1, ag_2, ag_3, ag_4	(2)	none	(3 4 2 5 1 6)
	$plan_3$	4010	ag_3, ag_4	(1)	$d_3 d_4$	(2 5 1 6)
	$plan_4$	3997	ag_1	(1)	$d_2 d_3 d_4$	(5 1 6)
22	$plan_1$	2748	ag_2	(1)	$d_2 d_3 d_4 d_5'$	(1 6)
	$plan_2$	306	ag_1, ag_2, ag_3, ag_4	(2)	none	(3 4 2 5 1 6)
	$plan_3$	4010	ag_3, ag_4	(1)	$d_3 d_4$	(2 5 1 6)
	$plan_4$	3997	ag_1	(1)	$d_2 d_3 d_4$	(5 1 6)
26	$plan_1$	2748	ag_2	(1)	$d_2 d_3 d_4 d_5'$	(1 6)
	$plan_2$	306	ag_1, ag_2, ag_3, ag_4	(2)	none	(3 4 2 5 1 6)
	$plan_3$	3857	ag_4	(1)	$d_2' d_3 d_4$	(5 1 6)
	$plan_4$	3997	ag_1	(1)	$d_2 d_3 d_4$	(5 1 6)
	$plan_5$	4162	ag_3	(1)	$d_2' d_3 d_4$	(5 1 6)
38	$plan_1$	2748	ag_2	(1)	$d_2 d_3 d_4 d_5'$	(1 6)
	$plan_2$	306	ag_1, ag_2, ag_3, ag_4	(2)	none	(3 4 2 5 1 6)
	$plan_3$	3857	ag_4	(1)	$d_2' d_3 d_4$	(5 1 6)
	$plan_4$	3997	ag_1	(1)	$d_2 d_3 d_4$	(5 1 6)
	$plan_5$	5089	ag_3	(1)	$d_1' d_2' d_3 d_4 d_5 d_6$	()

A problem environment is displayed, along with the possible solutions found by clustering the data and the acceptable solutions that can eventually be generated by the node. The plans at various node times are shown to indicate the evolution of the plans as problem solving progresses. For each plan is given its rating (out of 10000), the alternative-goals that it is expected to work toward, the Vehicle-event-classes of the vehicles it is attempting to track, the result it has generated to this point, and the pending i-goals in the order that they will be attempted.

Figure 31: Plan Summary for Experiment 5.2.9.

5.1.3 Experiment Set 5.3: Monitoring and Repairing Plans

The third experiment set uses the environment shown in Figure 32, where two solutions must be found, corresponding to two vehicles moving in parallel. Note that no areas are common to all alternative-goals. The experimental results for this environment are summarized in Table 3. Without the planner (E5.3.1), problem solving begins with the most strongly-sensed data (the noise in the

Table 3: Experiment Summary for Experiment Set 5.3.

Expt	Plan	STime	Rtime	Store	Comments
E5.3.1	no	74/78	20.1	699	-
E5.3.2	yes	46/57	14.7	443	-

Abbreviations

Plan:	Are the new planning mechanisms used?
Stime:	The simulated time when each of the two solutions is found (time-for-first/time-for-second).
Rtime:	The total runtime (computation time) to find solution (in minutes).
Store:	The total number of structures stored (storage costs).
Comments:	Additional aspects of the experiment.

center of the area) and works outward from there. Only after many incorrect decisions to form short tracks that cannot be incorporated into longer solutions does the node generate the two solutions. In contrast, the planner allows the node to explore alternatives more effectively and recover from failed actions better (E5.3.2).

The data is received over the first 5 times (Figure 32). The clustering functions then allow the planner to recognize the six alternative-goals, four of which pass through d_3'' (the most common area). At time 6, the planner initially forms $plan_1$, $plan_3$, and $plan_5$, beginning in d_3'', d_3, and d_3' respectively (it also triggers plans for the same data but with vehicle-event-class 2, and the lack of support causes these plans to be lowly rated). The time-order for these plans is (3 2 4 1 5): in $plan_1$ the planner prefers to begin at time 3 and work outward, and since this plan is divided to form $plan_3$ and $plan_5$ (initially all of the alternative-goals were grouped together), they inherit the same time-order. Since it works with more highly-believed data at time 3 and it has more alternative-goals, $plan_1$ is most highly rated. After developing d_3'' (time 9), $plan_1$ is divided into two plans to combine this data with either d_2 or d_2'. One of these equally-rated plans, in this case $plan_1$, is chosen arbitrarily and forms the track $d_2'd_3''$, which then must be combined with d_4 or d_4', so this plan is again divided (time 13). Because the goal to extend $d_2'd_3''$ increases the ratings of KSIs in d_4 (favoring vehicles not turning), $plan_8$ to develop that data is more highly rated. However, after forming $d_2'd_3''d_4$, $plan_8$ cannot extend this track into d_1' because of turning constraints. Only the result $d_1'd_2'$ can be formed, and the planner cannot repair the plan. The plan is aborted and $plan_1$ is pursued (time 21). This plan cannot join d_4' with $d_2'd_3''$, again because of turning constraints, and it thus is aborted (time 25).

Of the remaining plans, $plan_7$ is most highly rated and is pursued. With the goal to join d_2 to d_3'', the goal processor finds the track $d_3''d_4'$ formed by $plan_1$ on the blackboard. The combined track $d_2d_3''d_4'$ is unusable since d_4' is not consistent with both of $plan_7$'s alternative-goals (time 28). The plan repairing alternative-goals:

d_i = data for sensed time i

● = strongly sensed

= moderately sensed

= weakly sensed

$ag_1 = d_1 d_2 d_3 d_4 d_5$
$ag_2 = d_1' d_2' d_3' d_4' d_5'$
$ag_3 = d_1 d_2 d_3'' d_4 d_5$
$ag_4 = d_1 d_2 d_3'' d_4' d_5'$
$ag_5 = d_1' d_2' d_3'' d_4 d_5$
$ag_6 = d_1' d_2' d_3'' d_4' d_5'$

acceptable solutions: ag_1, ag_2

Time	Plan	Rating	A-goals	V-e-cs	Cur Result	Pend I-goals
6	$plan_1$	3732	ag_3, ag_4, ag_5, ag_6	(1)	none	(3 2 4 1 5)
	$plan_2$	562	ag_3, ag_4, ag_5, ag_6	(2)	none	(3 2 4 1 5)
	$plan_3$	3569	ag_1	(1)	none	(3 2 4 1 5)
	$plan_4$	428	ag_1	(2)	none	(3 2 4 1 5)
	$plan_5$	3569	ag_2	(1)	none	(3 2 4 1 5)
	$plan_6$	428	ag_2	(2)	none	(3 2 4 1 5)
9	$plan_1$	4093	ag_5, ag_6	(1)	d_3''	(2 4 1 5)
	$plan_7$	4093	ag_3, ag_4	(1)	d_3''	(2 4 1 5)
13	$plan_1$	4585	ag_6	(1)	$d_2' d_3''$	(4 1 5)
	$plan_8$	5168	ag_5	(1)	$d_2' d_3''$	(4 1 5)
20	$plan_8$ **	5168	ag_5	(1)	$d_1' d_2'$	(5)
21	$plan_8$ *	0	ag_5	(1)	$d_1' d_2'$	(5)
25	$plan_1$ *	0	ag_6	(1)	$d_3'' d_4'$	(5)
28	$plan_7$ **	4093	ag_3, ag_4	(1)	$d_2 d_3'' d_4'$	(4 1 5)
29	$plan_7$	4093	ag_3, ag_4	(1)	$d_2 d_3''$	(4 1 5)
30	$plan_7$	5061	ag_4	(1)	$d_2 d_3''$	(4 1 5)
	$plan_9$ **	5644	ag_3	(1)	$d_3' d_3'' d_4$	(1 5)
31	$plan_9$ **	5644	ag_3	(1)	$d_3'' d_4$	(1 5)
32	$plan_7$	5061	ag_4	(1)	$d_2 d_3''$	(4 1 5)
	$plan_9$ *	0	ag_3	(1)	$d_3'' d_4$	(1 5)
36	$plan_3$	3569	ag_1	(1)	none	(3 2 4 1 5)
	$plan_5$	3569	ag_2	(1)	none	(3 2 4 1 5)
	$plan_7$ *	0	ag_4	(1)	$d_1 d_2$	(5)
46	$plan_3$	3569	ag_1	(1)	none	(3 2 4 1 5)
	$plan_5$	7325	ag_2	(1)	$d_1' d_2' d_3' d_4' d_5'$	()
57	$plan_1$ *	0	ag_6	(1)	$d_3'' d_4'$	(5)
	$plan_3$	7325	ag_1	(1)	$d_1 d_2 d_3 d_4 d_5$	()
	$plan_5$	7325	ag_2	(1)	$d_1' d_2' d_3' d_4' d_5'$	()
	$plan_7$ *	0	ag_4	(1)	$d_1 d_2$	(5)
	$plan_8$ *	0	ag_5	(1)	$d_1' d_2'$	(5)
	$plan_9$ *	0	ag_3	(1)	$d_3'' d_4$	(1 5)

The plans at various node times are shown to indicate the evolution of the plans as problem solving progresses. Plans not included at a given time have not changed since the last time. For each plan is given its rating, alternative-goals, the types of vehicles, the result it has generated to this point, and the pending i-goals in the order that they will be attempted. Plans marked with a × have been aborted, and plans marked with ×× have deviated from expectations and are either repaired (e.g., $plan_7$ times 28 and 29) or aborted (e.g., $plan_9$ times 31 and 32).

Figure 32: Plan Summary for Experiment E5.3.2.

functions trigger the goal processor to form another KSI that combines only d_2 and d_3'', which is successfully accomplished (time 29). To pursue the different alternative-goals, the plan is divided, and the new plan, $plan_9$, is more highly rated and pursued. When attempting to join data in d_4 with d_2d_3'', the goal processor is only able to form a KSI involving hypothesis $d_2'd_3''$ (from $plan_1$ time 13) and the result formed by $plan_9$ is signaled by the plan monitor as deviating from the plan (time 30). The plan is repaired with a new KSI, and this time forms $d_3''d_4$ which also fails to include d_2 (time 31). The repairing functions cannot trigger any better KSIs, $plan_9$ is aborted, and $plan_7$ is pursued (time 32). This plan also aborts when it is unable to join d_1 to $d_2d_3''d_4'$ because of turning constraints (time 36). The planner then turns to $plan_5$, which it successfully completes (time 46). Finally, it also successfully completes $plan_3$ at time 57.

5.1.4   Experiment Set 5.4: Incorporating Data Over Time

In the previous experiments, the data for all n sensed times were simulated to arrive at the node at times 1 through n. The node and planner therefore started problem solving at time $n + 1$ with all of the problem information. In this experiment set, data arrives at the node over time. The DVMT allows the user to specify the speed of node processing relative to the "sensed" world: for each sensed time, the user can specify the simulated time when the data arrives. When data is simulated to arrive much faster than it can all be processed, a node needs intelligent control to process only the most important data as quickly as possible. When data arrives at widely spaced intervals, the node has more time to process data before more data arrives and control is not as much of an issue: when it has time to exhaustively process data, why should it spend time deciding what data to process first?

In this experiment set, a series of experiments are described where the relative rate of data arrival is varied. At one extreme is the case where sensed time equals node time. The previous experiment sets showed how the planner allows the data to be processed in a timely fashion to generate the solution. Experimental results for the environment without the planner (E5.4.1) and with the planner (E5.4.2) are summarized in Table 4.

When the node is simulated to work three times faster than before, it receives sensor data for sensed time 1 at simulated time 1, data for sensed time 2 at time 4, data for sensed time 3 at time 7, and so on until the final data for sensed time 6 is received at time 16. Without the planner (E5.4.3), the node finds the solution at the same node time as before, although the actual computation time and storage needs are reduced.[2] With the planner (E5.4.4), the node begins

---

[2] The reduction in computation and storage costs is a result of reduced goal processing costs when data is incorporated over time. When the data arrives all at once, the node builds

with less information about the problem and so the planner's decisions are less informed.

The behavior is summarized in Figure 33. To simplify this figure, the *eventual* alternative-goals are associated with plans even though the alternative-goals change (are extended) over time. After getting data for sensed time 1 (time 2), the planner forms 4 plans, one for each combination of data (d_1 and d_1') and vehicle types (1 and 2). It extends these plans for the data at sensed time 2 (time 5). When the data for d_3 arrives, the planner incorporates this into its plans and merges the plans together to pursue the common data (time 8). Note that even though d_1 has been developed, the plans can be merged since the plan cannot directly combine common data in d_3 with this result. The addition of data for sensed time 4 (time 11), sensed time 5 (time 14), and sensed time 6 (time 17) cause the plans to be extended. When the common data is processed, the plan is divided (time 18), with the past result for d_1 being associated only with the appropriate plan. The new plan's time-order (2 1 5 6) is patterned after the original plan's to most quickly generate a comparable result for sensed times 1–4. Since $plan_3$ is most complete, it is rated higher and is pursued and eventually aborted when it cannot form the track $d_1 d_2 d_3 d_4$ because of vehicle movement constraints (time 22). In turn, $plan_5$ is pursued, and is divided to pursue competing alternative-goals (time 30). For a while, the plan to develop correct data (d_5) is followed, but the planner is diverted by $plan_6$ because its next activities are more highly rated (time 34). After this plan is aborted because of vehicle movement constraints (time 38), the correct plan is pursued until the solution is generated (time 42).

Next, the node is simulated to be even faster by making the interval between sensed data arrivals equal 6 (data arrives at 1, 7, 13, 19, 25, 31). Without the planner, the node's performance is not much affected (E5.4.5). Having this larger interval does not much affect the overall performance of the node with the planner (E5.4.6), but it does affect whether plans are merged. The evolution of the plans is summarized in Figure 34. After the first sensed data is received (time 2), the same four plans are developed as in Figure 33. When the next data is received (time 8), these plans are updated. The next received data that in the last experiment caused plans to be merged this time is received too late to cause plan merging (time 14). Since $plan_3$ has already developed results in $d_1 d_2$, it cannot be merged with $plan_1$: when such a plan develops results in d_3 and combines them with past results, the track $d_1 d_2 d_3$ would be inconsistent with $plan_1$'s goals. The next data d_4 causes the plans to be further updated (time 20), but when $plan_3$ attempts to combine this data with $d_1 d_2 d_3$ it is unsuccessful and the plan aborts (time 23). Subsequent data for sensed time

---

up several initial islands of high belief (partial tracks) and the goal processing must generate goals and subgoals for each. When the data arrives over time, the node builds initial partial tracks only from the data it starts with, and then extends these into the data it receives later. Because it is extending fewer tracks at any given time, it is forming fewer goals and subgoals.

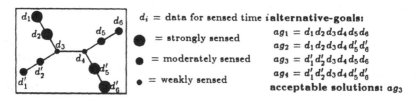

A problem environment is displayed, along with the possible solutions found by clustering the data and the acceptable solutions that can eventually be generated by the node. The plans at various node times are shown to indicate the evolution of the plans as problem solving progresses. Plans not shown at a given time are assumed to be unchanged since the previous time.

Time	Plan	Rating	A-goals	V-e-cs	Results	Pend I-gs
2	$plan_1$	3171	ag_3, ag_4	(1)	none	(1)
	$plan_2$	301	ag_3, ag_4	(2)	none	(1)
	$plan_3$	3569	ag_1, ag_2	(1)	none	(1)
	$plan_4$	454	ag_1, ag_2	(2)	none	(1)
5	$plan_1$	3171	ag_3, ag_4	(1)	none	(1 2)
	$plan_2$	301	ag_3, ag_4	(2)	none	(1 2)
	$plan_3$	3569	ag_1, ag_2	(1)	none	(1 2)
	$plan_4$	454	ag_1, ag_2	(2)	none	(1 2)
8	$plan_3$	3537	ag_1, ag_2, ag_3, ag_4	(1)	d_1	(3 2)
	$plan_4$	283	ag_1, ag_2, ag_3, ag_4	(2)	none	(3 2 1)
11	$plan_3$	3229	ag_1, ag_2, ag_3, ag_4	(1)	d_1	(3 4 2)
	$plan_4$	252	ag_1, ag_2, ag_3, ag_4	(2)	none	(3 4 2 1)
14	$plan_3$	3637	ag_1, ag_2, ag_3, ag_4	(1)	d_1, d_3	(4 2 5)
	$plan_4$	273	ag_1, ag_2, ag_3, ag_4	(2)	none	(3 4 2 5 1)
17	$plan_3$	3518	ag_1, ag_2, ag_3, ag_4	(1)	d_1, d_3	(4 2 5 6)
	$plan_4$	285	ag_1, ag_2, ag_3, ag_4	(2)	none	(3 4 2 5 1 6)
18	$plan_3$	4554	ag_1, ag_2	(1)	$d_1, d_3 d_4$	(2 5 6)
	$plan_5$	4213	ag_3, ag_4	(1)	$d_3 d_4$	(2 1 5 6)
22	$plan_3$	0	ag_1, ag_2	(1)	$d_1 d_2 d_3$	(5 6)
	$plan_5$	4213	ag_3, ag_4	(1)	$d_3 d_4$	(2 1 5 6)
30	$plan_5$	4785	ag_3	(1)	$d_1' d_2' d_3 d_4$	(5 6)
	$plan_6$	4715	ag_4	(1)	$d_1' d_2' d_3 d_4$	(5 6)
34	$plan_5$	4639	ag_3	(1)	$d_1' d_2' d_3 d_4 d_5$	(6)
	$plan_6$	4715	ag_4	(1)	$d_1' d_2' d_3 d_4$	(5 6)
38	$plan_5$	4639	ag_3	(1)	$d_1' d_2' d_3 d_4 d_5$	(6)
	$plan_6$	0	ag_4	(1)	$d_4 d_5'$	(6)
42	$plan_5$	5963	ag_3	(1)	$d_1' d_2' d_3 d_4 d_5 d_6$	()

Figure 33: Plan Summary for Experiment E5.4.4.

5 modifies the plans (time 26). When the data for sensed time 6 arrives, the plans are updated appropriately, and $plan_1$ also must be divided for competing alternative-goals (time 32). As in the past experiments, the correct plan is initially pursued, then the planner temporarily follows an incorrect plan with more highly-rated KSIs (time 36), and when this plan aborts (time 40) the correct plan is completed (time 44).

Table 4: Experiment Summary for Experiment Set 5.4.

Expt	Plan	STime	Rtime	Store	Comments
E5.4.1	no	57	17.5	519	data interval of 1
E5.4.2	yes	34	8.8	311	data interval of 1
E5.4.3	no	57	12.6	453	data interval of 3
E5.4.4	yes	42	11.3	345	data interval of 3
E5.4.5	no	60	12.8	484	data interval of 6
E5.4.6	yes	44	11.7	170	data interval of 6
E5.4.7	no	63	14.4	515	data interval of 10
E5.4.8	yes	56	15.1	387	data interval of 10
E5.4.9	yes	56	13.8	359	data interval of 10, allow idle node

Abbreviations

Plan: Are the new planning mechanisms used?

Stime: The simulated time when each of the two solutions is found (time-for-first/time-for-second).

Rtime: The total runtime (computation time) to find solution (in minutes).

Store: The total number of structures (hypotheses, goals, KSIs, clusters, plans) stored (storage costs).

Comments: Additional aspects of the experiment.

When data arrives even more infrequently—at intervals of 10—then not only does the planner have less information for making informed plans, but it also has less need for making informed plans: the node has enough time to exhaustively process data before new data arrives, so being intelligent about what data to process first is not as important. The last data arrives at time 51, and without the planner (E5.4.7), the node generates the solution at time 63. With the planner (E5.4.8), the node forms the solution at time 56—since it has already aborted the plan that uses d_6', it focuses on d_6 to generate the solution faster than if it did not have the planner. Note, however, that the computational overhead for planning exceeds the time saved in solving the problem only slightly faster. As a fail-soft mechanism, when the planner runs out of planned actions it invokes KSIs straight from the KSI queue based on their ratings. Thus, the node does not sit idle as long as there are any actions it can take. When it only invokes planned actions (and sits idle the rest of the time), the node still forms the solution at the same simulated time but computational needs are reduced (E5.4.9). In this experiment, the node only invokes 48 KSIs and is idle for the remaining 8 time units waiting for more data.

The utility of the planner is also affected by uncertainty in the data. When data has little uncertainty, the planner is not needed as much. For example, in Figure 35 is an environment similar to the other experiments in this set except that the strongly-sensed noisy data (d_1, d_2, d_5', and d_6') is not included. Without the planner (Table 5, E5.4.10), the node solves the problem in 33 time units while with the planner (E5.4.11) the node needs 30 time units. The planner has only a small effect on the number of KSIs invoked and also makes only minor

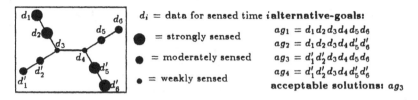

Time	Plan	Rating	A-goals	V-e-cs	Cur Result	Pend I-goals
2	$plan_1$	3171	ag_3, ag_4	(1)	none	(1)
	$plan_2$	301	ag_3, ag_4	(2)	none	(1)
	$plan_3$	3569	ag_1, ag_2	(1)	none	(1)
	$plan_4$	454	ag_1, ag_2	(2)	none	(1)
8	$plan_1$	3171	ag_3, ag_4	(1)	none	(1 2)
	$plan_2$	301	ag_3, ag_4	(2)	none	(1 2)
	$plan_3$	4800	ag_1, ag_2	(1)	d_1	(2)
	$plan_4$	454	ag_1, ag_2	(2)	none	(1 2)
14	$plan_1$	3015	ag_3, ag_4	(1)	none	(1 2 3)
	$plan_3$	4510	ag_1, ag_2	(1)	$d_1 d_2$	(3)
	$plan_4$	283	ag_1, ag_2, ag_3, ag_4	(2)	none	(3 2 1)
20	$plan_1$	3521	ag_3, ag_4	(1)	none	(1 2 3 4)
	$plan_3$	4581	ag_1, ag_2	(1)	$d_1 d_2 d_3$	(4)
	$plan_4$	283	ag_1, ag_2, ag_3, ag_4	(2)	none	(3 4 2 1)
23	$plan_1$	3521	ag_3, ag_4	(1)	none	(1 2 3 4)
	$plan_3$	0	ag_1, ag_2	(1)	$d_3 d_4$	()
	$plan_4$	283	ag_1, ag_2, ag_3, ag_4	(2)	none	(3 4 2 1)
26	$plan_1$	5368	ag_3, ag_4	(1)	d_1'	(3 4 2 5)
	$plan_4$	283	ag_1, ag_2, ag_3, ag_4	(2)	none	(3 4 2 5 1)
32	$plan_1$	5094	ag_3	(1)	$d_1' d_2' d_3 d_4$	(5 6)
	$plan_4$	283	ag_1, ag_2, ag_3, ag_4	(2)	none	(3 4 2 5 1)
	$plan_5$	4892	ag_4	(1)	$d_1' d_2' d_3 d_4$	(5 6)
36	$plan_1$	4887	ag_3	(1)	$d_1' d_2' d_3 d_4 d_5$	(6)
	$plan_5$	4892	ag_4	(1)	$d_1' d_2' d_3 d_4$	(5 6)
40	$plan_1$	4887	ag_3	(1)	$d_1' d_2' d_3 d_4 d_5$	(6)
	$plan_5$	0	ag_4	(1)	$d_4 d_5'$	(6)
44	$plan_1$	6308	ag_3	(1)	$d_1' d_2' d_3 d_4 d_5 d_6$	()

A problem environment is displayed, along with the possible solutions found by clustering the data and the acceptable solutions that can eventually be generated by the node. The plans at various node times are shown to indicate the evolution of the plans as problem solving progresses. Plans not shown at a given time are assumed unchanged from the previous time.

Figure 34: Plan Summary for Experiment E5.4.6.

reductions in the computational time needs and storage needs of the node.

Alternatively, when the data has a lot of uncertainty, the planner's overhead can increase because the possible combinations of data (potential solutions) increases. For example, in Figure 36, data for two vehicles moving in parallel is so close that the clustering mechanisms recognize tracks made by crossing between the lower and upper tracks as potential solutions. The planner thus

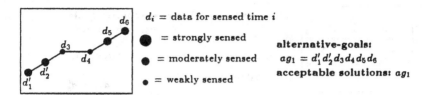

d_i = data for sensed time i

● = strongly sensed

● = moderately sensed

● = weakly sensed

alternative-goals:
$ag_1 = d_1' d_2' d_3 d_4 d_5 d_6$

acceptable solutions: ag_1

A problem environment is displayed, along with the possible solutions found by clustering the data and the acceptable solutions that can eventually be generated by the node.

Figure 35: Environment for Experiments E5.4.10-1.

Table 5: Experiment Summary for Experiment Set 5.4 Continued.

Expt	Plan	STime	Rtime	Store	Comments
E5.4.10	no	33	7.0	265	low uncertainty
E5.4.11	yes	30	5.8	206	low uncertainty
E5.4.12	no	66/67	20.9	767	high uncertainty
E5.4.13	yes	29/53	19.0	440	high uncertainty

Abbreviations

Plan:	Are the new planning mechanisms used?
Stime:	The simulated time(s) to find solution(s) (if more than one, time-for-first/time-for-second).
Rtime:	The total runtime (computation time) to find solution (in minutes).
Store:	The total number of structures (hypotheses, goals, KSIs, clusters, plans) stored (storage costs).
Comments:	Additional aspects of the experiment.

begins with 32 alternative-goals and must reason about their relationships and build plans to achieve them. Therefore, even though the node with the planner (E5.4.13) solves the problem faster than the node without the planner (E5.4.12), the computational overhead incurred by the planner is high: there may be times when planning should be postponed until the less sophisticated control mechanisms have brought the data to a point where the planning mechanisms are more effective.

5.1.5 Experiment Set 5.5: Dealing With Time Constraints

In the experimental environment shown in Figure 37, there are only two possible solutions: the vehicle can start either in the upper-left or lower-left corner. The track extending to the upper-left involves weak and strong data, but more weak than strong, while the lower track is moderately sensed throughout. The overall

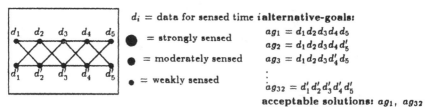

A problem environment is displayed, along with the possible solutions found by clustering the data and the acceptable solutions that can eventually be generated by the node.

Figure 36: Environment for Experiments E5.4.12-3.

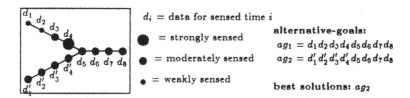

A problem solving environment is displayed, along with the possible solutions found by clustering the data and the best solutions that can eventually be generated by the node (since in this case both of the possible solutions are valid solutions but one is better than the other).

Figure 37: Environment for Experiment Set 5.5.

belief of the lower track is higher than the upper, and therefore represents the best solution. The experimental results are summarized in Table 6. For each experiment is shown the time when the best solution was found, the time the problem solving terminated, the sensed times of the solution track, the belief of the solution track, and comments about the experiment.

Depending on how conservatively it should solve the problem, the node may terminate problem solving only after it has explored every possible solution, or it may end as soon as it believes (based on its predictions) that it has found the best solution. In experiment E5.5.1, the node explores all possible solutions, and hence terminates problem solving much later than in experiment E5.5.2 where it stops as soon as it predicts that it has found the best solution. Although both experiments find the best solution equally fast, E5.5.1 spends time and energy verifying that it was the best solution while E5.5.2 predicted that the upper track would be inferior and did not pursue it. The predictions in these experiments are sufficiently accurate so that E5.5.2's termination decision is correct. In other situations such a decision might be premature—the predictions

Table 6: Experiment Summary for Experiment Set 5.5.

Expt	ST	TT	Track	Belief	Comments
E5.5.1	40	57	1-8	high	Explore all solutions
E5.5.2	40	40	1-8	high	Stop with best predicted solution
E5.5.3	-	36	-	-	No predictions, deadline = 36
E5.5.4	36	36	1-8	mod	Predictions, deadline = 36, large scope
E5.5.5	32	32	1-8	low	Predictions, deadline = 32, large scope
E5.5.6	30	30	2-8	low	Predictions, deadline = 30, large scope
E5.5.7	28	30	4-8	high	Predictions, deadline = 30, high belief

Abbreviations

Expt:	The experiment
ST:	Time at which the best solution was found
TT:	Time at which problem solving terminated
Track:	Times spanned by best solution track
Belief:	Belief in best solution track

might underestimate the quality of as yet undeveloped results and the best solution might be missed. How conservative a node's termination decisions should be depends on the situation and how much time it has.

In this environment, a highly-believed hypothesis spanning the entire track cannot be formed in less than 40 time units. A deadline of 36 time units was used in experiments E5.5.3 and E5.5.4. Since any partially developed track needs more work before it can be proposed as a solution (proposed solutions must be at the pattern blackboard-level, and the planner develops tracks at the vehicle blackboard-level), a node without prediction abilities has no solutions by time 36 (E5.5.3). When it can predict that there is insufficient time to form the best solution (E5.5.4), the planner revises the plan to meet the deadline: told by the experimenter to favor scope over belief, it removes enough plan steps (KSs for supporting hypotheses) so that it still forms a solution covering all the sensed times but with only a moderate belief. With only 32 time units to work with (E5.5.5), the planner removes plan steps so that the solution covers all the sensed times but with low belief.

Given a deadline of time 30 (E5.5.6), the planner must employ both mechanisms since it still expects to exceed the deadline after it has removed all the unnecessary plan steps. It reduces the scope of the goal, dropping the earliest sensed time (time 1), and generates a hypotheses with low belief spanning times 2-8. Finally, given the same deadline of time 30 but told by the experimenter to generate a solution with high belief, the planner no longer drops steps (that would reduce belief) but instead reduces the scope of the solution to span times 4-8 (E5.5.7). Note that in these environments where each plan step (KSI) takes one time unit, the planner can drop just enough plan steps to meet the deadline exactly (E5.5.3 – E5.5.5). When it needs to get high belief and drops entire i-goals for less important sensed times, the planner may not meet deadlines exactly (E5.5.7) since these i-goals take several steps to achieve.

5.2   Local Planning Evaluation

The planner is most useful when the node is receiving data faster than it can all be processed (within deadlines) and when the data is noisy but not so noisy that the planner cannot initially generate a reasonably small set of potential solutions to consider. Because these conditions often hold true, our planner is usually practical and effective for controlling a problem solver in our domain. However, in circumstances where these conditions do not hold, planning might be more costly than beneficial. There are two ways of addressing this problem: either to improve the planner's decisions about *when* and *how much* to plan, or to divide the data among several problem solvers when the amount of data becomes large enough to be potentially unmanageable. The latter approach of cooperative problem solving is the principal topic of the remaining chapters. The former approach means that *meta-level* control mechanisms are needed to control the planner. Just as the planner controls goal processing to get its benefits (stimulate important activities) while reducing its costs (avoid unnecessary goal processing), we expect that introducing control mechanisms such as the blackboard model of control developed by Hayes-Roth [Hayes-Roth, 1985] could promote a more intelligent use of the planner so that the benefits and costs of planning in a particular situation could be weighed and intelligent decisions about applying the planning mechanisms could be made. The development of such meta-level control components is an open area for future research (Chapter 9).

There are many other avenues for future research both to improve on the planner and to exploit it to improve other aspects of problem solving. These avenues include introducing parallelism into the plans (for nodes that are themselves multiprocessors), extending the mechanisms for meeting deadlines to achieve real-time problem solving [Lesser *et al.*, 1988], using failed plans to detect and diagnose errors in problem solving decisions or domain knowledge, and using the view provided by plans to better understand and describe problem solving behavior. Each of these directions is described in Chapter 9.

Chapter 6

Recognizing Partial Global Goals

Before they can plan activities to solve larger network problems, nodes must first identify that in fact they are working on subproblems of a larger problem. To plan for cooperation, the nodes need to communicate about their local goals and identify the larger goals that they are cooperating to achieve. These goals are called **partial global goals** (PGGs): they are *global* in the sense that they can encompass the local goals of several nodes, but only *part* of the entire network of nodes may contribute to a single PGG. To identify PGGs for groups of nodes, the planner needs a **network-model** to represent the plans and goals of individual nodes and of groups of nodes. The focus of this chapter is on how nodes model each other and the network as a whole, and use these models to recognize PGGs and determine *when* they should cooperate; in the next chapter, we describe how these nodes then plan *how* they should cooperate to achieve these PGGs.

6.1 Background

Modeling other agents is an important topic in distributed computing research in general: in distributed problem solving, each problem solver needs to know enough about others to coordinate problem solving; in distributed database systems, each local database manager needs to know whether other databases are accessible and where to look in case of inconsistencies in information; in a distributed operating system, each processor needs to know about the available resources at other nodes when determining how to assign computing tasks. Modeling is also used in fields such as natural language understanding where decisions about what information to communicate and how to communicate it are based on knowledge about how a recipient will respond.

The two most important aspects of one node's model of another are what type of information is stored in the model (at what level does one node view another) and how the node got that information. The type of information stored depends on how the model is to be used, determining how much detail one node needs about another. At one extreme, the information might be facts about what the other node knows and what it does with this knowledge. For example, in the system described by Konolige, a node's model of another node consists of the logical assertions it knows the other node believes and the inference operators that it knows the other node has for generating new assertions [Konolige, 1984]. Similarly, Rosenschein and Genesereth describe a system where a node's model of another consists of the logical statements it knows that the other possesses [Rosenschein and Genesereth, 1987]. A model with this much detail allows nodes to develop extremely specific expectations about each other since they can essentially duplicate each other's reasoning.

At the other extreme, the information might be very rough specifications about the general behavior of another node. In the DVMT, for example, the organizational structure gives each node a model of the others: the responsibilities for problem solving that each possesses and the general characteristics (spatial, temporal) of hypotheses and goals that each might produce. Based on this model, a node does not know how another node forms results, when those results will be formed, or if it is even forming any results at a given time. All a node knows is that *if* another node is forming results, *then* those results will meet the very general specifications.

Between these extremes are models of nodes' goals, plans, and behavior. For example, in Georgeff's process model approach, nodes only use specifications of each other's *outward* behavior to identify cases where their plans may interfere [Georgeff, 1984]. Cohen's speech acts system uses nodes' goals in their models of each other [Cohen, 1978]. Carver *et al.* describe an office information system that models the user in terms of the user's plans [Carver *et al.*, 1984]. In all of these systems, the level of detail was chosen so that interacting nodes could model their interactions without modeling the internal actions that others were taking to get to those interactions.

The other important aspect of modeling nodes is how a node gets its models of others. In some systems, nodes' models of each other are statically defined. For example, in the DVMT the organizational information is established during network creation (or at specific "reorganization" intervals) and is not maintained as part of basic network activity. It is because organizational information is so infrequently updated that it should be so underspecified, as discussed in Chapter 2. In other systems, a node builds a model of another by observing its activity and inferring its plans based on that activity. In an office automation system, for example, the user's actions are analyzed to hypothesize what the user's plans and intentions are [Carver *et al.*, 1984]. In most systems, however, a node builds a model of another based on what the other node tells it: the node communicates information about itself to help others model it better. Nodes that know they are cooperating (or interacting in some other way) can explicitly communicate information that will affect other nodes to better achieve their mutual (or selfish) goals. Because we are focusing on cooperative distributed problem solving, our approach currently expects nodes to communicate about their local plans and goals. By representing plans at both a long-term and short-term level of detail, the long-term information crucial for coordination (indicating what results nodes expect to form and when) can be extracted and exchanged easily.

6.2   Overview

A **network-model** has three types of information:

local plan: The representation of a plan maintained by a node that is pursuing the plan. Contains information about the plan's objective, its major plan steps, how long each step is expected to take, and detailed actions (KSs) that have been taken or will be taken.

node-plan: The representation of a plan that nodes communicate about. Contains information about the plan's objective, its major plan steps, and how long each step is expected to take. Details about short-term actions are not represented.

PGP: The representation of how several nodes are working toward a larger goal. Contains information about the larger goal, the major plan steps that are occurring concurrently, and how the partial solutions formed by the nodes should be integrated together.

An example network-model is shown in Figure 38. The node has the *local plans* that it forms based on its view of the problem situation. For example, node 1 in Figure 39 will have two local plans, and the one with the objective track d_4–d_{12} is outlined in Figure 38. The node's planner summarizes each of its local plans into a **node-plan** that specifies the objective of the plan, the major plan steps (order of intermediate-goals), and an estimate of how long each activity will take (based on the time costs of the plan's past and current activities). The planner uses this information to generate the node-plan's **plan-activity-map**: a series of activities, where each activity has a predicted starting time, ending time, and result (partial track). The node-plan for node 1's local plan to form track d_4-d_{12}, for example, is outlined in Figure 38. Since node-plans have much less detailed information than local plans and do not point to local data structures, nodes can cheaply exchange them and reason about others' node-plans as they can their own. Thus, nodes use node-plans to build models of each other [Corkill, 1979; Georgeff, 1984; Konolige, 1984].

A node's planner scans the model of the network to recognize **partial global goals** (PGGs). A PGG is global in that it may (but does not necessarily) encompass local goals of several nodes, and is partial in that only part of the network might participate in it. The planner compares local goals and uses approximate knowledge (the same used in clustering data) to determine whether they are part of a larger PGG (tracking the same vehicle). For each PGG, the planner forms a **partial global plan** (PGP) that represents the concurrent activities and intentions of all of the nodes that are working in parallel on different parts of the same problem (to potentially solve it faster). For example, the PGP to generate the overall track d_1-d_{15} (Figure 39) by combining the plans of nodes 1, 2, and 3 is outlined in Figure 38. The planner interleaves the participating node-plans' plan-activity-maps to recognize the relative timing of the nodes' activities and to discover how activities might be reordered to avoid harmful interactions (such as performing redundant activities) and to promote helpful interactions (such as providing predictive information sooner).

Given a suitably ordered set of activities for the participating nodes, the planner uses this view of concurrent actions to develop expectations about interactions. It estimates when a node will complete a group of activities that together form a sharable result, and forms a **solution-construction-graph** that indicates how and where results should be integrated. For example, in the situation of Figure 39, node 3's track d_1-d_3 and node 1's track d_4-d_9 may be combined at node 1 to form track d_1-d_9 (Figure 38). The planner uses its network-model to assign integration tasks to nodes with available computation resources or suitable expertise. Thus, while the plan-activity-map provides details about how each node will form its own results, the solution-construction-graph provides a high-level view of how the nodes are pooling resources and working together. This view of node interactions helps nodes better identify important communication actions (to send track d_1-d_3 from node 3 to node 1 as in Figure 38, for example).

A PGP can be formed for any number of nodes with compatible local goals. Initially, a node's PGPs correspond only to its local plans, but, as information from other nodes arrives, it builds larger, more encompassing PGPs. Because nodes build their network-models asynchronously and over time, they may be incomplete or out-of-date and cooperating nodes may have inconsistent PGPs. The extent and quality of a node's network-model and how it is formed depends on the **meta-level organization**: the communication topology, capacity, delay, and reliability; the coordination responsibilities of different nodes; the credibility that a node has in coordination information from other nodes (determining their authority relationships); and so on. The distributed

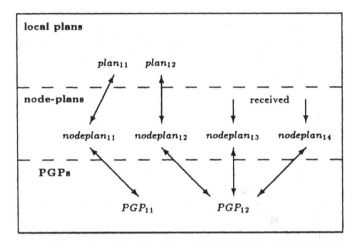

Structure	Generalized Attribute	DVMT Example Contents
$plan_{12}$:	objective alternative-goals	clusters $= (cl_{11} \ ... \ cl_{1n})$
	objective attributes	track $= ((4 \ region_4) \ ... \ (12 \ region_{12}))$
		eventual vehicle types $= (1 \ 2 \ ...)$
	long-term plan	i-goal times order $= (4 \ 5 \ ... \ 12)$
	long-term predictions	costs $= ((4 \ c_4) \ ... \ (12 \ c_{12}))$
	short-term record	$(4 \ action_1 \ ... \ action_i)$
	short-term actions	$(4 \ action_{i+1} \ ... \ action_n)$
$nodeplan_{12}$:	objective attributes	track $= ((4 \ region_4) \ ... \ (12 \ region_{12}))$
		eventual vehicle types $= (1 \ 2 \ ...)$
	long-term plan	i-goal times order $= (4 \ 5 \ ... \ 12)$
	long-term predictions	costs $= ((4 \ c_4) \ ... \ (12 \ c_{12}))$
	plan-activity-map	$((t_0, t_0 + c_4, d_4)$
		$(t_0 + c_4, t_0 + c_4 + c_5, d_4\text{-}d_5) \ ... \ )$
	pointers	local plan $= plan_{12}$
PGP_{12}:	participants	$(plan_{12} \ plan_{21} \ plan_{31})$
	objective attributes	track $= ((1 \ region_1) \ ... \ (15 \ region_{15}))$
		eventual vehicle types $= (1 \ 2 \ ...)$
	plan-activity-map	$((t_0, t_0 + c_4, d_4) \ (t_0, t_0 + c_1, d_1) \ ... \ )$
	solution-construction-graph	$(3 \ d_1\text{-}d_3) + (1 \ d_4\text{-}d_9) \rightarrow (1 \ d_1\text{-}d_9) \ ...$
	communication	$((3 \ 1 \ d_1\text{-}d_3) \ (1 \ 2 \ d_1\text{-}d_9) \ ... \ )$

The network-model of node 1 from Figure 39 is graphically depicted along with simplified views of the data structures. A **local plan** has pointers to local data clusters, a goal track (a region for each sensed time) and vehicle types, the long-term order for processing data (data for sensed time i, then j, etc) and the estimated cost for each (time-cost pairs), and finally the specific KSs to process the next data. A **node-plan** has the local plan's goals and long-term information, and has an plan-activity-map (each activity has a start-time, end-time, and result-track). A **PGP** points to participating plans, combines their goals, interleaves their node-plans' plan-activity-maps, and has a solution-construction-graph and communication predictions (for example, node 3 forms $d_1\text{-}d_3$ and node 1 forms $d_4\text{-}d_9$ and node 1 combines them into $d_1\text{-}d_9$).

Figure 38: An Example of a Node's Network-Model.

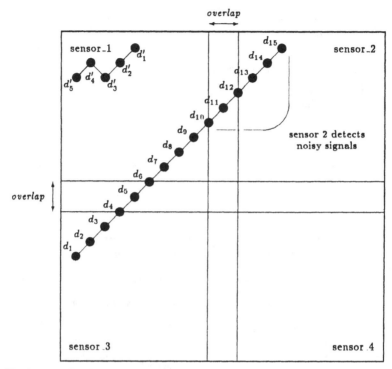

The four overlapping sensors detect signal data at particular locations for discrete sensed times (the dots with associated times). Sensor_2 is faulty and not only generates signal data at the correct frequencies for each location but also detects noisy signals at spurious frequencies for each location. Node i is connected to sensor i.

Figure 39: Four-Sensor Configuration with Sensed Data.

problem solving network is therefore organized both in terms of problem solving responsibilities (the domain-level organization) [Corkill, 1983; Corkill and Lesser, 1983] and coordination responsibilities (the meta-level organization).

The meta-level organization is statically defined during network creation, although our future research directions include developing organizational self-design mechanisms for the network. A node sends its node-plans to those nodes specified in the organization, perhaps to a particular coordinator-node, or maybe to all other nodes so that they recognize PGPs individually (as in Figure 38 where node 1 receives node-plans from 2 and 3 and forms its own PGPs). When it coordinates other nodes, a node may send them PGPs to guide their actions, but two nodes with equal authority may also exchange PGPs to negotiate about (converge on) a consistent view of coordination. A node that receives a node-plan or PGP considers the sending node's credibility when deciding how (or whether) to incorporate the new information into its network-model: it can follow a highly-rated PGP from a much trusted coordinator-node, but may disobey coordination requests if the credibility and ratings of its local information is superior. The meta-level organization therefore allows various levels of autocracy and democracy, obedience and insubordination.

Although they share many common attributes, node-plan and PGPs are kept separate for two reasons. First, a node-plan corresponds to only one node's plan, and having a different structure allows nodes to more quickly treat this information suitably (to modify a node-model). Second, the information might be used differently. In some organizations, a node might not have authority to locally change a received PGP even if it believes the changes represent improvement. By sending its local view as a node-plan, it might persuade a node with more authority to change the PGP, or it could persuade other low-authority nodes that they should all change their PGPs together (in a kind of "grass-roots" movement). PGP messages say how nodes *are* working together, while node-plan messages provide context for deciding how nodes *might* cooperate. Finally, nodes could send only some of a PGP's information (leaving out the planned activities of some participants) so that recipient nodes have insufficient context to recognize and suggest improvements. This enforces consistent views and reduces computation at recipient nodes, since they blindly follow the PGP and cannot explore alternatives.

6.3 Details

6.3.1 Data Structures for Modeling the Network

To determine whether and how they should cooperate with others, nodes exchange **node-plans**, which are summaries of their local plans. The attributes of a node-plan are shown in Figure 40. A node-plan has a name, and has attributes specifying the name of its corresponding local plan, the node with that plan, and the plan's rating and creation-time. To indicate the goals of the plan, the node-plan copies the plan's objective track and vehicle type information. To represent the long-term activities of the plan, the node-plan also contains the plan's time-order (order of i-goals), time-predictions (expected time needed to complete each i-goal), tracking-levels (how the i-goal results will be integrated), and activity-per-time (the basic types of KSs used to achieve an i-goal).

The planner uses the time-order, time-predictions, and objectives of the plan to generate an **plan-activity-map** that explicitly associates starting and ending times with activities. That is, given a time when the plan is started, the plan-activity-map indicates when the i-goals will be pursued and when different partial solutions will be generated. The plan-activity-map is a sequence of plan-activities, where each plan-activity summarizes the set of detailed actions that together achieve an i-goal. The attributes of a plan-activity are shown

name	A unique name (symbol) pointing at the node-plan structure	
plan-name	The name of the local plan summarized in this node-plan	
node	The node that has the local plan summarized in this node-plan	
rating	The rating of the local plan summarized in this node-plan	
creation-time	When the summarized local plan was created or last updated	
objective	track	The expected track for the local plan
	v-event-classes	The vehicle-event-classes (types of vehicles) being tracked by the local plan
long-term	time-order	The order the local plan will pursue i-goals, i-goal is identified by its sensed time
	time-predictions	The predicted or actual time needs of each i-goal and for the entire local plan
	tracking-levels	The blackboard-level(s) where hypotheses will be integrated into tracks
	activity-per-time	The basic activities (KSs) executed to achieve an i-goal
	plan-activity-map	Sequence of plan-activities: when i-goals are pursued and partial results formed
record	PGPs	The PGPs the node-plan participates in
	sent-to-nodes	Nodes sent this node-plan and the creation-time of sent node-plan
future	start-time	Expected start time of future node-plan
	planned-by	What node predicted the future node-plan
	triggering-PGP	The PGP that triggered the creation of the future node-plan
	basis	Names and creation-times of local plans on which future node-plan is based

Figure 40: The Attributes of a Node-Plan.

start-time	When the activities to achieve the i-goal are expected to begin
end-time	When the activities to achieve the i-goal are expected to end
node	The node performing the activities to achieve the i-goal
focus-area	The basic specifications (time-regions) of the data processed
expected-result	The expected results combining the new partial result from the focus-area with relevant results from previous plan-activities

Figure 41: The Attributes of a Plan-Activity.

in Figure 41. It has a start-time and an end-time, indicating when the first detailed action begins and when the last action that achieves the i-goal ends. Associated with a plan-activity is the node where the actions to achieve the i-goal take place. The plan-activity's principal area of focus—what information it is processing—is represented (in vehicle monitoring, this focus corresponds to the i-goal's sensed time and the possible regions where data may be developed). Finally, the plan-activity indicates its expected results, combining the results in its area of focus with results formed by previous plan-activities (in vehicle monitoring, the expected result is the partial track formed by combining the new time-regions with previously developed partial tracks).

A node-plan has attributes to record how it has been used. When the planner identifies a group of node-plans that together are working toward a PGG, it forms a PGP that points to each of these node-plans. The node-plans, in turn, have a record of the PGPs in which they participate. Recorded with a node-plan is also information about where and when it has been transmitted. When a node has a node-plan that another node might find useful, it should send it to that node; to avoid sending it repeatedly to the same nodes, it should record for each node-plan the nodes to which it has been sent. Moreover, because local plans can be modified and these modifications are propagated to the node-plans, some information about which version of the node-plan transmitted to each node should be maintained. Since the creation-times of local plans and node-plans are changed when the plans are altered, the node-plan associates with each node to which it has been sent the node-plan's creation-time. Thus, when a node-plan is modified and its creation-time changed, the planner can identify which nodes have obsolete versions of the node-plan and can respond by transmitting appropriate information to them.

The future attributes of a node-plan are also included in Figure 40. The future attributes are used when the node-plan is created because a PGP indicates that a node will likely develop a plan in the future: either it predicts that a vehicle will move into that node's sensed area, or it expects that tasks (data to process) will be passed to that node. For a future node-plan, the attributes specify when in the future the local plan is expected to start, what node formed the prediction (since one node may predict that another will have plans in the future), the name of the PGP that triggered the creation of the future node-plan, and the basis for the prediction. This last attribute indicates the names and creation-times for the plans that the PGP used when making the prediction, so that if the future node-plan is transmitted elsewhere the recipient nodes can check to see if the basis for the prediction is still valid considering their possibly more recent versions of these plans.

A node has a **node-model** for each node, including itself. When a node forms a node-plan locally or receives a node-plan from another node, it inspects the node-plan's node attribute and stores the node-plan in the appropriate node-model. A node-model thus represents one node's view of another, where the completeness and currency of this view depends on what node-plans it has received from the other node and when.

A node-model also contains information about a node's more general characteristics (Figure 42). Many of the more general characteristics of nodes are defined as part of the network organizational structure: what resources does the node have (KSs, sensors); what types of partial solutions is the node likely to produce (what spatial regions do its sensors cover); how long does the node take to perform various tasks (how efficient are its KSs); and what are the expected communication delays between nodes. In a node-model: the *ave-communication-delays* indicates for each of the other nodes the expected delay a message will incur when sent to or received from the node; the *expected-integration-costs* indicate the expected amount of time the node needs to in-

node	The node being modeled	
node-plans	A set of node-plans for the node	
general-characteristics	ave-communication-delays	Expected transmission delay between this and any other node
	expected-integration-costs	Expected time the node needs to integrate two partial solutions
	expected-processing-costs	Expected time the node needs to process sensor data into combinable results
	sensed-regions	Where node receives sensor data

Figure 42: The Attributes of a Node-Model.

tegrate two partial solutions (in the vehicle monitoring domain, to combine two tracks into a longer track); the *expected-processing-costs* estimates the expected amount of time a node needs to process (synthesize) sensor data; and the *sensed-regions* indicates the areas where a node can receive sensor data.

In this research, we assume that these more general characteristics of nodes are determined when the network is established and initially organized, and that this organization remains stable. Thus, the problem solving responsibilities and capabilities of nodes, the locations and ranges of sensors, and the communication topology linking nodes with sensors and with other nodes are constants that are accessible to the planner. Given an initial, general organization, the purpose of the planning mechanisms is to determine whether and how nodes can cooperate effectively in a specific situation, and for this purpose their models of each other change only when their local plans change.

A node's network-model is therefore composed of a set of node-models (one for each node including itself), and a set of PGPs representing groups of cooperating nodes. Given node-models of themselves and other nodes, the nodes identify any larger PGGs that they can achieve through cooperation, and a PGP is created for each. The PGG attributes are part of the PGP: just as local plans and node-plans have information about their objectives (goals), a PGP also has an objective, where its objective is to achieve a PGG. A PGP also has information about how the PGG can be achieved. In this chapter, our concern is building network-models that the planner uses to identify PGGs, so we only need consider a subset of a PGP's attributes (Figure 43). The other attributes of a PGP are discussed in the next chapter.

A PGP has a name, and attributes indicating what node formed the PGP and when it was created or last updated. The PGP also points to the node-plans that are pursuing parts of the overall PGG of the PGP, and what nodes are participating in achieving the PGG. The attributes of the PGG are represented as the PGP's objective information: the overall track that can be generated by combining the results of the individual node-plans, and the types of vehicles being tracked by the PGP. Because future node-plans are often based on the long-term information of a PGP, several of these attributes are briefly described

name	A unique name (symbol) pointing at the PGP structure	
participants	A list of the node-plans that participate in this PGP	
node	The node that created this PGP	
nodes	A list of the names of nodes participating in this PGP	
creation-time	When the PGP was created or last updated	
rating	The rating of the PGP	
objective	track	Expected complete track when pieces from separate node-plans are combined
	v-event-classes	Vehicle-event-classes (types of vehicles) being tracked
long-term	tracking-levels	Blackboard-level(s) where hypotheses will be integrated into tracks
	plan-activity-map	Sequence of plan-activities: when i-goals are pursued and partial results formed
	solution-construction-graph	What partial results will be integrated and indication of where and when

Figure 43: A Subset of the Attributes of a PGP.

here; a more complete description is given in the next chapter. Among the long-term attributes of the PGP are the tracking-levels where the node-plans will build partial solutions, the plan-activity-map that interleaves the plan-activities of the participating node-plans, and the solution-construction-graph that indicates where and when the separate partial solutions generated by the nodes will be integrated into the overall solution.

The nodes not only need to coordinate their problem solving, they also need to coordinate how they coordinate. Recognizing PGGs and building PGPs is itself a distributed problem solving task—a "meta-task" since solving the coordination problem influences how the domain problem is solved. Thus, although nodes could exchange node-plans indiscriminately and individually recognize PGGs and plans, they can more effectively solve the problem of how to coordinate if they are organized. To organize coordination activity, each node is provided with a copy of the meta-level organization, whose attributes are shown in Figure 44. The *node-plan-communication-alist* associates with each node the nodes that it should send node-plans to. Similarly, the *PGP-communication-alist* associates with each node the nodes that it should send PGPs.[1] To influence how nodes respond to received information, the meta-level organization specifies how much credibility a node gives to it. Authority is implemented in this way. For example, if $node_1$ gives low credibility to node-plans it gets from $node_2$, then PGPs that involve those node-plans will be less highly rated. On the other hand, if $node_1$ gives high credibility to node-plans from $node_2$, then it will give higher ratings to PGPs that involve them. Because a node pursues its most highly-rated PGPs, a node that has more credibility also has more in-

---

[1] In the future, we hope to extend the meta-level organization to allow the user to specify the characteristics of node-plans and PGPs that should be sent to a particular node so that communication about this information can be more selective.

node-plan-communication-alist	For each node, what nodes to send node-plans
PGP-communication-alist	For each node, what nodes to send PGPs
node-plan-credibility-factors	Credibility a node has in received node-plans
PGP-credibility-factors	Credibility a node has in received PGPs
coordination-responsibilities	What nodes each node should coordinate

Figure 44: The Attributes of the Meta-Level Organization.

fluence (authority) on the activities of others. The *node-plan-credibility-factors* specify for each node the credibility that node has in node-plans from each of the other nodes: the received node-plan's rating is multiplied by that factor. Similarly, the *PGP-credibility-factors* specify the same information for received PGPs. Finally, the *coordination-responsibilities* indicate for each node what nodes it is responsible for coordinating. Usually, it is responsible for coordinating itself, but it may be responsible for coordinating several nodes, as described in the next chapter.

6.3.2   Initializing Node-Models

Each node has a node-model for itself and each of the other nodes. The node-models are initially empty. When the node generates node-plans from its local plans, it inserts these into its model of itself. Similarly, when it receives node-plans from another node, it inserts these into its node-model of that node. Because nodes' plans and goals can change unpredictably over time, maintaining suitable node-models requires that nodes communicate about their node-plans to keep each other up to date.

The more general characteristics of a node are found in the organizational information when they are needed. To develop a sensible organization, any organization designer would have information about the nodes' communication topology, their capabilities for processing data and for integrating partial solutions, and what areas their sensors cover. Thus, as part of its static (or infrequently changing) domain-level organization, a node has this information, and nodes need not communicate about these attributes.

6.3.3   Building Node-plans

A node gets node-plans from three different sources: the planner may build them from local plans; the node may receive them from another node; or the planner may use PGPs to predict that a node will have a local plan at some future time. Moreover, to explicitly represent a lack of any local plans, a node may form an "idle" node-plan, which indicates that the node has no planned activities. Idle node-plans are useful when the nodes attempt to move tasks to balance their loads: if one node knows that another is idle, then it can safely pass tasks to it; without explicit idle node-plans, a node cannot be sure whether another node is idle or if it simply has not communicated about its plans.

Three ways of building node-plans—from local plans, from PGPs, and from a lack of local plans—are described in this section. The mechanisms for building node-plans from received information are described in the next section.

Building Node-plans from Local Plans

Given a freshly created or modified local plan, the planner updates its node-model of itself by creating or modifying a node-plan for that local plan. It begins by first identifying whether a node-plan already exists for an older version of the local plan (using the plan's name). If one is not found then a new node-plan structure is created to represent the local plan. The new or existing node-plan is then given some attributes directly from the local plan: plan-name, creation-time, objectives, and most of the long-term plan information. The node-plan's node is simply the name of the node that has this local plan (which is the current node). To compute the node-plan's rating, the planner takes the rating of the local plan and multiplies it by the node's credibility in its own node-plans (which it finds in the meta-level organization). Thus, a node's credibility in its own plans (and therefore its authority over itself) is determined by the meta-level organization.

Because the node-plan's plan-activity-map associates specific intervals of time with the plan's i-goals, the planner cannot compute this information until it knows when it will start working on the plan, which in turn depends on the other plans that it could work on. This attribute is therefore set later when the planner decides what local plan it will pursue next. However, if the node-plan is being modified because its local plan has been changed, then it may already have a plan-activity-map. In this case, the planner deletes from the plan-activity-map any plan-activities for the future. Since the local plan may have been pursued for a while and some i-goals completed, the plan-activities for those completed i-goals represent actual past activities, not potential future activities, and so should be permanently associated with the node-plan.

The attributes specifying what PGPs use the node-plan and where it has been sent are set later by the planner. Because the node-plan is based on an existing local plan, its future attributes are empty.

Building Future Node-Plans

A future node-plan is a prediction about future activities that, as yet, no local plan represents. By examining a PGP, the planner recognizes that a node currently not working on a part of the PGP may do so in the future. A future node-plan for a node is generated for any of three reasons:

- the objective track of a PGP indicates that the vehicle being tracked will likely move into the sensed area of the node, so that the node will begin receiving sensor data at some future time;

- the planned activities for integrating partial results (in the PGP's solution-construction-graph) indicate that the node will receive partial results (tracks) to combine at some future time;

- the planner has represented in the PGP a possible transfer of data (tasks), where some other node may pass data (tasks) to this node so that its computational capabilities or expertise are better used.

In the first case, the planner takes the current objective track of the PGP and uses expectations about how vehicles move to predict its likely future course. If this course passes through a node's sensed area, then a future node-plan can be hypothesized for that node. The future start-time for that node-plan would be when the new sensor data is expected to start arriving. The node-plan's objectives correspond to the expected course of the vehicle through the node's area, its long-term information and use are left empty, its future planned-by attribute is the name of the node that is building the node-plan, its future triggering-PGP is the name of the PGP, and its future basis is a list of the plan-names for the participating node-plans. Note that any node with the PGP could form the future node-plan for the node.

In the second case, the planner builds a future node-plan if a PGP indicates that certain integration tasks will take place at a particular node in the future. For example, two nodes that build partial solutions for a larger problem need to combine these somehow. One of them could pass its partial solution to the other, which would then combine them. Alternatively, they could each recognize that a third node has expertise or available computing power that makes it the best node to integrate the pieces, so both nodes pass their partial solutions to the third. A node with this PGP can build a future node-plan, specifying that the third node will have these integration activities in the future, and this node-plan is stored in the third node's node-model. By using the general characteristics about the nodes involved, the planner can estimate when the partial solutions will reach the third node, and so, can approximate the start-time for the future node-plan. The node-plan's objectives are those of the combined partial solutions, its long-term and use information are empty, and its future information is set as in the first case.

In the third case, the planner has identified that some tasks—some i-goals to achieve—could potentially be transferred from one node to another node. The proposed recipient node would be more capable of performing the tasks: it may be idle or performing unimportant activities, or it may have expertise for performing these tasks. When the planner recognizes such a situation, it can use PGPs to negotiate over task passing. The details are covered in the next chapter, but as part of this negotiation, a node might build a future node-plan representing its anticipated reception of a task.

Future node-plans are only constructed when they could affect current plans. The planner needs to predict future node-plans when it is deciding whether it should transfer tasks (i-goals) or partial solutions for integration because it should not transfer tasks that may interfere with activities that the node will need to perform in the future. Future node-plans are therefore most important when a transfer of tasks is being considered, and to reduce control overhead in the current implementation are not generated otherwise.

Building Idle Node-Plans

When a node has no local plans, either because it never had any or because those that it had have been completed or aborted, then it should model this inactivity in an idle node-plan. An idle node-plan has no objectives, and no long-term, use, or future information. It's plan-name is nil and its rating is 0. It does have a creation-time (when the node became idle) and the name of the node that is idle. The idle node-plan is locally incorporated in the node's model of itself, and can be transmitted to other nodes as well. When a node knows that another is idle, then its planner can develop PGPs that represent passing tasks to that node to make better use of its computational resources. However, when a node that was idle is no longer idle, it must inform other nodes of this fact so that they do not hypothesize further task-passing.

6.3.4 Meta-Level Communication About Node-plans

Each node is responsible for communicating about node-plans so that the nodes responsible for recognizing and responding to cooperative opportunities are adequately informed about other nodes' plans and goals. Because they are exchanging meta-level information about how they are solving the problem instead of domain-level information about the problem itself, this exchange of information is called meta-level communication. The meta-level organization specifies the coordination responsibilities of the nodes and the meta-level communication patterns that are the basis for deciding where node-plans should be sent and received. For example, if the network is organized so that a single node acts as coordinator, then each of the other nodes should direct their node-plans only to that node. Alternatively, if each node is responsible for coordinating itself, then nodes should broadcast their node-plans so that each can individually recognize when and how it should cooperate with others.

Meta-level communication also involves communicating about PGPs. Because the focus of this chapter is on building node-models and identifying PGGs, the discussion of how PGPs are communicated is delayed until the next chapter where the attributes and reasons for communicating PGPs are more fully explained. However, since node-plans can be transmitted in response to received PGPs, it is important to mention at this point that PGPs can be communicated.

Transmitting Node-Plans

A node transmits a node-plan for one of four reasons: to inform other nodes of a new or changed local plan of this node; to relay node-plans that it received on to other nodes; to inform other nodes of idle node-plans of this node, or to respond to coordination information (a PGP) that it received from another node. When determining which of its *local node-plans* (node-plans in its node-model of itself) to transmit, the node first must decide which of its node-plans are relevant: it identifies a set of highly-rated node-plans (where the width of the window between highest and lowest rated of these is a user supplied parameter *node-plan-communication-window) and determines whether any node-plans have changed since they were last sent to other nodes (specified in the meta-level organization), if sent before. The node-plan is sent to any recipient nodes that do not have a current version of the node-plan, and the node-plan's sent-to-nodes information is updated.

The planner also checks other nodes' node-models to see if any of their node-plans should be forwarded because the communication topology might not allow some nodes to communicate directly. To identify such node-plans, the planner scans through its models of other nodes and when it discovers that the most recent version of the node-plan has not been transmitted to a node that should know about it, then the planner transmits the node-plan to that node.

The third reason for sending a node-plan is to inform other nodes about idle node-plans, and the fourth reason for sending a node-plan is as a response to a received PGP that was requesting information about whether and when the node could perform transferred tasks. In the current implementation, future node-plans are only transmitted in response to requests for information about task-passing. Because future node-plans might never materialize (the expected events might not occur), the planner must inspect future node-plans regularly to determine whether they should be retracted. By having nodes avoid transmitting future node-plans, the number of node-plans in a node's node-models is minimized so the costs of keeping track of them and retracting them is minimized (see Section 6.3.5).

To transmit a node-plan, the planner extracts the attributes of the node-plan and builds a node-plan message with this information. The message has a predefined structure so that the recipient node knows how to extract the attributes out again to create a local copy of the node-plan.

Receiving Node-Plans

If a received node-plan message has no triggering-PGP attribute then it is not a response to a PGP, and the planner incorporates the received information into the appropriate node-model. It retrieves an earlier version of the node-plan, if any, and otherwise it generates a new node-plan structure and inserts it into the node-model. The attributes of the node-plan message are used to update the local version of the node-plan if the creation-time of the newly received node-plan is later than the creation-time of the local version. That is, it is possible that this node locally has more recent information about the plan summarized in the node-plan message (it received a more current message from somewhere else), and thus should not update its version of the node-plan with less current information.

To compute the node-plan's rating, the node multiplies the received rating and the credibility-factor for the transmitting-node from the meta-level organization. Thus, a received node-plan from a node with high (low) credibility has its rating raised (lowered). Because nodes pursue highly-rated PGPs, where a PGP's rating is based on the participating node-plans' ratings, node-plans from high-credibility nodes have more influence on a node's decisions, and thus exert authority. In addition, note that a node-plan that is received, incorporated, and later relayed on to other nodes may be passed on with a different rating than it had at the originating node: a node passes on not what it was told (the message it received) but what it believes (the node-plan it locally added). The meta-level organization determines how node-plans will be relayed, and thus can be used to have nodes pass on skewed views of others to influence other nodes' behavior.

When the received node-plan has a triggering-PGP, then it is a response to a transmitted PGP. The planner retrieves the PGP and stores the message in one of the PGP's fields. When the planner must decide whether to transfer tasks as proposed in the PGP, it examines the stored messages which represent counter-proposals indicating where and whether the tasks should be transferred.

6.3.5 Maintaining Node-Models

Nodes communicate about node-plans to build models of each other, but because their problem situations can change over time these models must be updated when needed. For example, when a node that has been working on one plan shifts to another, then it should send out node-plans that reflect this change: not only information about the node-plan that it is now working on, but also information about the node-plan that it has shifted away from. Since another node may have been expecting to coordinate with the original plan, it is important that this node be told when work on the original plan ceased and what parts of the plan had been completed. This information comes from the node-plan's creation-time (which is updated when this plan is no longer the one being followed) and from the node-plan's plan-activity-map (which contains plan-activities for all i-goals already achieved). If it knows what parts of the plan have been completed, the recipient node can better determine what parts it should work on or, if it expects that the node will resume work on the plan (because it believes that the node will receive information that will make the plan more attractive), the recipient node can hypothesize when future activities will take place because it knows what parts have already been accomplished.

Node-models therefore represent possibly incomplete, inconsistent, and out-of-date views of other nodes, and PGPs based on node-models are thus tentative. One node may have a model of another that indicates that that node is idle. If it later receives a node-plan indicating that that node is active (is pursuing actions), then it should delete the idle node-plan from its model of that node. Similarly, if it has a future node-plan as part of its model of another node, then the node must keep track of that node-plan and delete it either when it receives the node-plan from the other node (indicating that the future node-plan is now a node-plan based on a current local plan) or when sufficient time has elapsed that it should have gotten such a node-plan. In the latter case, the predicted future node-plan never materialized, and the node must respond to the failed assumption: it might change how it interacts with that node. If a node aborts a node-plan, then other nodes' node-models of this node must be updated accordingly: the node-plan should be removed from the node-model and any PGGs that the node-plan participates in must be adjusted accordingly.

Because node-models represent assumptions about other nodes' plans and goals, maintaining node-models is like maintaining any assumption-based information: sometimes assumptions are retracted and the effects of changed assumptions must be propagated. Because assumptions about a node's behavior are contained in any number of node-models distributed among nodes in the network, maintaining these models (propagating changes) is a complicated process. To simplify things in this research, nodes are not permitted to exchange especially volatile information (such as future node-plans based on possible extensions to PGPs' tracks), so that they only need communicate about what they are doing and have done in the past, not what they might do. The other simplification we make is that we allow nodes to transmit *all* of their updating information. Because these messages incur communication delays and because nodes only communicate about their most highly-rated node-plans, nodes still may have inconsistent, incomplete and out-of-date information. However, because we assume that communication between them allows useful update information to eventually reach nodes that need it, the planner does not need mechanisms to infer likely changes to other nodes' behavior. Making such inferences can be difficult and very costly, since one node is trying to model the problem solving of others. In Chapter 9, one of the future research directions discussed covers these issues further.

6.3.6 Recognizing Partial Global Goals

The process of recognizing PGGs from node-plans can be costly both in computation and storage. The computation costs can be high because the planner could compare many possible combinations of node-plans' objectives to identify all the possible PGGs. The storage costs can be high because the planner may have to save many **partial-combinations** of objectives as well. For example, in Figure 45 there are two PGGs, each represented as a sequence of track sections: *abc* and *abd*. When the planner constructs PGGs, it cannot simply merge new pieces into an existing PGG: if it merges *c* with the PGG it has so far constructed for *ab*, then it cannot merge *d* into the result and must rederive *ab*. Instead, the planner makes a copy of the PGG *ab* before merging it with *c* so

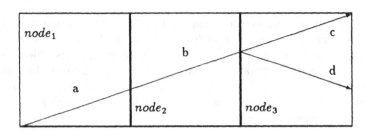

Figure 45: Alternative Plan Combinations.

that it can later merge it with *d* as well. Because copies of partial-combinations are saved, generating PGGs can be expensive in storage.

To identify PGGs and build PGPs, the planner begins with the new or modified node-plans in any of its node-models. For each, the planner generates a partial-combination whose objectives are the same as the node-plan's. Moreover, if a modified node-plan represents an aborted plan, then the planner finds all the PGGs that this node-plan participates in and treats each of the other participants of these PGGs as modified node-plans. This allows the planner to find alternative PGGs for them that do not include the aborted node-plan.

Because PGGs that only involve unmodified node-plans need not be changed, the planner only looks for PGGs involving the new and modified node-plans. It uses each of their partial-combinations as a starting point. For each, it compares the partial-combination with the node-plans in the node-models, and forms a new partial-combination when a node-plan can be combined with the partial-combination. A node-plan can be combined with a partial-combination if: it is potentially tracking vehicles of the same type as the other participants in the combination (the node-plan's vehicle-event-classes intersect with each of the participants' vehicle-event-classes), and its objective track can be combined with the partial-combination's objective track. Tracks can be combined if they meet the vehicle movement constraints that the clustering mechanisms use— if the same vehicle could be responsible for both tracks. When these criteria are met, the node-plan information is combined with the partial-combination's information into a new partial-combination: the planner combines the vehicle types as the union of the node-plan's and the old partial-combination's, and it combines the tracks together with the same functions it uses when it combines tracks of alternative-goals together (Chapter 4). In addition, the partial-combination records what node-plans participate in it.

Whenever a new partial-combination is formed, the planner adds it to the list of starting points and the process continues until every node-plan has been checked against the partial-combinations. At this point, subsumed partial-combinations are removed. For example, each of the 4 track sections in Figure 45 represents a separate node-plan (where $node_3$ has two node-plans). At the end of forming combinations, the partial-combinations are *a*, *b*, *c*, *d*, *ab*, *bc*, *bd*, *abc*, and *abd*. The planner removes any subsumed partial-combinations, leaving *abc* and *abd*. These are then compared with any existing PGPs, and if any represent modifications to a PGP the PGP is modified appropriately (its objectives are set to those of the new partial-combination). If any partial-combinations are not represented by existing PGPs, a new PGP is formed whose objectives are set to those of the new partial-combination, and whose participants are also retrieved from the partial-combination.

Because it only uses new and modified node-plans as starting points, the planner can avoid generating all possible combinations each time node-plans change. In Figure 45, for example, if the node-plan to build track section *d* is later modified (possibly extended with new data), then the planner generates partial-combinations *d*, *bd*, and *abd* only (since the PGGs involving *c* will be unaffected), and of these then *abd* will be used to modify the existing PGG. More examples are provided in Section 6.3.8.

Recognizing PGGs can be costly because, in the worst case, the planner might consider every possible combination of node-plans. This is why nodes restrict meta-level communication to only exchanging highly-rated node-plans: not only is communication resource usage reduced, but also the number of node-plan combinations at the recipient nodes is decreased. The possible drawback to restricting communication to only the best node-plans is that some combination of less highly-rated node-plans might together form a highly-rated PGP. Thus, the time needs of the planner are reduced at the potential cost of making worse decisions. The user supplied parameter *node-plan-communication-window can be adjusted to balance minimizing costs and minimizing risk.

Even when meta-level communication is restricted, there are potentially a large number of combinations. If we assume that node-plans in the same node-model need not be compared (because if they were part of a larger goal the local plans would be merged locally), then if there are n node-models with p node-plans each, the number of possible combinations of any length other than 0 is $[(1+p)^n - 1]$, or on the order of p^n. For a large number of nodes and node-plans, it can get extremely expensive to compute these combinations. Moreover, two locally unrelated goals might be part of the same PGG (a vehicle passes through a node's area twice). When all possible combinations of 1 or more of all $p \times n$ node-plans must be considered, there are $[2^{p \times n} - 1]$ such combinations possible. Ways of reducing the number of comparisons include having a node only find the PGGs that the node can participate in, making the maximum possible combinations with one node-plan per node $[p(p^n - 1)/(p-1) - 1]$ (which is still order p^n) and the maximum possible combinations of all node-plans $[2^{p \times n}/2^n - 1]$ (which is still exponential). Another way of reducing the number of combinations to consider is to restrict the set of nodes that the planner searches to find PGGs. The last way to reduce the number of combinations is to represent the combined activities of a group of nodes in a single "node-plan", and this is discussed as a future research direction in Chapter 9.

Node	Model	Entry	Participants	Track	V-types	Sent?
1	1	np_{1a}	-	d'_1–d'_5	(1)	yes
		np_{1b}	-	d'_1–d'_5	(2)	no
		np_{1c}	-	d_4–d_{12}	(1)	yes
		np_{1d}	-	d_4–d_{12}	(2)	no
	All	PGP_{1a}	np_{1a}	d'_1–d'_5	(1)	no
		PGP_{1b}	np_{1b}	d'_1–d'_5	(2)	no
		PGP_{1c}	np_{1c}	d_4–d_{12}	(1)	no
		PGP_{1d}	np_{1d}	d_4–d_{12}	(2)	no
2	2	np_{2a}	-	d_{10}–d_{15}	(1 2 3 4 5)	yes
	All	PGP_{2a}	np_{2a}	d_{10}–d_{15}	(1 2 3 4 5)	no
3	3	np_{3a}	-	d_1–d_6	(1)	yes
		np_{3b}	-	d_1–d_6	(2)	no
	All	PGP_{3a}	np_{3a}	d_1–d_6	(1)	no
		PGP_{3b}	np_{3b}	d_1–d_6	(2)	no
4	4	np_{4a}	-	nil	nil	yes

Figure 46: Initial Network-Models.

6.3.7 Network-Models

A node's network-model thus has two principal components: a set of node-models and a set of PGPs. The planner develops the node-models from local plans and from received messages about other node's node-plans. Nodes communicate to keep their node-models up-to-date. The planner develops PGPs by recognizing groups of node-plans that are working toward a single, larger goal. Because nodes can also exchange PGPs, they communicate to keep their views of cooperation among nodes consistent.

6.3.8 Examples of Finding Partial Global Goals

Consider the problem environment of Figure 39. There are four overlapping sensors, and each is assigned to a different node. $Sensor_2$ is faulty and generates data at correct frequencies but also forms noisy signals at spurious frequencies. $Node_1$ receives data d'_1–d'_5 and d_4–d_{12}, $node_2$ gets data d_{10}–d_{15}, $node_3$ gets data d_1–d_6, and $node_4$ gets no data at all. Each node uses its data to form local plans. Each then summarizes its plans into node-plans, and then forms PGPs based on its current node-models (which initially just contain information about its own plans). Assume that the data arrives at sequential node times, so that problem solving does not begin until after all of the data has arrived. When the nodes form local plans, therefore, they have all of their local data available. In Figure 46 are shown the initial network-models for each node: each node has models of the individual nodes (although if the model for a node is empty it is not shown in the figure) and of all nodes (its PGPs). $Node_1$ has formed four local plans, two for d'_1–d'_5 (with different vehicle types) and two for d_4–d_{12} (with different vehicle types). Each of these local plans is represented by a node-plan in its node-model of itself, and each serves as the basis for a PGP.

Node	Model	Entry	Participants	Track	V-types	Sent?
1	1	np_{1a}	-	$d'_1-d'_5$	(1)	yes
		np_{1b}	-	$d'_1-d'_5$	(2)	no
		np_{1c}	-	d_4-d_{12}	(1)	yes
		np_{1d}	-	d_4-d_{12}	(2)	no
	2	np_{1e}	-	$d_{10}-d_{15}$	(1 2 3 4 5)	yes
	3	np_{1f}	-	d_1-d_6	(1)	yes
	4	np_{1g}	-	nil	nil	yes
	All	PGP_{1a}	np_{1a}	$d'_1-d'_5$	(1)	no
		PGP_{1b}	np_{1b}	$d'_1-d'_5$	(2)	no
		PGP_{1c}	np_{1c},np_{1e},np_{1f}	d_1-d_{15}	(1 2 3 4 5)	no
		PGP_{1d}	np_{1d},np_{1e}	d_4-d_{15}	(1 2 3 4 5)	no
2	2	np_{2a}	-	$d_{10}-d_{15}$	(1 2 3 4 5)	yes
	1	np_{2b}	-	$d'_1-d'_5$	(1)	yes
		np_{2c}	-	d_4-d_{12}	(1)	yes
	3	np_{2d}	-	d_1-d_6	(1)	yes
	4	np_{2e}	-	nil	nil	yes
	All	PGP_{2a}	np_{2a},np_{2c},np_{2d}	d_1-d_{15}	(1 2 3 4 5)	no
	All	PGP_{2b}	np_{2b}	$d'_1-d'_5$	(1)	no
3	3	np_{3a}	-	d_1-d_6	(1)	yes
		np_{3b}	-	d_1-d_6	(2)	no
	1	np_{3c}	-	$d'_1-d'_5$	(1)	yes
		np_{3d}	-	d_4-d_{12}	(1)	yes
	2	np_{3e}	-	$d_{10}-d_{15}$	(1 2 3 4 5)	yes
	4	np_{3f}	-	nil	nil	yes
	All	PGP_{3a}	np_{3a},np_{3d},np_{3e}	d_1-d_{15}	(1 2 3 4 5)	no
		PGP_{3b}	np_{3b}	d_1-d_6	(2)	no
		PGP_{3c}	np_{3c}	$d'_1-d'_5$	(1)	no
4	4	np_{4a}	-	nil	nil	yes
	1	np_{4b}	-	$d'_1-d'_5$	(1)	yes
		np_{4c}	-	d_4-d_{12}	(1)	yes
	2	np_{4d}	-	$d_{10}-d_{15}$	(1 2 3 4 5)	yes
	3	np_{4e}	-	d_1-d_6	(1)	yes
	All	PGP_{4a}	np_{4c},np_{4d},np_{4e}	d_1-d_{15}	(1 2 3 4 5)	no
		PGP_{4b}	np_{4b}	$d'_1-d'_5$	(1)	no

Figure 47: Subsequent Network-Models.

$Node_2$ has formed a single local plan for $d_{10}-d_{15}$, where this plan encompasses several vehicle types: because the spurious frequency data formed by $sensor_2$ corresponds to several types of vehicles, $node_2$ is unable to narrow down the possible vehicle types. This local plan is summarized in $node_2$'s node-model of itself, and a PGP is formed from this. $Node_3$ has two local plans for data d_1-d_6, each with a different vehicle type, and $node_4$ forms an idle node-plan that it stores in its node-model of itself.

Nodes exchange their most highly-rated node-plans to build up models of each other, and each of the node-plans sent to other nodes are indicated in Figure 46. When a node receives node-plans from others, it incorporates them into the appropriate node-models and modifies the PGPs. The situation where nodes have exchanged highly-rated node-plans is shown in Figure 47. Each node has some information about the others and can build up more global

PGPs, but nodes do not necessarily have identical network-models since they do not communicate every node-plan. $Node_1$ builds node-models for the other nodes, and recognizes more global PGPs: PGP_{1c} where nodes 1, 2, and 3 all participate in forming the complete track d_1–d_{15} (since the participating node-plan's tracks are compatible and they share the objective of tracking a vehicle of type 1); and PGP_{1d} where nodes 1 and 2 participate in forming the track d_4–d_{15} (because $node_3$ does not send its node-plan for vehicle type 2, the track does not extend into its area). $Node_2$ builds node-models for the other nodes and recognizes PGP_{2a} where nodes 1, 2, and 3 participate in forming the track d_1–d_{15} (since they all share node-plans with vehicle type 1). $Node_3$ and $node_4$ similarly recognize the same PGP.

The nodes initially had different network-models, and even after meta-level communication about their node-plans their network-models are not identical because they selectively exchange their most highly-rated node-plans. However, the nodes all recognize two highly-rated PGPs: to generate a track covering d_1–d_{15} where nodes 1, 2, and 3 participate; and to generate a track covering d_1'–d_5' where node 1 is the lone participant.

Note that the common PGP covering d_1–d_{15} has numerous vehicle types. Even though two of its participant node-plans are of vehicle type 1, one of its participant node-plans is for several vehicle types including type 1. When $node_2$ receives node-plans from 1 and 3 (which it locally represents as np_{2c} and np_{2d}), it could divide its local plan into two—one for vehicle type 1 and the other for the remaining vehicle types. In the current implementation, it does *not* divide the plan based on received meta-level information; it must wait to receive domain-level messages (hypotheses) that provide concrete, predictive information. Forcing nodes to exchange predictive domain-level information allows us to emphasize and explore issues in planning cooperative activities: one node must plan actions to generate results that it can send to another node to help that node better solve its problems.

As problem solving proceeds, $node_1$ forms and transmits a predictive partial solution to $node_2$: using the mechanisms described in the next section, it forms and sends a track covering d_8–d_9 with vehicle type 1. $Node_2$ uses this data to divide its local plan into a plan to form the track d_8–d_{15} with vehicle type 1, and another plan to form the track d_{10}–d_{15} with the remaining vehicle types. These changes are reflected in its node-model of itself and in its PGPs, as is shown in Figure 48. The node-plans for these changed local plans are communicated, but because of communication delays the nodes will have somewhat different views of important PGPs before the changed node-plans are received (Figure 48).

Finally, when these node-plans are received by other nodes and their node-models are updated, then the view of highly-rated PGPs becomes consistent once again, as is shown in Figure 49.

The previous example assumes a meta-level organization where each node broadcasts its most highly-rated node-plans, and the nodes individually form PGPs to recognize when they should cooperate. In an alternative meta-level

Node	Model	Entry	Parts	Track	V-types	Trans
1	All	PGP_{1a}	np_{1a}	$d'_1-d'_5$	(1)	no
		PGP_{1b}	np_{1b}	$d'_1-d'_5$	(2)	no
		PGP_{1c}	np_{1c},np_{1e},np_{1f}	d_1-d_{15}	(1 2 3 4 5)	no
		PGP_{1d}	np_{1d},np_{1c}	d_4-d_{15}	(1 2 3 4 5)	no
2	2	np_{2a}	-	d_8-d_{15}	(1)	yes
		np_{2f}	-	$d_{10}-d_{15}$	(2 3 4 5)	yes
	All	PGP_{2a}	np_{2a},np_{2c},np_{2d}	d_1-d_{15}	(1)	no
	All	PGP_{2b}	np_{2b}	$d'_1-d'_5$	(1)	no
	All	PGP_{2c}	np_{2f}	$d_{10}-d_{15}$	(2 3 4 5)	no
3	All	PGP_{3a}	np_{3a},np_{3d},np_{3e}	d_1-d_{15}	(1 2 3 4 5)	no
		PGP_{3b}	np_{3b}	d_1-d_6	(2)	no
		PGP_{3c}	np_{3c}	$d'_1-d'_5$	(1)	no
4	All	PGP_{4a}	np_{4c},np_{4d},np_{4e}	d_1-d_{15}	(1 2 3 4 5)	no
		PGP_{4b}	np_{4b}	$d'_1-d'_5$	(1)	no

Node-plans and PGPs not listed from the previous figure are unchanged.

Figure 48: Later Network-Models.

organization, consider what happens when nodes 1, 2, and 3 send node-plans to $node_4$, and $node_4$ forms PGPs and sends them back to the other nodes. The

Node	Model	Entry	Parts	Track	V-types	Trans
1	1	np_{1c}	-	d_4-d_{12}	(1)	yes
		np_{1d}	-	d_4-d_{12}	(2)	no
	2	np_{1c}	-	$d_{10}-d_{15}$	(1)	yes
		np_{1b}	-	$d_{10}-d_{15}$	(2 3 4 5)	yes
	All	PGP_{1a}	np_{1a}	$d'_1-d'_5$	(1)	no
		PGP_{1b}	np_{1b}	$d'_1-d'_5$	(2)	no
		PGP_{1c}	np_{1c},np_{1e},np_{1f}	d_1-d_{15}	(1)	no
		PGP_{1d}	np_{1d},np_{1h}	d_4-d_{15}	(2 3 4 5)	no
2	2	np_{2a}	-	$d_{10}-d_{15}$	(1)	yes
		np_{2f}	-	$d_{10}-d_{15}$	(2 3 4 5)	yes
	All	PGP_{2a}	np_{2a},np_{2c},np_{2d}	d_1-d_{15}	(1)	no
	All	PGP_{2b}	np_{2b}	$d'_1-d'_5$	(1)	no
	All	PGP_{2c}	np_{2f}	$d_{10}-d_{15}$	(2 3 4 5)	no
3	2	np_{3e}	-	$d_{10}-d_{15}$	(1)	yes
		np_{3g}	-	$d_{10}-d_{15}$	(2 3 4 5)	yes
	All	PGP_{3a}	np_{3a},np_{3d},np_{3e}	d_1-d_{15}	(1)	no
		PGP_{3b}	np_{3b}	d_1-d_6	(2)	no
		PGP_{3c}	np_{3c}	$d'_1-d'_5$	(1)	no
	All	PGP_{3d}	np_{3g}	$d_{10}-d_{15}$	(2 3 4 5)	no
4	2	np_{4d}	-	$d_{10}-d_{15}$	(1)	yes
		np_{4f}	-	$d_{10}-d_{15}$	(2 3 4 5)	yes
	All	PGP_{4a}	np_{4c},np_{4d},np_{4e}	d_1-d_{15}	(1)	no
		PGP_{4b}	np_{4b}	$d'_1-d'_5$	(1)	no
	All	PGP_{4c}	np_{4f}	$d_{10}-d_{15}$	(2 3 4 5)	no

Node-plans and PGPs not listed from the previous figure are unchanged.

Figure 49: Final Network-Models.

Node	Model	Entry	Participants	Track	V-types	Sent?
1	1	np_{1a}	-	$d'_1-d'_5$	(1)	yes
		np_{1b}	-	$d'_1-d'_5$	(2)	no
		np_{1c}	-	d_4-d_{12}	(1)	yes
		np_{1d}	-	d_4-d_{12}	(2)	no
	All	PGP_{1a}	np_{1a}	$d'_1-d'_5$	(1)	no
		PGP_{1b}	np_{1b}	$d'_1-d'_5$	(2)	no
		PGP_{1c}	np_{1c}	d_4-d_{12}	(1)	no
		PGP_{1d}	np_{1d}	d_4-d_{12}	(2)	no
2	2	np_{2a}	-	$d_{10}-d_{15}$	(1 2 3 4 5)	yes
	All	PGP_{2a}	np_{2a}	$d_{10}-d_{15}$	(1 2 3 4 5)	no
3	3	np_{3a}	-	d_1-d_6	(1)	yes
		np_{3b}	-	d_1-d_6	(2)	no
	All	PGP_{3a}	np_{3a}	d_1-d_6	(1)	no
		PGP_{3b}	np_{3b}	d_1-d_6	(2)	no
4	4	np_{4a}	-	nil	nil	no
	1	np_{4b}	-	$d'_1-d'_5$	(1)	no
		np_{4c}	-	d_4-d_{12}	(1)	no
	2	np_{4d}	-	$d_{10}-d_{15}$	(1 2 3 4 5)	no
	3	np_{4e}	-	d_1-d_6	(1)	no
	All	PGP_{4a}	np_{4c},np_{4d},np_{4e}	d_1-d_{15}	(1 2 3 4 5)	yes
		PGP_{4b}	np_{4b}	$d'_1-d'_5$	(1)	yes

Figure 50: Centralized Example Network-Models.

initial situation is identical to the previous example (Figure 46), except that $node_4$ does not transmit is idle node-plan. After it receives node-plans from the other nodes, $node_4$ forms PGPs; meanwhile, the other nodes' network-models have not changed, as shown in Figure 50. Note that the node-plans in $node_4$'s node-models are not transmitted, but the two PGPs that it forms are both sent to the other nodes, when relevant.

The mechanisms for communicating about PGPs, which are more fully described in the next chapter, are used by $node_4$ to decide where to send PGPs: it sends a PGP to each node that participates in it. Other nodes do not need the PGP since $node_4$ is coordinating the nodes (if each node is forming PGPs and coordinating with others, then each may need to know about all highly-rated PGPs whether or not they participate in them). When the other nodes receive the PGPs from $node_4$, they incorporate these into their network-models. They match a received PGP to any local participating node-plans, and through these node-plans find any existing PGPs to modify. If the received PGP is unrelated to any local node-plans a new PGP is created for it. The resultant network-models are shown in Figure 51.

Once again, when $node_2$ receives a predictive partial solution from $node_1$, it divides its local plan into two. It sends the changed node-plans to $node_4$, which then modifies the PGPs and distributes them. The advantage of using $node_4$ as a coordinating node is that the other nodes need not process and store as much information; but the disadvantage is that the other nodes do not get the more global PGPs as early when they must wait for $node_4$ to send back PGPs

Node	Model	Entry	Participants	Track	V-types	Sent?
1	1	np_{1a}	-	$d'_1-d'_5$	(1)	yes
		np_{1b}	-	$d'_1-d'_5$	(2)	no
		np_{1c}	-	d_4-d_{12}	(1)	yes
		np_{1d}	-	d_4-d_{12}	(2)	no
	All	PGP_{1a}	np_{1a}	$d'_1-d'_5$	(1)	no
		PGP_{1b}	np_{1b}	$d'_1-d'_5$	(2)	no
		PGP_{1c}	np_{1c}	d_1-d_{15}	(1 2 3 4 5)	no
		PGP_{1d}	np_{1d}	d_4-d_{12}	(2)	no
2	2	np_{2a}	-	$d_{10}-d_{15}$	(1 2 3 4 5)	yes
	All	PGP_{2a}	np_{2a}	d_1-d_{15}	(1 2 3 4 5)	no
3	3	np_{3a}	-	d_1-d_6	(1)	yes
		np_{3b}	-	d_1-d_6	(2)	no
	All	PGP_{3a}	np_{3a}	d_1-d_{15}	(1 2 3 4 5)	no
		PGP_{3b}	np_{3b}	d_1-d_6	(2)	no
4	4	np_{4a}	-	nil	nil	no
	1	np_{4b}	-	$d'_1-d'_5$	(1)	no
		np_{4c}	-	d_4-d_{12}	(1)	no
	2	np_{4d}	-	$d_{10}-d_{15}$	(1 2 3 4 5)	no
	3	np_{4e}	-	d_1-d_6	(1)	no
	All	PGP_{4a}	np_{4c},np_{4d},np_{4e}	d_1-d_{15}	(1 2 3 4 5)	yes
		PGP_{4b}	np_{4b}	$d'_1-d'_5$	(1)	yes

Figure 51: Distributing PGPs Among Nodes.

instead of forming PGPs locally.

6.4 Generalizing

Most distributed computing systems have network-models: at least one of the computing agents has a model of network activity. Computing agents use the model to make control decisions about how the tasks in the network should be assigned and pursued for the network as a whole to work as effectively as possible. Sometimes these models are very general (the basic responsibilities and capabilities of each agent), while at other times they are extremely detailed (exactly what tasks each node is doing). The choice as to what level of representation is needed in a network-model depends on the characteristics of the network and the task domain, such as the cost of communication, the speed of communication, the rate at which tasks are completed, and the rate at which capabilities and responsibilities evolve.

If a computing node takes an average of t time units to complete a task, then, to coordinate individual tasks, nodes must be able to exchange coordination messages in time less than t. Otherwise, by the time the messages are exchanged they are obsolete. Similarly, if nodes communicate about individual tasks, then they must be able to exchange messages every t time units. Nodes that communicate details about individual tasks need communication channels that are faster than the individual tasks and that have sufficient bandwidth to communicate separately about each task. When communication channels are slower, then nodes should communicate about groups of tasks for their more extended future. Also, when communication channels have less bandwidth, then nodes should not exchange details about individual tasks but instead should summarize groups of tasks.

The level of detail for modeling the network chosen in this research is based on assumed relationships between the communication channels and the local node capabilities. We assume that communication is generally slower than the time needed to perform a primitive task (execute a KS), so that nodes should not exchange messages about individual KSIs but should communicate about groups of tasks. We also assume that communication is sufficiently expensive to warrant being selective about what coordination information to exchange, but where it is less expensive for nodes to communicate needed coordination information than it is to have nodes infer that information by duplicating each other's reasoning. As a result, our mechanisms were developed to communicate about entire plans and the long-term activities being taken in those plans: the level of detail allows nodes to reason about coordinating the construction of entire solutions without detailing the construction of each hypothesis along the way to those solutions. Because they exchange only the long-term and objective information about plans, the nodes reduce communication costs: the contents of each message are decreased (since detailed short-term information is not exchanged) and the number of messages is decreased (since the objectives and long-term plans change less often than the short-term details).

If the costs and delays of communication decrease, then the level of detail should be changed: it may be advantageous for nodes to coordinate individual actions (KSs). In the extreme situation where communication is extremely cheap and rapid, nodes can be so closely coupled that they resemble a parallel processing system where they schedule tasks as a group. On the other hand, if the costs and delays of communication increase, then nodes may need to communicate at another level of detail, exchanging information not about individual plans (which may be completed by the time the message arrives at its destination) but about groups of plans. In the limit where communication becomes very costly and slow, nodes should only communicate about general capabilities and responsibilities—they should only maintain a basic organizational framework and not coordinate their more specific activities.

Useful representations of node activities all have one thing in common, however, no matter what the characteristics of the communication channels and task domain are. Although there is no such thing as a completely "general" representation for network-models, all useful network-models simultaneously represent activities at different levels of detail. The detail needed for making local control decisions is different from that needed for identifying when nodes are working on larger, shared goals, which in turn is different from that needed to determine where future tasks are likely to occur.

Our network-models enable nodes to represent information at appropriate levels of detail depending on how that information will be used. With its models of local and network activity, a node can not only make informed decisions about its local activities, but can also recognize when it should cooperate with others, how it should cooperate with others, and what the basic capabilities of others are. Because it has knowledge at the right level of detail for each type of control decision it must make, a node can make better control decisions.

Although the contents of most of the fields in the various network-model data structures are domain-dependent, the basic concepts behind what is being represented and why are more general: node-plans summarize local plans so only the aspects that affect outward behavior (interactions with other nodes) are represented; a plan-activity-map represents a view of how the node will behave (what results it will produce and when); the more general characteristics of a node represent its basic capabilities and responsibilities; PGPs represent the shared objectives and planned interactions between cooperating nodes; and the meta-level organization identifies the coordination responsibilities and communication patterns among nodes. Thus, although the specific *form* that the knowledge represented in these structures takes is domain-dependent, the *type* of knowledge represented is domain-independent.

The plans generated locally by nodes are easy to summarize because they explicitly represent the plans' objectives, long-term plans, and short-term detailed plans. Building node-plans is therefore a relatively simple task of extracting the appropriate information. Since most planners in other domains develop plans hierarchically, the relevant information about plans at different levels is generally accessible. Planners without such a representation would need mechanisms to cluster primitive actions into larger groups. Similarly, the mechanisms for meta-level communication and for maintaining network-models are straightforward and generally useful: their main function is to keep track of information being exchanged. Finally, the mechanisms for recognizing PGGs involve domain information, since identifying objectives that are part of a larger goal necessitates domain knowledge about how local goals could be related. The principal issue involved in these mechanisms is in reducing the combinatorics involved in identifying when and how nodes should cooperate.

When tasks are decomposed by some central authority, their relationships with other tasks can be distributed with them. In many domains, however, tasks (subproblems) are inherently distributed among nodes. Nodes therefore must solve the association problem by communicating information in order to associate their individual subproblems and recognize opportunities for cooperation. This chapter has shown how nodes can build network-models to identify shared PGGs; the next chapter describes how they coordinate their actions better.

The highest and best form of efficiency is the spontaneous coopera-tion of a free people. –Woodrow Wilson

Chapter 7

Coordination Through Partial Global Planning

To cooperate more effectively, nodes should use their views of network activity (from their network-models) and their knowledge about the goals of cooperation. Using this information, nodes alter their local actions and their interactions to work as a more effective team. This chapter focuses on how nodes develop their more coordinated plans, including techniques for negotiating over coverage of shared tasks and over transfers of tasks to use network resources and expertise better. A second focus of this chapter is on consistency: nodes might have somewhat different network-models because of domain dynamics and communication delays and limitations, and thus might develop inconsistent views of how they should coordinate. We focus on how the network as a whole should develop and distribute coordination information (how it should be organized) so that nodes develop, pursue, and maintain reasonably consistent views, and how the nodes can cooperate despite inconsistencies.

7.1 Background

Issues and approaches in coordination were discussed in Chapter 1. Recall that previous approaches have stressed particular styles of cooperation, such as having a centralized coordinator, or forming contracts, or exchanging local information based on organizational knowledge to eventually converge on solutions. Each of these approaches was also geared to different goals of cooperation, such as ensuring against resource conflicts, or decomposing and distributing tasks, or exploring how local results should be combined into more global results. Our approach, in contrast, represents a more general framework that lets nodes cooperate in different styles and pursue a variety of cooperative goals.

Our mechanisms view coordination as a planning task. Nodes need to plan complementary actions and anticipate their interactions, even though in dynamically changing environments each may have a somewhat different view of cooperation than the others. Coordinating through a centralized leader (that plans for the group), or through contracts (which are plans shared by the manager and contractor), or through exchanging partial results to converge on solutions (where nodes share an organizational plan about what types of information to exchange), all involve plans. The partial global planning framework lets nodes coordinate in any of these styles without resorting to different mechanisms for different styles. Moreover, by reasoning about how local plans fit together into partial global plans and about the concurrent actions and interactions of nodes, the nodes can cooperate to achieve any of a number of goals such as avoiding redundant or conflicting activities, transferring activities from overburdened to underutilized nodes, or integrating local results into more global results.

7.2   Overview

A node invokes its partial global planner (also referred to as its **PGPlanner**) to find current plans and activities for the set of nodes that it is responsible for coordinating (based on the meta-level organization). Unlike the local planner which is typically invoked after each problem solving action to monitor, repair, and update plans, the PGPlanner can be invoked less often, depending on the dynamics of the problem and network. Moreover, because it is working in a dynamic world, the PGPlanner should not completely map out every future action and interaction. However, because decisions about current activities can depend on projected future activities, the PGPlanner must develop a sufficient view of how nodes will act and interact to determine which of their possible activities nodes should pursue. The PGPlanner thus may consider several PGPs at a given time and project the future interactions between nodes involved in each as it makes decisions about which of its plans a node should pursue and whether it should alter that plan to cooperate more effectively.

When the PGPlanner is invoked, it begins by processing any node-plan and PGP messages and by updating node-plans of any changed local plans. If its network-model has changed, the PGPlanner scans the network-model to recognize new or modified PGGs, and creates or modifies PGPs as needed. The PGPs are stored on the PGP queue based on their ratings (where their ratings are a function of the ratings of the participating node-plans). Unlike local plans

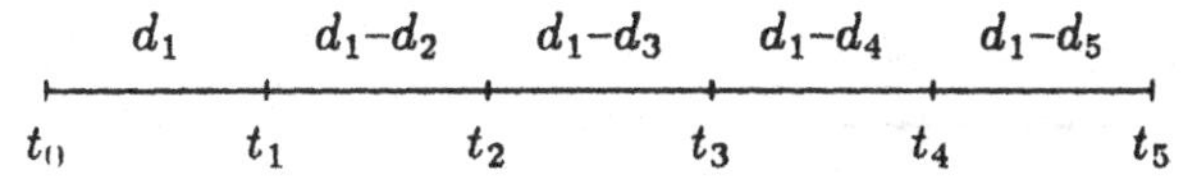

$$d_1 \qquad d_1{-}d_2 \qquad d_1{-}d_3 \qquad d_1{-}d_4 \qquad d_1{-}d_5$$

$$t_0 \qquad\quad t_1 \qquad\quad t_2 \qquad\quad t_3 \qquad\quad t_4 \qquad\quad t_5$$

Activity begins at time t_0. From $t_0{-}t_1$, the node works on data in d_1, from $t_1{-}t_2$ the node works on data in d_2 and combines it with past results to form $d_1{-}d_2$, and so on until it forms the result $d_1{-}d_5$ at time t_5.

Figure 52: An Example Node-Plan Plan-Activity-Map

(or KSIs) where only one can be current at any time, PGPs can be pursued concurrently by different groups of nodes so a *set* of active PGPs must be found by the PGPlanner. Depending on the node's coordination responsibilities (represented in the meta-level organization), its PGPlanner is responsible for finding PGPs for some subset of the nodes in the network: if it is a coordinator, it must find enough PGPs so that each of the nodes it should coordinate is accounted for, while if nodes plan for themselves, then a node must scan through PGPs until it finds what it should currently be doing. Note, however, that even a node that only plans for itself may have to examine several PGPs because it must see whether the nodes it expects to cooperate with are also cooperating in other PGPs, and if so how that may affect this node's PGP.

For the most highly-rated active PGP, the PGPlanner first builds the PGP **plan-activity-map** to interleave the activities of the participating nodes. Each of the PGP's participating node-plans contains information about the local plan's i-goals, the order they will be pursued in, and predictions about how much time each requires. The PGPlanner builds a plan-activity-map from this information: it assumes that the activities begin at the current time, and builds a sequence of plan-activities where the next plan-activity begins after the previous one ends. For example, a plan-activity-map for a node that builds a track with data $d_1{-}d_5$ is graphically depicted in Figure 52. The PGPlanner builds plan-activity-maps for each node-plan to recognize the concurrent activities of the nodes. An example is shown in Figure 53.

Next, the PGPlanner uses a hill-climbing algorithm to reorder the activities to improve network performance. It rates each activity based on attributes such as expected time cost, expected result quality, how it will be affected by earlier activities, and how it will affect later activities. It then swaps activities to move the most highly-rated ones earlier. Because their ratings depend on the ordering, the activities are rated in the new order, and the process repeats until a reordering does not increase the sum of the activities' ratings. Thus the algorithm *cheaply* finds a better but not necessarily optimal ordering.

Rating and reordering activities depends on the network's goals of cooperation. For example, a goal of cooperation may be to avoid redundantly deriving partial solutions. In the example in Figure 53, $node_1$ and $node_2$ share activities d_1 and d_2, and $node_2$ and $node_3$ share activities d_7 and d_8. To avoid redundancy

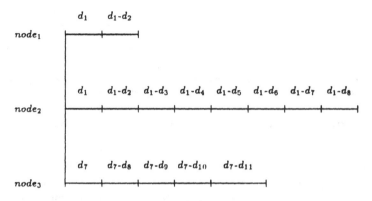

Figure 53: Concurrent Plan-Activity-Maps for Three Nodes.

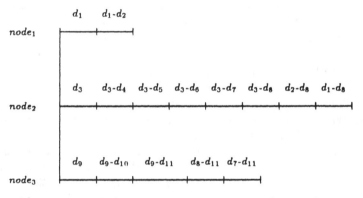

Figure 54: Final Reordering of Concurrent Plan-Activity-Maps.

between $node_1$ and $node_2$, the activities of $node_2$ are reordered to move redundant activities to a later time, and to avoid the possible redundancy between $node_2$ and $node_3$ (since the predicted durations of activities may be somewhat off), $node_3$'s activities can be reordered to move d_7 and d_8 to later times (Figure 54). With this reordering, the nodes anticipate the possibility of incorrect estimates about when they will perform certain activities: each concentrates on the activities only it can do first and then works towards others, committing to common activities only when needed.

When it has found a reasonable ordering of plan-activities, the PGPlanner finds sequences of activities that all contribute to forming a larger partial solution, and represents this group as a **PGP-partial-solution**. For example, given the plan-activities in Figure 54, the PGPlanner recognizes that $node_1$ will form partial solution d_1–d_2 over the interval spanned by both activities. Similarly, it recognizes that $node_2$ will form d_3–d_7 (its other activities work on

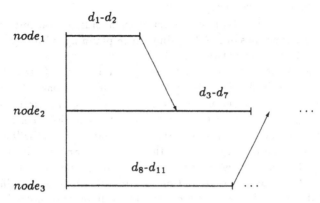

Figure 55: Proposed Solution Construction Activities.

data that will already be processed) and $node_3$ will form d_8-d_{11} (d_7 will have already been covered by $node_2$). These partial solutions and their intervals are shown in Figure 55. With this representation, the PGPlanner can then determine how the various partial solutions should be integrated. Since $node_1$ completes its partial solution soonest, it sends it off to $node_2$ (so that $node_2$ continues working on its partial solution while the partial solution from $node_1$ is in transit). Similarly, $node_3$ completes its partial solution before $node_2$ and so should send that partial solution on to $node_2$. When $node_2$ has completed its partial solution, it will have received or will be about to receive the other partial solutions and can integrate the pieces into an overall solution.

The PGPlanner thus represents how the nodes can construct a solution as a **solution-construction-graph**, and with this view it can reason about what hypotheses need to be exchanged and where, so communication decisions can be made more intelligently than when using only local criteria [Durfee *et al.*, 1985b; Durfee *et al.*, 1987]. The PGPlanner explicitly represents as part of the PGP the basic specifications of hypotheses to transmit, what nodes should send them, and what nodes should receive them. Once this is complete, the PGPlanner has roughly mapped out how the nodes will act (what activities they take and approximately when) and how the nodes will interact (what hypotheses they exchange and what nodes integrate partial solutions).

The PGPlanner also uses the reordered plan-activity-map to modify any local plans: it changes their major plan steps to reflect the improved ordering. Once it has formed PGPs that specify the current plans and activities for all the nodes it must coordinate, therefore, the PGPlanner has updated the local plans that participate in these PGPs. The local plan corresponding to the node's current PGP is selected and the local planner triggers its next KSI as the node's next problem solving action. Finally, the PGPlanner also transmits any new or modified information about its plans and PGPs to interested nodes, as specified in the meta-level organization.

This simple view of the PGPlanner's activities avoids several important issues, especially the dynamics of PGPlanning (since planning is interleaved with execution), the interactions between PGPs that may concurrently be active, and how the PGPlanner recognizes when tasks should be transferred. First, as problem solving proceeds the PGPlanner must represent the past, present, and future plan-activities for node-plans. To avoid recomputing plan-activity-maps, the PGPlanner stores the plan-activity-map that it generates for a node-plan with that node-plan. Thus, for plans that do not change, the PGPlanner can simply extract the plan-activity-map for the node-plan and use it to form a PGP's plan-activity-map. However, when a node changes its plans (new information arrives, actions fail, time predictions are modified), these modifications are propagated to its node-plans, which in turn will be transmitted to pertinent nodes. The modifications to a node-plan include an updating of the plan-activity-map (if any has yet been formed). The PGPlanner removes from the plan-activity-map any *future* plan-activities which should be recomputed, while any past plan-activities are left in the plan-activity-map since the past cannot be changed.

Therefore, when building a PGP's plan-activity-map, the PGPlanner may have some plan-activities as part of a node-plan's plan-activity-map, and must compute the others. A node that forms a PGP and updates a node-plan for one of its own local plans can send out the node-plan's plan-activity-map with that node-plan. Although this increases communication costs (more information to transmit), it saves on computation costs (since the recipient node's PGPlanner need not derive the plan-activity-map itself) and it better reflects the actual times when plan-activities will occur (since the node performing the local plan knows more exactly when activities will be pursued).

The second important issue concerns dealing with several active PGPs. Since PGPs are rated, the PGPlanner considers them one at a time starting with the most highly rated. However, this does *not* mean that all nodes involved in the most highly-rated PGP should currently follow plans associated with that PGP. Some of the nodes may have completed their local plans that participate in the PGP, and so the PGPlanner must look at other PGPs to determine what these nodes should be doing. Furthermore, it may be advantageous to delay activities by some of the nodes working on the best PGP so that they can form important results for other PGPs (such as predictive results). The PGPlanner must determine whether such activities exist for a node and whether they can be pursued without affecting the more highly-rated PGPs.

For example, in the situation in Figure 56, $node_1$ participates in two PGPs: to form d_1–d_{10} and to form d'_1–d'_{10}. Because the data for d_1–d_{10} is more strongly rated, the plans of $node_1$ and $node_3$ to develop their partial solutions are highly rated and the PGP to form the overall solution has a higher rating than the PGP to form d'_1–d'_{10}. The PGPlanner develops this PGP first, and identifies the partial solutions being formed by $node_1$ and $node_3$ (Figure 57).

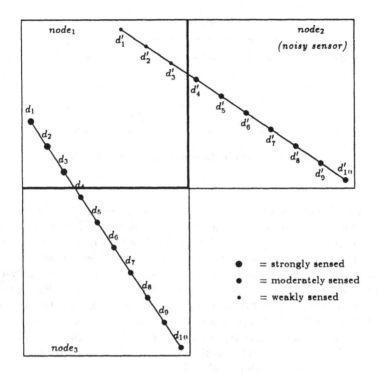

Figure 56: An Example With Alternative PGPs.

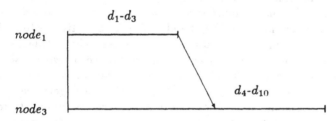

Figure 57: Proposed Solution Construction for Better PGP.

The PGPlanner recognizes that $node_1$'s partial solution provides no predictive information (since $node_3$'s data has little ambiguity) and thus arrives well before $node_3$ needs it. The PGPlanner treats the time between when $node_1$ begins to form its partial solution and when it must send this partial solution to $node_3$ (Figure 58) as a time-window [Vere, 1983]. Because the PGP is the most highly rated and should thus be achieved as quickly as possible, the PG-Planner must plan to pursue the activities that generate this partial solution within the time-window, but it can use any extra time to pursue other PGPs. When it examines its other PGP (to form d'_1–d'_{10}), it recognizes that $node_1$ may

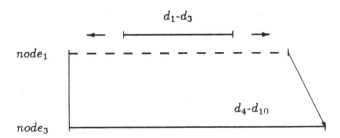

Figure 58: Time-Window for Node 1's Activities.

provide predictive information to $node_2$. As a result, the PGPlanner decides to postpone $node_1$'s activities on the more highly-rated PGP,[1] and will perform activities for the more lowly-rated PGP until it has used up the available time. Hopefully, it can perform enough activities to form and send predictive information to $node_2$ before it must work on its activities for the more highly-rated PGP. If not, it has not lost anything since it still forms and transmits the partial solution for the more highly-rated PGP so that $node_3$ receives it by the time it is needed. Thus, a PGP's solution-construction-graph not only represents how nodes should exchange partial results but also represents the flexibility they have in their local activities while still interacting effectively with others. The PGPlanner exploits this flexibility when possible.

The third important issue to address is task-passing. The PGPlanner as outlined above determines how nodes should pursue their local activities and exchange partial solutions to improve cooperation, but did not consider how cooperation might be further improved if nodes transferred activities to make better use of their computational resources and expertise. The PGPlanner makes simple decisions about whether tasks (groups of related activities) should be transferred for better load balancing, and uses the meta-level organization to find nodes with appropriate expertise for these tasks. Once again, the PGPlanner bases these decisions on a PGP's solution-construction-graph: it identifies whether there is a **bottleneck-node** that takes substantially longer to form its partial solution than the other cooperating nodes. If it finds such a node and can find nodes that are underutilized (based on its network-model) and that could potentially perform some of the bottleneck-node's activities, then it modifies the PGP to propose a possible transfer of tasks. This PGP is sent to the underutilized nodes, which respond with node-plans that represent counter-proposals. The original node compares replies to find which (if any) of the nodes should receive the tasks, or to generate new proposals.

---

[1] Because the predicted durations of the activities might be somewhat off, the PGPlanner can add an extra time-cushion to the expected time needs for forming the partial solution to avoid the situation where a node exceeds the window.

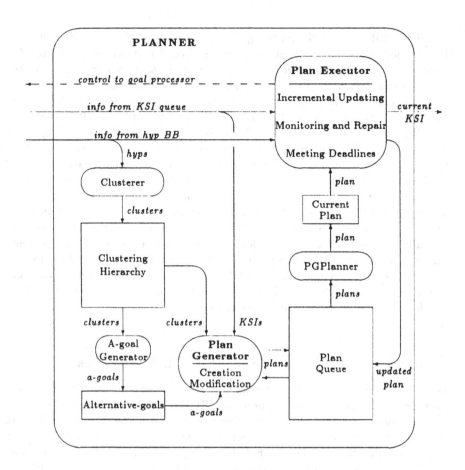

Figure 59: The Architecture of the Planner With the PGPlanner.

7.3   Details

The partial global planning mechanisms extend the local planning mechanisms in much the same way that the local planning mechanisms extend a node's basic control scheme. Because local plans combine individual actions into purposeful, coherent sequences, control decisions are working toward local long-term goals. In a similar way, PGPs combine several local plans into coordinated groups, so that control decisions are based on how local plans and their actions work toward network long-term goals. Schematically, the dispatcher in the local planner that simply chooses the most highly-rated local plan (Figure 19) is replaced with the partial global planning mechanisms that determines the local plan to pursue based on the PGPs (Figure 59).

The architecture of the partial global planner is sketched in Figure 60. The PGPlanner's network-model is composed of several node-models and the PGP queue. How node-models are generated and maintained was described in the previous chapter: node-plans are formed from the node's local plans and from received node-plan messages. The PGP generator scans the node-plans in the node-models to recognize PGGs, and it forms and maintains PGPs, as was also described in the previous chapter. This chapter examines the remaining mechanisms. The PGP communication mechanisms allow nodes to exchange PGPs to update each other's network-models and to converge on consistent views of cooperation when possible. The dispatcher finds a set of highly-rated PGPs that can be active concurrently (that are being pursued by different groups of nodes). The PGP executor then generates additional information about active PGPs: how the activities of the participating nodes may interact and could potentially be reordered to better achieve the PGP's objectives; where and when the partial solutions being formed at various nodes should be combined to construct the entire solution; what partial solutions should be communicated and where to generate the entire solution; how local plans associated with the PGPs should be altered to reflect the better ordering of activities, and what local plan to pursue next.

7.3.1   Partial Global Planning Data Structures

When the PGP generator scans the node-models to form and modify PGPs, it is identifying opportunities for cooperation (PGGs). The description of PGPs in the previous chapter therefore focused on the attributes necessary for indicating *when* a group of nodes should cooperate. This section describes PGPs more fully, discussing the representation of *how* this group of nodes should cooperate.

The attributes of a PGP are shown in Figure 61. Several of these attributes were described in the last chapter: the PGP has a name, a list of participating node-plans, the name of the node that formed the PGP, a list of the nodes that participate in the PGP, the time when the PGP was created or last modified, a rating (combining the ratings of the participating node-plans), and objectives (the expected track and vehicle types of a solution). The PGP's long-term information includes a specification about what type of results will be integrated (the blackboard-levels for combining tracks), and representations of the concurrent activities of nodes and how they should cooperate.

The plan-activity-map is an ordered list of plan-activities, where each plan-activity represents a separate i-goal for a node to achieve. The attributes of a plan-activity were discussed in the previous chapter (Figure 41), and include a begin-time, an end-time, the node performing the activity, an area of focus, and an expected result (partial solution). The PGP's plan-activity-map interleaves plan-activities from each of the participating nodes based on their *end-times*— to coordinate the nodes, the PGPlanner needs to identify when they will form partial results, not when they will start to form them. By scanning through

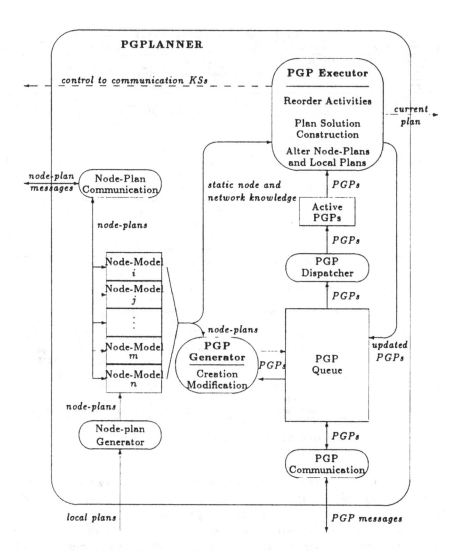

Figure 60: The Architecture of the PGPlanner.

the plan-activity-map, the PGPlanner can recognize the concurrent activities of the various nodes at an appropriate level of detail: instead of recognizing what specific actions they take concurrently (which would entail a large amount of quickly outdated information), the PGPlanner only needs to identify which i-goals are being pursued concurrently.

The PGPlanner forms a solution-construction-graph from the plan-activity-map. It finds groups of plan-activities for a node and summarizes them as a **PGP-partial-solution** (Figure 62). Each PGP-partial-solution has a begin-

name	A unique name (symbol) pointing at the PGP structure	
participants	A list of the node-plans that participate in this PGP	
node	The node that created this PGP	
nodes	A list of the names of nodes participating in this PGP	
creation-time	When the PGP was created or last updated	
rating	The rating of the PGP	
objective	track	Expected complete track when pieces from separate node-plans are combined
	v-event-classes	Vehicle-event-classes (types of vehicles) being tracked
long-term	tracking-levels	Blackboard-level(s) where hypotheses will be integrated into tracks
	plan-activity-map	Sequence of plan-activities: when i-goals are pursued and partial results formed
	solution-construction-graph	What partial results will be integrated and indication where and when
	communication	What partial solutions will be exchanged between nodes
record	sent-to-nodes	Nodes sent this PGP and the creation-time of sent PGP
	node-and-plans	Name(s) of the local plan(s) for each participating node
	plans-and-times	Creation-times for participating the local plans
future	to-nodes	Where PGP sent to elicit future node-plans
	sent-time	When PGP sent to elicit future node-plans
	responses	Node-plans received in response to PGP
	respond-to	Node receiving future node-plan responses
	response-label	Label (PGP-name) for responses
	source-node	Where tasks to be passed come from
	communication	What tasks to send, from where to where

Figure 61: The Attributes of a PGP.

time (when the group of plan-activities begin), an end-time (when the group of plan-activities end), a duration (how much time the plan-activities require), a list of nodes (the node(s) that are building the partial solution), an expected result (a partial track), a list of supporting PGP-partial-solutions (the PGP-partial-solutions that were integrated to form this PGP-partial-solution), and a list of supported PGP-partial-solutions (the PGP-partial-solutions in which this PGP-partial-solution is a component). The leaves of the solution-construction-graph thus represent partial solutions formed at individual nodes, the root of the graph represents the complete solution, and the paths between leaves and the root indicate how and where partial solutions should be integrated. The mechanisms for forming the solution-construction-graph are outlined later, along with discussions about why the duration may be less than the difference between the begin-time and end-time and why several nodes may build the same partial solutions.

The long-term communication information explicitly represents the communication expectations developed in the solution-construction-graph. By scan-

begin-time	When the activities to form the partial solution begin
end-time	When the activities to form the partial solution end
duration	How much time the activities need to form the partial solution
nodes	A list of the nodes that are forming the partial solution
expected-result	The basic specifications (time-regions) of the partial solution
supporting-pss	PGP-partial-solutions combined in this PGP-partial-solution
supported-pss	PGP-partial-solutions this PGP-partial-solution is combined into

Figure 62: The Attributes of a PGP-partial-solution.

ning through the solution-construction-graph, the PGPlanner identifies what partial solutions must be transmitted from one node to another, and builds a communication expectation of the form (from-node to-node time expected-result). From-node and to-node indicate the source and destination of the message, time is an estimate of when the message will be transmitted (based on the PGP-partial-solution's end-time), and expected-result has specifications of the hypothesis to be transmitted (its time-locations). The long-term communication information also represents communication that is intended for purposes other than solution construction. For example, if the PGPlanner recognizes that a earlier version of some partial solution should be transmitted for predictive purposes, it represents this exchange in the long-term communication information as well.

The PGP contains a record of where and when it itself has been transmitted in the past, so that the PGPlanner can determine where and when a new or modified PGP should be sent. The PGP also contains a record that indicates the local plans from which it is built, what nodes created those local plans, and when those local plans were created or last updated. Because nodes communicate about PGPs, it is important that they be able to recognize when a received PGP corresponds to an existing local PGP, and to do this they need to compare the information on which each is based. Since they each give local names to PGPs and node-plans, they record the original names given to local plans by the nodes that created them (and transmitted as the plan-name attribute of a node-plan), and use these names as a common basis for determining whether two PGPs correspond to cooperation among the same plans. Thus, each PGP has a node-and-plans attribute that associates with each node the name(s) of its local plan(s) that are participating in the PGP. The PGP also has a plans-and-times attribute that associates with each local plan name the creation-time of that plan (so that given PGPs for the same plans, the PGPlanner can determine which was built from the more recent information).

Finally, the PGP contains information about potential future cooperation. The principal use of this information is for task-passing: when these attributes are set, the PGP includes information proposing a transfer of tasks, and a node that receives such a PGP will generate a future node-plan in response to it. The PGP's future attributes include: a list of to-nodes where tasks could be transferred, the time when the PGP was sent to those nodes, a list of responses in the form of node-plan messages received for the PGP, the name of the node where responses should be sent, a label for the responses so that the node can associate a received response with the appropriate PGP, the name of the node where the tasks to transfer currently reside (which may or may not be the same as the node proposing the transfer), and the communication expectations representing the exchange of tasks once this has been determined.

Besides the PGP data structures, the PGPlanner uses the data structures for network-models described in the previous chapter, including the meta-level organization and the general characteristics of nodes.

To decide how to modify local plans to improve cooperation, the PGPlanner also needs to know the goals of cooperation. Preferences for how to cooperate are currently represented numerically in the **cooperation-parameters** (Figure 63), which are part of the meta-level organization (so all nodes have identical cooperation-parameters). The PGPlanner uses these parameters to determine a cost for each of the various activities that a node can perform. By using numeric parameters, the PGPlanner can make simple comparisons for conflicting goals of cooperation. For example, if the nodes have a goal of influencing each other only when by doing so they can significantly improve network coordination, then balancing the conflicting goals of improving coordination and maintaining autonomy is difficult. If the cost of maintaining autonomy is half that of improving coordination, then for activities to be reordered the expected quality of coordination (network solution time) by reordering must be at least twice what would have been achieved otherwise. With numeric values indicating the cost of each of these goals, the overall costs of activities strike a balance between them.

The current set of factors that affect how (and whether) the PGPlanner reorders tasks are redundancy, reliability, duration, predictiveness, locally-predicted, independence, and diversity. *Redundancy* is the cost associated with redundantly deriving results, so that redundant activities are more costly than those that are not. Conversely, *reliability* is the cost of *not* verifying results through rederivation, so activities that rederive previous results are less costly than those that do not. Thus, to avoid rederiving redundant results, the redundancy cost should be high and the reliability cost low, while the opposite settings promote verification. *Duration* is the cost of performing more expensive (time-consuming) activities before less expensive activities, and it favors ordering activities so that cheaper activities are pursued sooner. *Predictiveness* is the cost of generating results that are not predictive ahead of those that are, to promote orderings where predictive results are formed earliest. *Locally-predicted* is the cost of generating results that do not extend previous results: since problem solving is most effective when previously formed results are extended into new areas, this factor penalizes orderings where a node forms separate pieces of its result and later merges them. *Independence* is the cost of moving an activity from its position in the initial ordering (formed locally by a node based on the cluster information as described in Chapter 4). Since a node orders its activi-

redundancy	Cost of redundantly deriving results
reliability	Cost of not verifying results through rederivation
duration	Cost of performing more expensive (longer duration) activities before less expensive
predictiveness	Cost of generating predictive results later
locally-predicted	Cost of not locally pursuing adjacent activities
independence	Cost of deviating from the locally generated order for activities
diversity	Cost of working on results near to results being developed at other nodes
time-cushion	Acceptable amount of time deviation between when actions and interactions were predicted to occur and when they actually occur
solution-construction-redundancy	Number of nodes that should redundantly integrate results to increase reliability
min-task-duration	The minimum expected time a task must require to consider transferring it to another node
task-strategy	The strategy for extracting information (bids) for tasks (focused or broadcast)
task-redundancy	The number of nodes from which information should be requested (for focused strategy)

Figure 63: The Cooperation-Parameters.

ties based on local information that is not available to the PGPlanner (not part of a node-plan message since it is very context dependent), the independence factor specifies how costly it is to change that ordering. Finally, *diversity* is the cost of performing an activity "near" activities done at other nodes. To avoid redundantly deriving results in the future, a node should develop results as far as possible from those being developed by other nodes, where "nearness" of activities is measured by how close the sensed time of their data is. How these cost parameters are used is more completely described in Section 7.3.2.

Another important piece of information affecting cooperation is the time-cushion that represents the network's view of a "significant" amount of time. The time-cushion is the largest amount of time that a node's predictions about when actions or interactions will take place can deviate before it should react to those deviations. The time-cushion balances predictability and responsiveness, since a small time-cushion forces nodes to respond more frequently to deviations while a large time-cushion allows them to continue working on their plans in essentially the way that they had expected to despite deviations.

The **solution-construction-redundancy** indicates how many nodes should be responsible for integrating a pair of partial solutions. In a reliable network (where nodes do not fail), no redundancy is needed and this parameter is set to 1. However, in less reliable networks, the nodes should not depend on one node successfully developing a combined solution. When the solution-construction-redundancy is set to n, it means that partial results will be sent to n different nodes, each of which will integrate the pieces into larger results. Obviously, n should not be larger than necessary to ensure that some node successfully combines the partial results, since having more than 1 node form the combined result is a duplication of effort.

The other information in the cooperation-parameters is used by the PG-Planner to make task-passing decisions, where a task is some set of related activities. The *min-task-duration* indicates the minimum size (expected time needs) of a task that is worth transferring. Because transferring a task requires communication and computation overhead, it should not be done when the costs (time spent by a node) of the task are small. The *task-strategy* specifies whether the PGPlanner should request information (bids) from selected nodes or from all nodes. Since the PGPlanner has a model of the network, it usually focuses requests to those nodes that it believes are underutilized. However, if its network-model is substantially incomplete or out-of-date, broadcasting the request may be appropriate. Finally, the *task-redundancy* parameter indicates the number of underutilized nodes from which the PGPlanner should request information (in the focused task-passing strategy). A low value reduces the communication and computation of task-passing (since fewer nodes must process and respond to the request), but a high value makes finding the best node more likely. The task-passing mechanisms that use these parameters are more fully discussed in Section 7.3.7.

7.3.2   Generating a PGP Plan-Activity-Map

After scanning its network-model and finding a set of PGPs, the PGPlanner processes them one at a time starting with the most highly-rated one. By working from the best PGP down and reasoning about one before considering the next, the PGPlanner avoids the cost and complication of considering several PGPs together, with the result of possibly coordinating nodes suboptimally. In general then, when the PGPlanner processes a PGP, it may have already processed some set of more highly-rated PGPs. The PGPlanner thus goes through three phases when generating a PGP's plan-activity-map: first, it forms an initial plan-activity-map by interleaving the plan-activities of the participating nodes; second, it modifies this plan-activity-map based on the any more highly-rated PGPs to avoid expecting nodes to do two things at once; and third, it determines whether the plan-activities could be reordered to improve group problem solving, and if so, generates a new, improved plan-activity-map.

Forming the Initial PGP Plan-Activity-Map

When building a PGP's plan-activity-map, the PGPlanner finds a sequence of plan-activities for each participating node (whenever possible). These plan-activities can come from any of several sources. If the participating node's node-plan is not in its node-model, then the PGP must have been received (this node could not have identified the PGG involving that node) and the plan-activity-map for the node is extracted from the PGP's plan-activity-map. If the plan-activities for this node were not included in the received PGP message, then the PGPlanner cannot compute the PGP's plan-activity-map, and must follow it exactly as received. By holding back plan-activity information, therefore, the node sending the PGP can enforce adherence to the PGP since a recipient lacks sufficient context to develop alternative ways of achieving the PGP.

If the node-plan for the participating node is in its node-model, then it is used to generate the plan-activity-map. The PGPlanner may have already formed a plan-activity-map for the node-plan and stored it with the node-plan, so it simply must retrieve this plan-activity-map. Similarly, the node that formed the node-plan (from a local plan) may have computed the plan-activity-map and included it in the node-plan message, so again the PGPlanner simply retrieves the plan-activity-map. If the plan-activity-map for the node-plan does not already exist, however, then the PGPlanner must compute it.

To compute a plan-activity-map, the PGPlanner uses three pieces of information: the past activities for the node-plan, the order in which it will pursue i-goals, and the time-predictions for these i-goals. If a node has already completed some activities, then these are permanently part of its plan-activity-map. The long-term:time-order provides predictions about the order in which the remaining i-goals will be pursued, and the long-term:time-predictions roughly estimate how long each of those i-goals will take. The PGPlanner uses this information to build plan-activities for the remaining i-goals. If nodes have exchanged node-plans so that each believes the others currently have the same view, then the plan-activity to pursue the first pending i-goal begins at the current time and the remaining i-goals follow one after the other. If the node is coordinating others, however, the plan-activity-maps estimate when the actual activities will be pursued based on when the PGP could be received by others. In more general terms, whenever a node first recognizes some PGG and develops a PGP to achieve it, the node cannot be completely aware of whether other nodes are simultaneously recognizing and forming equivalent PGPs. The plan-activity-map that one node forms for another thus represents an estimate of that node's activities, and inconsistencies between how nodes view coordination can result from differing estimates. Rather than building in synchronization mechanisms to prevent such inconsistencies, the PGPlanning mechanisms allow nodes to cooperate despite them and to exchange information to converge on more consistent PGPs.

The PGPlanner interleaves the plan-activity-maps for the participating node-plans into a single plan-activity-map for the PGP based on the end-times for the plan-activities (and when plan-activities end at the same time, the name of the node performing the activity is used to order them). By ordering the plan-activity-map based on end-times, the PGPlanner can step through the plan-activity-map and develop a view of which partial solutions will be developed before others and of the relative times of their development.

Modifying a PGP Plan-Activity-Map Using Better PGPs

After it forms an initial plan-activity-map, the PGPlanner checks it against the plan-activity-maps of any more highly-rated PGPs to recognize situations where the same node is expected to be pursuing two different node-plans at the same time. When such a conflict occurs, the more highly-rated PGP takes priority, and the plan-activities for the less highly-rated PGP are usually moved to non-conflicting times in the future. However, the plan-activities for the more highly-rated PGP can be moved when doing so will not interfere with when its overall solution will be developed. An example of this was shown in Section 7.2, Figure 58. The PGPlanner expands the solution-construction-graph by working backwards from the integrated solution to find the latest time that any separate partial solution could be formed without affecting when the complete solution could be formed. We represent the flexibility that nodes have in when they develop partial solutions as **time-windows** [Vere, 1983]. The time-window for a PGP-partial-solution is represented by its begin-time and end-time: if its duration is less than the interval between the begin-time and end-time, then the activities can be moved around within that window to improve flexibility.

Determining an optimal arrangement of activities within windows is a complex (and costly) process. Moving a node's activities within a window for one PGP can affect when that node expects to interact in other PGPs. For example, a node might participate in two PGPs, and the decision to work first on one PGP will postpone its activities on the other, which in turn might widen the time-windows available to other nodes working on the second PGP. They in turn might schedule their activities differently as a result, which might cause the original node to alter its decisions. Propagating the effects of arranging activities can therefore be extremely complicated and costly.

For these reasons, and for the underlying assumption that unexpected changes to the situation may occur that will make any optimal arrangement void, the PGPlanner uses a much simpler approach to scheduling activities within their windows. It begins with the premise that the only reason for moving a highly-rated PGP's activities to a later time is if the activities *do not* generate predictive results (so generating them earlier will not help other nodes) and if the activities of inferior PGPs do. So if the most highly-rated PGP is generating predictive results or no more lowly-rated PGPs are generating predictive results then the activities are scheduled to begin right away, otherwise the activities are scheduled to begin at the latest possible time to still provide partial solutions when they are needed. The activities for subsequent PGPs are fit in around assigned times for previous PGPs, possibly being scheduled earlier when the activities for previous PGPs were postponed. The end result is that a PGP's plan-activity-map is altered based on the previously pursued PGPs to reflect when nodes are likely to pursue the activities considering how they are already tentatively committed to cooperating with others. Because the plans, goals, and data of nodes change over time, this tentative postponing of some actions in favor of others can be changed when new information arrives and the activities and ratings of PGPs change.

Reordering the PGP Plan-Activity-Map to Improve Cooperation

To reorder the PGP plan-activity-map in order to improve cooperation, the PGPlanner must find the cost of the various plan-activities in the plan-activity-map, and move less costly activities earlier. The PGPlanner considers cost to be the opposite of rating, and uses costs to simplify the mechanisms because it can use a cost of 0 for plan-activities that have already been completed (they now cost nothing to complete). The PGPlanner computes a cost for each pending plan-activity as:

$$c_{pa} = (rdf \times rd) + (rlf \times rl) + (drf \times dr) + (prf \times pr) + (lpf \times lp) + (inf \times in) + (dvf \times dv)$$

where rdf is the redundancy factor, rlf is the reliability factor, drf is the duration factor, prf is the prediction factor, lpf is the locally-predicted factor, inf is the independence factor, and dvf is the diversity factor. Each of these is specified in the cooperation-parameters (as part of the meta-level organization). The redundancy value rd is computed as the number of nodes that could perform the plan-activity (that have data for the specified area). Thus, the redundancy cost increases as more nodes are able to perform the activity. In contrast, the reliability value rl is the total number of nodes minus the number that could perform the activity, and so the reliability cost decreases as more nodes are able to perform the activity. The duration value dr is simply the duration of the plan-activity (the difference between its end-time and begin-time), and the duration cost increases with duration.

The predictiveness value pr is computed by comparing the plan-activity with the uncompleted plan-activities for other nodes and determining whether the plan-activity might provide the others with predictive information (there is no point in providing predictive information for completed activities). This decision is based on the durations of the plan-activities: a plan-activity that has a shorter duration may provide predictive information for an plan-activity with a longer duration (assuming that the longer duration is because of ambiguity). For each such plan-activity, the PGPlanner determines the *activity-distance* between them as the absolute value of the difference between the sensed times for the data they work on. For example, if one works on data d_1 (sensed at time 1) and the other on data d_4 (sensed at time 4), then the activity-distance between them is 3. If either or both plan-activities process data for several sensed times, then the minimum distance between these sensed times is used. The minimum activity-distance between the plan-activity and the others that it can provide predictive information for is used as the predictiveness value. If it does not provide predictive information then the maximum possible activity-distance (difference between the first and last sensed time for the PGP's objective track) is used. Thus, the closer a plan-activity is to plan-activities that need its predictive information, the lower its predictiveness cost.

The locally-predicted value lp is computed by comparing the plan-activity with *earlier* plan-activities for the same node. If there are none, then the value is 0. Otherwise, the minimum activity-distance between these plan-activities and the plan-activity whose cost is being computed is calculated. This minimum is used as the locally-predicted value: the closer the plan-activity is to previous plan-activities performed by the same node, the lower the locally-predicted cost. Note, furthermore, that when plan-activities are reordered this value can change because a plan-activity might have different previous plan-activities.

The independence value in is computed as how many plan-activities for the node are performed before this plan-activity *in the initial plan-activity-map*. For a given node, later plan-activities have a higher independence cost than earlier ones do, and these costs are constant whatever the reordering. The independence cost thus represents a form of inertia, preventing the PGPlanner from finding an ordering far from the original ordering and therefore minimizing the PGPlanner's effects on local plans.

Finally, the diversity value dv is computed by comparing the plan-activity with earlier plan-activities and determining whether it will derive redundant results. If not, the diversity value is 0. Otherwise, the PGPlanner examines the later plan-activities for the same node and determines if any do not represent redundant activity. If all are redundant, then the diversity value is 0 (since nothing better can be found), but if some are not redundant, than the activity-distance between this plan-activity and those are computed and the minimum is used as the diversity value. A plan-activity thus has a higher diversity cost when it is redundant and farther away from non-redundant plan-activities for the same node. Note once again that the diversity cost of a plan-activity can change when the plan-activity-map is reordered because it is based on which plan-activities are performed earlier and which later.

The PGPlanner works its way down the plan-activity-map and computes the total cost for each plan-activity (c_{pa}). The cost for the entire map is the sum of the plan-activities' costs. It then iteratively attempts to reorder the plan-activity map until it cannot find a better one, using the hill-climbing algorithm:

1. for the current (initial) plan-activity-map, compute the cost of each plan-activity and compute the current-plan-activity-map-cost as the sum of the plan-activity costs;

2. for each plan-activity in the current plan-activity-map examine the later plan-activities for the same node to find the one with the lowest cost, and if the lowest cost later plan-activity has a lower cost than the current plan-activity, then swap them in the new plan-activity-map;

3. if the new plan-activity-map is different from the current plan-activity-map then compute the cost of each plan-activity in the new plan-activity-map and compute the new-plan-activity-cost as the sum of the plan-activity costs;

4. if the new plan-activity-map is different from the current plan-activity-map and the new-plan-activity-cost is lower than the current-plan-activity-cost then set the current plan-activity-map equal to the new plan-activity-map and the current-plan-activity-cost to the new-plan-activity-cost and go to step 2, and otherwise return the current plan-activity-map.

Since a new plan-activity-map must have a strictly lower cost than any earlier versions of the plan-activity-map, and because the same plan-activity-map will have the same overall cost if encountered twice in the algorithm, the algorithm cannot get into indefinite cycle. Also, because the number of possible orderings of a plan-activity-map with a set number of plan-activities is finite, the algorithm must terminate. In fact, the algorithm generally needs to iterate only a few times (less than 5 in our experiments) before it generates a plan-activity-map that is not an improvement over earlier ones. The number of iterations is small because each iteration can swap any number of plan-activities: if instead it were constrained to swap only one pair at each iteration, then many more iterations might be needed. By swapping several pairs in an iteration, the algorithm might miss a locally optimal ordering because it would "overshoot" that peak (if the good swaps are outweighed by the bad). The more conservative approach of swapping one pair per iteration is less likely to overshoot the optimal ordering, but is also much more expensive because so many more iterations are needed. The computation of costs for the plan-activities can be expensive (since comparisons between each pair of plan-activities must be done) so reducing the number of iterations is important. The less conservative approach is thus used in the implementation.

Even though the algorithm attempts to minimize the number of times that the costs of plan-activities must be determined, the expense of this calculation must be reckoned with. Because the cost of a plan-activity depends on what plan-activities precede it and which succeed it, computing this cost means that, in the worst case, a plan-activity must be compared with every other plan-activity. Thus, the complexity of computing the cost for a plan-activity-map increases quadratically with the number of plan-activities in that plan-activity-map. For a sizable plan-activity-map containing on the order of one hundred plan-activities, this complexity can make reordering the plan-activity-map very expensive. In the experiments studied to date, these costs are still acceptable, but future research will need to deal with this issue.

Having found an acceptable ordering, the PGPlanner uses the new ordering to alter any local plans that participate in the PGP. It modifies the order in which they will pursue i-goals to reflect any new ordering, and if the ordering does change it triggers the local planner to recompute the plan's other attributes. The PGPlanner also extracts out the plan-activities for each participating node-plan and assigns these to that node-plan to avoid having to recompute them later.

7.3.3   Building a Solution-Construction-Graph

After it has determined what activities the cooperating nodes should perform and when, the PGPlanner next must determine how the nodes will interact to form the overall solution. By roughly estimating future interactions, the PGPlanner recognizes cases where some nodes have extra time before they need to form their piece of the overall solution, and the mechanisms described in the last section use this view to decide whether in fact a node should pursue an inferior PGP because it has extra time before it must generate its pieces of the overall solutions for better PGPs. The PGPlanner also uses information about interactions when deciding what partial solutions should be exchanged between nodes and what tasks should be transferred between nodes. The interactions are represented as a solution-construction-graph, which is built by first finding the partial solutions being formed by each node and then by determining how they should be integrated.

Finding the Initial PGP-Partial-Solutions

The PGPlanner scans down the plan-activity-map and removes irrelevant plan-activities. In the current implementation, a plan-activity is irrelevant if it generates results that a previous activity (at another node) has already generated *and* if the redundancy cost is greater than the reliability cost. This allows the PGPlanner to let nodes avoid informing each other of results that they have already derived or received from elsewhere. When rederivation is important, on the other hand, the PGPlanner does not remove these activities since nodes should exchange results covering the same areas in order to compare their results (and have higher confidence if their results agree). In addition, the PGPlanner does not remove a plan-activity that generates results that were formed earlier somewhere else if it determines that the earlier results could not arrive at the node performing the later activity before the later activity is finished. That is, communication delays might mean that a node could locally form a duplicate result sooner than if it waits to receive that result.

With the possibly filtered plan-activity-map, the PGPlanner next groups together related activities being performed by the same node. For example, if a node performs a sequence of activities to form a single partial solution, then these activities are grouped together (see Figures 54 and 55 for an example). For each node, any number of such groups are possible, each corresponding to a separate partial solution that cannot be combined with any other local partial solutions (otherwise their combined activities would be grouped together). Since some plan-activities may be removed to avoid redundancy, some nodes may not have any groups at all.

Each group of activities is used to form a PGP-partial-solution. First, the overall partial solution of the activities is represented as an expected result (the activities' combined time-regions) and this expected result is compared to any PGP-partial-solutions that have already been developed to determine if another node is already forming these results. When no such PGP-partial-solutions exist, then a new PGP-partial-solution is formed for the group of activities. If such PGP-partial-solutions do exist, then the PGPlanner uses the solution-construction-redundancy to decide whether to form a PGP-partial-solution for this group of activities or whether they are already being performed elsewhere. If generating a new PGP-partial-solution will not exceed the solution-construction-redundancy then a new PGP-partial-solution is formed. Alternatively, if the possible new PGP-partial-solution would represent too much redundancy, then it replaces an existing PGP-partial-solution if its expected end-time (the end-time of its last plan-activity) is much less than the existing PGP-partial-solution's, or if their end-times are within the time-cushion specified in the cooperation-parameters and the possible new PGP-partial-solution is begin performed on a less congested node.

To decide whether one node is less congested than another, the PGPlanner examines the PGPs that it knows about. It first looks at any PGPs that are more highly rated than the current PGP, and the node that should complete its activities earlier is less highly used. If no more highly-rated PGPs exist, or if both nodes complete their activities at the same time, then the PGPlanner examines less highly-rated PGPs. Since these may not yet have solution-construction-graphs, the PGPlanner scans them until it finds one where only one of the two nodes participates. If it finds such a PGP, the PGPlanner assumes that the other node is less highly utilized (pursues less highly-rated PGPs) and assigns responsibility for the partial solution to that node. Finally, if the PGPlanner cannot choose between the nodes on this basis (they participate in the same PGPs), then it arbitrarily chooses one of them (the one with the higher number in the current implementation).

Forming the Solution-Construction-Graph from Initial PGP-Partial-Solutions

From the initial set of PGP-partial-solutions, the PGPlanner determines when and where these should be combined to eventually form complete solutions. This is performed by an iterative procedure:

initialize the PGP-partial-solution-set to the initial set

while the PGP-partial-solution-set contains two or more elements

> **for** each pair of entries in the PGP-partial-solution-set, find the earliest time they can be combined and at what node
>
> **for** the pair with the earliest combination time
>
> > **form** a new PGP-partial-solution for their combination and add it to the PGP-partial-solution-set
> >
> > **remove** the PGP-partial-solutions that have been combined from the PGP-partial-solution-set depending on the solution-construction-redundancy

return the single entry in the PGP-partial-solution-set

To find when and where a pair of PGP-partial-solutions could be combined, the PGPlanner uses their end-times, information about communication-delays between nodes, and models of other nodes' time needs for combining results (the expected-integration-costs in the node-model). Using the communication topology, it determines which nodes could possibly receive the two partial solutions to combine. For each of these, the PGPlanner determines the earliest that the possible combining node could receive the partial solutions (based on the end-time of each PGP-partial-solution and communication-delays to send it to the possible node), and adds to that the expected time needed by the node to combine the results. If only one of the possible nodes is capable of combining the results, then this node and the combination time is returned. When several nodes could combine the results, all at about the same time (determined by the time-cushion), then the procedure outlined in the previous section is used to find the least utilized node and assign the integration activities to it. In this case, the procedure takes an additional step before choosing one of the nodes arbitrarily. If the nodes participate equally in the PGPs, then preference is given to nodes that are forming the partial solutions that must be combined: when one of these nodes can receive the other partial solution and form the combination, then less communication is needed. If both such nodes could combine the partial solutions, then one of them is chosen arbitrarily.

For the pair of PGP-partial-solutions that can be combined earliest, the PGPlanner forms a new PGP-partial-solution which gets its node and end-time (combination time) from the information for the pair. Its duration is the node's time needs for combining results and the begin-time is the difference between the end-time and duration. The PGP-partial-solution's result is the combined time-regions of the pair of PGP-partial-solutions. The new PGP-partial-solution points to the two combined PGP-partial-solutions as supporting partial solutions, and they in turn point to it as a supported partial solution. The new PGP-partial-solution is then added to the set of PGP-partial-solutions.

The set of PGP-partial-solutions is further updated by possibly removing the PGP-partial-solutions that have been combined. If these are removed once they have been combined, then the solution-construction-graph becomes a binary tree: each PGP-partial-solution points to only one supported partial solution formed at a single node. This is the simplest representation of constructing a solution, and in a reliable system is a reasonable way of forming overall solutions. However, in less reliable networks, more redundancy may be desirable so that if a node that is to combine partial solutions has hardware failure, other node's can form the desired partial solutions. To allow various degrees of reliability, the PGPlanner removes PGP-partial-solutions from the set only when the number of PGP-partial-solutions it supports equals the solution-construction-redundancy. Because the algorithm ends when a single PGP-partial-solution remains in the set, a PGP-partial-solution is also removed if it is combined in a PGP-partial-solution that represents the same track: once the solution-construction-graph contains several complete solutions, these may be "combined" at nodes so that the solution-construction-graph has a single root (to simplify its representation and use).

To illustrate the formation of a solution-construction-graph, consider the examples shown in Figure 64 based on the three partial solutions that must be combined in the environment shown in Figure 39. In Figure 64a, the solution-construction-redundancy equals 1. Tracks d_1–d_6 and d_7–d_{11} can be combined slightly earlier at node 1 than they can be combined at other nodes, and node 1 forms d_1–d_{11}. Because node 2 lags behind, it should be sent this result which it combines with its own result into d_1–d_{15}. Alternatively, if the time-cushion is larger, the PGPlanner identifies that node 4 can combine results at an acceptably later time (since communication delays affect when it can start combining partial results). As shown in Figure 64b, nodes 1, 2, and 3 send their results to node 4 for integration because node 4 does not otherwise participate in highly-rated PGPs. Node 4 similarly would have been chosen if it had superior combination expertise (KSs) so that it could combine results sooner despite receiving them later. Finally, if the solution-construction-redundancy equals 2, and the time-cushion is small, then the solution-construction-graph is no longer a simple binary tree. Shown in Figure 64c, each of the initial partial solutions are combined at two different nodes. Tracks d_1–d_6 and d_7–d_{11} are combined at both nodes 1 and 3. Track d_1–d_{11} formed at node 1 is sent to node 2, which forms the complete track d_1–d_{15}, but node 2 also sends its partial track d_{12}–d_{15} to node 3 which also forms the complete track.

7.3.4 Determining Domain-Level Communication

To decide what domain-level information (hypotheses) should be communicated among nodes for a given PGP, the PGPlanner considers the goals of cooperation and several attributes of the PGP. First, since the purpose is to integrate partial solutions into complete solutions, the PGPlanner uses the solution-construction-graph to determine what hypotheses should be transmitted, where they should be transmitted, and approximately when they should be transmitted. Besides communicating to form the overall solution, nodes may also communicate about hypotheses for reasons such as to provide predictive information that helps others resolve their uncertainty, or to corroborate results when they wish to verify work on the same data. The PGPlanner therefore examines both a PGP's solution-construction-graph and its plan-activity-map to make intelligent communication decisions based on the goals of cooperation.

If the cooperation-parameter for reliability is greater than that for redundancy, then the PGPlanner scans the PGP's plan-activity-map to find verifying activities (plan-activities at different nodes forming results with common time-region characteristics). When it finds two matching plan-activities, the PGPlanner builds a communication expectation to send the results of the earlier plan-activity to the other node (if possible), or to find a common integrating

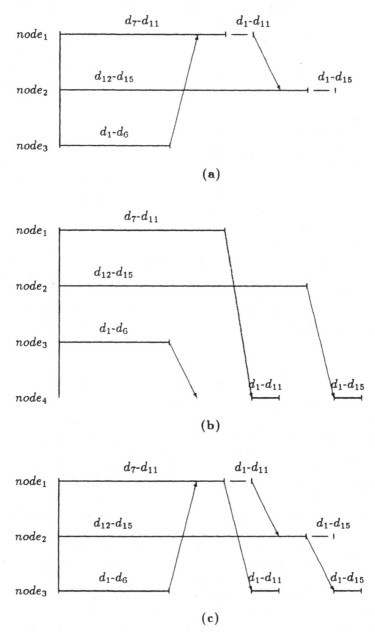

Figure 64: Example Solution-Construction-Graphs.

node where both results are sent and compared. Comparison means that the hypotheses are merged, and their combined belief might be higher (but not in the current implementation of the DVMT which simply assigns the merged hypothesis the maximum belief of the separate hypotheses).

If the cooperation-parameter for predictiveness is greater than the parameter for independence, then the PGPlanner should build communication expectations to send predictive results as well. To find predictive results, the PGPlanner scans the PGP's plan-activity-map to find plan-activities performed by one node that border on those being performed by another node. If these plan-activities are less costly (have shorter duration) than the other node's, then the other node may be facing ambiguity in its data. By sending the bordering result to the other node, this node may provide useful predictive information that helps the other node form results sooner (unless the other node takes longer because it has inferior expertise (KSs)). For example, in the situation in Figure 39, the PGPlanner builds a communication expectation for node 1 to send the hypothesis it forms for d_8–d_9 to node 2, because this predictive information can help node 2 focus its attention on a smaller subset of its data.

When it forms a hypothesis that it could potentially send (a KSI to send the hypothesis is instantiated), a node compares this hypothesis to the communication expectations for its PGPs, and only executes that KSI if the transmission corresponds to some communication expectation. Similarly, given a potential received hypothesis (a KSI to receive the hypothesis is instantiated), the node compares this hypothesis message to the communication expectations for its PGPs, and only executes that KSI if the reception corresponds to an expectation. By being more selective about what hypotheses are sent and received, the nodes reduce the amount of domain-level communication in the network while still exchanging important hypotheses.

7.3.5 Coordinating Current Activities

The PGPlanner must balance two opposing needs: it should avoid planning too far into the future since unpredictable events (failed actions, new data) may cause plans to change, but it should plan far enough so that it can make intelligent decisions about current actions. Planning future actions and interactions (in the form of the solution-construction-graph) is important for making good control decisions. For example, without making estimates about when nodes will form their partial solutions and when they are needed for integration, the PGPlanner cannot recognize situations where it can safely postpone actions for a more highly-rated PGP so that it can take useful actions for a more lowly-rated PGP. The results of these actions may provide predictive information to other nodes, and the earlier this predictive information is supplied, the less time those nodes will waste when forming their partial solutions.

To balance these needs, the PGPlanner may generate several PGPs, but discontinues its activities as soon as it has found current actions for each of the nodes that must be coordinated. It begins with a list of nodes to coordinate, as specified in the meta-level organization. It then steps through the PGPs, starting with the most highly-rated and ending when it has found current actions for each of these nodes. For each PGP, it checks to see whether any information about that PGP has changed since it was last reasoned about (whether any node-plans have more recent creation-times than the PGP's creation-time). If so, the PGPlanner updates the PGP's plan-activity-map, solution-construction-graph, and communication expectations, and resets its creation-time to the current time. It then examines the solution-construction-graph to identify which nodes should be pursuing plans associated with the PGP: if the PGP-partial-solutions associated with a node indicate that the node has activities that it must pursue, then the node is removed from the list of nodes to coordinate. A node has activities that it must pursue if there is a PGP-partial-solution associated with that node whose duration equals the difference between its begin-time and end-time (so the node has no time to spare), or if there is a PGP-partial-solution associated with that node which indicates there is time to spare but none of the less highly-rated PGPs has possible actions that the node could take that would provide predictive information.

After each PGP is successively processed, the PGPlanner may remove some nodes from the list of nodes to coordinate. The PGPlanner stops processing PGPs when the list of nodes becomes empty or the set of PGPs is exhausted, whichever comes first. The PGPlanner therefore generates views of actions and interactions for groups of nodes so that it roughly predicts the current activities of the nodes that it should coordinate. If the PGPlanner is coordinating nodes besides the current node, then it should inform these nodes about relevant PGPs. By sending them PGP information, the coordinating node can give other's a more global view of network activity. Moreover, a node may send PGPs to another node even if it is not coordinating that node: by exchanging PGPs, nodes communicate about how they view network cooperation, and thus can resolve inconsistent views.

7.3.6   Meta-Level Communication of PGPs

The meta-level organization specifies which nodes exchange PGPs. In fact, the communication of PGPs is very similar to the communication of node-plans as described in the previous chapter. First, the PGPlanner decides which PGPs could potentially be transmitted: it scans the queue of PGPs and any that involve other nodes are potential candidates. It then compares the creation-time of each of these PGPs with the record of what versions of the PGP other nodes already have (from the PGP's record:sent-to-nodes information). If any have obsolete versions, then the appropriate PGPs are transmitted.

The PGPlanner constructs a PGP message from a PGP's attributes. Depending on where the PGP is to be sent and how that node is related to the sending node, some information about the PGP may be eliminated. For example, if the sending node is supposed to coordinate the receiving node, then it might send a plan-activity-map whose plan-activities for other nodes have been removed. By doing so, the coordinating node does not give the recipient the ability to form alternative plan-activity-maps (since it does not have all the relevant plan-activities). This decreases the recipient's computation costs (since it is not attempting to reorder network activities) and increases network consistency (since the recipient blindly follows the PGP). On the other hand, if two nodes are peers (with equal coordination authority), then they would exchange complete plan-activity-maps so that they could reason about each other's PGPs in an attempt to converge on consistent PGPs. They exchange PGPs to *negotiate* about network coordination, since they could adopt the most highly-rated PGP or might form a new compromised PGP by combining the best (most up-to-date) information from each.

When a node receives a PGP that does not represent a possible task transfer (see the next section), then it incorporates the PGP into its network-model. The PGPlanner first checks to see if the PGP already exists: it compares PGPs' record information about the names of participating plans to see if any match the received PGP. If not, then a new PGP is formed. If a matching PGP already exists, then the PGPlanner combines the received information with the existing information. First it determines which PGP is more highly rated (where the received PGP's rating is modified based on the recipient node's credibility in the sending node). It then steps through the PGPs' attributes and modifies the existing PGP based on their contents and the more highly-rated PGP. Many of the attributes must match if the PGPs match: the PGP's nodes and its record:node-and-plans, for example. However, for attributes that do not match, the values of the more highly-rated PGP are adopted, including its objectives and rating. If the PGPs have different plan-activity-maps, then the PGPlanner examines their record:plans-and-times attribute to determine which PGP has the more current view of each node's activities. The PGPlanner combines the most current plan-activities from the two PGPs to form a compromised plan-activity-map (of course, the received PGP might be from the same node (a coordinator node) as the existing PGP, and therefore its entire plan-activity-map is more recent and is adopted).

Once the PGPlanner forms a new PGP or modifies an existing PGP from the message, it links this PGP to the local environment. This linking is simply done by using the new PGP's record information about the names of participating plans and, if any of these plans are modeled by node-plans at the recipient node, then these node-plans are updated to point to the PGP and the PGP to point to these node-plans as participants. In addition, the PGPlanner examines the PGP to determine whether any local plans for the current node must be modified. It extracts plan-activities for the current node from the PGP's plan-activity-map, and compares them with the participating local plan's long-term information (time-order and time-predictions). If the PGP represents a reordering of the local plan's intermediate-goals, then the plan is modified.

7.3.7   Coordinating Future Activities: Prediction and Task-Passing

To plan coordinated actions and interactions better, the PGPlanner should anticipate possible future events that might lead to additional subproblems to solve. In addition, it should recognize situations where tasks currently at one node should be transferred to another node to make better use of network resources and expertise. Whether caused by events or deliberate transfers, nodes should coordinate future activities.

Anticipating Future Activities

Subproblems often indicate potential future subproblems. In the DVMT, the PGPlanner extrapolates the objective tracks of PGPs to determine whether a vehicle that is being tracked by some nodes will likely pass through other nodes' sensed areas. This extrapolation is based on the assumption that the vehicle will approximately maintain its current course (although assumptions based on such things as likely maneuvers or terrain to be encountered could also be used). By building a view of a vehicle's future course and identifying when that course intersects the sensed areas of other nodes, the PGPlanner builds future node-plans indicating that these nodes will likely be performing activities to track the vehicle in the future. Because these are future node-plans, the PGPlanner sets certain future attributes. The future:start-time can come from two sources. If the simulated environment has signals detected at known intervals, then the PGPlanner simply computes when a node will begin receiving data. To enlarge the range of problems that the system can study, however, the start time can instead be retrieved directly from the environment file which specifies when data will be simulated to arrive. This flexibility allows the user to simulate data arriving in bursts or out of order, and the PGPlanner as currently implemented uses this information to determine the start time of a predicted future node-plan.

Future node-plans point to the PGPs that triggered their creation. The PGPlanner forms plan-activities for predicted activities, so that when reordering the PGP's plan-activity-map it avoids giving responsibility for some tasks to a node that will soon receive other important data to process. However, the cost of extrapolating tracks and forming future node-plans can be high and possibly unnecessary, since other unexpected changes to the nodes' problem solving may cause PGPs to be changed over time: rather than anticipating future node-plans, the PGPlanner might be better off simply reacting to these node-plans when the data actually arrives. In the current implementation, therefore, the PGPlanner does not typically generate future node-plans in the process of coordinating nodes' current activities. When nodes exchange tasks, however, this investment of time is more worthwhile. Because exchanging tasks can be a costly process (both in computation and communication), the PG-

Planner should determine whether a node that is currently underutilized (not participating in important PGPs) is likely to remain underutilized long enough to perform tasks for other nodes. Tasks should not be passed to a node that will soon receive data from its sensors that it will have to process, because either it will not process this data in a timely manner or else it will postpone the received task (possibly making the exchange of information unnecessary).

Task-Passing

Before it can transfer tasks, a node must solve the decomposition problem. In some applications, a node might use only local knowledge such as static procedures for how to *always* decompose certain types of tasks. More generally, however, a node cannot intelligently decompose a task without knowledge about other nodes, so that it can decide whether to pursue the task (it might be unimportant relative to other nodes' tasks) and, if so, what nodes might be able to assist it. Before task-passing begins, therefore, nodes could share local views. In our framework, nodes form and exchange node-plans so that some nodes develop more global views. These activities are shown graphically in Figure 65, steps 1 and 2. Note that these steps are optional, but they help a node make better decisions about decomposing and announcing tasks.

In step 3 (Figure 65), a node steps through its PGPs, which can represent local activities or activities of several nodes if steps 1 and 2 were taken. The node's PGPlanner checks the solution-construction-graph to detect a bottleneck-node that expects to finish its partial result much later (greater than the min-task-duration cooperation-parameter) than other nodes working on the PGP. A node working alone on a task longer than min-task-duration is always a bottleneck. In Figure 66a, node 2 is a bottleneck because it expects to finish its activities (to process data d_5–d_{13}) much later than node 1. If it finds a bottleneck-node, the node initiates task-passing if it is responsible for coordinating the bottleneck-node, based on the meta-level organization. Thus, in a network with a centralized coordinating node, that node initiates task-passing, while in a broadcast organization where each node has equal responsibility, the bottleneck-node itself initiates task-passing. Unlike protocols where only nodes with tasks can initiate task-passing, our framework permits a node to have an "agent" negotiate for it.

The initiating node's PGPlanner forms a task to pass, where the task is to generate some piece of the bottleneck-node's partial result, represented as a sequence of plan-activities. Before it decides on a decomposition, the PGPlanner scans its network-model to identify underutilized nodes that might perform this task. A node is underutilized if it participates only in lowly-rated PGPs or is idle (indicated by an idle node-plan), and if the PGPlanner does not anticipate any future node-plans that could interfere with the passed task. Thus, the PGPlanner avoids passing tasks that could interfere with a node's responsibilities to process its own data, but if the expected tasks fail to materialize or are

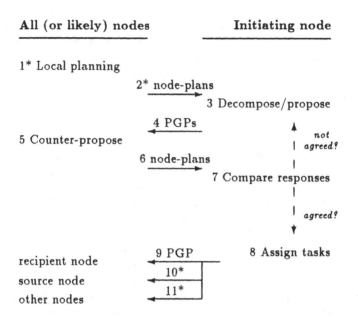

The major steps in task-passing are shown. Steps marked with a * are optional.

Figure 65: Task-Passing Steps.

unimportant, then the PGPlanner can reinitiate task-passing to this node.

When the PGPlanner finds underutilized nodes, or when the meta-level organization specifies that nodes should attempt to pass tasks despite incomplete network views, then the PGPlanner forms a task to pass from the bottleneck-node's activities. It roughly divides the pending plan-activities (some might already be complete) in half, and those that were to be performed by the node later are grouped together into the task to pass. For example, given the situation in Figure 66a, the PGPlanner decides that it would reduce the bottleneck by assigning plan-activities to process data d_{10}–d_{13} elsewhere (Figure 66b). Note that the node receiving the passed task could later divide it and transfer half, so as to decompose the overall subproblem into pieces for every available node. In the future, we hope to modify these mechanisms to instead let the PGPlanner divide the bottleneck activities into an arbitrary number of roughly equal portions for each possibly available node.

When it has a task to send and potential recipients, the PGPlanner copies the task's plan-activities and modifies these copies by altering their begin and end times based on expectations about when a recipient node could pursue them (considering communication delays). It also changes the name of the

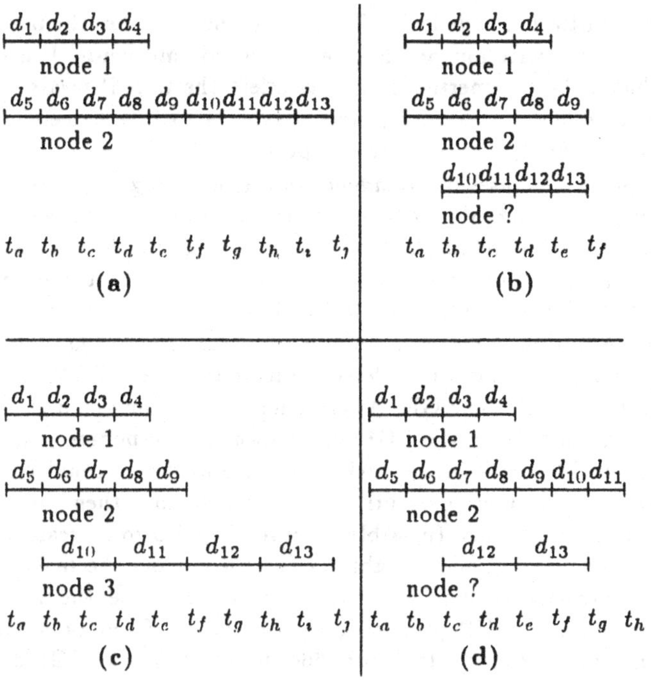

In (a) node 2 is a bottleneck-node, and (b) indicates a possible transfer of tasks to an unknown node. Node 3 provides the counter-proposal in (c), and this triggers the new proposal in (d).

Figure 66: Task-Passing Example.

node performing these plan-activities to a special *unassigned* marker and inserts these new plan-activities into the PGP's plan-activity-map. For example, in Figure 66b, an unknown node is expected to start the transferred task at time t_b (because of communication delays). The PGPlanner also modifies the PGP's future attributes: the to-nodes are set to the possible recipients, the respond-to attribute is set to the current node (initiating the task-passing), and the response-label is set to the local name for the PGP. The modified PGP is sent to the potential task recipients or broadcast if specified in the meta-level organization (Figure 65 step 4).

When it gets the PGP (step 5), a recipient node's PGPlanner checks the future:to-nodes attribute to determine if it should submit a bid or counter-proposal. If so, it extracts the unassigned plan-activities and builds a node-plan from them with this node's name replacing the special marker. The PGPlanner then examines its current set of PGPs and node-plans to determine the earliest that it could begin working on the plan-activities. During this computation, it also uses its own information to form future node-plans since it might have information the initiating node lacks. The PGPlanner modifies the plan-activities to avoid interfering with any actual or expected commitments. It also modifies them if it has or lacks expertise that may affect the time it needs to complete them. In Figure 66c, for example, node 3 expects to take twice as much time for each plan-activity because it lacks expertise.

The recipient node uses its confidence in the initiating node (from the meta-level organization) to modify the future node-plan's rating, sets the future:start-time as the begin time of the first plan-activity, sets the future:planned-by as the received PGP's future:respond-to node, and sets the triggering-PGP to the received PGP's future:response-label. It sends the resultant future node-plan to the initiating node as a counter-proposal (Figure 65 step 6). As it receives node-plan messages that have a future:triggering-PGP, the initiating node stores them with the PGP. When it has waited long enough (depending on communication delays), the PGPlanner scans the responses (step 7) to find which nodes could complete the task earliest, and if any could complete the task sooner than the node currently with the task can, then the PGPlanner decides to transfer the task (possibly to several nodes to increase reliability). Otherwise, the initiating node might give up on passing the task, or it might further negotiate over problem decomposition. To negotiate, the initiating node modifies and sends a PGP proposing that nodes do fewer or different plan-activities (returns to step 3). In Figure 66d, for example, the PGPlanner might propose to transfer a smaller task covering data d_{12}–d_{13} (note that the extra round of negotiation further delays the task's expected starting time). Because PGPs indicate why and how nodes could cooperate, nodes need not simply accept or reject tasks, but instead can engage in multistage negotiation [Conry *et al.*, forthcoming]. Alternatively, the larger task could be passed, and node 3 could then subcontract out parts of it to other nodes.

Once an assignment has been negotiated, the initiating node updates the PGP to represent the assignment (Figure 65 step 8). It sends this PGP to the chosen node(s) (step 9), and either sends the task (data corresponding to the subproblem to solve) if it has it, or sends the PGP to the source node (that has the task) so it will send it (step 10). The node that sends the task also keeps a copy in case communication errors, node failures, or poor coordination cause a need to reassign the task. Note that the task-assigning PGP might include a solution-construction-graph to indicate where the result of the task should be transmitted. However, once the recipient node has the task, it can negotiate over result-sharing as if the task had been locally developed.

The initiating node might also send the PGP to unchosen nodes, depending on the meta-level organization. Whether they explicitly receive the PGP (Figure 65 step 11), or they learn that they were not chosen because the task does not arrive when expected, the unchosen nodes remove the future node-plan they formed and adjust other future node-plans. For example, if it had responded to several PGPs and had modified plan-activities based on possibly receiving tasks, then once a task is awarded elsewhere the PGPlanner may modify and transmit other future node-plans to indicate that it could pursue tasks earlier. This way, nodes can respond to multiple requests and update their responses when tasks are assigned, although because of communication delays the updated information may not reach an initiating node before the task is assigned and a less than optimal assignment might be made. In a network with communication delays, potentially errorful channels, and asynchronous activities at the different nodes, such incoherence is unavoidable.

In summary, the task-passing mechanisms essentially go through basic contracting steps: a node builds a task that could be passed elsewhere, it sends out bid-requests (in the form of PGPs) to those nodes that it believes could potentially do the tasks, it receives bids (future node-plans) from those nodes, it chooses the best bid(s) (if any), and it stimulates the passing of tasks between nodes (by transmitting the PGP to the source and recipient nodes). Our current mechanisms are limited in the task-passing situations they can recognize: they cannot find task swaps between two equally-loaded nodes to make better use of each node's resources and they cannot pass resources and expertise among nodes. However, the important thing to recognize is that contracting is really a type of partial global planning because it is a PGP shared by two (or more) nodes indicating how they can work together by exchanging tasks, so the same representation that allows nodes to coordinate their current activities also allows them to identify and coordinate future activities caused by passing tasks.

7.3.8 Putting It All Together

To understand how the partial global planning, local planning, and problem solving mechanisms all work together, we examine the activities of a node through a node execution. The basic activities of the node can be broken down into four major phases: incorporating new information, reasoning about local and network activity to find a local action, transmitting information that affects coordination, and pursuing the local action.

Incorporating Information

The node starts by processing new domain-level information (from sensors or other nodes): the local planner updates the clustering hierarchy and changes the local plans based on any new or modified alternative-goals (detailed in Chapter 4). The PGPlanner then updates the node's network-model based on received coordination information and on changes to local plans. Received node-plans and PGPs are incorporated into node-models and the network-model respectively, as previously described. In addition, any PGPs that represent possible task transfers are processed (possibly triggering new future node-plans to be sent back), as are PGPs indicated agreed upon transfers (possibly triggering the node to send subproblem data).

If a new local plan is formed, a node-plan summarizing that plan is generated and added to the node's model of itself. If highly-rated enough, this node-plan may later be transmitted to other nodes. An existing local plan may be updated either because new data arrives or because the short-term actions of the plan are modified (actions to repair the plan or to work on the next i-goal). In either case, the plan's corresponding node-plan may or may not be altered, depending on the significance of the change to the local plan. Significance of change is determined from a more global perspective: the PGPlanner examines the PGPs that the node-plan participates in and determines whether the change to the local plan will substantially affect the activities of nodes and their expected interactions. A change to a local plan should be propagated to that plan's node-plan if: the objectives of the plan have changed in *unexpected* ways (ways that were not predicted by a PGP); the order of activities being pursued by the plan have changed (so that expected interactions may be affected); or the predicted time when partial solutions will be formed deviates substantially from what is expected in the PGP's solution-construction-graph.

The first reason for propagating changes handles the situation where new data, especially new sensor data, arrives at the node. If the possible solution that the plan is working toward changes unexpectedly, then it is important that network-models reflect this change. However, sometimes a plan's objectives change in expected ways. A node that is expected to integrate two partial solutions (based on a PGP's solution-construction-graph) should not update its node-plans and network-model when it receives the expected partial solutions and modifies its local plans to find actions to integrate them. Only when the changes to its local plans are not predicted by PGPs should the node update its node-plans and transmit these updated node-plans to others.

The second reason for propagating changes is when the local planner has changed the order in which activities will be pursued. Since PGPs are based on expectations about the order in which nodes will generate partial results, it is important that network-models reflect any changes to such an ordering. However, if the order is simply extended with expected new information (such as a partial solution to integrate), then the change is expected and the network-model need not be updated.

The final reason for propagating changes in local plans to node-plans is generally the most common. Node-plans and their resulting PGPs involve temporal expectations based on rough predictions of likely durations of activities (see Chapter 4). As a plan is pursued, the actual durations of activities often deviate from the expected durations, and the predictions for remaining activities might be updated. The PGPlanner must decide whether the changes could affect network activity by comparing the local plan's new predictions with the predictions recorded in the node-plan. By using the time-cushion as the definition of "significant" time, the PGPlanner determines whether the deviation is significant. If so, then the node-plan is updated; otherwise, the minor differences are not considered important from the more global perspective. The time-cushion thus determines how and whether nodes will respond to the feedback [Arbib, 1972] provided by the node's actual performance. Nodes can react to changes and modify how they coordinate appropriately, but overcompensating for minor variations can lead to oscillating behavior where nodes bounce from one way of coordinating to another instead of converging on a stable view. Since planning and execution are interleaved in our system, such oscillations degrade performance but eventually stop, because with each oscillation some problem solving occurs so that eventually nodes complete their activities. A smaller time-cushion leads to more changes to node-plans and network-models, possibly causing oscillations and increasing communication and computation overhead as nodes recompute how they should coordinate. A larger time-cushion, on the other hand, reduces oscillations and costs but at the possible price of having the network generate solutions in a less effective manner because nodes were less responsive to changes. The time-cushion thus represents how nodes balance predictability and responsiveness.

Reasoning About Local Plans and PGPs

The PGPlanner updates the PGPs if the network-model has changed due to received information. It steps through the PGPs as described previously until it has found current activities for each of the nodes that it should plan for based on the meta-level organization. It records which PGP each node is pursuing, and can thus return the PGP for the local node. Through the pointers between PGPs, node-plans, and local plans, the PGPlanner finds the local plan associated with the PGP. The local planner then works with this plan: it finds the next action to pursue, possibly updating, repairing, or aborting the plan in the process. If it successfully finds an action (with a KSI), the local planner triggers the KSI for execution. When local planning must further alter the plan, then once the local plan is changed the PGPlanner once again goes through the steps of updating network-models and PGPs if necessary. The control mechanisms thus cycle through local planning and PGPlanning (although depending on the changes caused by local planning, PGPlanning may do very little) until the next action can be found. As a failsoft mechanism, moreover, if after trying all the PGPs the node still cannot find an action, the PGPlanner drops out of this loop and the node simply pursues its best local plan. Similarly, if unable to find a local plan to pursue, the local planner drops out of the loop and the node simply pursues the most highly-rated KSI.

Meta-level Communication

Once the next action for the node has been found, the PGPlanner transmits to appropriate nodes any new and freshly modified PGPs and node-plans, including node-plans that it formed in response to PGPs that request task-passing information. The PGPlanner also invokes the task-passing mechanisms to identify any new opportunities for transferring tasks and to find any previously transmitted PGPs that have received responses. If the PGPlanner finds suitable responses, the tasks are awarded as previously discussed.

Problem Solving

Finally, the KS associated with the next action is invoked and the node takes the next step toward solving the problem.

Summary

The sequence of control activities that a node invokes to find another action is substantial and possibly costly. At times the overhead of local and partial global planning is simply not worth the cost when it steals too much computation time from actual problem solving. The mechanisms have been developed so that they can be scaled down: the node can bypass the partial global planning or both the local and partial global planning mechanisms, and fall back on the simpler mechanisms which could possibly be more cost effective (achieve acceptable control with much less overhead). In the next chapter, we evaluate the mechanisms and explore some cases where less sophistication is better.

7.3.9   Detailed Example

This example illustrates the internal reasoning performed by the local planner and PGPlanner when a single coordinating node identifies a PGP for an important overall solution, recognizes how nodes should pursue their local activities and exchange results to work as an effective team, and distributes these PGPs to coordinate nodes. Experiments covering issues such as pursuing more than one solution, using different meta-level organizations, working in more dynamic situations, coordinating larger networks, passing tasks, using heterogeneous nodes, and improving reliability are discussed in the next chapter.

The example has the environment of Figure 39 with four cooperating nodes that track a vehicle passing among them. We assume in this environment that: each node can communicate with any other node with a delay of two time units; each KS execution takes one time unit; the data arrives over the first 15 time intervals so that problem solving begins at time 16; and that nodes have the same KSs (expertise). The meta-level organization assigns the principal coordination responsibilities to node 4 (since it has no data of its own). Nodes 1, 2, and 3 send node-plans to node 4, which forms PGPs and sends them back to the other nodes. The time-cushion in this experiment is 0 time units, so that nodes update and transmit their node-plans any time their local plans deviate from the PGP expectations in any way. Finally, the min-task-duration is set very high (to 100) so that nodes do not pass tasks.

At time 16, each node's local planner generates plans to process the data local to that node: node 1 has one plan to form the track d'_1–d'_5 and another plan to form the track d_4–d_{12}; node 2 has the plan to form the track d_{10}–d_{15}; node 3 has the plan to form track d_1–d_6; and node 4 has no local plans. This discussion ignores the lowly-rated plans for unlikely vehicle types. The PGPlanner at each node summarizes these local plans into node-plans and adds them to the network-model. It forms PGPs based solely on the local node-plans (each node's initial view of group activity is just its own activity), and pursues the most highly-rated PGP which is equal to the most highly-rated local plan. The PGPlanner at each node except 4 transmits its node-plans to node 4.

At time 18, node 4 receives these node-plans and identifies that there are two PGPs in the network: to form the overall track d_1–d_{15}, and for node 1 to form the track d_1'–d_5'. The first of these PGPs is more highly rated (since three nodes participate in it), and so the PGPlanner starts with that PGP. It constructs the plan-activity-map by interleaving the plan-activity-maps of each of the participating node-plans. For example, from node 1 it received a node-plan without a plan-activity-map (because locally node 1 is pursuing its other plan based on the more strongly-sensed data d_1'–d_5'). However, the node-plan does indicate that node 1 intends to start at sensed time 4 and work across to sensed time 12. It also has rough predictions about how long node 1 expects to take for each of these activities. With this information, the PGPlanner builds a plan-activity-map for node 1, where it assumes node 1 will start the first activity when it becomes aware of the PGP (which will be two time-units from now since the PGP must be sent back to node 1). By assuming the next plan-activity will start after the previous one ends, the PGPlanner constructs the plan-activity-map for node 1. On the other hand, node 4 receives plan-activity-maps for the node-plans from nodes 2 and 3: since these plans are currently being pursued at those nodes, the PGPlanner at those nodes constructed and sent the plan-activity-maps with those node-plans.

The PGPlanner interleaves the plan-activities in order of their end-times, so that it can identify the order in which results will be completed. Since this is the most highly-rated PGP, it need not check against other PGPs to find conflicts. The PGPlanner therefore next applies the mechanisms for reordering plan-activities to find better coordination. The cooperation-parameters are such that nodes assign higher costs to actions that are redundant or that generate less predictive results. The reordering sequence is shown in Figure 67. The initial ordering of actions for each node and their costs is shown in Figure 67a. The PGPlanner swaps less costly plan-activities for more costly plan-activities for a node, as shown in Figure 67b, and modifies the begin and end times of the plan-activities to reflect their change of position. The PGPlanner computes the costs of each plan-activity in this new ordering, and the total cost of the new sequence is less than the initial sequence. The process is then repeated, resulting in the ordering shown in Figure 67c, which is better (has lower cost) than the previous ordering. In this ordering, no more costly actions precede less costly actions at the same node, so the algorithm terminates and the ordering is returned as the chosen reordering of node activities.

Node 1	actions	d_4	d_5	d_6	d_7	d_8	d_9	d_{10}	d_{11}	d_{12}	
	costs	286	281	276	171	166	161	276	261	266	total = 2144
Node 2	actions	d_{10}	d_{11}	d_{12}	d_{13}	d_{14}	d_{15}				
	costs	493	538	533	408	413	418				total = 2803
Node 3	actions	d_1	d_2	d_3	d_4	d_5	d_6				
	costs	267	272	277	412	427	442				total = 2097
											sum = 7044

(a)

Node 1	actions	d_9	d_8	d_7	d_{11}	d_{12}	d_{10}	d_6	d_5	d_4	
	costs	115	130	145	215	220	210	320	345	370	total = 2070
Node 2	actions	d_{13}	d_{14}	d_{15}	d_{10}	d_{12}	d_{11}				
	costs	372	377	382	537	507	523				total = 2698
Node 3	actions	d_1	d_2	d_3	d_4	d_5	d_6				
	costs	246	251	256	361	366	371				total = 1851
											sum = 6619

(b)

Node 1	actions	d_9	d_8	d_7	d_{10}	d_{11}	d_{12}	d_6	d_5	d_4	
	costs	114	129	144	209	214	219	319	344	369	total = 2061
Node 2	actions	d_{13}	d_{14}	d_{15}	d_{12}	d_{11}	d_{10}				
	costs	371	376	381	506	522	536				total = 2692
Node 3	actions	d_1	d_2	d_3	d_4	d_5	d_6				
	costs	245	250	255	360	365	370				total = 1845
											sum = 6598

(c)

Figure 67: Example of Plan-Activity-Map Reordering.

With the reordered PGP plan-activity-map, the PGPlanner next forms the solution-construction-graph. Because the cooperation-parameters lead the PG-Planner to avoid redundancy, it steps through the plan-activity-map and groups together plan-activities for each node that have not yet been developed at other nodes. In this case, node 1 expects to form d_7–d_{12}, node 2 d_{13}–d_{15}, and node 3 d_1–d_6. The PGPlanner then considers each pair of these and finds that the PGP-partial-solutions from nodes 1 and 3 can be combined earliest, and they should be combined at node 1. This new PGP-partial-solution could then be combined at node 2 with node 2's PGP-partial-solution. The PGPlanner also determines that, in the only other PGP there is no possibility for predictive results to be formed earlier (since only one node participates in it). Thus, it decides that each of the participating nodes should pursue activities for the shared PGP first.

Next, the PGPlanner builds the set of communication expectations. It uses the solution-construction-graph to recognize that the result d_1–d_6 should be passed from node 3 to node 1, and that the result d_1–d_{12} should be passed from node 1 to node 2. The PGPlanner also scans the plan-activity-map to recognize any additional communication that could help network problem solving. Because the cooperation-parameters indicate that providing predictive information is more important than refraining (to improve independence), the PGPlanner scans down the plan-activity-map and recognizes that node 1 will develop results in an area bordering on node 2 (since their sensors overlap) and that the duration of its activities in these areas is substantially less than node 2's (indicating that perhaps node 2 could use predictive information). The PGPlanner finds the earliest partial track that node 1 will develop that borders on node 2's information: since node 1 will work on d_9 and d_8 and form d_8–d_9, the PGPlanner builds an expectation for node 1 to transmit this result to node 2. If the cooperation-parameters had indicated that verification was desirable (instead of avoiding redundancy), then the PGPlanner would also scan the plan-activity-map to find the earliest cases where duplicate tracks are formed and would build communication expectations to transmit these (so that the recipient node(s) could verify results as soon as possible, and if the results are incompatible the plans can be abandoned as soon as possible).

At this point, the PGPlanner has completed the PGP, and must do two more things. First, it should modify any relevant local plans based on the reordered plan-activity-map. Since node 4 has no participating plans for the PGP, it does not need to change anything. Second, the PGPlanner must transmit the PGP to the relevant nodes, which in this meta-level organization are nodes 1, 2, and 3. Instead of transmitting the PGP as is, node 4's PGPlanner modifies the plan-activity-map differently for each message so that it only sends a node the plan-activities for that node. As a result, the recipient node cannot reason about alternative orderings. This helps enforce consistent views, and reduces communication overhead (a smaller plan-activity-map is sent) and computation overhead (since the recipient does not explore alternatives).

Finally, node 4's PGPlanner examines any other PGPs since it has not yet found current activities for itself. Since it has no local plans, it does not find such a PGP. Once it exhausts the set of PGPs, it completes its activities. No local plan (or KSI) is invoked at node 4.

The PGP messages arrive at time 20. Before they arrive, some nodes have already changed their node-plans. Node 1 has finished developing d'_1 and begins working on d'_2, but finds that its predictions about how long each i-goal (other than d'_1) will take were off by one time unit because they did not include time for integrating new data with previously formed results (d'_1 was formed before any other results and so did not have to be integrated). Similarly, the predictions made by node 3 were off by one time unit. Node 2 has not changed its plans yet since each of its i-goals takes so much longer. Because the time-cushion is 0, the changes to local plans made by nodes 1 and 3 cause them to propagate these changes to their node-plans, and these node-plans are sent at time 19 to node 4, where they will arrive at time 21.

At time 20, the PGP messages from node 4 arrive at nodes 1–3. Each node incorporates the received PGP into its queue of PGPs, and it links the PGP with the local environment. In particular, each finds out which local node-plans and local plans participate in the PGP. When the PGPlanner for each of these nodes begins its activities, it finds the new PGP information. Because it only receives plan-activities for itself and has no node-plans for other nodes, the PGPlanner does not attempt to change the received PGP's attributes, but instead follows the received plan-activity-map, solution-construction-graph, and communication expectations. However, because its local plans participate in the PGP, each node does update its local plans if necessary. The PGPlanner at node 1 alters the plan to form d_4–d_{12} so that its long-term time-order is now (9 8 7 10 11 12 6 5 4), as indicated by the PGP. Similarly, the PGPlanner at node 2 alters its plan so that it works on data at times 13, 14, and 15 first. Node 3 does not change its local plan. Both nodes 1 and 2 propagate the changes to their node-plans and transmit these updated node-plans to node 4.

At time 21, node 4 receives the node-plans that nodes 1 and 3 sent at time 19. The node-plan from node 1 is not part of the highly-rated PGP and so does not affect it. However, the node-plan from node 3 indicates that node 3 will take longer than previously expected to form its results. The PGPlanner checks to see if the plan-activity-map should be reordered and finds that the nodes should not change the order of their activities but that the relative times they will complete activities has changed. These changes affect the solution-construction-graph because now node 1 is expected to form its PGP-partial-solution earlier than node 3. The solution-construction-graph and the communication expectations are altered so that now node 1 sends its result d_7–d_{12} to node 3 which then sends d_1–d_{12} to node 2. This modified PGP is then sent by node 4 to nodes 1, 2, and 3, which receive it at time 23.

Node 4 receives node-plans from nodes 1 and 2 at time 22, indicating that they have changed the order of their i-goals. These updated node-plans correspond the node 4's expectations, and node 4's PGPlanner does not alter the highly-rated PGP based on them.

At time 23, nodes 1–3 receive the modified PGP from node 4. They incorporate this PGP, which does not alter their local plans since their plan-activities are not reordered. Node 1 also has completed developing d_9 and, when it plans for d_8, it discovers that its predictions were off by one time unit for the same reasons as discussed above. It therefore updates the corresponding node-plan and sends this off to node 4.

Node 4 receives this node-plan at time 25, and once again changes the PGP's plan-activity-map because the relative times that results will be formed have changed. The solution-construction-graph and communication expectations are changed back again to their initial values: node 3 sends its partial result to node 1, which sends their combined results to node 2. This updated PGP is sent to nodes 1–3, which receive it at time 27.

At time 29, the predictive result d_8–d_9 is received by node 2. It had been formed by node 1 at time 27 and transmitted because it met the communication expectations. With this new information, node 2 makes major revisions to its local plans. It divides its original plan that involved a large amount of ambiguity into two plans: it modifies the existing plan to only develop results that are consistent with the received result (track the same type of vehicle) and forms a new plan to develop the other possible results. It updates its existing node-plan to reflect the change and forms a new node-plan for the new local plan. Both of these are sent to node 4.

At time 31, node 4 receives this information from node 2 and changes the PGP appropriately. Because node 2 has changed its plan to process a more selective subset of the data at each time frame, the predicted durations for its plan-activities are substantially reduced. Its plan-activities are expected to complete earlier and are moved to earlier parts of the PGP's plan-activity-map. The solution-construction-graph is altered as a result: now node 2 is expected to process data in d_{12} before node 1 does, so node 1 should form track d_7-d_{11} while node 2 forms $d_{12}-d_{15}$. In fact, node 2 should form its PGP-partial-solution before node 1, so the solution-construction-graph and the communication expectations now have node 3 sending d_1-d_6 to node 1 and then node 2 sending $d_{12}-d_{15}$ also to node 1, so that node 1 is now responsible for forming the overall result. The modified PGP is sent to the nodes which receive it at time 33.

The nodes follow this PGP until they form the solution at time 45. For most of this time, the local plans do not change. However, when first node 3 and then node 2 finish their partial solutions, they begin exploring their other local plans (to develop tracks for other vehicle types). Because the better plans have been completed, these local plans now become the most highly-rated local plans and these nodes begin sending node-plans to node 4. Node 4 cannot combine them into a larger PGP (since the node-plan that would join them would come from node 1 which is still working on the more highly-rated plans). As a result, the communication of node-plans and PGPs peaks in the early stages of problem solving (when nodes are developing an initial cooperative strategy) and at the late stages of problem solving (when some nodes are looking for alternative ways to cooperate since they have fulfilled their initial activities). The amount of coordination activity drops off during the middle stages of problem solving in this environment.

When the time-cushion is set to 1 in this environment, the amount of meta-level communication decreases: where before the nodes updated node-plans when the predicted duration of i-goals was off by 1 time unit, this deviation is now acceptable. The result is that fewer updates to node-plans are made and this reduces the coordination overhead, but the nodes might not interact as crisply as before. The larger time-cushion also affects integration. Node 4 can combine the results from nodes 1 and 3, but because it must wait for both it generally integrates the results 1 or 2 time units later. With the time-cushion equal to 0, node 4 is not called on to do the integration. However, with the larger time-cushion the PGPlanner recognizes that node 4 can form results soon enough and that it is underutilized (does not otherwise participate in important PGPs). In this case, node 4 is chosen to integrate results so that its computational resources can be used more effectively.

When the example environment with this variation is run, the same activities occur at times 16 and 18, except now the PGP calls for nodes 1–3 to all send their partial results to node 4 for integration. At time 19, the changes to local plan predictions are not propagated to the node-plans, so these are not sent to node 4. Nodes 1–3 receive the PGP at time 20, nodes 1 and 2 change their local plans accordingly, and the modified node-plans are sent to node 4. The PGP is *not* changed at time 21 since node 4 does not get updated node-plans from 1 or 3. Node 4 receives node-plans from 1 and 2 at time 22 but as before these do not alter the PGP. The nodes do not exchange PGPs and node-plans until node 2 alters its local plans based on the predictive information from node 1. The altered node-plan is sent to node 4, which updates the PGP and sends it back to the other nodes, where it still expects results to be integrated at node 4 but now node 2 provides results including d_{12} instead of node 1. The nodes follow this PGP, and the overall solution is formed at node 4 at time 46— slightly later than in the earlier version, but in this case the communication and computation overhead was reduced because less PGPlanning was needed. The costs and benefits of changing the time-cushion are more completely explored in the experiments of the next chapter.

7.4   Generalizing

A general view of coordination mechanisms can be misleading because, from a high-level, many crucial details might be missed—details that affect whether the mechanisms do, in fact, represent a viable approach in a practical system. By describing in detail how the partial global planning concepts have been implemented in the DVMT, we have attempted to make more clear what they do and how they do it, addressing issues not only in how concepts translate to particular mechanisms but also the issues we faced and the decisions we made while implementing these mechanisms. Because we cannot foresee all possible variations of domains and implementations, we have detailed our experience so that others can hopefully extract aspects of the mechanisms that they need. However, in this section we attempt to generalize the mechanisms and the approach as a first step in helping others implement partial global planning mechanisms in different systems, and we suggest ways to apply partial global planning in other domains.

7.4.1   Generalizing the PGPlanner

The Data Structures.   The whole point of representation in the planner and the PGPlanner is finding the right level of detail, and our particular decisions about what the right level is has been biased by our problem domain. In a closely-coupled environment where communication is fast and inexpensive, nodes might cooperate effectively by coordinating specific actions: they could essentially form a global schedule of actions to follow. In an environment with extremely loose-coupling, nodes might communicate only about overall local plans, so that they can decide how the final results of a plan might affect network activity. Our view rests between these extremes, because we want nodes to coordinate larger groups of actions (intermediate-goals) within plans, without coordinating any specific actions. No matter what the particular aspects of the environment are, however, the data structures for control need the ability to represent activities at different levels of detail: a node needs a lot of detail about its own activities (to choose a specific action to achieve its goals), and less detail about the basic activities of others (what their goals are and how their actions to achieve these goals could affect this node).

Our PGPs allow a node to represent information at different levels of detail, so that it has suitable views for the different decisions it must make. For example, to recognize how nodes should cover data that they both sense (whether to avoid duplication of effort or to verify each others results), they need to have a rough view of what data each will be working on and when. This view is provided by the plan-activity-map. On the other hand, to decide how they should interact to combine individual results, they do not need details about the order in which each constructs its local result, but instead simply need to know when the desired local result will be formed. This view is provided by the solution-construction-graph. Both of these data structures provide information at the right level of detail for making some control decisions, and the purpose of the PGP representation is to give nodes these different views.

In more general terms, a PGP contains some representation of group objectives. In the vehicle monitoring case, this is where vehicles are being tracked and what types of vehicles they are. In other domains, the objective might be to cooperatively construct a bridge, to cooperatively explore a region, or to cooperatively diagnose a network fault. A PGP also contains a plan-activity-map to represent the concurrent activities of nodes. Depending on the environment, these activities could be simple actions or they could each be complex sequences of actions. Because the nodes may interact infrequently (rather than after each activity), the PGP represents their interactions in a separate structure—the solution-construction-graph. Finally, because nodes may want to explore possible future cooperative activities (such as transferring tasks so that new nodes can join in important group activities), the PGP allows nodes to represent possible future activities so that they can reason about how these could influence local and network activity.

The other important data structure used for partial global planning is the cooperation-parameters structure. The choice of important cooperation parameters is in many ways domain-dependent, influenced by which ways of cooperating are desirable (or undesirable) in a domain. However, the choices made for our implementation also have a certain degree of task independence. In any domain, for example, cooperating agents need information about the importance of duplicating activities (redundancy and reliability), of helping each other out (predictiveness), of staying out of each other's way (independence and diversity), and of committing to group activity versus adapting to changed local views (time-cushion). *What* information is represented in the cooperation-parameters, though by no means exhaustive of all possible information, is therefore fairly general. *How* the information is represented—as numerical parameters—is less likely to be the best representation in other domains. In fact, the PGPlanner in the vehicle monitoring domain could make better decisions if this information had a richer, symbolic representation, but for the purposes of developing an initial implementation, the numeric view has been satisfactory.

Plan-Activity-Map Generation and Manipulation. Representations similar to the plan-activity-map have been used to represent concurrent activities in other domains [Allen, 1983; Allen, 1984; Cheeseman, 1984; Dean, 1986; Vere, 1983], and using begin and end-times for activities to coordinate nodes is a generally useful mechanism (so long as time t means about the same thing to one node as it does to another). Moreover, given a representation of local plans that allows nodes to summarize and selectively exchange information (as discussed in Chapter 6), our method of generating the plan-activity-map using expected durations of activities is very straightforward.

The mechanisms for manipulating plan-activity-maps to avoid interference can also be generalized. Scanning through a pair of plan-activity-maps to find cases where they expect a node to be doing two things at once means simply comparing intervals for activities of the same node. When such a situation occurs, then activities are shifted to other times by altering their begin and end times. The techniques for moving activities of particular duration around within a window of time is a common problem in scheduling [Stankovic *et al.*, 1985] and in planning [Vere, 1983]. However, using plans about likely interactions between cooperating nodes to determine the extents of time-windows is still a little understood topic that our mechanisms contribute to exploring.

Finally, our mechanisms for reordering activities find a cost for each and iteratively move them around to minimize total cost. Cooperating nodes must have a basis for considering some activities better (less costly) than others based on how the activities fit into the overall network activities. Our mechanisms represent this preference numerically and simply move better activities to earlier times, postponing worse activities until later (if ever). Assuming that a suitable rating function (combining all important considerations into a single value) can be found in other domains, the hill-climbing algorithm used in the current implementation could be more generally applied. In our future research, we hope to improve on these techniques to find an alternative way to reorder activities (based on symbolic representations of their utility) that is more intelligent and less costly. It is important to note that the choice of algorithms used to reorder the activities is irrelevant to the rest of the PGPlanning mechanisms which simply use whatever plan-activity-map is generated, so different techniques can be incorporated modularly into the PGPlanner.

Solution-Construction-Graph and Domain-Level Communication.
The mechanisms for generating the solution-construction-graph assume that
the preferences for network redundancy, that communication delays, and that
estimates of nodes' integration expertise are known so that it can formulate
a reasonable (though not necessarily optimal) prediction about how results
should be combined into the complete solution. It begins by grouping together
sequences of related activities to identify the combinable results made locally
by the nodes. In more general terms, it finds groups of activities, where each
group triggers some form of interaction. For example, in an assembly domain
the group of activities may lead to a complete sub-assembly, and the next step
would be to combine this with a sub-assembly made by another agent. Similarly,
in a diagnosis task the group of activities might lead to a local hypothetical diagnosis which must then be sent to other nodes for corroboration. The criteria
for grouping activities depends on how the nodes expect to cooperate and the
relative time that nodes are performing activities, and is domain-dependent.

Once these groups have been found, the simple mechanisms for determining
when and where each pair of groups could be joined and for building up larger
and larger combinations are applied. These mechanisms are more generally applicable in other domains. In an assembly domain, for example, the mechanisms
would identify when and where sub-assemblies could be united into a larger sub-
assembly, and through iteration would determine how all of the pieces should
be combined into the overall result. However, the mechanisms may need to be
extended in some domains since they only consider pairwise combinations of
pieces—some domains may need a group of more than two pieces at the same
place and time before they can be combined. Such extensions are not needed
in the vehicle monitoring domain (since the KSs combine two pieces at a time).
They would be fairly easy to add to the mechanisms, but may raise issues in
additional complexity: when considering pairs of partial results, the number
of combinations to consider rises quadratically with the number of pieces; but
when considering all combinations of two or more, the number of combinations
rises exponentially with the number of pieces.

Task-Passing and Prediction. Partial global planning exploits the fact that
negotiation over the decomposition and transfer of tasks is similar to negotiation
over which subsets of local tasks nodes should pursue. A PGP is a representation for goals, actions, and interactions that nodes can use as a protocol for
negotiating for both local assignments and task-passing, so the partial global
planning framework provides a unified view of coordination. Because they allow
nodes to form contracts (shared PGPs), these mechanisms for task-passing are
generalizable to other domains where task-passing is important for effective use
of network resources. When the tasks at different nodes are interdependent, a
PGP indicates how the potentially cooperating nodes should coordinate their

tasks. However, the mechanisms are also useful in domains where tasks are independent, since a PGP for task-passing would simply reduce to information about the specific task to pass. The types of tasks to be represented and exchanged would have to be extended for other domains so that nodes can move more diverse tasks around, but, in any domain, nodes would want to represent possible transfers of tasks using PGPs. Before it can propose a task transfer, a node must have enough knowledge of the task to recognize how it fits into the more global perspective (whether it is relevant and not being done elsewhere) and what other nodes need to know to make intelligent decisions about whether they can perform the task. PGPs provide a useful representation for indicating the relevance of a task and how the task could be performed.

The mechanisms for predicting future tasks are very domain dependent, as well as being rudimentary in the current implementation. How our mechanisms in the vehicle monitoring domain predict tasks is less important than the PG-Planner's more general ability to represent and use these future plans. The ability to represent possible future tasks based on current tasks can be useful in domains where tasks arrive over time and where future tasks might be predicted from the current tasks. By representing and reasoning about predicted future activity, the PGPlanner can make better decisions about current actions (and about receiving tasks from others) so that the node is better prepared to pursue those future tasks. Finally, note that the mechanisms represent the possible reception of tasks from other nodes the same way that they represent the possible local development of tasks. By viewing plans for future activities in a uniform way despite their different sources, the PGPlanner can more effectively reason about relationships between current problem solving and possible future activities.

Meta-Level Communication.   The meta-level communication mechanisms transfer information about node-plans and PGPs. Viewed very simply, these mechanisms extract the attributes of a local data structure, build a message structure from them, and send this message structure to another node which builds a local copy of the data structure with the attributes provided. One of the issues that complicates these mechanisms is the need to timestamp information so that nodes can compare different views of the same information (node-plans for the same local plan, PGPs for the same group of local plans) to decide which views are more current. These techniques are more generally used in networks (for example, distributed database systems) where time-dependent information must be propagated among nodes. Another issue is the balance between maximizing the currency of views while minimizing communication, which is struck by tolerating some degree of deviation from expectations. The technique of specifying a time-cushion is generally applicable to other systems where nodes should coordinate plans but can still achieve network goals when their plans get somewhat out of phase.

Connection Between PGPlanning, Local Planning, and Problem Solving. The PGPlanner, local planner, and problem solver are distinct parts of an overall node and, although they interact, the interface between them allows the implementation of one of these components to be changed without major revisions to the others. The purpose of the PGPlanner is to alter the local plans on the plan queue so that the best plan *from a global perspective* rises to the top of the queue. How this manipulation is done is irrelevant to the local planner, since it simply takes the top local plan from the queue and pursues it. Similarly, the local planner alters the KSI queue so that the best KSI *to work toward longer term goals* is invoked next. The implementation of the local planner is irrelevant to the problem solver itself when it invokes this KSI. The local planner needs to know about the problem solver's representation of hypotheses, goals, and KSIs, and the PGPlanner must know about the local planner's representation of plans. However, the different components reason about these representations independently.

This view of control in different but interacting levels is more generally applicable to other cooperating systems. The more a node needs to reason about how nodes interact, the more it needs to reason about its own actions. Besides its mechanisms to control basic activities, therefore, a node needs more levels of control to represent and reason about its own behavior and the behavior of others. Our mechanisms provide an initial pass at these levels of control: a level for controlling local actions to achieve immediate goals, a level for controlling sequences of local actions to achieve long-term goals, and a level for controlling concurrent sequences of actions at different nodes to achieve network goals. Although it may well be that other applications need a larger (or smaller) number of levels, the levels we have developed are likely to be some part of the control mechanisms in cooperative systems.

7.4.2 Other Applications of Partial Global Planning

The PGPlanner could be useful in a cooperative assembly task, where several robots work together to build products. Each robot may have a store of parts and knowledge about ways that it could combine those parts into larger assemblies. Each can therefore recognize local long-term goals—possible sub-assemblies—and can locally plan actions to achieve these goals. The plans can be ranked based on how important each sub-assembly is (perhaps giving preference to sub-assemblies that use the most parts or a particular type of part). By communicating about these local plans, the robots can recognize larger combined assemblies that they could cooperatively form, and they generate PGPs to represent these. Moreover, they could use the local plans to determine their concurrent activities and to decide when and where to combine their sub-assemblies, considering the time it takes for one robot to transport a sub-assembly to another robot. As they pursue their plans and their expectations change (tasks take longer than expected, parts do not fit together properly), they can update and exchange their plans to reconsider how (or whether) to cooperate. They could also recognize how, by providing some parts of sub-assemblies ahead of time, they can constrain each other's activities (since the recipient would have to build a compatible sub-assembly). Finally, by identifying important PGPs, they can also identify underutilized robots and develop modified PGPs that reflect how these robots could better participate.

As a second example, consider cooperating diagnostic systems that are monitoring a communication network. Each has a view of part of the network and can locally recognize aberrant behavior within its view. The nodes must cooperate to diagnose network faults. They begin by forming plans to diagnose local errors, and then exchange summaries of these plans. Given information about several nodes plans, a node can recognize when they are individually diagnosing errors that could be part of a more global problem, and would form PGPs to represent the cooperative diagnostic activity. By reasoning about their concurrent activities, nodes can avoid duplicating each other's efforts (such as testing a communication link), can verify each other's partial diagnoses (such as hypothesizing common faults), and can provide predictive information (such as a symptom that any diagnoses must account for). In an uncertain and dynamic environment like large communication networks, partial global planning represents a promising approach for diagnosing (and possibly repairing) failures.

As a final application, a network operating system must coordinate the processing and resource use of a group of nodes. Tasks arrive at the various nodes asynchronously and possibly unpredictably (although repetitive tasks might also be part of the domain). Each task has certain resource needs, may be related to other tasks (such as by precedence), and may have a deadline. A node might consider groups of tasks (related by deadlines or some other attribute) and plan roughly when it will pursue each group. Nodes could exchange summaries of their plans and build PGPs: they could reorder local activities, could share task results, and could move tasks to underutilized nodes.

Many hands make light work. –Heywood

Too many cooks spoil the broth. –Anonymous

Chapter 8

Partial Global Planning: Experiments and Evaluation

8.1 Partial Global Planning Experiments

Experimental Environments

The majority of the experiments are conducted on four-node networks, although experiments involving both larger and smaller networks are also discussed. The two principal environments are shown in Figure 68. Environment A was used for examples in the previous two chapters. Its important features are the track shared by several nodes (d_1–d_{15}), the much less globally-important moderately-sensed data of node 1 (d_1'–d_5'), and the ambiguity introduced into node 2's data by its sensor. Environment A thus focuses on issues of giving preference to more globally-important plans, providing predictive information, and avoiding redundant processing.

Environment B has two vehicles. To better emphasize issues in coordination (rather than in resolving local uncertainty about what data to combine), we assume that the vehicles are far enough apart so that there is no confusion about which data belongs together. Unlike similar environments described

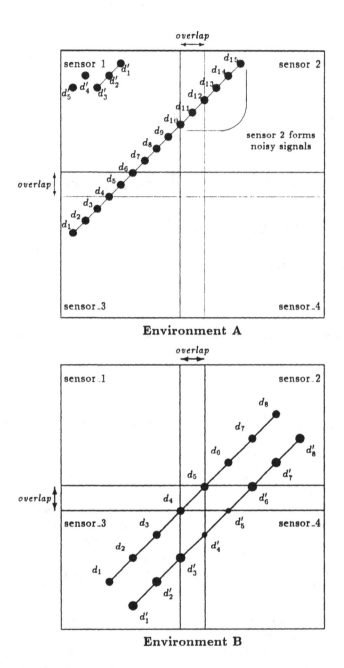

Figure 68: Four-Sensor Configurations with Sensed Data.

in other papers [Corkill, 1983; Corkill and Lesser, 1983; Lesser and Corkill, 1983], the nodes *cannot* form cross-tracks that connect data in different solution tracks together. The data for one of the vehicles is moderately-sensed at each sensed time, while the data for the other has strongly and weakly sensed sections. When the node combines the data into overall tracks, the track made of moderately-sensed data (d_1-d_8) is a little more highly-believed than the track with strong and weak parts $(d'_1-d'_8)$. We therefore consider d_1-d_8 to be the better solution and $d'_1-d'_8$ to be the worse solution. The network should find both solutions, but should find the better solution first. Environment B focuses on issues of promoting work on each solution while avoiding redundancy and giving preference to the better solution.

Assumptions and Default Values in the Experiments

Many assumptions and default values for environmental attributes hold throughout the experiments except where changes are explicitly noted. Each KS takes 1 time unit to execute, so that each time unit corresponds to a local control decision. Domain-level communication is limited to vehicle-track hypotheses (to reduce communication), the only exception being during task-passing when nodes can also exchange signal-location hypotheses. Domain-level and meta-level communication between nodes is broadcast, message delay is 2 time units (for all messages, no matter what their size), and messages are not lost. Although broadcast communication means that messages sent by one node arrive at all other nodes, a node only incorporates a hypothesis message if specified by the PGPs, or domain-level organization if the node has no PG-Planner. Messages that are not incorporated are saved and checked again if PGPs change, but to reduce storage, any subsumed messages (the hypotheses they represent are subsumed by hypotheses of other messages) are deleted. A node only incorporates a meta-level message (node-plan or PGP) if allowed by the meta-level organization.

Nodes are permitted to use all control mechanisms—including goal processing—in all experiments, although nodes with local and partial global planning might only selectively apply these other mechanisms. Network problem solving terminates after every solution has been found by at least one node. To simplify the experiments, we use the termination criterion of specifying the desired solutions beforehand. Although they do not use this information to guide control decisions, the nodes compare the hypotheses they form against this information to determine when they have found the answer(s) and can stop problem solving. In environment A, the network ends problem solving as soon as one node has formed the track d_1-d_{15} at the pattern blackboard-level, while in environment B, problem solving ends as soon as some node has formed d_1-d_8 and some (possibly different) node has formed $d'_1-d'_8$, both at the pattern blackboard-level. Using this termination criterion also lets us compare networks with and without the local and partial global planning mechanisms, since the more advanced termination techniques are only possible with planning.

The default goals of cooperation cause the PGPlanner to avoid redundancy and to promote the formation and exchange of predictive information (the redundancy and predictiveness cooperation-parameters are greater than the reliability and independence parameters). The time-cushion is 1, so nodes tolerate minor plan deviations. The solution-construction-redundancy is also 1 (no redundancy). To avoid complications of task-passing (except in the specific experiments designed to study task-passing), the min-task-duration defaults to a large value (100) where possible tasks in these environments always fall short of this value. The default meta-level organization has nodes broadcast node-plans and form their own PGPs. Finally, in the experiments that do not use the new PGPlanning mechanisms, the domain-level organization constrains communication decisions by having nodes *choose* to receive hypotheses only when they can extend those hypotheses. Thus, the communication channels are broadcast but nodes are selective about what communicated hypotheses they actually incorporate locally, and this saves them the expense of processing hypotheses that they are less likely to find useful (which is crucial in larger networks to avoid overwhelming nodes with information to be processed). With the PGPlanning mechanisms, these constraints are removed so that an idle node can receive results to integrate (when specified in its PGPs) regardless of whether it can locally contribute to the overall result.

Experimental Measurements

Simulated Solution Time. By assigning a simulated time cost of 1 time unit to each KS, we can equate simulated time with control decisions: since each KS takes 1 time unit, a node that works for t time units has made t control decisions. Because each node maintains a separate clock, the nodes are simulated to perform KSs in parallel. If the network finds the solution at time t, therefore, it means that *each node* has invoked as many as t KSs (although some nodes may have invoked fewer KSs if they ran out of data to process). We measure simulated network performance as how quickly the network finds the solution(s) in simulated time. With local and partial global planning, network performance should hopefully improve since nodes should invoke fewer unnecessary KSs and should exchange partial solutions in a more timely manner. Network performance is based on how quickly the network forms all solutions *and* how quickly it forms better solutions (if there are more than one). That is, we view the network as supplying solutions to some consumer of solutions whenever it forms them, so the network should generate and send better solutions as soon as possible rather than timing its activities to form and send all solutions at once.

Computation Costs. While simulated solution time lets us measure the benefits of our new mechanisms (in improving control and coordination), we also must measure the computation costs of these mechanisms since the time a node spends on control activities is time lost to actual problem solving. To measure the computation costs in the network, we use the actual computation time needed to simulate network problem solving. The time needed by the simulator, running in CLisp on a VAX 11/750, represents how much computation the network needed as a whole, including time spent on both problem solving and control (the time spent context switching between nodes is negligible). By measuring the overall computation time of DVMT experiments, we can compare the computation needed by networks using the various control mechanisms to determine whether the additional computation overhead introduced by local and partial global planning is compensated for by a reduction in computation spent on other aspects of problem solving (since fewer KSs are invoked and less goal processing is done).

An advantage of this measure is that it reflects the costs in a real (albeit preliminary) implementation. Another advantage is that it makes the simulation less complicated. If the costs of control were to affect simulated runtime, then it would be much more difficult to separate out the benefits and costs of the mechanisms, and it would also make description of concurrent activity in nodes a much harder task. A disadvantage of measuring computation cost as actual runtime is it only allows us to measure overall computation in the network, and does not reflect possible parallelism in control. For example, if several nodes are forming similar PGPs instead of having a single coordinator, then the network is doing more *computation*, but is not necessarily spending more *time* on control. In our discussions, a higher computation cost implies more resources spent on computation but not necessarily more time spent in the simulated network. Another disadvantage is that the computation spent on control cannot affect when nodes interact: a node that spends time on control will pursue its problem solving actions later, and so may be delayed in when it sends expected partial results to other nodes. Hence, without the ability to simulate different costs for the various control activities, an experimenter cannot explore the ramifications of having more or less costly control activities.

Communication Costs. Communication involves the cost for accessing communication channels, and the cost for processing communicated information—for building messages from local information at one end and for building and incorporating local information out of messages at the other. Incorporating received information can be especially costly because it can trigger substantial amounts of control activity so that a node knows what to do with that information. Simply measuring the number of messages transmitted therefore may not adequately reflect all of the costs of communication, so instead we count the number of messages that are received *and incorporated* by nodes in the network. Our measure of communication neglects aspects such as the size of the messages exchanged and how this affects contention for the channel as a function of time. Hypotheses, node-plans, and PGPs can have varying size, and the size of their messages depends on how the information is encoded. Since encoding issues are not a focus of this research, we disregard actual message size and concentrate instead on the number of times nodes need to exchange information to coordinate and solve problems.

Storage Costs. We measure storage costs by counting the number of major data structures that the nodes build both for planning and for problem solving. For problem solving, these structures are hypotheses, goals, and KSIs, while for planning these structures are clusters (in the clustering hierarchy), plans, node-plans, and PGPs. The actual size of the different structures vary with their contents and encoding: some hypotheses are bigger than other hypotheses; some hypotheses are bigger than some plans; some plans are bigger than some hypotheses; etc. Since we do not focus on encoding issues, we get a preliminary view of storage costs by simply counting the total number of structures in the network.

8.1.1   Experiment Set 8.1: Different Levels of Partial Global Planning

In the first set of experiments, we explore how the addition of the new mechanisms affect the quality and costs of cooperation in environments A and B (Figure 68). For each of these environments we run four experiments: (1) without any planning; (2) with only local planning; (3) with local planning and meta-level communication but no PGPlanning; and (4) with all local and PGPlanning mechanisms.

The experimental results are summarized in Table 7. In environment A, the lack of any planning mechanisms causes very poor performance (E8.1.1). The control decisions are based on local views and the need for node 1 to provide predictive information to node 2 is not recognized. Node 2 receives predictive information only after it has already spent a lot of time on its ambiguous data, and as a result, the nodes generate and exchange many partial results before they converge on a solution. Not only does the network take longer (more KSs) to generate the solution, but the actual runtime, the amount of communication, and the amount of storage are also very high.

With local planning (E8.1.2), the nodes form their local partial solutions more efficiently and the network finds the solution more than twice as quickly (in simulated time). Moreover, the actual runtime was dramatically lowered, so the savings in problem solving (fewer KSs executed and less goal processing) much more than outweigh the overhead costs of planning (including forming and maintaining the clustering hierarchy). Local planning also reduces communication because nodes form fewer partial solutions that could be exchanged, and it reduces the number of hypotheses, goals, and KSIs, to more than offset

Table 7: Experiment Summary for Experiment Set 8.1.

Expt	En	Mec	STime	Rt	H-r	N-r	T-r	Hyp	Goal	KSI	Cl	Pl	NP	PGP	Store
E8.1.1	A	none	171	465	44	-	44	1124	1771	698	-	-	-	-	3593
E8.1.2	A	local	81	76	17	-	17	761	268	373	222	13	23	28	1688
E8.1.3	A	pgg	62	124	23	90	113	706	236	384	224	9	45	42	1646
E8.1.4	A	pgp	46	64	5	54	59	593	202	296	186	9	32	34	1352
E8.1.5	B	none	84/44	221	117	-	117	749	1962	545	-	-	-	-	3256
E8.1.6	B	local	30/44	42	24	-	24	504	175	236	193	15	20	30	1173
E8.1.7	B	pgg	30/49	100	57	204	261	591	195	294	252	15	73	74	1494
E8.1.8	B	pgp	25/34	37	5	54	59	411	144	202	154	14	35	46	1006

Abbreviations

En:	The problem solving environment
Mec:	Which of the new planning mechanisms are used: none, local (no exchange of plans), pgg (exchange, no reordering), pgp (all)
Stime:	The simulated time to find solution(s); if more than one, earliest time for each is given (better-sol/worse-sol)
Rt:	The total runtime (computation time) to find solution(s) (in minutes).
H-r:	The total number of hypotheses messages received and incorporated by nodes.
N-r:	The total number of node-plans messages received and incorporated by nodes.
T-r:	The total number of messages received and incorporated by nodes.
Hyp:	The number of hypotheses formed by nodes.
Goal:	The number of goals formed and processed by nodes.
KSI:	The number of KSIs formed by nodes.
Cl:	The number of clusters in nodes' clustering-hierarchies.
Pl:	The number of plans formed by nodes.
NP:	The number of node-plans in nodes' network-models.
PGP:	The number of PGPs formed by nodes.
Store:	The total number of structures stored (storage costs).

the additional storage needs for clusters, plans, node-plans, and PGPs.[1]

When nodes exchange node-plans to recognize PGGs, they can pursue plans that work toward the best PGGs (E8.1.3). As a result, the nodes (and in particular node 1 which locally prefers a plan that does *not* contribute to the best PGG) pursue better plans and the network finds the solution in less simulated time (fewer KSs are needed). However, this improvement incurs substantial overhead. The computation overhead of forming PGGs makes the overall runtime greater than with only local planning even though local planning ran more KSs. Communication is also dramatically increased by the exchange of node-plans, and to a lesser extent by the exchange of more hypotheses: without PGGs, the nodes only send the end result of their local plans; with PGGs, the nodes send several short partial tracks to each other for integration because they cannot reorder activities to better divide the data so they each build one

---

[1] Local planning was caused by having nodes not send any node-plans and PGPs, but they still form these from their local plans. The fact that there are more node-plans and PGPs than local plans is due to idle node-plans and the PGPs they trigger.

larger partial result. Overall storage needs are slightly reduced despite the fact that nodes maintain node-plans for each other and more PGPs, because fewer hypotheses and goals are formed. Thus, the ability to form PGGs introduces significant amounts of computation and communication overhead, while reducing storage and improving control decisions.

Finally, when all of the new mechanisms are added (E8.1.4), the control decisions improve still further, so even fewer KSs need to be run. In particular, nodes coordinate their activities to more quickly provide predictive results (from node 1 to 2) and to avoid redundant integration of results. Computationally, the overhead of PGPlanning is justified by this improvement in problem solving, since the runtime is less than in any other combination of mechanisms. Nodes also make much more intelligent communication decisions about hypotheses than before; however, the communication of node-plans adds overhead so that, on the whole, the nodes communicate more than if they had just planned locally (E8.1.2) or had not planned at all (E8.1.1). The overall storage needs of nodes are reduced despite the need to store node-plans and PGPs, thanks to the reduction in hypotheses and goals. Thus, with all of the PGPlanning and local planning mechanisms, the network is substantially more coordinated, uses less computation, and uses less storage, but the cost of these improvements is in additional communication.

Environment B shows the same basic trends (E8.1.5–E8.1.8), although there are some differences caused by characteristics of the environment. In particular, this environment contains much less ambiguity because every data point is involved in one solution or the other. The experiment summaries in Table 7 give the simulated time when each of these solutions is found, with the time for the more highly-rated solution (d_1–d_8) given first. Note that without the planner, the nodes form the poorer solution first because they initially focused on its strongly-sensed data. Also, nodes exchange many hypotheses because several nodes often could potentially extend a given hypothesis (for example, d_1–d_3 formed by node 3 could be extended by any of the nodes).

As in environment A, local planning substantially reduces the simulated time (number of KSs run), and especially lets the nodes form the overall better solution earlier thanks to the ability of each to roughly predict beliefs of future results (E8.1.6). As a consequence, the solution time for forming both solutions is nearly half that of the network without any planning. Despite the computation overhead for planning, overall computation needs are significantly reduced. So is the communication in the network, since nodes form and exchange fewer short partial solutions. Finally, storage is also dramatically reduced.

With the additional ability to exchange node-plans, network performance actually degrades (E8.1.7). Not only do PGGs not help local decisions (since nodes do not need to be directed to plans that they should pursue), but they lead nodes into performing redundant tasks on the better PGG. For example, node 2 forms d_7'–d_8' later than with only local planning because it is part of the more lowly-rated PGG, and so, node 2 exhausts its activities in d_4–d_8 first. The computation overhead is increased because of the additional redundancy and because of the costs of correlating node-plans into PGGs. The communication overhead is increased because of the exchange of node-plans and because the poorly-coordinated PGPs (since nodes' activities are not reordered) cause nodes to form and exchange more short partial solutions. For example, the PGGs cause nodes to prefer working on data for d_1-d_8, and because they cannot reorder activities, node's 1, 2, and 4 all redundantly form and send d_4-d_5. Storage costs are also increased, so this level of partial global planning is not justified in any way for this case.

When nodes have all of the PGPlanning mechanisms (E8.1.8), they avoid redundant work in their overlapping areas and redundant integration of results. Simulated runtime to find both solutions is thus reduced and nodes still find the better solution earlier. The overall computation and the storage needs are also reduced, even with the added overhead of forming and saving PGPlanning information. However, although PGPlanning once again makes the exchange of hypotheses more selective, the communication of node-plans increases overall communication resource use.

8.1.2   Experiment Set 8.2: Different Organizations and Their Overhead

Broadcasting coordination information and individually forming PGPs introduces considerable overhead into the nodes' activities. Altering the meta-level organization to change nodes' coordination responsibilities can reduce this overhead, but usually at some cost (such as reliability and node autonomy). We here analyze the costs and benefits of several meta-level organizations.

Once again, the experiments are based on environments A and B (Figure 68). For each environment, we explore four meta-level organizations. The first is the broadcast organization used in experiment set 8.1, where nodes broadcast their node-plans and individually form PGPs. The second is a centralized organization, where nodes send node-plans to a coordinating node (the least busy node is used—in environment A this is node 4 while in environment B this is node 1), which in turn forms the PGPs and sends these back to the other nodes. Since communication is more focused, this organization can reduce communication overhead, and since only one node maintains a full network-model and generates PGPs, the computation and storage needs of the overall network can be decreased. However, centralization decreases reliability (since the network depends on the single coordinating node) and the coordinating node may become a bottleneck. In addition, the extra lag caused by communication delays (node-plans must get to the coordinator and then PGPs must come back) can slow down the rate at which nodes respond to new or changing situations.

The third meta-level organization allows each node to pass node-plans only to its clockwise neighbor, so we refer to this as a "ring" organization. Nodes pass on these node-plans, but the extra delay as messages get passed around the ring can cause nodes to have less consistent network-models than in the broadcast organization, and poorer coordination can result. Thus, this organization explores what happens when communication patterns are limited and when nodes may have more inconsistent views of each other. Finally, in the fourth organization, nodes still communicate in a ring but with two important differences: they pass PGPs, and the organization limits when they can send these PGPs through the use of a predicate.[2] In this "pgp-ring" organization, the predicate causes nodes to pass a single group of PGPs around, where each modifies the group before passing it on: node 1 initially send its PGPs to node 2, which then adds to these PGPs and sends them to node 4 (its clockwise neighbor), and so on. The point of this organization is to see how passing a single set of PGPs can reduce communication but might also slow down the rate at which coordination information becomes available to nodes.

The experimental results are summarized in Table 8. In environment A, the broadcast organization promotes the best control decisions, allowing the network to find the overall solution faster than in other organizations (E8.2.1). However, the overhead costs (computation, communication, and storage) are lower in a centralized network (E8.2.2) than in any other: only node 4 maintains a full network-model (reducing network storage costs); only node 4 generates multi-node PGPs (reducing network computation costs); and communication is more directed, node-plans to node 4 and PGPs from node 4 (reducing communication costs). The ring network finds the overall solution later than the broadcast but earlier than the centralized organization, despite the fact that node 1 sends predictive results to node 2 later than in the previous organizations. This is because the more asynchronous formation and modification of PGPs (because of different delays in getting node-plans from each other) causes the nodes to update their node-plans and PGPs more often, and since this triggers nodes to communicate more often about their node-plans, the nodes develop a more current view of network activity. As the results indicate, the cost of this additional exchange of coordination information is an increase in the amount of communication and a dramatic rise in the computation overhead of coordination (since nodes are updating their PGPs more often). Finally, in the pgp-ring organization, the delays in propagating PGPs substantially degrades coordination, and the additional problem solving adds to computation and storage overhead. However, the restriction in how often nodes pass coordination information (a single set of PGPs is circulated, where each node receives

---

[2] We define a predicate that limits when a given node can send PGPs, and it is checked whenever the node determines that it has PGPs to send. The predicate in these experiments allows each node to send PGPs once every 8 time units, and the allowed sending times are offset for the different nodes to achieve the receive-modify-send behavior desired. In essence, the predicate is part of the meta-level organization, but to maintain flexibility during evolution of the mechanisms we did not define a particular attribute of the organization that contains this information. An important area for future research is to develop a more encompassing, less *ad hoc* representation for the meta-level organization.

Table 8: Experiment Summary for Experiment Set 8.2.

Expt	Env	Org	STime	Rtime	H-r	M-r	T-r	Store
E8.2.1	A	broadcast	46	64	5	54	59	1352
E8.2.2	A	central	48	52	4	48	52	1331
E8.2.3	A	ring	47	77	8	58	66	1339
E8.2.4	A	pgp-ring	62	77	4	27	31	1447
E8.2.5	B	broadcast	25/34	37	5	54	59	1006
E8.2.6	B	central	26/35	32	7	49	56	985
E8.2.7	B	ring	27/38	41	8	59	67	1089
E8.2.8	B	pgp-ring	27/44	44	9	33	42	1063

Abbreviations

Env: The problem solving environment

Org: Which of the meta-level organizations are used: broadcast, centralized, ring, or pgp-ring

Stime: The simulated time to find solution(s); if more than one, earliest time for each is given (better-sol/worse-sol).

Rtime: The total runtime (computation time) to find solution(s) (in minutes).

H-r: The total number of hypothesis messages received and incorporated by nodes.

M-r: The total number of meta-level messages (node-plan and PGP) received and incorporated by nodes.

T-r: The total number of messages received and incorporated by nodes.

Store: The total number of structures stored (storage costs).

them, updates them based on its local plans, and passes them on to the next) significantly reduces the number of messages exchanged in the network.

In environment B, the same types of issues arise. The broadcast organization promotes the best control decisions and the solutions are found in the least amount of (simulated) time, but the centralized organization incurs less overhead (computation, communication, and storage). The ring organization once again performs fairly poorly relative to the others. Finally, as in environment A, the pgp-ring organization has inferior coordination and incurs higher computation and storage costs because of the additional problem solving, but the communication overhead is reduced because nodes send coordination information less often.

8.1.3   Experiment Set 8.3: Different Organizations in More Dynamic Environments

Even when nodes begin their problem solving with all the data, they are still uncertain about how and when problem-solving activities will take place. They change their plans as hypotheses are exchanged or predictions improve, and they dynamically recompute PGPs. Issues in dynamic coordination are further compounded when data arrives over time. In this experiment set, we briefly explore these issues. Our purpose is to determine first of all how well the

Table 9: Experiment Summary for Experiment Set 8.3.

Expt	Env	Org	STime	Rtime	H-r	M-r	T-r	Store
E8.3.1	A	none	187	957	56	0	56	3847
E8.3.2	A	broadcast	55	93	6	151	157	1348
E8.3.3	A	central	68	70	4	109	113	1368
E8.3.4	B	none	71/58	109	57	0	57	2495
E8.3.5	B	broadcast	33/42	42	4	141	145	1067
E8.3.6	B	central	39/49	43	6	99	105	1108

Abbreviations

Env: The problem solving environment
Org: Which of the meta-level organizations are used: broadcast,
         centralized, or none (if none, then no planning at all)
Stime: The simulated time to find solution(s); if more than one,
         earliest time for each is given (better-sol/worse-sol).
Rtime: The total runtime (computation time) to find solution(s) (in minutes).
H-r: The total number of hypothesis messages received an incorporated by nodes.
M-r: The total number of meta-level messages (node-plans and PGPs)
         received and incorporated by nodes.
T-r: The total number of messages (hypothesis and meta-level)
         received and incorporated by nodes.
Store: The total number of structures stored (storage costs).

PGPlanning mechanisms can adapt to unexpected changes caused by new data, and second of all the costs and benefits of using PGPlanning in such a domain. To do this, we once again turn to environments A and B, but this time we alter these environments so that all data does not arrive before problem solving begins. We instead have data arrive at intervals of three time units: data for sensed time 1 arrives at simulated time 1, data for sensed time 2 arrives at simulated time 4, sensed time 3 at simulated time 7, and so on. This arrival rate is slow enough so that nodes can perform some problem solving between arrivals, but fast enough so that control of actions and interactions are still important and nodes cannot exhaustively explore the data (see Chapter 5).

The experimental results are summarized in Table 9. For each environment, we run three experiments: without any planning (no local or PGPlanning); with the new mechanisms and a broadcast meta-level organization; and with the new mechanisms and a centralized meta-level organization.

The incorporation of data over time has an effect on problem solving without the mechanisms (E8.3.1). In particular, the computation time needed by the network is nearly twice that needed when the data arrives all at once (E8.1.1 in Table 7). This can be attributed to the later start that node 2 gets: since it does not begin getting data until time 28, node 1 has more time to develop tracks of both the correct and incorrect vehicle types, which it provides to node 2 which spends time working with each. Moreover, the extra hypotheses communicated (12 more than in E8.1.1) trigger additional problem solving and control activities. Once again, the broadcast organization provides better coordination than the centralized control, but is more costly in network computation and communication (recall, however, that some of the additional computation could occur in parallel).

Comparing the broadcast and centralized organizations, note that this time they are more different than when data came in at once (E8.2.1 and E8.2.2 in Table 8). In particular, the control decisions are substantially worse in the centralized case. In the broadcast organization, node 1 initially works on the data for the undesirable track $d'_1-d'_5$, node 2 has no data, and node 3 works on the early data for the important track. However, node 1 switches to working on the important track as soon as it starts getting data at d_4 because it has received a node-plan from node 3 covering data d_1-d_3 and can form a PGP to cooperate with node 3. In the centralized organization, when node 1 gets data for d_4 it does not begin to work with it because it cannot locally form the PGP to cooperate with node 3. Instead, node 4 forms this PGP and sends it back. In the mean time, however, node 1 has further progressed with the plan to form $d'_1-d'_5$, and the plan's rating rises as the fraction completed increases. The PGP to pursue this plan thus becomes more highly rated than the PGP received from node 4, and node 1 does not assist node 2 until much later.

Turning now to environment B, we first note that in this case the delays between data arrivals actually reduced the time needed to find both solutions (compare E8.3.4 with E8.1.5 in Table 7). The computation, communication, and storage were also reduced. Unlike environment A, there is little ambiguous data in this environment so delays do not trigger exploration of unpromising alternatives. In addition, receiving data over time improves local problem solving because nodes build fewer initial tracks (from the earlier data) and extend them (see Chapter 5), hence the improved performance and reduced cost. With the PGPlanning mechanisms, we once again see that the broadcast organization makes better control decisions than the centralized organization. This time, however, the computation needs of broadcast are also slightly less because the additional problem solving done by the centralized environment in this case offset the lower coordination overhead. The centralized organization does, however, reduce the amount of communication more substantially than in previous experiments.

8.1.4 Experiment Set 8.4: Predictability and Responsiveness

This experiment set studies the balance between predictability and responsiveness. Recall that this balance is struck by the value chosen for the time-cushion, which represents how much plans can deviate from what others have been told (through node-plans) before the changes must be told to others. In the previous experiments with PGPlanning, the time-cushion had a value of 1. By exploring how lower and higher values for the time-cushion affect the costs and benefits of PGPlanning, we can gain a fuller understanding of how predictability and responsiveness can be balanced. We again focus on environments A and B, with the broadcast and centralized meta-level organizations. For each combination of environment and organization, we describe three experiments: with a time-cushion of 0, a time-cushion of 1 (the default), and a time-cushion of 2. The results are summarized in Table 10.

We begin with environment A using a broadcast organization (E8.4.1 – E8.4.3). As the time-cushion increases, several trends become apparent. First, the quality of coordination decreases somewhat because nodes are adapting less to deviations—they continue with PGPs that may not be the best they could form. Second, the computation overhead is substantially reduced, since nodes do not spend as much time recalculating how they should coordinate. Third, the communication overhead is also significantly reduced, since nodes update each other's network-models (by passing node-plans) less often. Fourth, the storage overhead slightly increases due to the extra problem solving caused by less precise coordination: the extra storage is attributable to more hypotheses, goals, and KSIs, while the coordination storage is essentially the same (since updated node-plans replace earlier versions). The same trends are seen with the centralized organization (E8.4.4 – E8.4.6).

With environment B, different phenomena are encountered. In the broadcast organization, the best time-cushion is 1 (E8.4.8). A lower time-cushion (E8.4.7) does not improve coordination (solution time) while it does introduce substantially more computation and communication overhead (because nodes unnecessarily update their node-plans and PGPs more often). Meanwhile, a higher time-cushion (E8.4.9) degrades coordination because nodes do not adequately adapt to incorrect predictions about when they will exchange results. By the time nodes do respond to inappropriate PGPs, they have already wasted time on unnecessary actions (usually duplicating each others results) so network computation is increased due to this extra work. In addition, when a node does finally react to deviations in its local plans and updates its node-plans and PGPs, the exchange of the changed node-plans causes other nodes to change their plans and node-plans, and these cause other nodes to further change—so the net result is that once the nodes start changing their plans the effect snowballs, and that is why meta-level communication is also increased in this experiment. Most of this extra communication activity occurs near the end of network problem solving when some nodes have finished their local responsibilities for important PGPs and begin pursuing and communicating about less highly-rated plans.

With a centralized organization, a lower time-cushion actually degrades coordination (E8.4.10), because nodes are *too* responsive. Specifically, the more constant stream of updated node-plans received by node 1 (the coordinating node) causes it to change the network PGPs and nodes oscillate between coordinating one way and then another. For example, the expectation about whether

Table 10: Experiment Summary for Experiment Set 8.4.

Expt	Env	Org	T-C	STime	Rtime	H-r	M-r	T-r	Store
E8.4.1	A	bc	0	43	76	5	63	68	1280
E8.4.2	A	bc	1	46	64	5	54	59	1352
E8.4.3	A	bc	2	47	57	4	42	46	1357
E8.4.4	A	cn	0	45	59	6	65	71	1306
E8.4.5	A	cn	1	48	52	4	48	52	1331
E8.4.6	A	cn	2	49	50	4	35	39	1347
E8.4.7	B	bc	0	25/34	45	6	95	101	1015
E8.4.8	B	bc	1	25/34	37	5	54	59	1006
E8.4.9	B	bc	2	26/39	39	7	63	70	1093
E8.4.10	B	cn	0	32/41	42	8	85	93	1057
E8.4.11	B	cn	1	26/35	32	7	49	56	985
E8.4.12	B	cn	2	32/47	39	4	41	45	1136

Abbreviations

Env: The problem solving environment

Org: Which of the meta-level organizations are used: bc = broadcast,
       cn = centralized

T-C: The time-cushion used

Stime: The simulated time to find solution(s); if more than one,
       earliest time for each is given (better-sol/worse-sol).

Rtime: The total runtime (computation time) to find solution(s) (in minutes).

H-r: The total number of hypothesis messages received and incorporated by nodes.

M-r: The total number of meta-level messages (node-plan and PGP)
       received and incorporated by nodes.

T-r: The total number of messages (hypothesis and meta-level)
       received and incorporated by nodes.

Store: The total number of structures stored (storage costs).

node 3 or node 4 will integrate d'_1–d'_2 and d'_3–d'_6 changes several times, where sticking to either decision would have resulted in better performance. These oscillations eventually end because nodes make progress with each oscillation until one or more of them produces the desired result. A higher time-cushion (E8.4.12) also degrades coordination, but this time because nodes are not responsive enough. In the broadcast organization (E8.4.9), nodes build their own PGPs and this introduces inconsistencies that cause nodes to send substantial amounts of modified node-plan information back and forth whenever one node changes its node-plans. With a centralized organization, node 1 forms PGPs for the network, and by imposing consistent views of cooperation on the nodes, it prevents them from triggering these rounds of updates. As a consequence, the nodes pass fewer node-plans (decreasing the amount of communication). In turn, the PGPs formed by node 1 are modified much less frequently, so the nodes pursue PGPs based on outdated information and solution time suffers as a result. Because the network needs to invoke more KSs, overall network computation increases as well. Whether the savings in communication warrant this choice of time-cushion over the time-cushion of 1 (E8.4.11) depends on the

Table 11: Experiment Summary for Experiment Set 8.5.

Expt	Env	Org	STime	Rtime	H-r	M-r	T-r	Store
E8.5.1	A (4 integrator)	bc	47	65	6	48	54	1369
E8.5.2	A (4 integrator)	cn	45	49	4	39	43	1295
E8.5.3	B (4 integrator)	bc	26/37	39	7	60	67	1048
E8.5.4	B (4 integrator)	cn	28/39	37	7	71	78	1048
E8.5.5	A (redun)	bc	43	134	15	81	96	1333
E8.5.6	A (redun, 4 fails)	bc	43	128	11	63	74	1301
E8.5.7	A (redun, 4 int+fails)	bc	65	127	11	77	88	1439
E8.5.8	B (redun)	bc	25/34	63	14	116	130	1087
E8.5.9	B (redun, 4 fails)	bc	25/34	59	11	109	120	1041
E8.5.10	B (redun, 4 int+fails)	bc	26/60	83	21	141	162	1117

Abbreviations

Env:	The problem solving environment (with comments about whether there is solution construction redundancy, whether node 4 is an integrator, and whether node 4 fails)
Org:	Which of the meta-level organizations are used: broadcast, centralized, or none (if none, then no planning at all)
Stime:	The simulated time to find solution(s); if more than one, earliest time for each is given (better-sol/worse-sol).
Rtime:	The total runtime (computation time) to find solution(s) (in minutes).
H-r:	The total number of hypothesis messages received and incorporated by nodes.
M-r:	The total number of meta-level messages (node-plans and PGPs) received and incorporated by nodes.
T-r:	The total number of messages (hypothesis and meta-level) received and incorporated by nodes.
Store:	The total number of structures stored (storage costs).

available network resources.

8.1.5   Experiment Set 8.5: Heterogeneous Nodes and Reliability

This experiment set briefly addresses issues in how nodes can work together when they have different expertise and how they can coordinate to remain more robust in the face of node failures. We once again use environments A and B to illustrate how the PGPlanning mechanisms help nodes coordinate in these situations, and the experiments are summarized in Table 11.

As an initial investigation into issues in differing node expertise, we alter the environments so that a particular node is substantially better at integration than other nodes. This causes the PGPlanning mechanisms to generate PGPs where this node is the chosen integrator for the partial results. To establish one node as a better integrator, we alter the time needs of KSs at some nodes: parameters for integration KSs (to merge partial solutions) are changed in the non-integrating nodes so that they take 10 time units to run (as opposed to taking 1 time unit in the integrating node). This means that the other nodes take 10 times as long to integrate partial results. This information in reflected in the node-models (see Chapter 6) where the expected-integration-costs for the non-integrator nodes is 10 and for the integrator node is 1.

Node 4 was chosen as the integrating node for environment A, since it is otherwise idle. With a broadcast organization (E8.5.1), the network is not quite as effective as when nodes were equally capable of integrating results (E8.2.1 in Table 8). The communication delay for node 1 to send its partial result d_7–d_{12} to node 4 causes the network to take slightly longer than before (in simulated and real time). However, in the centralized organization, heterogeneity improves coordination slightly (comparing E8.5.2 with E8.2.2 in Table 8). When nodes were equally good integrators, the network expected node 1 to integrate its result d_7–d_{11} with node 3's result d_1–d_6, where the result from node 3 was expected to arrive before it was needed. In fact, the result from node 3 arrived later and node 1 waited for it and then combined the results. When all results are sent to node 4, the extra delay is avoided: the two results are at node 4 two time units after the later of the two is formed (because of communication delays) instead of node 4 receiving the combination 5 time units after the later piece is formed (delay of 2 for d_1–d_6 to get to node 1, 1 time unit to combine them, and then a delay of 2 for the combination to get to node 4).

In environment B, node 1 is least busy, but to see what happens when a node that has local data to process is also the best integrator, we once again make node 4 the integrating node. In the broadcast organization, this slows down the solution time for the better solution by one time unit because of the extra communication delay. Node 4 is interrupted by the integration tasks (to combine d_1–d_3 from node 3, d_4–d_5 from node 1, and d_6–d_8 from node 2) and forms its own piece of the less highly-rated solution (d_3'–d_6') later than it would have. Consequently, the simulated time when the less highly-rated solution is formed increases compared to when nodes integrate equally well (E8.2.5 in Table 8). Similar results hold with the centralized organization (E8.5.4).

When nodes can fail, plans should be more robust—more resilient to un-expected failures—through redundancy so that any important tasks are being performed at more than one node. An alternative way of addressing node fail-ure is to plan without redundancy but to monitor node interactions to detect when failures occur and then reassigning important tasks. A combination of the two methods could also be employed. Our initial implementation focuses on building more robust PGPs by increasing redundancy.

With environments A and B, we simulate a failure by dropping node 4 from the network after simulated time 30. For each environment, we examine three cases: where nodes have equivalent expertise and no nodes fail, where nodes have equivalent expertise and node 4 fails at time 30, and where node 4 has much better integration expertise (as in the earlier experiments in this set) but fails at time 30. In particular, when node 4 has better integration expertise (and thus attracts integration tasks), it is crucial that partial results are also sent to other nodes just in case node 4 fails. For each of the six experiments (E8.5.5–E8.5.10), the solution-construction-redundancy is set to 2, so that any partial solution is sent to at least 2 nodes for integration. We also only explore the broadcast meta-level organization since a centralized meta-level organization would be inappropriate where node failures are probable.

In environment A where nodes have equivalent expertise (E8.5.5), the solution is formed at simulated time 43 which is comparable to when it would be formed without the extra redundancy (see E8.4.1 and E8.4.2, for example). In fact, it is slightly better: without the redundancy, the nodes changed the PGPs several times as local plans changed and the changing views about which node should integrate results delayed completion; with redundancy, PGPs changed over time but possible integrators changed less frequently (because two integrators rather than one are found at any time). However, the redundancy causes two nodes to generate this solution at the same time, and thus increases the computation and communication overhead (comparing E8.5.5 with E8.4.1 and E8.4.2). In the same environment but when node 4 fails (E8.5.6), redundancy allows the solution to be found at the same simulated time. When node 4 fails, it stops using network resources so the network computation, communication, and storage are slightly reduced. When node 4 has more expertise (E8.5.7), the solution is formed much later in simulated time, because node 4 fails and nodes with inferior KSs (that take ten times as long to run) must integrate partial results. At least the result was formed, however, which would not have been the case without the extra solution-construction-redundancy since nodes 1–3 would send partial results to node 4 and not know that node 4 had failed. As before, redundancy significantly increases the computation and communication overhead (comparing E8.5.7 with E8.5.2).

In environment B with equivalent expertise where no nodes fail (E8.5.8), the network performance in simulated time is once again comparable with the time needs without the more robust PGPs (E8.4.8) because node 4 is not responsible for integrating results. The redundancy once again increases the computation and communication overhead (comparing E8.5.8 with E8.4.8). When node 4 fails (E8.5.9), the network can still find the solution at the same simulated time and the computation, communication, and storage are slightly reduced since node 4 is idle. When node 4 has better integration expertise (E8.5.10), several things happen. The solution time for the better solution is not seriously affected because node 4 generates it before failing. The solution time for the second solution is very much affected, however, because node 4 fails and it is up to another node (in this case node 2) to integrate the results using its inferior KSs. Fortunately, before it failed node 4 did send its piece of this solution off to 3; without the extra redundancy introduced into the PGP, node 4 would not have shared this partial result since it would expect to do integration itself. The costs of the additional redundancy are once again high (more computation and overhead comparing E8.5.10 with E8.5.3), but the additional resiliency of the PGPs enabled the network to find the solutions despite node 4 failing.

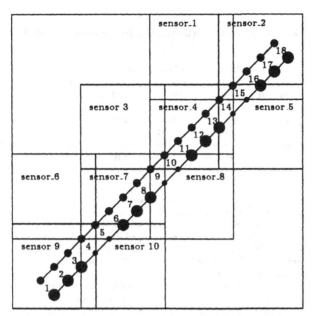

The sensors' ranges overlap, there are 18 data points in both of the tracks, and the size reflects how strongly sensed the data point is.

Figure 69: Ten-Sensor Configuration with Sensed Data.

8.1.6 Experiment Set 8.6: Larger Networks

The experiments in this set are based on the sensor and data configuration shown in Figure 69. There are 10 sensors, arranged diagonally, whose regions have some degree of overlap. In what is essentially an extension of environment B (Figure 68), two vehicles move in parallel among the nodes, but while one vehicle consistently generates moderately-sensed data, the other vehicle track alternates between strongly and weakly-sensed sections. From this sensor and data configuration we develop two networks. One network is composed of 10 nodes, where node *i* receives data from sensor *i*. In this network, the nodes are organized at the domain-level as a *lateral* network: the nodes pass hypotheses among themselves so that one or more of them eventually forms overall solutions. To reduce communication, nodes only exchange hypotheses with adjacent nodes (otherwise the large number of hypotheses exchanged degrades network performance). The other network is composed of 11 nodes, where the 10 nodes connected to different sensors send hypotheses to the eleventh node which is solely responsible for integrating results. The domain-level organization in this network is thus *centralized*, since node 11 does high-level (integration) activities using the low-level (synthesis) results from the other nodes.

The experimental results for the larger networks are summarized in Table 12.

Table 12: Experiment Summary for Experiment Set 8.6.

Expt	Nds	D-L-O	M-L-O	STime	Rtime	H-r	M-r	T-r	Store
E8.6.1	10	lateral	none	86+/58	2005	329	0	329	6738
E8.6.2	10	lateral	local	49/65	583	216	0	216	4238
E8.6.3	10	lateral	broadc	42/57	429	19	396	415	3264
E8.6.4	10	lateral	central	42/50	208	41	322	363	3073
E8.6.5	10	lateral	hierarc	41/51	161	19	384	403	2864
E8.6.6	11	central	none	81/54	186	119	0	119	4197
E8.6.7	11	central	central	47/54	146	14	222	236	2721
E8.6.8	11	central	broadc	40/51	262	14	370	384	2914

Abbreviations

Nodes:	The number of nodes in the network
D-L Org:	Which of the domain-level organizations are used: lateral (any node forms result) or centralized (node 11 forms result)
M-L Org:	Which of the meta-level organizations are used: broadcast, centralized, hierarchical, local (no PGPlanning), or none (no planning at all)
Stime:	The simulated time to find solution(s); if more than one, earliest time for each is given (better-sol/worse-sol).
Rtime:	The total runtime (computation time) to find solution(s) (in minutes).
H-r:	Total number of hypothesis messages received and incorporated by nodes.
M-r:	The total number of meta-level messages (node-plan and PGP) received and incorporated by nodes.
T-r:	The total number of messages received and incorporated by nodes.
Store:	The total number of structures stored (storage costs).

We begin with the 10-node network (lateral domain-level organization) without any of the new local and partial global planning mechanisms (E8.6.1). We also do not allow subgoaling because the huge number of subgoals would use up all available memory and cause the computer to crash. This experiment was terminated after nearly 24 hours of CPU time, when the progress being made was deemed insignificant because of memory thrashing. Despite only communicating with neighbors, nodes exchange large numbers of hypotheses and excessive time is spent incorporating received information. Hence, although the simulated time is not extremely high, the actual computation time needed to perform the simulation is. Because the nodes prefer the strongly-sensed data, they redundantly form d'_1–d'_{18} first. With local planning (E8.6.2), the better solution is found much sooner (to the detriment of the worse solution) because nodes are individually better problem solvers. Fewer useless hypotheses are formed and exchanged, so the computation time, communication, and overall storage are all reduced.

With a broadcast meta-level organization (E8.6.3), nodes essentially duplicate each other's PGPlanning, and to reduce the overhead incurred we set the time-cushion to 5 so that nodes change node-plans and PGPs less often. PGPlanning leads to better simulated performance for finding both solutions. Its computation overhead is acceptable, since the overall computation costs are reduced (comparing E8.6.3 with E8.6.2), and the reduction in the number of KSIs invoked reduces the storage needs. However, to build and maintain the PGPs does require substantial communication (we measure the messages received so a single broadcast node-plan triggers 9 receptions). We use a centralized meta-level organization to reduce the network communication and the computation overhead incurred by having nodes redundantly derive PGPs (E8.6.4). Node 1 receives node-plans from the other nodes, builds PGPs, and sends these PGPs back to the other nodes. Because fewer nodes are building PGPs, we allow the network to be more responsive by setting the time-cushion to 1, improving network performance because the less highly-rated solution is found earlier. Network computation is substantially reduced because only one node is recognizing PGGs and building PGPs. Moreover, this meta-level organization reduces meta-level communication, although more hypotheses are sent because decisions about where to integrate results change several times (due to the low time-cushion). Because it must correlate node-plans from all 10 nodes (and incurs the combinatorics associated with finding all possible combinations), however, node 1 does require substantial computation to build the PGPs.

As a final experiment with the 10 node network, we try a hierarchical meta-level organization to relieve the coordinating node from having to deal with so many combinations (E8.6.5). Half the nodes send their node-plans to one node (nodes 2–5 send to node 1) and the other half send to another node (nodes 6–9 send to node 10). Each of these nodes builds PGPs for its subset (including itself) and sends its PGPs to a higher-level coordinator (node 6). The top-level coordinator combines and modifies the PGPs it gets and sends the revised PGPs back to the middle-level nodes, which in turn send PGP information on to the bottom-level nodes. The organization is thus a multi-level hierarchy. Nodes 1 and 10 each correlate node-plans for half the network, which is much simpler than correlating node-plans for the entire network because the number of possible combinations rises exponentially with the number of node-plans. Node 6 gets these PGPs which "pre-digest" the node-plans, so node 6 needs only to recognize that the PGPs should be combined and to reorder activities appropriately for the complete PGPs. Although the simulated performance is not substantially changed from the centralized meta-level organization (E8.6.4), the overall computation costs are reduced because the coordination problem is decomposed into simpler problems that are distributed among the nodes in the multi-level hierarchy. Having a multi-level hierarchy does increase communication, however, since the nodes in the hierarchy must communicate more (less encompassing) PGPs. We could further improve coordination in multi-level hierarchies by allowing nodes to summarize the activities of a group of nodes as if they were a single node so higher-level coordinators need not reason about individual nodes (see Chapter 9).

In the 11 node network where nodes have neither local nor partial global planning mechanisms (E8.6.6), it is clear that the centralized domain-level organization performs much better than the lateral organization (comparing E8.6.6 with E8.6.1), not so much in simulated performance but in actual computation. This is attributable to the more focused communication. By concentrating communication on node 11, only one node is receiving hypotheses and performing all of the control tasks (goal processing) associated with these hypotheses. Consequently, the simulation takes one-tenth the time to run. Its simulated performance, however, is not substantially different, and once again the less highly-rated solution is found significantly earlier.

If the domain-level organization is centralized, then reliability will not suffer if the meta-level organization is centralized as well (E8.6.7). Node 11 is thus responsible for both integration of problem information and coordination of the network. As expected, this coordination improves simulated performance. The computation costs were also reduced, because the savings in problem solving more than compensated for the additional coordination overhead. The savings in problem solving also reduces the storage since fewer unneeded hypotheses are formed. Once again, however, communication costs are increased since nodes must communicate meta-level information in order to coordinate their plans.

A centralized domain-level organization imposes more structure on how nodes work together on the problem than a lateral organization does because roles and responsibilities are more compartmentalized among the nodes. Given so much structure, the nodes probably could not take as much advantage of the local autonomy and responsiveness that a broadcast meta-level organization provides. However, to illustrate how our new mechanisms separate meta-level from domain-level organization, we impose a broadcast meta-level organization over a centralized domain-level organization (E8.6.8). Because of the increased responsiveness (nodes need not wait for the coordinator), the simulated performance is somewhat improved (compared to E8.6.7). However, the network computation overhead incurred for coordination is high—and even exceeds the computation needs when no local or partial global planning mechanisms are used (E8.6.6). The communication costs are also substantially increased. Thus, this experiment shows both that the mechanisms are flexible (allowing different combinations of domain-level and meta-level organizations) and that their application should be controlled in certain complex situations since their costs may exceed their benefits.

8.1.7   Experiment Set 8.7: Task-Passing

To illustrate how task-passing is done with the PGPlanner, we begin with a simple two node environment (7A), with sensors and data as shown in Figure 70. A vehicle moves through the area sensed by node 1 and does not at all enter the area sensed by node 2. This is a situation where task-passing is definitely appropriate to improve simulated concurrency: node 1 should pass some of its tasks (data to process) off to node 2, which would otherwise sit idle. Note, however, that passing tasks does not reduce the amount of problem solving

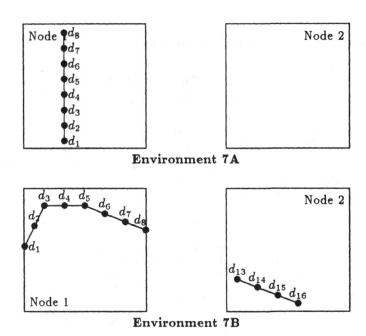

Figure 70: Task-Passing Environments.

in the network, but only redistributes it. Task-passing will not reduce overall computational needs of the network, and may actually increase computation, communication, and storage costs since nodes incur overhead as they decide where to send tasks, send them, and then store received tasks.

The experimental results are summarized in Table 13. With a meta-level organization where nodes do not communicate about local plans, the network (node 1) needs 41 simulated time units to generate the solution (E8.7.1). In a broadcast meta-level organization (E8.7.2), the nodes exchange node-plans—where node 2 builds an idle node-plan—and form PGPs. The data arrives over the time interval 1–9, so local planning is done at time 9 and, because of communication delays, the nodes have models of each other at time 11. At this point, each of them modifies its PGP to represent a possible exchange of tasks. Since node 1 possesses those tasks and there is no coordinating node specified by the meta-level organization, node 1 initiates task-passing by sending its modified PGP to node 2. Node 2 receives this at time 13, extracts out the expected tasks, checks them against any future node-plans (it has none), and sends the future node-plan back indicating that it can carry out the tasks right away. Node 1 gets this reply at time 15 and passes the task by sending the data (hypotheses) and the PGP assigning the task to node 2. At time 17, node 2 receives this data, builds a local plan to process it, and fits this local plan into the PGP (including determining when and where it should send the results it

Table 13: Experiment Summary for Experiment Set 8.7.

Expt	Env	Org	STime	Rtime	H-r	M-r	T-r	Store
E8.7.1	7A	local	41	8.6	1	0	1	305
E8.7.2	7A	broadcast	32	12.2	16	15	31	408
E8.7.3	7A	central	30	11.9	16	15	31	400
E8.7.4	7B	broadcast	44/34	13.6	0	21	21	483
E8.7.5	7B	central	44/34	13.8	0	17	17	475
E8.7.6	7B (local future)	broadcast	44/34	13.8	0	23	23	483
E8.7.7	7B (local future)	central	44/34	13.8	0	17	17	475
E8.7.8	A (task-passing)	broadcast	48	97	77	65	142	1652
E8.7.9	A (task-passing)	central	52	120	81	139	220	1841

Abbreviations

Env:	The problem solving environment
Org:	Which of the meta-level organizations are used: broadcast, centralized, or local (if local, then no PGPlanning)
Stime:	The simulated time to find solution(s); if more than one, earliest time for each is given (better-sol/worse-sol).
Rtime:	The total runtime (computation time) to find solution(s) (in minutes).
H-r:	The total number of hypothesis messages received and incorporated by nodes.
M-r:	The total number of meta-level messages (node-plan and PGP) received and incorporated by nodes.
T-r:	The total number of messages received and incorporated by nodes.
Store:	The total number of structures stored (storage costs).

forms from the data). It builds the track d_6–d_8 and sends it back to node 1, where the track d_1–d_5 has been formed.

In a centralized meta-level organization with node 2 as coordinator (E8.7.3), the node making task-passing decisions (node 2) is not the same as the node with tasks to pass (node 1). Local planning once again occurs at time 9, and this time node 1 sends its node-plans to node 2. At time 11, node 2 forms the more global PGPs and recognizes that it itself is underutilized. Not only does it modify the PGP to represent an exchange of tasks from node 1 to node 2, but it also forms the future node-plan in response to this PGP and decides to award the task to itself. At this point, it sends the modified PGP to node 1 since node 1 must supply the tasks. Node 1 receives this PGP at time 13 and immediately sends the hypotheses to node 2. Thus, node 2 begins its task at time 15 (instead of time 17 as in E8.7.2) and the nodes form the overall solution 2 time units earlier.

While environment 7A represents a case where task-passing is appropriate, environment 7B does not (Figure 70). As in environment 7A, the two nodes have different sensor areas, but now the vehicle that first passes through node 1's area eventually passes through node 2's area as well. Because it spends time between the nodes' areas, (in an area possibly sensed by some other node not simulated here), the vehicle causes node 2 to sense data later than node 1:

we simulate the sensed time occurring at the corresponding simulated time, so node 2 does not begin getting its own data until time 13. Initially, therefore, node 2 is idle when it attempts to coordinate with node 1, but it later will be getting data of its own.

We begin once again with a broadcast organization (E8.7.4). As in environment 7A, the time interval from 1 to 9 is used to incorporate the sensed data (by node 1). At time 9 the nodes build local plans and transmit them, so at time 11 they both recognize that node 2 is currently underutilized. Before node 1 modifies and sends the PGP requesting node 2 to bid on the tasks, it first checks the PGPs to see if node 2 might get data in the near future. By extending the projected track of the vehicle to later time frames, it determines that the vehicle may pass through node 2's area, and that node 2 should start getting data at time 13. As a consequence, node 1 does not modify and send a PGP because there would not be time for node 2 to complete the task before it got data of its own. No tasks are passed, and node 1 forms d_1–d_8 on its own while node 2 forms d_{13}–d_{16} by itself.

Much the same thing occurs with a centralized organization (E8.7.5). At time 11, node 2 forms the more global PGP and determines that task-passing may be in order. Before modifying the PGP, it checks to see if it might get new data in the future based on projected vehicle movements and discovers that it should. Thus, it builds a future node-plan to represent this probable future activity and does not modify the PGP since it could not complete the tasks before the future activities are expected to begin.

As a variation, consider what would happen if the node that modifies the PGP has an incomplete view and is unaware of possible future node-plans for task recipients. We simulate this by simply not allowing a node to form future node-plans for anyone but itself. Thus, with the broadcast meta-level organization (E8.7.6), node 1 builds the PGP at time 11 and modifies it because it cannot project future node-plans for node 2. When node 2 receives this PGP, however, it builds the future node-plan before it replies to the PGP. Since it predicts that local data is about to arrive, node 2 builds a node-plan indicating that it will pursue the passed tasks when it is done with the local tasks it expects to get. When node 1 receives this counter-proposal and compares it with the PGP, it recognizes that the tasks will be done sooner where they are (at node 1) than they would be if they were passed (to node 2). Consequently, node 1 modifies the PGP to indicate that the tasks will not be passed, and each node pursues its local plans. This shows how the mechanisms can be robust in the face of incomplete information, since both the sending and potential recipient nodes' views affect task-passing. A centralized organization, with node 2 as coordinator (E8.7.7), has the same behavior as before (E8.7.5) because node 2 recognizes its own future node-plan when deciding whether to modify the PGP.

Finally, consider the four-node environment A. With a broadcast organization, the nodes exchange node-plans and each builds more global PGPs at time 18. Each node recognizes that node 2 is currently a bottleneck: given the ambiguity of its data, it is expected to form d_{13}–d_{15} well after nodes 1 and 3 form their pieces. In addition, each node identifies node 4 as being underutilized (idle) and capable of performing some of node 2's tasks. Each node modifies the relevant PGP to indicate a possible transfer of tasks (to process data d_{14} and d_{15}), and node 2 sends its PGP to node 4. At time 20, node 4 responds, indicating that it could do the tasks as expected since it has no other future node-plans. Node 2 gets this information at time 22 and immediately sends those tasks—which entails a fairly large amount of communication to send the ambiguous data. At time 24, node 4 gets this data, forms local plans to process it, links these plans to the more global PGP, and begins processing this data. However, node 2 receives the predictive information from node 1 at time 27, and when it changes its local plans it is no longer a bottleneck-node. Now no node is a substantial bottleneck (nodes 1, 2, and 3 expect to form their pieces of the solution at about the same time), and node 4 need not receive any new tasks. Instead, it simply discontinues pursuing its local plan since it expects node 2 to form the relevant piece sooner. From this point on, problem solving is essentially the same as when no task-passing is done.

In a centralized meta-level organization, node 4 as coordinator determines that it should receive tasks from node 2 and receives these tasks at time 22. When node 2 gets the predictive information from node 1, node 4 recognizes that task-passing was unnecessary. The extra delays in coordinating nodes and the extra problem solving performed in the network (because coordination is not as effective as in the broadcast meta-level organization) add to the computation, communication, and storage overhead. Therefore, these experiments show that, while task-passing can often improve network performance, it can also sometimes waste resources when task-passing decisions are based on simple criteria. Our mechanisms need more sophistication to anticipate how future problem solving might affect current task-passing decisions, and how to redistribute tasks even when there are no bottleneck-nodes (see Chapter 9).

8.1.8   Experiment Set 8.8: Miscellaneous Experiments

This experiment set uses certain environments to point out some of the PG-Planner's additional capabilities—and costs. To show some of these capabilities, we begin with environment 8A, shown in Figure 71. This is a four-node network, where two vehicles move among the nodes. Node 1 senses data for both vehicles, node 2 only senses one of the vehicles, node 3 only senses the other vehicle, and node 4 senses neither of the vehicles. Once again, node 2's sensor detects ambiguous data, so that it expects to take more time to generate partial solutions, unless node 1 provides predictive results to help it.

The experimental results are summarized in Table 14, E8.8.1–E8.8.4. First, without any of the planning mechanisms at all (E8.8.1), the network performs so badly that the experiment was aborted after 14 hours of runtime because the thrashing of memory was making progress on problem solving very slow. After

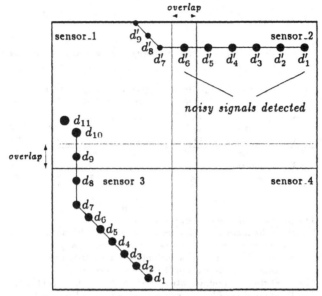

Environment 8A

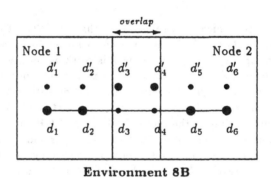

Environment 8B

Figure 71: Miscellaneous Environments.

it had found the more highly-rated solution (d_1-d_{11}), the network had difficulty forming the other solution $(d'_1-d'_9)$ because of the ambiguous data. The addition of local planning (E8.8.2) substantially improves network performance because each node forms its local solutions more effectively. Once node 1 forms $d'_6-d'_9$ and sends this predictive information to node 2, node 2 modifies its local plans so that it finds the compatible track $d'_1-d'_5$ more effectively. However, node 1 forms d_9-d_{11} before $d'_6-d'_9$ because it is more strongly sensed, and so node 2 gets predictive information later than it otherwise might.

With the PGPlanning mechanisms and a broadcast meta-level organization

Table 14: Experiment Summary for Experiment Set 8.8.

Expt	Env	Org	STime	Rtime	H-r	M-r	T-r	Store
E8.8.1	8A	none	62/294+	840+	116+	0	116+	5189+
E8.8.2	8A	local	45/56	55	17	0	17	1457
E8.8.3	8A	broadcast	45/41	53	5	42	47	1299
E8.8.4	8A	central	51/43	58	4	67	71	1323
E8.8.5	8B	none	78	87	47	0	47	1420
E8.8.6	8B	local	72	361	28	0	28	1808
E8.8.7	8B	broadcast	40	564	7	69	76	1339

Abbreviations

Env:	The problem solving environment
Org:	Which of the meta-level organizations are used: broadcast, centralized, or none (if none, then no planning at all)
Stime:	The simulated time to find solution(s); if more than one, earliest time for each is given (better-sol/worse-sol).
Rtime:	The total runtime (computation time) to find solution(s) (in minutes).
H-r:	The total number of hypothesis messages received and incorporated by nodes.
M-r:	The total number of meta-level messages received and incorporated by nodes.
T-r:	The total number of messages received and incorporated by nodes.
Store:	The total number of structures stored (storage costs).

(E8.8.3), node 1 recognizes several things: that the PGP to form d_1–d_{11} is more highly rated; that node 3 will take much longer to form its piece of the overall solution for this PGP; that node 2 is working on the other PGP (d'_1–d'_9) and might benefit from predictive information from node 1; and that node 1 could possibly develop this predictive information early on without hurting cooperation on the more highly-rated PGP. In short, node 1 sees that it has time to spare for working on the more highly-rated PGP, and so it could try to help out node 2 in that spare time. Node 1 thus forms and sends d'_7–d'_8 to node 2 early on, and still sends d_9–d_{11} to node 3 soon enough to avoid disrupting coordination. As a result, the network finds the better solution no later and the other solution substantially earlier (comparing solution times for E8.8.3 and E8.8.2). The improved decisions reduce overall computation and storage needs, but the improved coordination does add communication overhead. Finally, with a centralized organization (E8.8.4), node 1 once again helps out node 2 early on, although the extra communication delays to and from the coordinator (node 4) cause this help to be delayed by 2 time units. The better solution is not found as quickly, however, because node 3 takes longer to form its partial solution than node 4 expected (since this deviation was within the time-cushion). This imperfect coordination comes about because of the extra time needed to modify PGPs (delays to and from the coordinator). It delays solution construction and also increases the computation, communication, and storage costs, compared to the broadcast organization.

In environment 8B (Figure 71), we complicate things to increase our understanding of the costs and limitations of the local and partial global planning mechanisms. In this environment, the actual vehicle track d_1–d_6 is paralleled by a "ghost" track d'_1–d'_6, possibly caused by reflections of sound in the environment. The actual and ghost data are close enough to lead to confusion, so that nodes can build tracks incorporating both actual and ghost data. This confusion leads the planning mechanisms into proposing a much larger number of possible local plans and into forming many more PGPs for different combinations of these plans. Thus, the planning overhead may not be worthwhile given the combinatorics.

When neither local nor partial global planning is used (E8.8.5), the nodes each form hypotheses based on local criteria (KSI ratings) and problem solving is essentially data-driven. Without a long-term view of potential solutions to work toward, the nodes make poorer control decisions and must invoke more KSIs, but the overhead in making control decisions is lower. Giving the nodes the ability to form local plans (E8.8.6) allows them to make better control decisions, which reduces the simulated time needs compared to the experiment without planning (E8.8.5). However, each node has two data points for each of the four sensed times, and thus locally forms 16 alternative-goals (combinations of data). Although the local planner does not initially form plans for each alternative-goal because it can pursue several concurrently, over time more plans are generated for smaller subsets of these alternative-goals. The planner must reason about more information, and thus the computation overhead is substantially increased. Local planning allows nodes to make better control decisions and to reduce communication costs, but it increases computational needs (and also adds to storage since the number of additional planning structures exceeds the number of hypotheses, goals, and KSIs that are not generated because of the better control decisions).

When nodes are also given PGPlanning abilities (E8.8.7), the control decisions improve even more. However, the combinatoric problems are compounded: in a worst case view, each node forms 16 plans, and every possible combination of plans leads to a PGP, meaning that there are 16^2 (256) PGPs. Not only is finding and storing all of these combinations expensive, but also reasoning about all of these PGPs can be very costly as seen in E8.8.7. The amount of computation is extremely high, the communication about plans is very costly, and the savings in storage caused by making the much better control decisions (forming fewer hypotheses, goals, and KSIs) is practically offset by the additional storage needs for all the plans and PGPs.

8.2 Evaluation

The experiments show that partial global planning improves network coordination, but at a price. In most of the situations we explored, the benefits of partial global planning typically outweighed the costs: better control of actions and interactions reduces the overall amount of computation needed to solve the problem despite the computation overhead needed for that control. We also saw, however, that in particularly complex or ambiguous situations, the cost of control may not be worthwhile. Sometimes a brute force approach to problem solving is more cost-effective than a more controlled approach.

Another important cost of the mechanisms is in communication. By dynamically coordinating their interactions, the nodes reduce their domain-level communication because they have more knowledge about what results are worth exchanging in the current situation. To develop this knowledge, however, requires nodes to communicate meta-level information, and the amount of additional meta-level communication usually exceeds the amount of domain-level communication saved. Communication is unavoidable if nodes are to form more dynamic views of network activity, but meta-level communication decisions could be more selective than they currently are, and this is an area for further research described in the next chapter.

The additional storage costs of the plan and PGP information are usually offset by savings in domain-level storage, since better control reduces the amount of domain-level information generated and stored. However, in particularly pathological cases where many plans and PGPs are possible, these costs also may not be worthwhile.

When applied *judiciously*, therefore, partial global planning can be cost-effective. The mechanisms have limitations, especially in complex or ambiguous situations where it is impossible or overly time-consuming to form an adequate view for control. An important avenue of future research is the development of meta-level control to control the control mechanisms, so that the planning mechanisms are applied only when they will be of use. Partial global planning is also flexible: it allows cooperation in different styles through different meta-level organizations; and promotes a variety of goals of cooperation, such as avoiding unnecessary redundancy, balancing load, exploiting expertise, and improving reliability through redundancy. Having this flexibility in a single approach to dynamic coordination is both practical (since coordination should adapt to different distributed problem situations) and conceptually pleasing (since a single framework promotes cooperation in a variety of situations to meet different goals). Moreover, our framework allows nodes to coordinate flexibly depending on the meta-level organization, which is important because different situations demand coordination in different ways. Based on the preliminary experimental results, therefore, partial global planning is a suitable approach to coordination in a wide (but bounded) range of cooperative computing situations. Although further experimentation may reveal other costs, benefits, limitations, and capabilities of the approach, the initial evaluation shows that the approach shows promise and warrants further exploration.

If to do were as easy as to know what were good to do, chapels had been churches, and poor men's cottages princes' palaces. It is a good divine that follows his own instructions; I can easier teach twenty what were good to be done, than to be one of the twenty to follow mine own teaching. –Shakespeare *(The Merchant of Venice)*

Chapter 9

Conclusions

9.1 Summary

The overall objective of this research has been to develop, implement, and evaluate an approach for coordinating cooperating problem solvers, and this was done in two major phases. In the first phase (Chapters 3–5), the control mechanisms for an individual problem solver were modified to improve its self-awareness of goals and plans. It uses simplified domain knowledge to cheaply generate an abstract view of the problem situation so that it can recognize potential solutions and predict their long-term significance and cost. By reasoning about how the potential solutions are related, the problem solver plans actions that work toward one or more of them, and that at the same time generate information that helps resolve uncertainty about which potential solutions to pursue. Because the results of earlier actions may affect how (and whether) a plan should be pursued, the planning mechanisms interleave plan generation, monitoring, and repair with plan execution, leading to more versatile planning where actions to achieve problem solving goals and actions to resolve uncertainty are integrated into a single plan. The experiments indicate that this self-awareness improves the problem solver's control decisions, and the additional control overhead (computation and storage) is generally compensated for by resources saved in problem solving since fewer incorrect actions are taken.

The second major phase of the research (Chapters 6–8) extended the local planning mechanisms so that problem solvers can communicate summaries of their own plans and thus can increase each other's network awareness. With this additional knowledge, problem solvers identify when they are working on parts of some larger (partial global) goal, and represent their combined efforts as a partial global plan. How information is exchanged and processed depends on the meta-level organization, which indicates the coordination roles of the different problem solvers. By following this organization, one or more problem solvers forms partial global plans and reasons about how the cooperating problem solvers could alter their actions to improve coordination. These partial global plans are distributed among the problem solvers, which individually change their local plans to reflect the more global view. Since local plans may change dynamically, coordination information is propagated around the network over time, and the problem solvers must cooperate despite possibly inconsistent partial global plans. An important aspect of the approach is that it emphasizes planning *during* problem solving (while problem and network characteristics are changing) and allows problem solvers to cooperate well enough (but not necessarily optimally) to form acceptable solutions. Our experimental evaluation showed the benefits and costs (in overhead) of the approach, and especially how it allows coordination in a changing world. The upshot of the experiments is that partial global planning represents a flexible, versatile, and practical approach to dynamic coordination, but that indiscriminate application of the mechanisms can result in excessive overhead in certain complex situations where the nodes cannot distinguish a small set of possible goals.

9.2   Research Issues Revisited

9.2.1   Sophisticated Local Control

A problem solver needs self-awareness about its local goals and plans so that it can anticipate its actions and interactions as part of a coordinated group. By sharing their local views, nodes can develop network-awareness and can plan as a group. However, our research has shown that coordination is not a new layer of control that surrounds individual problem solvers and controls their interactions. Instead, coordination mechanisms must be an integral part of a problem solver's internal control mechanisms: decisions about coordination affect local control decisions and *vice versa*, so nodes must consider both local and network needs when deciding on actions and interactions. The local and partial global planning mechanisms we have introduced provide this sophisticated decision-making. Control moves back and forth between these planning mechanisms so that each can influence the other's options and choices, and a node's decisions are thus based on a more complete view of local and network needs and expectations. Unlike approaches that add coordination mechanisms as an afterthought to individual systems, our approach recognizes that both local and network needs must be considered simultaneously when coordinating multiple problem solvers.

9.2.2 Goals of Cooperation

In Chapter 1, we listed a number of possible goals of cooperation that a network of problem solvers might possess. In Chapters 6–8, we described and evaluated the partial global planning mechanisms that are intended to provide sufficient flexibility so that nodes might cooperate to achieve these various goals. To understand how well these mechanisms succeed in meeting this objective, we address the different goals of cooperation and briefly indicate how each can be achieved through the partial global planning mechanisms.

- *To increase the solution creation rate by forming subsolutions in parallel.* The inherent distribution of tasks among nodes allows them to work on tasks in parallel. When tasks are not well distributed initially, the new mechanisms allow computation load to be balanced in any of several ways: the meta-level organization can give additional coordination responsibilities to an underutilized node by making it form PGPs for others; the PGPs can assign integration tasks to an underutilized node; or the task-passing mechanisms can move data to be processed from an overburdened node to an underutilized node.

- *To minimize the time agents must wait for results from each other by coordinating activity.* The PGPlanner reorders the nodes' activities so that nodes generate more globally-important results earlier. In addition, the PGPlanner explicitly represents how nodes should interact to form overall solutions: which node provides which partial solution and when. Not only does this allow nodes to exchange important partial solutions in a timely manner, but it also lets them recognize when they can delay work on one result in favor of another so that they cooperate more effectively (as shown in some experiments in experiment set 8.8 in Chapter 8).

- *To improve the overall problem solving by permitting agents to exchange predictive information.* Among the cooperation-parameters is the importance of providing predictive information, and the PGPlanner uses this parameter when reordering activities so that activities that are likely to generate predictive results are performed earlier. The PGPlanner also uses this information when deciding what results should be exchanged between nodes so that predictive results are transmitted. Many of the experiments in Chapter 8, and in particular those involving environments where one of the nodes has a faulty sensor, had providing predictive information as one of the goals of cooperation.

- *To increase the probability that a solution will be found despite agent failures by assigning important tasks to multiple agents.* The PGPlanning mechanisms allow increased reliability in several ways. First, if reliability is more important than avoiding redundancy, the PGPlanner allows nodes to generate duplicate results. Second, the meta-level organization allows decentralization of PGPlanning so that nodes can coordinate despite agent failures. Third, the integration-redundancy cooperation-parameter indicates how many nodes should have responsibility for integrating results, and if a result is sent to several nodes for integration, that integration is more likely to be done despite node failures. Some experiments in experiment set 8.5 (Chapter 8) illustrated how these mechanisms allow a network to find solutions even when an integrating node fails.

- *To improve the use of computing resources by allowing agents to exchange tasks.* The PGPlanning mechanisms provide task-passing capabilities. When some nodes are underutilized while others are overburdened (and represent bottlenecks in overall network problem solving), the nodes can exchange node-plans and PGPs to negotiate about the possible transfer of tasks. Experiment set 8.7 in Chapter 8 illustrated these mechanisms.

- *To improve the use of individual agent expertise by allowing agents to exchange tasks.* The PGPlanning mechanisms allow nodes to represent each other's expertise as part of their node-models. As shown in some experiments in experiment set 8.5 (Chapter 8), the PGPlanner uses this information when deciding where results should be sent for integration: nodes that are "experts" at integration (for example, they can combine results fastest) are chosen. The PGPlanning framework could also support having nodes find possible task swaps so that a node that could do a task might pass it to a node that could do it better.

- *To reduce the amount of unnecessary duplication of effort by letting agents recognize and avoid useless redundant activities.* The importance of avoiding redundancy is represented in the cooperation-parameters, which the PGPlanner uses when reordering activities: those that could be done by other nodes are typically postponed to avoid redundancy. The PGPlanner also considers redundancy avoidance when deciding how the overall solution will be constructed. Most of the experiments in Chapter 8 had avoiding redundancy as one of the goals of cooperation.

- *To increase the confidence of a (sub)solution by having agents verify each other's results through rederivation using their potentially different expertise.* The cooperation-parameters specify the relative importance of verification (reliability) versus redundancy avoidance. If it is more important to verify results than to avoid redundancy, the PGPlanner reorders node activities to concentrate on overlapping data first and it plans solution construction and communication to exchange these partial results.

- *To increase the variety of solutions by allowing agents to form local solutions without being overly influenced by other agents.* The cooperation-parameters include parameters affecting the relative importance of independence. When the independence is high, the cost of changing local plans based on global views is high and a node is much less likely to modify its local plans based on other agents. By striking a balance between independence and the other factors, the network allows nodes to balance their local desires against more global pressures.

- *To reduce the communication resource usage by being more selective about what messages are exchanged.* Because it develops a view about exactly which results should be combined and where, the PGPlanner can dramatically reduce the number of messages about partial results passed between nodes, as illustrated in the experiments in Chapter 8. As was also seen, however, the exchange of messages about node-plans and PGPs adds to the communication resource usage, and future research must be directed toward making more selective meta-level communication decisions.

9.2.3 Styles of Cooperation

The style of cooperation between nodes—whether centralized or decentralized, hierarchical or lateral, task-sharing or result-sharing—is very situation dependent. A style that works well for one situation may be bad in another situation. In the PGPlanning mechanisms, the style of cooperation is dictated by the meta-level organization and the cooperation-parameters. The PGPlanner uses this specification of the coordination roles and responsibilities of nodes to determine, for instance, what coordination information (node-plans and PGPs) to send and where, how to treat received coordination information (how credible it is), and what nodes it is responsible for coordinating. In the experiments in Chapter 8, we examined a number of different meta-level organizations, indicating their advantages and disadvantages. Many more meta-level organizations are possible, especially in larger, more complex networks, and an important advantage of the PGPlanning mechanisms is that they are versatile enough to work in wide variety of styles of cooperation.

9.2.4 Predictability and Responsiveness

The experiments in Chapter 8 briefly explored some of the tradeoffs between having nodes be predictable versus having them be responsive. The PGPlanning mechanisms do not dictate a particular balance between these conflicting demands because the decision about the relative costs and benefits of predictability and responsiveness depend on the network characteristics. As shown in the experiments, increasing predictability (by enlarging the time-cushion in which nodes' plans can deviate from expectations without the node responding) reduces the overhead for coordination (nodes modify their node-plans and PGPs less often) but can also lead to poorer network problem solving. On the other hand, increasing responsiveness can improve network problem solving but at the cost of more coordination overhead, and being too responsive can sometimes degrade network performance because PGPs change too rapidly for nodes to develop similar views of coordination. Where the line between when to be predictable and when to be responsive should be drawn is thus a difficult and situation-dependent question, but the PGPlanning mechanisms allow predictability and responsiveness to be balanced flexibly within a single coordination framework.

9.2.5   Negotiation

Partial global planning provides a protocol—the PGP—for communicating about coordination. In our research, we have described reasoning mechanisms that can use this protocol to negotiate about goals, actions, and interactions in order to improve network performance. Our mechanisms address the association problem by allowing nodes to exchange coordination information and recognize when they are working on related subproblems. With this view, nodes then rearrange their local actions and interactions to work as a more effective team. Our mechanisms address the connection problem by allowing nodes to form proposals and counter-proposals concerning the transfer and assignment of subproblems among them. Finally, our mechanisms address, in a preliminary way, the decomposition problem by allowing nodes to divide and distribute subproblems based on awareness of the capabilities, plans, and goals of the nodes in the network. By incorporating negotiation in all of these forms as part of the partial global planning approach, we have begun to understand the relationships and similarities among them.

9.3   Future Research Directions

Improving the Existing Mechanisms.   To improve the existing mechanisms, we must address some of the simplifications and assumptions made in our initial implementation. For instance, we noted that the combinatorics of forming PGPs and reasoning about the actions of many nodes in larger networks could be prohibitive, so we need to introduce PGPlanning mechanisms that allow nodes to summarize the goals and activities of a group of nodes as if the group were a single node. We also need to improve our ability to simulate different costs for control activities to understand better the tradeoffs in control and problem solving and also the effects that time spent on control has on coordination. In addition, although local and partial global planning are well integrated, they could be combined more completely so that local planning is even more influenced by knowledge about the network. Another improvement would be to the meta-level organization: it is currently a fairly amorphous collection of information, and we hope to develop a more structured view so that

its design (and re-design) could be automated. Included in the improvements
to the meta-level organization would be improvements to the network-model
so that nodes can more completely reason about each other's capabilities and
biases. We also should improve the PGPlanner to monitor and repair PGPs,
so that nodes can respond when expected interactions (exchanges of results)
do not occur either because some node is unable to form a result or because
of errors in communication. Task-passing can also be improved so that nodes
can recognize task swaps to make better use of resources even when there is no
bottleneck node, so that nodes can form and distribute an arbitrary number
of subproblems from a problem to make more complete use of the network,
and so that nodes can move resources and expertise as well as subproblems if
appropriate. Nodes could also be more selective about meta-level communication, and we need to improve meta-level communication decisions to include
not only information from the meta-level organization but also from expectations about how sending a particular message might affect other nodes. Finally,
the mechanisms evolved over time, and we should recode them to reflect our
current view—concentrating specifically on separating out the more domain-
independent aspects in order to build a more generic framework much like the
reimplementation of the underlying blackboard architecture has led to the development of GBB (a generic blackboard development system) [Corkill *et al.*,
1986].

Goal Processing.   The planner uses a high-level, long-term view of the problem situation that has insufficient detail for determining exactly what KSs
should be applied to what data. The planner depends on the goal processor for this more detailed view. By being more discriminating about applying
goal processing, the planner reduces goal processing overhead. A future research direction is to better understand the interactions between detailed goal
processing [Hernandez *et al.*, 1987] and more abstract planning, and to better
integrate them into a multi-level control paradigm.

Real-Time Problem Solving.   indexlocal plan¿deadlines
   Planning and its ability to predict how and when results will be formed
has opened new areas for research in real-time problem solving [Lesser *et al.*,
1988]. An important future research direction will be to further explore how
a problem solver can modify its plans so that it balances conflicting needs of
forming good results and of meeting deadlines. In addition, we also hope to explore techniques for forming meta-level organizations that better meet deadlines
by reducing redundancy, and understanding the costs of such organizations in
terms of reliability.

Node Parallelism.   If each problem-solving node were a multi-processor, it
could exploit the parallelism in its local tasks. We would like to explore how

local and partial global planning could be used to make intelligent decisions about the concurrent activities of a node, and how that decision-making differs from decision-making in the more loosely-coupled network of problem solvers. One use of parallelism would be to have local problem solving, local planning, and partial global planning all proceed concurrently (recall Figure 1 in Chapter 1). These activities could occur asynchronously and in parallel, although some synchronization might lead to better overall performance (for example, if the problem solver sometimes waits for the planner to monitor and repair plans). Another use of parallelism would be to invoke several problem-solving actions concurrently. Each processor could be assigned a separate plan, so that the problem solver pursues several plans concurrently but each of these plans serially. At a finer-grained level, each processor could be assigned a different intermediate-goal for the same plan. Because parts of this plan are achieved concurrently, the overall results of the plan are achieved faster. However, the sequences of actions to achieve intermediate-goals are still serial. At an even finer-grained level, each processor could be assigned a different KSI for the same intermediate-goal, to increase the rate at which the intermediate-goal is achieved. Parallelism introduced at any of these levels can cause difficulties. Since the planner decides which action, intermediate-goal, or plan to pursue next based on previous results, the scheduling decisions for each processor might be poorer. Thus, mechanisms that use parallelism effectively must choose the granularity of concurrent tasks carefully, and this is an important future research topic.

Satisficing. The nodes cannot expect to form optimal plans and PGPs, both because the costs of finding optimal plans and PGPs can be prohibitively large, and because the environment is dynamic and uncertain. Our mechanisms thus strive for acceptable (satisficing [March and Simon, 1958]) control rather than optimal control. To make better satisficing decisions, the local and partial global planning mechanisms should consider other factors such as balancing quality and quantity of results. Instead of always giving preference to the most highly-rated PGP, for example, our mechanisms could be extended to pursue a satisfactory set of PGPs that meet some other criteria.

Communication. A node need not receive information from another node if it could infer that information locally, but making such inferences requires computation. Our current implementation concentrates on using communication resources: a node monitors and modifies only its own plans, and communicates about important changes. In the future, we hope to extend the mechanisms so that nodes can reason about probable changes in each other's plans, and can weigh the additional computation overhead against the saving in communication to find a suitable balance for maintaining network-models. We would also like to explore issues in more errorful communication channels. Although PGPs provide a basis for recognizing when domain-level messages have been lost, they do not help nodes recognize when meta-level messages have been lost. Although the PGPlanning mechanisms allow nodes to tolerate a certain amount of inconsistency in their PGPs, issues in how much inconsistency (caused by message losses) can be tolerated should be studied.

Heterogeneous Systems. The mechanisms that we have developed allow for some heterogeneity in the network (nodes may have different expertise) but they do assume that nodes have much in common in terms of their architecture and control structure. An area for future research concerns how different nodes can be before coordination becomes impossible. We must explore the intimate relationship between local control and coordination, how this relationship affects cooperation among more heterogeneous systems, and whether a more generic framework for cooperation is possible when these systems are so different that they cannot reason about each other.

Fault Detection and Diagnosis. Although plans and PGPs are tentative, the failure of several highly-rated plans or PGPs may be indicative of some fault in the problem solver or network. Planning thus provides a starting place for detecting faults. By analyzing the failed plans, the source of the failure might be found. Perhaps they all failed for similar reasons, such as while invoking a particular KS, and this could be a starting point for further diagnosis. In essence, the plans represent models of expected system behavior, and by comparing the actual behavior with these plans, initial steps toward diagnosis can be taken (although a more detailed model may be needed to completely isolate the fault [Hudlicka, 1986; Hudlicka *et al.*, 1986]).

Understanding Problem Solving Behavior. A complex problem solver is often difficult to understand: the myriad actions taken seem to have little in common so the larger implications and goals of actions are obscure [Pavlin and Corkill, 1984]. The local and partial global planning mechanisms help alleviate this difficulty because they group actions together into plans and plans together into PGPs. Using plans and PGPs as a frame of reference, the experimenter can more easily grasp the intentions of the problem solvers. A future research direction is to develop techniques that exploit this information to generate high-level explanations of local and network behavior.

Organizations. A crucial assumption made throughout this research has been that, somehow, the nodes have been organized both for problem solving and for coordination. By using the static domain-level and meta-level organizations, the planning and PGPlanning mechanisms were able to dynamically coordinate nodes to work as an effective team in a particular situation. An important area for future research is developing mechanisms for forming organizations, and this research will benefit from the planning and PGPlanning mechanisms because plans and PGPs provide a basis for detecting poor organizations and for proposing new organizations.

Meta-Level Control. Making better control decisions introduces overhead, and in particularly complex or ambiguous situations the increase in overhead might not justify the improvement to control. To balance the time spent on control with the time spent on actual problem solving, a node needs meta-level control (for control of control). Meta-level control examines the current situation and decides what if any control mechanisms should be applied, just like control decides what actions should be taken. An important future research direction is to build meta-level control mechanisms, perhaps based on the blackboard model of control developed by Hayes-Roth [Hayes-Roth, 1985].

Other Applications. The detailed description of how our mechanisms have been implemented serves not only as a basis for evaluation but also an exemplar for other applications. When we generalized the different mechanisms in the preceding chapters, we indicated other application domains that might implement versions of the same mechanisms. However, the emphasis of this research has been on building a complete implementation in one domain so that we could evaluate the promise of our approach. Our evaluation has shown that our approach is indeed a practical means for improving coordination among cooperating problem solvers in our domain. In the future, we hope to use our experience in this domain to explore how our approach works in other domains like those outlined in the earlier chapters, and we would like to encourage others to apply similar mechanisms as well, especially in real (not simulated) networks. No doubt our mechanisms will need substantial modification before they can be more generally used for coordination in a variety of domains, but our initial experiments show that our approach is practical and worth pursuing.

9.4   Contributions

Distributed problem solving, and more generally distributed artificial intelligence, is an important meeting ground between artificial intelligence and distributed computing. As the complexity of distributed computing applications grows, so does the need to control the distributed systems more intelligently. As artificially-intelligent systems are introduced into environments where they interact with other intelligent agents (whether artificial or natural), they need to reason about and plan coordinated actions and interactions with those other agents. In short, we contend (and we are not alone [Nilsson, 1980]) that distributed artificial intelligence will become an increasingly important area for study in both the AI and the distributed computing communities.

As an investigation into many important issues in cooperation in a distributed problem solving network, this research contributes to extending our limited view of the field. By proposing, developing, implementing, and evaluating an approach to coordination, this research has built on past efforts and has gone beyond. Although it explores a limited part of the larger issues in distributed AI and distributed computing systems, it provides one more reference point from which to base future exploration.

We have laid down a conceptual foundation that views control of both local and group activity as a planning task, where planning is worthwhile only insofar as it improves the system's ability to achieve its domain goals. Our approach is therefore *not* a distributed planning system, because nodes may solve their domain problems without ever forming a complete plan, particularly in dynamic environments where they should plan incrementally to avoid detailing actions that may never come to pass. Instead, nodes plan actions and interactions as domain problem solving proceeds. They exchange only relevant information about their local plans, determine when changes to local plans should be communicated, and use whatever information they have locally to individually decide how best to cooperate at any given time.

Conceptually, therefore, this research has explored the types of knowledge and reasoning methods that are needed for coordination in a dynamic world. An important conceptual contribution is our view of coordination as a partial global planning process. Whereas previous approaches to coordination developed separate techniques for coordination depending on what was to be gained through cooperation, our new approach provides a unified framework where diverse goals and styles of cooperation can be achieved. Using this framework and a variety of meta-level organizations, we have explored how different styles of cooperation affect network performance and control overhead. Moreover, we have examined how nodes can dynamically exploit available resources and expertise, and how they can develop partial global plans that are more robust when some nodes may fail.

Our research has also made contributions to understanding control in complex problem solvers. We have recognized the need to apply approximate processing to form a representation uniquely suitable for control so that control decisions can be based on more long-term views. We have also examined the role of incremental planning as a technique to control problem solving when long-term goals are uncertain and dynamic. As artificially-intelligent systems are applied to more complex domains, we expect that the role of approximate processing and incremental planning in control will become increasingly important.

Since our research methodology focuses on implementing and evaluating our approach, our research also makes several practical contributions. One of these contributions is simply experience. Although many approaches to coordination have been proposed in the literature, only a handful have been implemented. Implementation points out issues that may be inapparent or ignored in more speculative treatments. By implementing our approach, we came upon many issues that we had not anticipated, and by sharing our experience in the previous chapters, we hope to provide an example that others can build on. Implementation also leads to evaluation, and another important contribution of this research has been exploring the practicality of the approach: it does improve coordination as expected, but the costs for better control must also be considered, especially in complex and dynamic situations.

Finally, an important contribution of this research is that it raises new questions about cooperation and provides an implementation so that future research can build upon it both conceptually and experimentally. By opening new avenues for exploration into planning, control, coordination, communication, and organization, this research acts as a springboard for diving deeper into distributed AI and distributed computing. Because it provides an implementation in which to test new ideas, this work also allows subsequent researchers to not only theorize about issues in cooperation, but to experiment with them as well.

Acknowledgments

This book is a revised and shortened version of the dissertation I wrote at the University of Massachusetts, and these acknowledgments are derived from that dissertation.

I'd like to thank Victor Lesser, my advisor, for all of his help as I pursued this research. He has led me sometimes, followed me other times, encouraged me to keep going, applauded my successes, asked tough questions when I thought I had all the answers, supplied insights when I got stuck, greeted my insights with delight, and throughout has radiated a contagious enthusiasm for this research. It has been a pleasure to have collaborated with him.

I also owe a great debt to Dan Corkill, another of my committee members. It was he who introduced me to the implementation and simulation of distributed problem solving networks. Because he shared so much of his practical knowledge and expertise with me, I was much better prepared to turn my own ideas into realities. Dan's conceptual insights, moreover, have continually helped me recognize interesting research issues in distributed problem solving.

My other committee members have made important contributions to this research. Krithi Ramamritham helped open my eyes to the ties between distributed AI and distributed operating systems. His interest in my work as it applies to other aspects of computer systems has encouraged me to consider some of the more general aspects of coordinating cooperating computers. Reid Smith has provided an alternative view, since he has approached distributed problem solving from a different angle. His questions and comments have helped me see relationships between different approaches to control and coordination, and have led me to better understand the limitations and costs of my approach, where I might have otherwise not looked beyond its benefits.

The past and present members of the distributed problem solving lab here at UMass have helped this research and researcher in many different ways, and I would like to thank them all. In particular, Joe Hernandez and I have had many brainstorming (and other types of) discussions which have helped me better understand issues and channel my energies. Others that have contributed ideas, criticisms, or technical help to this research are Joe Walters, Dave Hildum, Anil Rewari, and Dave Westbrook (and Teri Westbrook often provided dinners that helped break up the monotony of my typical bachelor fare).

Many others inside and outside of the UMass COINS community deserve thanks as well. Among those who have had an influence on my work here at UMass are Jim Kurose, Jack Stankovic, Peter Bates, Paul Cohen, and Michael Arbib. Discussions with other DAI researchers, especially Les Gasser of USC, have also helped me mature my ideas. I'd also like to thank Michele Roberts for her administrative help so that I could more fully concentrate on my research. The many people that maintain the computer facilities here deserve credit as well for providing a relatively reliable and stable environment in which to compute. Finally, this research was sponsored, in part, by the National Science Foundation under Grant MCS-8306327, by the National Science Foundation under Support and Maintenance Grant DCR-8318776, by the National Science Foundation under CER Grant DCR-8500332, and by the Defense Advanced Research Projects Agency (DOD), monitored by the Office of Naval Research under Contract NR049-041. I was also partially supported in the 1985-6 academic year by a University Fellowship sponsored by the University of Massachusetts, and in the 1986-7 academic year by an IBM Graduate Fellowship.

Many others have helped and encouraged me over the years, even though not directly with this work. I'd like to thank Ed Heideman, Mr. V, and Fred Snyder for many lessons in science, in self-discipline, and in teamwork. I'd also like to thank the friends and colleagues I had while I was a chemist at GE. Although I wasn't cut out to be a chemist, I learned invaluable lessons in self-motivation and self-organization, especially from George Loucks.

Thanks to my other friends who, though working in unrelated areas, have helped me in their own ways. These include Jane and Nigel, the Esch, and Blaise. I'd also like to thank Mary, who has reminded me of the other fine things in life (besides computers), who has inspired me in many ways to complete this work, and who has made this difficult process much more bearable.

My family has helped me throughout. I'd like to thank my sister Sue and her family: Sue for wonderful meals and her cheerful outlook on life; her husband David for bike rides and for helping me keep my Volvo running through most of my graduate career; and the nieces for hours of play and entertainment that distracted me, for a while, from the other demands I faced. My brother Ken, as the other computer professional in the family, has helped by being someone that does not look completely baffled when I explain what I do at family get-togethers. My sister Rachel, by being an undergraduate while I was in school, helped me avoid being the only student in the family, so I wasn't alone in being accused of not having a "real" job.

Finally, I'd like to thank my parents for more things than I can mention. They have always been there, supporting and encouraging me; and though they have not pushed me, somehow their influence makes me want to do my best and make them proud. Thanks, folks.

Glossary

alternative-goal: A possible long-term solution that a node can work toward. Corresponds to a top-level cluster in the node's clustering hierarchy. Related to other alternative-goals that share clusters at lower levels of the clustering hierarchy.

belief: The confidence in a hypothesis. In the DVMT, belief is represented as in integer (to avoid floating-point calculations) between 0 and 10000, where 0 equals no confidence and 10000 equals full confidence.

blackboard: A data structure organized for efficient storage and retrieval of information by knowledge sources. Typically has multiple blackboard-levels corresponding to different amounts of processing knowledge applied to data.

blackboard-level: Level of abstraction of data. Low blackboard-levels correspond to relatively raw data, while information at higher blackboard-levels has undergone processing (application of knowledge) that groups data into entries that abstract the attributes of the data.

cluster: An entry in the clustering hierarchy. Combines data related by some set of relationships and summarizes their attributes and the past and pending actions that can be taken on the data. Emphasizes aspects that influence control decisions.

clustering hierarchy: A hierarchy of clusters, where clusters at higher levels represent combinations of clusters at lower levels. Formed by combining clusters using a succession of relationships, to emphasize different relationships that affect control at different levels.

cooperation-parameters: A set of numeric parameters that affect how the PG-Planner coordinates nodes. Gives relative importance of redundancy versus reliability, of independence versus predictiveness, and so on (see Figure 63). Also specifies information about integration redundancy and task-passing.

DVMT: See distributed vehicle monitoring testbed.

distributed problem-solving network: A network of communicating problem solvers that can work independently but that must cooperate to achieve larger network goals due to their individual limitations.

distributed vehicle monitoring testbed: The experimental testbed in which the new mechanisms are implemented and evaluated. Simulates a network of vehicle monitoring problem solvers where each problem solver monitors an area and problem solvers must cooperatively track vehicles that pass through more than one of their areas.

environment: A network problem-solving situation, specified by an environment file. Indicates both the characteristics of the network (number and location of nodes, communication topology and delay, sensed areas) and of the problem (what data arrives where and when).

event-class: Characterizes information in a hypothesis. At low blackboard-levels in the vehicle monitoring task, an event-class corresponds to a particular frequency or group of frequencies, while at higher blackboard-levels an event-class corresponds to a type of vehicle or vehicle formation.

goal: An explicit representation indicating a possible way that a hypothesis could be used. Stored on a separate goal blackboard and used to reason about relationships between possible actions (KSIs) and their results.

goal processor: Forms and manipulates goals. Responsible for generating goals based on new hypotheses, forming subgoals of important goals, and generating KSIs to satisfy goals.

goals of cooperation: Different and often conflicting objectives of cooperation, such as to provide predictive information, avoid interference, verify results, avoid duplication of effort, and exchange only useful information.

hypothesis: A partial solution at some blackboard-level. Represents some combination of sensory data that meets criteria specified by one or more KSs. Given a belief depending on how well it meets those criteria, and also has time-locations and an event-class.

i-goal: See intermediate-goal.

incremental planning: Interleaving planning with execution so that plans are formed over time. Useful when later steps of a plan depend on earlier steps, but where the outcome of the earlier steps cannot be predicted with certainty. Avoids detailing actions for future situations that may never occur but plans actions for the near future based on long-term strategic objectives.

interest area: Specifies a problem-solving responsibility of a node as part of the domain-level organization. Includes information about blackboard-levels, sensed times, spatial regions, and event-classes where the node should prefer developing hypotheses.

intermediate-goal: A major subgoal of a long-term problem-solving goal. In the vehicle monitoring task, an intermediate-goal is to develop data for a particular sensed time and incorporate that data into existing partial solutions. Each intermediate-goal may require several actions (KSIs) to achieve it.

KS: See knowledge source.

KSI: See knowledge source instantiation.

knowledge source: Contains domain problem-solving knowledge. Takes goals to achieve and hypotheses (data) to use as input, searches the blackboard for other relevant hypotheses, applies domain knowledge, and forms new hypotheses as output.

knowledge source instantiation: Represents the potential application of a KS on specific hypotheses to achieve certain goals. Rated and stored on a queue.

local control: Control of an individual computing node. Determines what action(s) that node will take at any given time.

local node-plan: A node-plan that corresponds to a plan at the node. The node can also have node-plans for other nodes.

local planner: A node's mechanisms for identifying its long-term goals and planning its own problem-solving actions.

meta-level organization: Static information that guides nodes coordination activities. Specifies coordination roles and where coordination information should be transmitted for some nodes in the network to develop partial global plans.

network control: Control of network activity. Determines actions and interactions for nodes in the network.

network-model: A node's view of the network. Contains node-models for each of the nodes that are known to this node (including whatever node-plans it has received from them) and partial global plans for groups of nodes.

node: An independent, often artificially-intelligent, problem solver that can develop partial solutions from its local information. Must cooperate with others to form more complete solutions.

node execution: A sequence of activities performed by a node that it repeats each time it invokes a KSI. These activities include incorporating any received information into its data structures, modifying its view for control (goals, KSIs, plans, PGPs), transmitting any messages, and invoking a KSI. The DVMT simulates concurrent activity in the network by interleaving node-executions for the various nodes.

node-model: Represents what a node knows about the plans and characteristics of another node. Contains node-plans for that node that have been received (and are updated through communication) and more static information about communicating with that node and about its problem-solving capabilities.

node-plan: Summarizes a plan. When nodes communicate about their individual (local) plans, they summarize these plans into node-plans to convey the information that is most relevant for coordination, including the objectives and the long-term aspects of how the plan will be pursued.

organization: Information about the roles and responsibilities of nodes. The domain-level organization guides problem-solving activities while the meta-level organization guides coordination activities. In the current implementation, an organization is assumed to be static and known to all nodes.

PGG: See partial global goal.

PGP: See partial global plan.

PGPlanner: See partial global planner.

PGP-partial-solution: A representation used when forming a solution-construction-graph. Represents a partial solution formed by some node(s) in achieving the PGP's objective.

partial global goal: Specifies an objective that one or more nodes should plan to achieve. Combines the objectives of one or more local plans into a possibly larger objective (to track a vehicle moving among a group of nodes).

partial global plan: Represents the concurrent actions and expected interactions of nodes pursuing a PGG.

partial global planner: Mechanisms that are part of a node that the node uses to develop PGGs, to form PGPs, and to modify local plans based on PGPs so that it better contributes to network problem solving.

plan: Represents how a node expects to achieve one or more local long-term goals (alternative-goals). Includes long-term plans about sequences of i-goals to achieve and short-term plans about specific KSIs to invoke in the near future.

plan-activity-map: A representation of what activities nodes will pursue over various expected intervals. When part of a node-plan, indicates the sequence of actions the node will take to achieve the plan and when it will form partial results. When part of a PGP, shows the concurrent activities of nodes and when they will individually form partial results.

solution-construction-graph: An attribute of a PGP. Indicates when and where partial solutions formed by nodes should be integrated into larger partial solutions until the overall solution is formed.

time-cushion: A numeric value indicating a "negligible" time difference. Used in several ways by the PGPlanner. When a plan deviates from predictions in terms of *when* results are formed, the PGPlanner compares the deviation to the time-cushion to determine whether the difference is significant enough to require changes to PGPs. When two partial solutions could be combined at more than one node, the PGPlanner uses the time-cushion to decide whether the combination could be formed *substantially* earlier somewhere, or whether the difference is negligible.

time-locations: A series of times and locations, each indicating where a vehicle was at a particular sensed time.

time-order: Represents a sequence of i-goals to achieve. Since an i-goal in the DVMT domain corresponds to processing data for a certain sensed time, an i-goal can be identified by that sensed time. The time-order is a sequence of sensed times where each represents an i-goal.

time-predictions: A list of time-predictions, one for each i-goal in the time-order. Each time-prediction indicates the predicted time needed to achieve a particular i-goal.

Bibliography

[Aikins, 1980] Jan S. Aikins. *Prototypes and Production Rules: A Knowledge Representation for Computer Consultations.* PhD thesis, Stanford University, 1980. (Also published as Technical Report STAN-CSD-80-814, Computer Science Department, Stanford University.).

[Allen, 1983] James F. Allen. Maintaining knowledge about temporal intervals. *Communications of the ACM*, 26(11):832–843, November 1983.

[Allen, 1984] James F. Allen. Towards a general theory of action and time. *Artificial Intelligence*, 23:123–154, 1984.

[Arbib, 1972] Michael A. Arbib. *The Metaphorical Brain.* Wiley, 1972.

[Axelrod, 1984] Robert Axelrod. *The Evolution of Cooperation.* Basic Books, 1984.

[Barto, 1985] Andrew G. Barto. *Learning by Statistical Cooperation of Self-Interested Neuron-Like Computing Elements.* Technical Report 85-11, Department of Computer and Information Science, University of Massachusetts, Amherst, Massachusetts 01003, April 1985.

[Bruce and Newman, 1978] Bertram Bruce and Denis Newman. Interacting plans. *Cognitive Science*, 2:195–233, 1978.

[Cammarata et al., 1983] Stephanie Cammarata, David McArthur, and Randall Steeb. Strategies of cooperation in distributed problem solving. In *Proceedings of the Eighth International Joint Conference on Artificial Intelligence*, pages 767–770, August 1983.

[Carver et al., 1984] Norman F. Carver, Victor R. Lesser, and Daniel L. McCue. Focusing in plan recognition. In *Proceedings of the Fourth National Conference on Artificial Intelligence*, pages 42–48, August 1984.

[Chandrasekaran, 1981] B. Chandrasekaran. Natural and social system metaphors for distributed problem solving: Introduction to the issue. *IEEE Transactions on Systems, Man, and Cybernetics*, SMC-11(1):1–5, January 1981.

[Cheeseman, 1984] Peter Cheeseman. A representation of time for automatic planning. In *Proceedings of the IEEE Conference on Robotics*, pages 513–518, 1984.

[Chien and Weissman, 1975] R. T. Chien and S. Weissman. Planning and execution in incompletely specified environments. In *Proceedings of the Fourth International Joint Conference on Artificial Intelligence*, pages 169–174, August 1975.

[Clancey and Letsinger, 1981] William J. Clancey and Reed Letsinger. NEOMYCIN: Reconfiguring a rule-based expert system for application to teaching. In *Proceedings of the Seventh International Joint Conference on Artificial Intelligence*, pages 829–836, August 1981.

[Cohen, 1978] Philip R. Cohen. *On Knowing What to Say: Planning Speech Acts*. PhD thesis, University of Toronto, Department of Computer Science, University of Toronto, Toronto, Canada, January 1978. Technical Report 118.

[Cohen and Levesque, 1986] Philip R. Cohen and Hector J. Levesque. Persistence, intention, and commitment. In *Proceedings of the 1986 Workshop on Reasoning About Actions and Plans*, July 1986.

[Conry et al., forthcoming] S. E. Conry, R. A. Meyer, and V. R. Lesser. Multistage negotiation in distributed planning. In A. Bond and L. Gasser, editors, *Readings in Distributed Artificial Intelligence*, Morgan Kaufmann Publishers, forthcoming.

[Corkill, 1979] Daniel D. Corkill. Hierarchical planning in a distributed environment. In *Proceedings of the Sixth International Joint Conference on Artificial Intelligence*, pages 168–175, August 1979.

[Corkill, 1983] Daniel David Corkill. *A Framework for Organizational Self-Design in Distributed Problem Solving Networks*. PhD thesis, University of Massachusetts, Amherst, Massachusetts 01003, February 1983. (Also published as Technical Report 82-33, Department of Computer and Information Science, University of Massachusetts, Amherst, Massachusetts 01003, December 1982.).

[Corkill and Lesser, 1983] Daniel D. Corkill and Victor R. Lesser. The use of meta-level control for coordination in a distributed problem solving network. In *Proceedings of the Eighth International Joint Conference on Artificial Intelligence*, pages 748–756, August 1983.

[Corkill and Lesser, 1987] Daniel D. Corkill and Victor R. Lesser. Distributed problem solving. In *Encyclopedia of Artificial Intelligence*, John Wiley & Sons, 1987.

[Corkill et al., 1986] Daniel D. Corkill, Kevin Q. Gallagher, and Kelly E. Murray. GBB: A generic blackboard development system. In *Proceedings of the Fifth National Conference on Artificial Intelligence*, pages 1008–1014, 1986. (Also to appear in *Blackboard Systems*, Robert S. Engelmore and Anthony Morgan, editors, Addison-Wesley, in press, 1987).

[Corkill et al., 1982] Daniel D. Corkill, Victor R. Lesser, and Eva Hudlicka. Unifying data-directed and goal-directed control: An example and experiments. In *Proceedings of the Second National Conference on Artificial Intelligence*, pages 143–147, August 1982.

[Davis, 1981] Randall Davis. *A Model for Planning in a Multi-Agent Environment: Steps Toward Principles of Teamwork*. Technical Report MIT AI Working Paper 217, Massachusetts Institute of Technology Artificial Intelligence Laboratory, Cambridge, Massachusetts, June 1981.

[Davis and Smith, 1983] Randall Davis and Reid G. Smith. Negotiation as a metaphor for distributed problem solving. *Artificial Intelligence*, 20:63–109, 1983.

[Dawkins, 1976] Richard Dawkins. *The Selfish Gene*. Oxford University Press, 1976.

[Dean, 1986] Thomas L. Dean. Intractability and time dependent planning. In *Proceedings of the 1986 Workshop on Reasoning About Actions and Plans*, July 1986.

[Drummond *et al.*, 1987] Mark Drummond, Ken Currie, and Austin Tate. Contingent plan structures for spacecraft. In *Proceedings of the Space Telerobotics Workshop*, January 1987.

[Durfee, 1987] Edmund Howell Durfee. *A Unified Approach to Dynamic Coordination: Planning Actions and Interactions in a Distributed Problem Solving Network*. PhD thesis, University of Massachusetts, Amherst, Massachusetts 01003, September 1987. (Also published as Technical Report 87-84, Department of Computer and Information Science, University of Massachusetts, Amherst, Massachusetts 01003, September 1987.).

[Durfee and Lesser, 1986] Edmund H. Durfee and Victor R. Lesser. Incremental planning to control a blackboard-based problem solver. In *Proceedings of the Fifth National Conference on Artificial Intelligence*, pages 58-64, August 1986.

[Durfee and Lesser, 1987] Edmund H. Durfee and Victor R. Lesser. Using partial global plans to coordinate distributed problem solvers. In *Proceedings of the Tenth International Joint Conference on Artificial Intelligence*, pages 875-883, August 1987.

[Durfee *et al.*, 1984] Edmund H. Durfee, Daniel D. Corkill, and Victor R. Lesser. Distributing a distributed problem solving network simulator. In *Proceedings of the Fifth Real-Time Systems Symposium*, pages 237-246, December 1984.

[Durfee *et al.*, 1985a] Edmund H. Durfee, Victor R. Lesser, and Daniel D. Corkill. *Coherent Cooperation Among Communicating Problem Solvers*. Technical Report 85-15, Department of Computer and Information Science, University of Massachusetts, Amherst, Massachusetts 01003, April 1985. Also to appear in *IEEE Transactions on Computers*.

[Durfee *et al.*, 1985b] Edmund H. Durfee, Victor R. Lesser, and Daniel D. Corkill. Increasing coherence in a distributed problem solving network. In *Proceedings of the Ninth International Joint Conference on Artificial Intelligence*, pages 1025-1030, August 1985.

[Durfee *et al.*, 1987] Edmund H. Durfee, Victor R. Lesser, and Daniel D. Corkill. Cooperation through communication in a distributed problem solving network. In Michael N. Huhns, editor, *Distributed Artificial Intelligence*, chapter 2, pages 29-58, Pitman, 1987. (Also to appear as Chapter 7 in Scott P. Robertson, Wayne Zachary, and John Black, editors, *Cognition, Computing, and Cooperation: Collected works on cooperation in complex systems*, in press).

[Erman *et al.*, 1980] Lee D. Erman, Frederick Hayes-Roth, Victor R. Lesser, and D. Raj Reddy. The Hearsay-II speech understanding system: Integrating knowledge to resolve uncertainty. *Computing Surveys*, 12(2):213-253, June 1980.

[Fehling and Erman, 1983] Michael Fehling and Lee Erman. Report on the third annual workshop on distributed artificial intelligence. *SIGART Newsletter*, 84:3-12, April 1983.

[Feldman and Ballard, 1982] J. A. Feldman and D. H. Ballard. Connectionist models and their properties. *Cognitive Science*, 6:205-254, 1982.

[Feldman and Sproull, 1977] Jerome A. Feldman and Robert F. Sproull. Decision theory and artificial intelligence II: The hungry monkey. *Cognitive Science*, 1:158–192, 1977.

[Fennell and Lesser, 1977] Richard D. Fennell and Victor R. Lesser. Parallelism in artificial intelligence problem solving: A case study of Hearsay II. *IEEE Transactions on Computers*, C-26(2):98–111, February 1977.

[Fikes and Nilsson, 1971] R. E. Fikes and N. J. Nilsson. STRIPS: A new approach to the application of theorem proving to problem solving. *Artificial Intelligence*, 2:189–208, 1971.

[Fox, 1983] Mark S. Fox. *Constraint-Directed Search: A Case Study of Job-Shop Scheduling.* PhD thesis, Carnegie-Mellon University, December 1983. (Also published as Technical Report CMU-CS-83-161, Computer Science Department, Carnegie-Mellon University, Pittsburgh, PA 15213, December 1983.).

[Georgeff, 1983] Michael Georgeff. Communication and interaction in multi-agent planning. In *Proceedings of the Eighth International Joint Conference on Artificial Intelligence*, pages 125–129, August 1983.

[Georgeff, 1984] Michael Georgeff. A theory of action for multiagent planning. In *Proceedings of the Fourth National Conference on Artificial Intelligence*, pages 121–125, August 1984.

[Grosz and Sidner, 1985] Barbara J. Grosz and Candace L. Sidner. Discourse structure and the proper treatment of interruptions. In *Proceedings of the Ninth International Joint Conference on Artificial Intelligence*, pages 832–839, August 1985.

[Halpern and Moses, 1984] Joseph Y. Halpern and Yoram Moses. Knowledge and common knowledge in a distributed environment. In *Third ACM Conference on Principles of Distributed Computing*, 1984.

[Hanson and Riseman, 1978] A. R. Hanson and E. M. Riseman. *Computer Vision Systems (CVS).* Academic Press, 1978.

[Hayes-Roth, 1985] Barbara Hayes-Roth. A blackboard architecture for control. *Artificial Intelligence*, 26:251–321, 1985.

[Hayes-Roth and Lesser, 1977] Frederick Hayes-Roth and Victor R. Lesser. Focus of attention in the Hearsay-II speech understanding system. In *Proceedings of the Fifth International Joint Conference on Artificial Intelligence*, pages 27–35, August 1977.

[Hernandez et al., 1987] Joseph A. Hernandez, Daniel D. Corkill, and Victor R. Lesser. *Goal Processing in Blackboard Architectures.* Technical Report 87-24, Department of Computer and Information Science, University of Massachusetts, Amherst, Massachusetts 01003, March 1987.

[Hewitt, 1977] Carl Hewitt. Viewing control structures as patterns of passing messages. *Artificial Intelligence*, 8:323–364, 1977.

[Hudlicka, 1986] Eva Hudlicka. *Diagnosing Problem-Solving System Behavior.* PhD thesis, University of Massachusetts, February 1986. (Also published as Technical Report 86-03, Department of Computer and Information Science, University of Massachusetts, Amherst, Massachusetts 01003, February 1986.).

[Hudlicka et al., 1986] Eva Hudlicka, Victor R. Lesser, Jasmina Pavlin, and Anil Rewari. *Design of a Distributed Diagnosis System.* Technical Report 86-63, Department of Computer and Information Science, University of Massachusetts, Amherst, Massachusetts 01003, December 1986.

[Jagannathan and Dodhiawala, 1986] V. Jagannathan and Rajendra Dodhiawala. Distributed artificial intelligence: An annotated bibliography. *SIGART Newsletter,* (95):44–56, January 1986.

[Konolige, 1984] Kurt Konolige. A deductive model of belief. In *Proceedings of the Eighth International Joint Conference on Artificial Intelligence,* pages 377–381, August 1984.

[Kurose et al., 1985] J. F. Kurose, M. Schwartz, and Y. Yemini. A microeconomic approach to optimization of channel access policies in multiaccess networks. In *Proceedings of the Fifth International Symposium on Distributed Computing Systems,* pages 70–80, May 1985.

[Lansky, 1985] Amy L. Lansky. *Behavioral Specification and Planning for Multiagent Domains.* Technical Report 360, SRI International, Menlo Park, CA 94025, November 1985.

[Lesser and Corkill, 1981] Victor R. Lesser and Daniel D. Corkill. Functionally-accurate, cooperative distributed systems. *IEEE Transactions on Systems, Man, and Cybernetics,* SMC-11(1):81–96, January 1981.

[Lesser and Corkill, 1983] Victor R. Lesser and Daniel D. Corkill. The distributed vehicle monitoring testbed: A tool for investigating distributed problem solving networks. *AI Magazine,* 4(3):15–33, Fall 1983.

[Lesser and Erman, 1980] Victor R. Lesser and Lee D. Erman. Distributed interpretation: A model and experiment. *IEEE Transactions on Computers,* C-29(12):1144–1163, December 1980.

[Lesser et al., 1988] Victor R. Lesser, Jasmina Pavlin, and Edmund H. Durfee. Approximate processing in real-time problem solving. *AI Magazine,* 9(1):49–61, Spring 1988.

[Lowrance and Friedman, 1977] John D. Lowrance and Daniel P. Friedman. Hendrix's model for simultaneous actions and continuous processes: An introduction and implementation. *International Journal of Man-Machine Studies,* 9:537–581, 1977.

[Malone and Smith, 1984] Thomas W. Malone and Stephen A. Smith. *Tradeoffs in Designing Organizations: Implications for New Forms of Human Organizations and Computer Systems.* Technical Report Sloan Working Paper 1541-84, Sloan School of Management, Massachusetts Institute of Technology, Cambridge, Massachusetts 02139, March 1984.

[March and Simon, 1958] James G. March and Herbert A. Simon. *Organizations.* Wiley, 1958.

[McCalla et al., 1982] Gordon I. McCalla, Larry Reid, and Peter F. Schneider. Plan creation, plan execution, and knowledge acquisition in a dynamic microworld. *International Journal of Man-Machine Studies,* 16:89–112, 1982.

[McDermott, 1982] Drew McDermott. A temporal logic for reasoning about processes and plans. *Cognitive Science,* 6:101–155, 1982.

[Nilsson, 1980] Nils J. Nilsson. Two heads are better than one. *SIGART Newsletter*, (73):43, October 1980.

[Pattison *et al.*, 1985] H. Edward Pattison, Daniel D. Corkill, and Victor R. Lesser. *Instantiating Descriptions of Organizational Structures*. Technical Report 85-45, Department of Computer and Information Science, University of Massachusetts, Amherst, Massachusetts 01003, December 1985.

[Pavlin, 1983] Jasmina Pavlin. Predicting the performance of distributed knowledge-based systems: A modeling approach. In *Proceedings of the Third National Conference on Artificial Intelligence*, pages 314–319, August 1983.

[Pavlin and Corkill, 1984] Jasmina Pavlin and Daniel D. Corkill. Selective abstraction of AI system activity. In *Proceedings of the Fourth National Conference on Artificial Intelligence*, pages 264–268, August 1984.

[Ramamritham and Stankovic, 1984]
Krithivasan Ramamritham and John 'A. Stankovic. Dynamic task scheduling in hard real-time distributed systems. *IEEE Software*, 1(3):65–75, July 1984.

[Rosenschein, 1985] Jeffery Solomon Rosenschein. *Rational Interaction: Cooperation Among Intelligent Agents*. PhD thesis, Stanford University, October 1985.

[Rosenschein and Genesereth, 1985] Jeffrey S. Rosenschein and Michael R. Genesereth. Deals among rational agents. In *Proceedings of the Ninth International Joint Conference on Artificial Intelligence*, pages 91–99, August 1985.

[Rosenschein and Genesereth, 1987] Jeffrey S. Rosenschein and Michael R. Genesereth. Communication and cooperation among logic-based agents. In *Proceedings of the Sixth Phoenix Conference on Computers and Communications*, pages 594–600, February 1987.

[Sacerdoti, 1977] Earl D. Sacerdoti. *A Structure for Plans and Behavior*. American Elsevier, 1977.

[Sacerdoti, 1979] Earl D. Sacerdoti. Problem solving tactics. In *Proceedings of the Sixth International Joint Conference on Artificial Intelligence*, pages 1077–1085, August 1979.

[Shortliffe, 1976] E. H. Shortliffe. *Computer-Based Medical Consultations: MYCIN*. American Elsevier, 1976.

[Shubik, 1982] Martin Shubik. *Game Theory in the Social Sciences: Concepts and Solutions*. MIT Press, 1982.

[Smith, 1980] Reid G. Smith. The contract-net protocol: High-level communication and control in a distributed problem solver. *IEEE Transactions on Computers*, C-29(12):1104–1113, December 1980.

[Smith and Davis, 1981] Reid G. Smith and Randall Davis. Frameworks for cooperation in distributed problem solving. *IEEE Transactions on Systems, Man, and Cybernetics*, SMC-11(1):61–70, January 1981.

[Stankovic, 1984] John A. Stankovic. A perspective on distributed computer systems. *IEEE Transactions on Computers*, C-33(12):1102–1115, December 1984.

[Stankovic *et al.*, 1985] John A. Stankovic, Krithivasan Ramamritham, and ShengChang Cheng. Evaluation of a flexible task scheduling algorithm for distributed hard real-time systems. *IEEE Transactions on Computers*, C-34(12):1130–1143, December 1985.

[Steeb et al., 1986] Randall Steeb, Stephanie Cammarata, Sanjai Narain, Jeff Rothenberg, and William Giarla. *Cooperative Intelligence for Remotely Piloted Vehicle Fleet Control*. Technical Report R-3408-ARPA, Rand Corporation, October 1986.

[Stefik, 1981] Mark Stefik. Planning with constraints. *Artificial Intelligence*, 16:111–140, 1981.

[Tate, 1975] Austin Tate. Interacting goals and their use. In *Proceedings of the Fourth International Joint Conference on Artificial Intelligence*, pages 215–218, August 1975.

[Tate, 1977] Austin Tate. Generating project networks. In *Proceedings of the Fifth International Joint Conference on Artificial Intelligence*, pages 888–893, August 1977.

[Vere, 1983] Steven A. Vere. Planning in time: Windows and durations for activities and goals. *IEEE Transactions on Pattern Analysis and Machine Intelligence*, PAMI-5(3):246–267, May 1983.

[Waldinger, 1977] Richard Waldinger. Achieving several goals simultaneously. In *Machine Intelligence 8*, pages 94–136, 1977.

[Wesson, 1977] Robert B. Wesson. Planning in the world of the air traffic controller. In *Proceedings of the Fifth International Joint Conference on Artificial Intelligence*, pages 473–479, August 1977.

[Wilkins, 1984] David E. Wilkins. Domain-independent planning: Representation and plan generation. *Artificial Intelligence*, 22:269–301, 1984.

[Woods, 1977] W. A. Woods. Shortfall and density scoring strategies for speech understanding control. In *Proceedings of the Fifth International Joint Conference on Artificial Intelligence*, pages 13–26, August 1977.

[Zhao, 1986] Wei Zhao. *A Heuristic Approach to Scheduling Hard Real-Time Tasks with Resource Requirements in Distributed Systems*. PhD thesis, University of Massachusetts, Amherst, Massachusetts 01003, February 1986.

[Zhao et al., 1987] Wei Zhao, Krithi Ramamritham, and John A. Stankovic. Preemptive scheduling under time and resource constraints. *IEEE Transactions on Computers*, C-36(8):949–960, August 1987.

Index

— A —

abstraction hierarchy, *see*
    • clustering, hierarchy
ACTOR, 17
Aikins, J. S., 46
Allen, J. F., 70, 204
alternative-goal, 60
approximate processing, *see*
    • clustering
Arbib, M. A., 195
association problem, 15, 158, 244
authority, 134, 137, 141, 147, 187
Axelrod, R., 23

— B —

Ballard, D. H., 16
Barto, A. G., 24
belief, 29
biological models, 24
blackboard, 17, 29
blackboard-level, 29
bottleneck-node, 166, 189
Bruce, B., 25

— C —

Cammarata, S., 2, 4, 13, 20
Carver, N. F., 132–133
Chandrasekaran, B., 23
Cheeseman, P., 70, 204
Chien, R. T., 68
Clancey, W. J., 46, 104
clustering, 45ff
    base-clusters, 53

cluster attributes, 51ff
cluster-data, 52
    example, 61ff
    functions, 55ff
    generalized, 63ff
    hierarchy, 49, 51ff
    relationships, 48
    updating, 59ff
Cohen, P. R., 24, 132
computer vision, 47
connection problem, 15, 244
connectionism, 16, 24
Conry, S. E., 192
contracting, 13, 18, 22, 193, 205; *see also*
    • task-passing
control
    meta-level, 130, 238, 248
control levels, 6, 207
cooperation
    goals of, 2, 12, 161, 172, 212, 241
    style of, 2, 13, 243
cooperation-parameters, 172
Corkill, D. D., 4, 13, 16, 19–20, 27,
    29, 32, 34, 36–37, 47, 134,
    136, 211, 245, 247
cost-heuristic-weight, 81, 113

— D —

DAI, 16ff
    closely-coupled, 16
    contracting, *see*
        • contracting
    formalisms, 21
    multi-agent planning, *see*
        • planning, multi-agent

organizational, *see*
  • organization
data-driven, 45ff
Davis, R., 13–14, 18, 26–27, 68
Dawkins, R., 24
deadlines, 98, 108, 127, 245; *see also*
  • local plan, deadlines
Dean, T. L., 204
decomposition problem, 15, 189, 244
diagnosis, 46, 104, 208, 247
distributed AI, *see*
  • DAI
distributed data-bases, 23
distributed operating systems, 21ff
distributed problem solving, 2, 27
  applications, 2
distributed scheduling, 22
distributed vehicle monitoring, *see*
  • DVMT
Dodhiawala, R., 16
Drummond, M., 68
Durfee, E. H., 3, 19, 36, 38, 51, 59,
  114, 163
DVMT, 27ff
  environment, 37, 209
  limitations, 42, 185
  network simulation, 38
  node, 29ff
  simulated time, 38, 212

— E —

economic models, 23
Erman, L. D., 2, 17, 83
event-class, 29

— F —

Fehling, M., 2
Feldman, J. A., 16, 68
Fennell, R. D., 17
Fikes, R. E., 68
Fox, M. S., 24
Friedman, D. P., 70

— G —

game theory, 23
Genesereth, M. R., 20–21, 24, 132
Georgeff, M., 20–21, 132, 134
goal
  blackboard, 33
  long-term, 45ff
  processor, 33, 73, 94, 113, 245
  rating, 33
  subgoal, 34, 40, 47
goal-directed, 45ff
grammar, 29
Grosz, B. J., 25

— H —

Halpern, J. Y., 21
Hanson, A. R., 47
Hayes-Roth, B., 46, 130, 248
Hayes-Roth, F., 98
Hearsay-II, 17
Hernandez, J. A., 245
heterogeneous nodes, 224, 247
Hewitt, C., 17
Hudlicka, E., 247
hypothesis, 29

— I —

i-goals, 71
implementation details, 6
intermediate-goals, *see*
  • i-goals

— J —

Jagannathan, V., 16

— K —

knowledge source, *see*
  • KS
Konolige, K., 20–21, 132, 134
KS, 29ff

communication, 31
integration, 31
models, 83
synthesis, 29
KSI, 32
Kurose, J. F., 23

— L —

Lansky, A. L., 21
Lesser, V. R., 2, 4, 16–17, 19, 27, 29,
        34, 36, 98, 108, 130, 136,
        211, 245
Letsinger, R., 46, 104
Levesque, H. J., 24
local plan
        attributes, 75
        creating, 78
        deadlines, 98, 127
        examples, 100
        generalized, 104
        long-term, 79
        modifying, 95, 122
        monitoring, 92, 119
        objectives, 78
        predictions, 88
        rating, 90, 114
        repairing, 93, 119
        short-term, 82
        time-order, 79
        updating, 94
local sophistication, 11, 240
Lowrance, J. D., 70

— M —

Malone, T. W., 24
March, J. G., 24, 246
McCalla, G. I., 68
McDermott, D., 70
meta-level communication, 145, 186,
        195, 206, 238, 246
meta-level organization, see
                • organization, meta-level
Moses, Y., 21

— N —

natural language, 24
negotiation, 15, 18, 136, 144, 187,
        189, 192, 205, 242, 244
network-model, 131, 133ff, 151
        attributes, 140
        generalizing, 156
Newman, D., 25
Nilsson, N. J., 68, 248
node
        architecture, 32, 74
        definition, 2
        execution, 38
        heterogeneous, 224
        parallelism, 245
node-model, 139
        initialization, 142
        maintaining, 147
node-plan, 133, 164
        attributes, 137
        construction, 142
        future, 143, 188
        idle, 145
        local, 146
        updating, 194

— O —

organization, 25, 247
        coordination through, 19, 42
        domain-level, 4, 6
        generality, 19, 36, 43, 132
        meta-level, 4, 8, 134, 141, 172,
                189, 211
        experiments, 217
        structure, 35
        theory, 24
overhead, 164, 188, 195–196, 201,
        214ff, 238
        communication, 150, 213
        computation, 42, 112, 125, 179,
                212
        control, 38, 42, 94, 148
        storage, 112, 214

— P —

partial global plan, *see*
  • PGP
partial-combinations, 148ff
Pattison, H. E., 36
Pavlin, J., 88, 247
PGG, 131ff, 134
  examples, 151
  generalizing, 156
  recognizing, 148
PGP, 3, 134–135, 160ff
  attributes, 140, 168
  communication, 170, 183, 205;
      see also
        • meta-level
          communication
  example, 196
  experiments, 209
  generalized, 202
  modifying, 219
PGP-partial-solution, 162, 180
  attributes, 169
PGPlanner, *see*
        • planner, partial global
PGPlanning, *see*
        • planning, partial global
plan
  aborted, 94
  local, *see*
        • local plan
  partial global, *see*
        • PGP
  suspended, 95
plan-activity, 168ff
  attributes, 137
plan-activity-map, 133, 137, 161, 204
  generation, 174
  reordering, 161, 177, 197
planner
  local, 6, 67ff
    architecture, 75, 167
  partial global, 7, 160
    architecture, 168
planning
  incremental, 11, 104
  local, 67ff
    experiments, 112

heuristics, 71
local and partial global, 193, 207
multi-agent, 19
partial global, 207
  experiments, 209
  overview, 3ff
reactive, 69
strategic, 69
temporal, 70
predictability, 14, 105, 195, 221, 243

— R —

Ramamritham, K., 23
real-time environments, 122, 219
redundancy, 173, 212, 224
research methodology, 10
responsiveness, 14, 195, 221, 243
Riseman, E. M., 47
Rosenschein, J. S., 16, 20–21, 24, 132

— S —

Sacerdoti, E. D., 68
Shortliffe, E. H., 46
Shubik, M., 23
Sidner, C. L., 25
Simon, H. A., 24, 246
Smith, R. G., 2, 4, 13–14, 18, 27
Smith, S. A., 24
solution-construction-graph, 134, 163,
    180ff, 205
Sproull, R. F., 68
Stankovic, J. A., 22–23, 204
Steeb, R., 13, 20
Stefik, M., 69, 71, 106

— T —

task-passing, 166, 174, 189, 205, 230;
    see also
      • contracting
Tate, A., 68
time-cushion, 166, 173, 181, 183, 194,
    201, 206, 221, 243
time-locations, 29

time-windows, 165, 176, 236

— V —

Vere, S. A., 70, 165, 176, 204

— W —

Waldinger, R., 68
Weissman, S., 68
Wesson, R. B., 68–69
Wilkins, D. E., 68
Woods, W. A., 98

— Z —

Zhao, W., 22